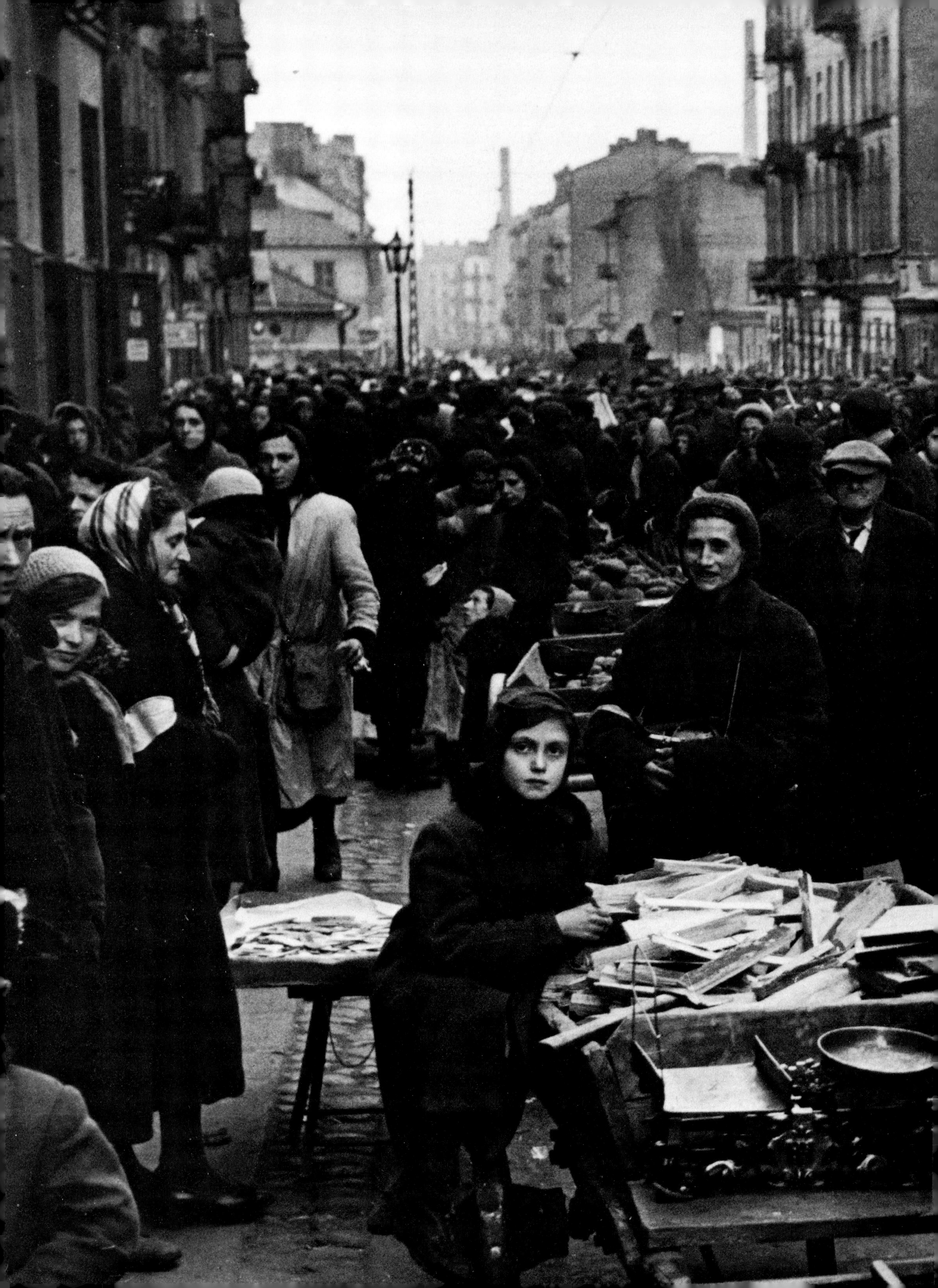

THE WARSAW GHETTO

IN PHOTOGRAPHS

206 Views Made in 1941

Edited by
ULRICH KELLER

Department of Art History
University of California, Santa Barbara

DOVER PUBLICATIONS, INC.
New York

Published in Canada by General Publishing Company, Ltd., 30 Lesmill Road, Don Mills, Toronto, Ontario.
Published in the United Kingdom by Constable and Company, Ltd., 10 Orange Street, London WC2H 7EG.

The Warsaw Ghetto in Photographs: 206 Views Made in 1941 is a new work, first published by Dover Publications, Inc., in 1984. The publisher is grateful to the Bundesarchiv, Koblenz, West Germany, for making its photoprints available for reproduction.

Manufactured in the United States of America
Dover Publications, Inc., 31 East 2nd Street, Mineola, N.Y. 11501

Book design by Carol Belanger Grafton

Library of Congress Cataloging in Publication Data
Main entry under title:

The Warsaw ghetto in photographs.

Includes bibliographical references.
1. Jews—Poland—Warsaw—Persecutions—Pictorial works.   2. Holocaust, Jewish (1939–1945)—Poland—Warsaw—Pictorial works.   3. Warsaw (Poland)—Ethnic relations—Pictorial works.   4. Warsaw (Poland)—Description—Views.   I. Keller, Ulrich, fl. 1977–
DS135.P62W39   1984   940.53′15′0392404384   83-20540
ISBN 0-486-24665-5

CONTENTS

INTRODUCTION

AN official German document of 1941 offers the following information about the Warsaw ghetto:

> The Jewish district covers an area of 403 hectares [995 acres]. The Jewish Council, which claims to have conducted a census, estimates the population of this area at ca 410,000 Jews while our own observations and calculations point to ca 470,000—590,000 Jews. Adopting the statistical figures of the Jewish Council and subtracting empty lots and cemeteries, the population density equals 1108 persons per hectare of built-up territory, or 110,800 per square kilometer [247 acres]. The corresponding figures for the city of Warsaw as a whole are 14,000 persons per square kilometer of the total metropolitan district and 38,000 persons per square kilometer of built-up and inhabitable space. . . . The Jewish quarter comprises ca 27,000 apartments with an average number of 2½ rooms each. Consequently, the average occupancy can be put at 15 persons per apartment and 6 to 7 persons per room. The Jewish quarter is separated from the rest of the city by walled-in streets, windows, doors and empty lots, fire and partition walls having been incorporated. The walls are 3 meters high; another meter is added by a parapet of barbed wire. Furthermore, surveillance is provided by police patrols on horseback and in motor vehicles.[1]

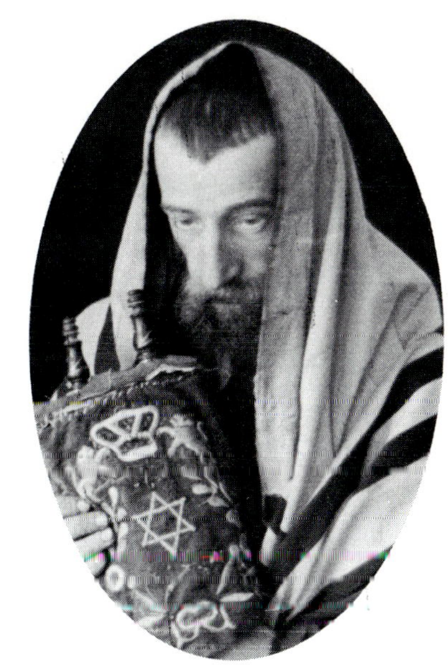

Three years after this document was written, not a single inhabitant was left in Warsaw's "Jewish district," and the ghetto streets had vanished from the map. When a Jewish survivor returned in 1946 to the place that once had been his home, he found that in this desert of "battered bricks and twisted iron bars only the sky had remained unchanged."[2]

Memories cling to locations, and if there is any place evoking more forcefully than others the tragedy of the Holocaust it is the Warsaw ghetto, the last refuge for hundreds of thousands of European Jews on their way to destruction by hunger, typhus and gas. Looking at the Warsaw ghetto means encountering the Jewish genocide in all its dimensions.

The historical facts of the Holocaust have been meticulously researched.[3] Until September 1, 1939, the "final solution" of the Jewish presence in Europe had been a vaguely phrased chapter of Nazi ideology, taken seriously by very few people. Only the outbreak of the Second World War created the abnormal conditions which put the Nazi leaders in a position to translate their chimerical concepts into gruesome reality. Methodically, they followed a two-step approach that culminated in the horrors of Auschwitz, Belsen and Treblinka. In a preliminary phase, however, the European Jews were concentrated in several Polish ghettos. That is, for political and economic reasons, the great genocide was preceded by a grace period of sorts during which the Jews were economically exploited, physically undermined and psychologically harassed. But by and large they were allowed to live, and to a degree their forced coexistence in overpopulated, sealed-off ghetto districts even helped to strengthen the very cultural identity that the Nazis sought to stamp out.

Established in October 1939 as an open "quarantine" area but later enclosed by a high wall, the Warsaw ghetto became the center of these preliminary events.[4] As the biggest Jewish prison city it developed the most elaborate self-administration and the most complex economic infrastructure. It also suffered the most. In spite of the constant influx of Jewish families from other European countries and outlying Polish districts, the ghetto's population figure of about 450,000 remained more or less stable because of the excessive mortality rate caused by severe food shortages and unsanitary conditions.

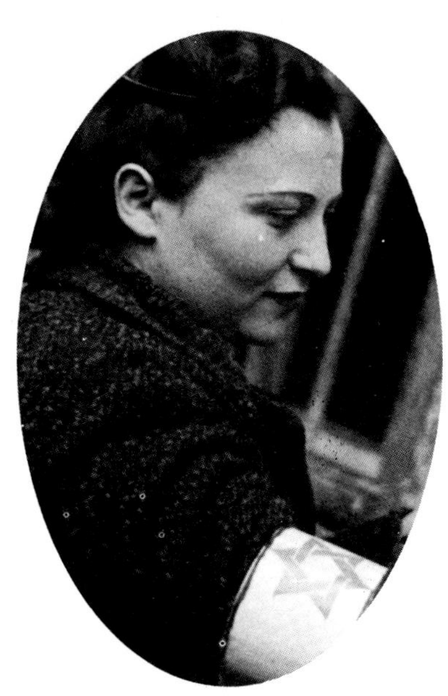

In the winter of 1941/42 the Nazi leadership replaced the policy of concentration by the policy of extermination. Officially labeled as a "resettlement" operation, the liquidation of the Warsaw ghetto began on July 22, 1942. Street by street, at a rate of 6000 to 9000 persons per day, the ghetto population was rounded up, put on trains to Treblinka and killed by the infusion of Cyclon B gas in chambers camouflaged as shower facilities. By October 1942, the ghetto had been reduced to some 45,000 able-bodied men and women employed for slave labor in a couple of German factory complexes.

The final attack on the Warsaw ghetto came on April 19, 1943, when the remaining territory was sealed off by German troops, and a column of 2000 SS men, heavily armed with tanks, artillery and machine guns, began to purge the ghetto of its last inhabitants. The invasion was answered by the bullets and handmade grenades of the Jewish Combat Organization (ŻOB), which had been formed under the leadership of M. Anielewicz in autumn 1942, after the last illusions about German intentions had dissipated. For several weeks the group fought effectively from rooftops, windows and basements, inflicting severe casualties on the invasion forces. Eventually, however, the better-armed and numerically superior German troops prevailed. On May 8 the ŻOB headquarters was surrounded, but along with about 100 other resistance fighters Anielewicz preferred suicide to capitulation. A few days later the last signs of life had been extinguished, allowing J. Stroop, the German commander, to announce in his notorious report: "Warsaw's Jewish district is no more."[5]

The Lodz ghetto—the second largest created by the Nazis—shared a similar fate. Sealed off from the rest of the city in May 1940, it comprised a population of over 160,000. Here, the "resettlement" operation began several months earlier than in Warsaw, but it proceeded at a different pace. Until 1944, about half of the inhabitants continued to work in the local armament industry. In the summer of that year they, too, were sent to the extermination camps—while the Russian army stood 75 miles away on the outskirts of Warsaw.

These are some of the bare chronological facts. Obviously, they give only a very inadequate idea of the annihilation of the Polish ghettos, and even with many more pages at our disposal the inadequacy would persist. Indeed, even though the Holocaust has been subjected to enormous research efforts, it can be said that its *history*—that is, a human understanding of the facts—has not yet emerged, and perhaps never will.[6]

Even if the Holocaust transcends our understanding, Karl Jaspers' dictum remains valid: "To forget it is guilt."[7] Considering the monstrosity of the event and how deeply it has traumatized all of us, the likelihood is small, of course, that we will forget in the near future. The main question is how we will deal with this trauma, one which may be too fundamental to be placated by rational strategies alone. After decades of collecting and studying the documentary evidence, amassing archives, reconstructing chains of events, organizing symposia and public demonstrations, teaching children and teaching whole nations; that is to say, after a generation of historical/educational struggling with the Holocaust, we have in recent years seen a shift toward the smoother fictional mode of dealing with the past. What is strange about this is not that it has occurred at all, but that it occurred at such a late point, many years after other World War II events such as the Normandy invasion or the battle for the Pacific islands, and even the nuclear pulverization of Hiroshima, were turned into screen epics. There was something about the Holocaust that held the movie producers in check: awe of the magnitude of the crime, reluctance to exploit the sufferings of the victims, the obvious inadequacy of any attempt to recreate the events before the camera—these and similar factors made it inconceivable for decades to "dramatize" the Holocaust.

Yet the fact of the Holocaust had made its mark in human memory, it had left a deeply ingrained shock and anxiety which the rational historical approach could never fully deal with. As every psychologist knows, such fundamental traumata need to be brought to the surface, not to be rationally known, but to be emotionally confronted, to be shaped and reshaped into plausible stories until they stop hurting. In short, we need to transform fact into fiction, which is, after all, the most effective way of coping with mental pain.

Today the powerful public institution known as "the media" undertakes for us to fictionalize and neutralize those emotional injuries that most of us have in common: the big historical traumata. Thus the TV dramatization of the Holocaust had to happen eventually. And the available evidence suggests that both recent screen epics, *Holocaust* and *The Wall*, were rather successful productions from the media point of view: an audience of millions was confronted with the truth; millions were warned, millions would remember—at least that is how the media assess the impact of their programs. What really happened, of course, was that the movie industry fictionalized the facts so as to make them acceptable. By literally bringing the Holocaust home to us, it absolved us from latent, lingering trauma.

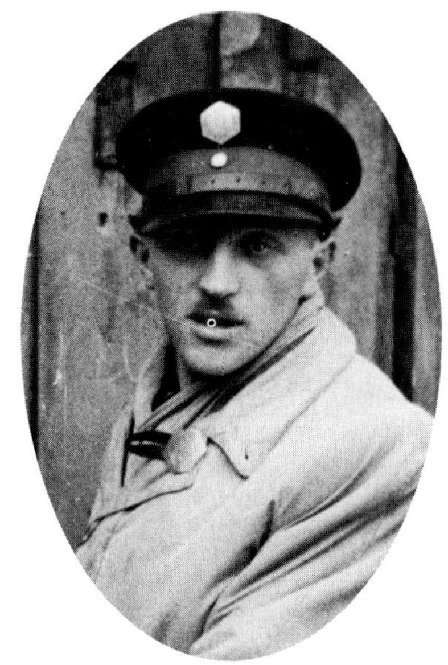

We were shown plausibly constructed examples of aggression and suffering, heroism and cowardice, hope and desperation, death and survival, violently reduced to the simplified categories which most Hollywood products boil down to: the mythical categories of the "individual" and "the family." And running through it all we found a chain of explanations, a precious red thread of meaning. We seemed to understand, we were moved, and with our tears our deepest anxieties were exorcised. That historical facts were distorted in the process, that *The Wall*, especially, furthered the story line by confusing both the nature and the course of the actual events (for example, by providing false information in the form of "documentary" subtitles)—this is only a side issue. Even a story line more in accordance with the facts would still be fiction, it still would suggest meaning where history itself is opaque, offer consolation where the evidence remains disturbing.

In the end, the television version of the Holocaust may have clarified at least this: if the choice is between historical reconstruction and fictional recreation, the first option, while psychologically less satisfactory to us, seems more respectful toward the victims, whose fate is not of the kind that can be reconciled with Hollywood drama and intermittent food commercials.[8]

Paradoxically, the pictures in this volume seem to lend themselves to both modes of coping with the past. Taken in the Warsaw ghetto under Nazi occupation, they are authentic documents rather than posthumous reenactments of the Jewish tragedy. In other words, these pictures are undeniably "historical" in character, yet it is also possible, in fact tempting, to read them on an emotionally gratifying, more or less fictional, level, as if they were stills from *The Wall* or *Holocaust*—some of whose stage scenery was fashioned after the photographs. Upon closer examination the streak of fiction that runs through the predominantly factual, historical texture of the photographs appears less surprising than it may seem at first. After all, they were made by German army reporters who resorted to the camera not just to record the Holocaust but rather to explain it to themselves and to posterity. As a medium which since its invention has oscillated between objective documentation and personal interpretation, photography was certainly the ideal tool to accomplish both purposes, that of personal explanation and that of plain record-keeping. For a critical reading of the present pictures it will be essential to keep this ambiguity in mind.

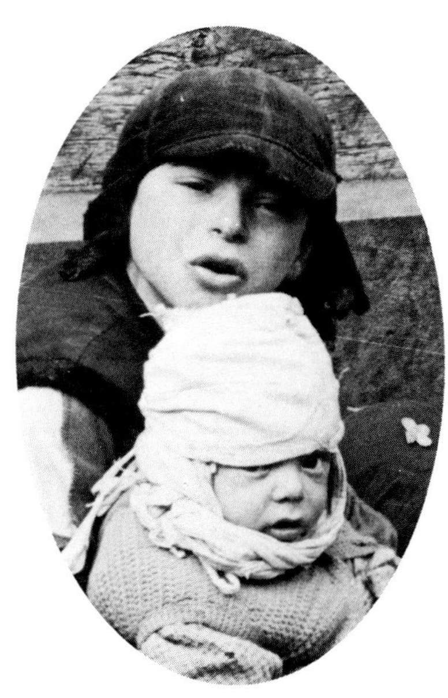

ONE might expect that the Warsaw ghetto, as a place of unspeakable horror and misery, was avoided by photographers, but the contrary is true.[9] Numerous sarcastic entries in Jewish ghetto diaries leave no doubt that a steady stream of German visitors poured into the ghetto, shamelessly inspecting and photographing sufferings which in their distorted view seem to have been perceived as proof of Jewish decadence rather than German inhumanity.[10]

The majority of these picture-hungry tourists came from the ranks of soldiers on furlough and workers on organized "Strength through Joy" trips. To them the Warsaw ghetto was simply a kind of Baedeker sight, and they recorded its "picturesque" scenes with monstrous innocence for display in souvenir albums, as we must assume. Several diarists agree that the Jewish burial ground near Okopowa Street was the principal point of attraction for the German visitors. According to M. Zylberberg:

> . . . it was not only the funeral processions that made the cemetery so strangely lively, but the constant presence of hundreds of German soldiers. They gleefully photographed the dead and the accompanying relatives, and even went as far as taking snapshots of the corpses as they were laid out in the mortuary. The Nazis were particularly active in this respect on Sundays, when they would visit the cemetery with their girl friends. This, rather than a cinema, was a place of amusement for them. The bereaved regarded them with scorn and loathing, but in the circumstances silence was the only protest.[11]

But not all German cameramen in the ghetto were tourists. Goebbels' ministry of propaganda, for example, proceeded to "document" it from a different point of view. Two months before the "resettlement" operation began, and presumably to obtain anti-Jewish picture material in defense of the operation, a German team of movie technicians and "experts" on Jewish culture appeared in the ghetto, generating a flurry of activities.[12] The misery in the streets, of course, could be filmed without special preparations. Contrasting scenes of dancing and banqueting, on the other hand, were carefully staged by the Germans with the help of hundreds of actors recruited from the general population. Dignified old Jews with Vandyke beards and elegant young ladies with heavy makeup were particularly sought out, even though key roles seem to have been reserved for Aryan actors in costume.

"I posed the question to them as to why our schools were not being filmed," noted Adam Czerniakow, the chairman of the Jewish Council, in his diary, not bothering to record the answer.[13] Czerniakow himself had to participate in enacting a scene of "petitioners and rabbis entering my office." Following that, "all paintings and charts were taken down [and] a nine-armed candlestick with all candles lit was placed on my desk." To complete the documentation of ghetto culture, "20 orthodox Jews with earlocks and 20 upper class women" were herded into a ritual bathing establishment, stripped naked and filmed, even though Jewish tradition demanded the separation of men and women in the *mikva*.[14] In short, for five weeks the German film crew was busy to prove the decadent presence of "Asia in Central Europe," and much of the footage was later included in an anti-Jewish propaganda movie under this title.[15]

In addition to Goebbels' movie men the ghetto was periodically combed by the military press units (Propaganda-Kompanien) that were routinely attached to every German army division and included writers and filmmakers as well as still photographers, the latter working with 35-millimeter cameras of the Leica or Contax type.[16] Several photo stories composed of such official picture material were published at the time by magazines such as the *Illustrierter Beobachter* or the *Berliner Illustrierte Zeitung*.[17] With their one-sided emphasis on Jewish poverty and sickness, and with their tendentious captions, these aimed at a hardly less blatant distortion of the ghetto reality than the above-mentioned movies.

A rather puzzling exception to the rule is a ghetto reportage of some 720 pictures which is today preserved at the Bundesarchiv in Koblenz, West Germany.

The reportage was compiled by the photographers Albert Cusian and Erhard Josef Knobloch (Warsaw) and Zermin (Lodz), who were members of Propaganda-Kompanie 689, but worked without obvious bias or prejudice and frequently even seem to express sympathy for the ghetto inhabitants. The question of how we can explain this surprisingly positive attitude must be postponed for the moment, primarily because we possess very little external information about the pictures. Among other things, it is impossible to reconstruct the specific purpose for which the reportage was undertaken. Moreover, the loss of the captions makes the identification of the represented scenes difficult and sometimes doubtful.

Not the least problem is the date of the reportage, but here a fairly accurate conclusion can be reached through careful picture analysis. G. Deschner, who published a selection of the images in 1969, assumes that they were taken over a course of two years, beginning in 1939.[18] However, while a prolonged or repeated presence of Propaganda-Kompanie 689 in Warsaw is a distinct possibility, the photographs reflect such uniform social, economic and weather conditions that they must have been taken in the span of a few weeks. On the basis of numerous factual picture details it can safely be determined that the period in question is late winter and early spring, 1941; and the presence of German camera teams in Lodz and Warsaw around this time is indeed confirmed by entries in Ringelblum's and Czerniakow's diaries.[19]

The numerous extant ghetto diaries and similar authentic documents not only help us to date the present pictures with reasonable certainty; they also offer abundant information about daily life in the ghetto, thus making up to a certain degree for the unfortunate loss of the picture captions. The following description of the Warsaw ghetto conditions during the spring of 1941 is largely based on these very eloquent and moving sources.[20] In writing the following paragraphs, it seemed important to mention many aspects of the complex ghetto reality that are absent from the photographs, either because the German press team chose to ignore them or because they were inaccessible to outsiders.

THE GHETTO AT FACE VALUE

To an unprepared visitor—such as a young German army photographer freshly arriving from Hamburg or Munich—the sight of the Warsaw ghetto under Nazi rule must have been staggering. Upon passing one of the tightly guarded entrances, he would immediately find himself engulfed by a noisy, confusing mass of humanity milling about in woefully narrow streets. The houses were old and decrepit, if not altogether ruined by the German bombardment of Warsaw. The air was bad, parks did not exist and hardly a single tree could be seen anywhere. Since the automobiles had been requisitioned and the horses had either been eaten, traded or expropriated, half a million ghetto inhabitants were left without transportation, except for a surreptitious streetcar line marked by the Star of David and a taxi service in the form of "rickshaws" propelled by "human motors" (photographs 83–87)—a luxury that few could afford.[21] The vast majority of the population had no choice but to spend hours every day traversing the ghetto on foot, either going to and from work, searching for something edible or simply trying to escape the dreary, overcrowded apartments.

That the Jewish religion was the one tie that this multitude of people had in common was not immediately apparent. Except for the mandatory white armband with the blue star, most ghetto inhabitants tried to look as un-Jewish as possible. Only staunch and intrepid conservatives continued to wear long beards, frock coats, starched hats and other ethnic insignia prone to invite German harassment. For similar reasons, fine clothes were shunned; after all, nobody wanted to incite "the plundering Nazi's lust," to put it in C. Kaplan's words.[22] As the ghetto's isolation from the outside world deepened, all clothes were reduced to the same shabby quality, anyway.

But the ghetto streets revealed more fundamental problems. Even first-time

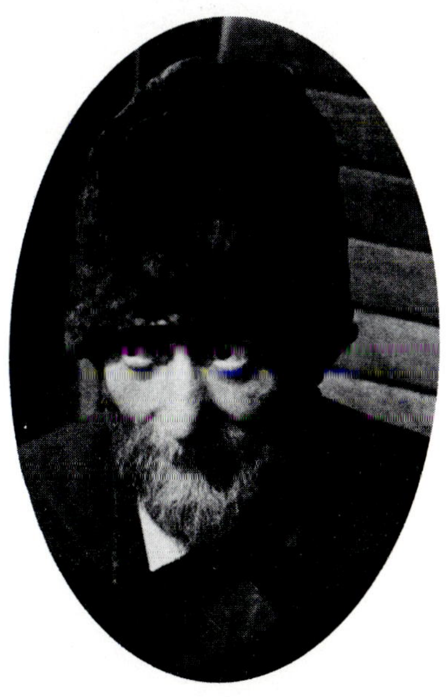

visitors quickly realized that for most inhabitants—the poor, the unemployed, the refugees, the orphaned children—the whole business of daily life revolved around a few economic transactions: a penny for a warm drink, a shirt for a loaf of bread. The main thoroughfares assumed a new function, that of a large, many-laned marketplace, kept in constant commotion by a prodigious amount of bartering and bargaining. So many people's livelihood depended on this primitive economic exchange that in some places the peddlers outnumbered the pedestrians.

The uncontested center of these activities seems to have been Gesia Street, if we can trust Ringelblum's diary entry of May 20, 1941: "The whole length of Gesia street has become a gigantic bazaar. Everything from the Jewish part of Warsaw is sold in that street. You can find linens, shirts, handkerchiefs, underwear, suits, shoes—principally linens. There are at least a thousand people standing around trading in it" (photo nos. 116–122).[23] According to M. Berg's recollections, Grzybowska Street vendors specialized in a different trade: "Hot iron or brick stoves are set up at every few steps. Large pots of water are boiling on them. Near by, at little tables or benches, there are thin slices of bread. Here, for forty groszy one can get a glass of hot water with saccharine and a slice of bread" (nos. 99, 130).[24]

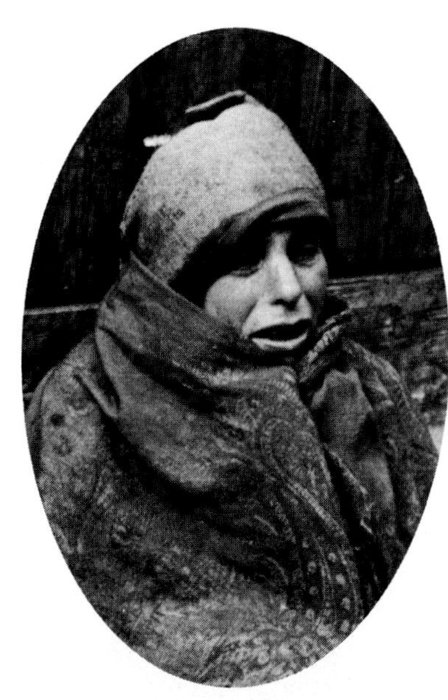

While the streets thus represented a lifeline for many impoverished Jews, it also became their deathbed when all personal possessions had been sold, begging failed and hunger and fever slowly claimed their due. At the same time, no passerby could overlook the bizarre irony that plenty of fine food was available to those who could pay the price. The store windows on Karmelicka Street, for example, were filled with pastries, cold meats and other delicacies which reached the ghetto through food parcels from neutral countries. "The Jewish Council tried repeatedly to cut down the lavishness of the displays in order to avoid provoking both the Germans and the starving people of the Ghetto. It was not unusual for people dying of starvation to be found right beside those shop windows." (Donat;[25] compare nos. 139, 150).

By spring 1941, when the photographs in this volume were most likely taken, the ubiquity of death was in fact the most striking feature in the Warsaw ghetto streets—the public death of thousands stranded without shelter, income or relatives to look after them. According to official statistics, 1700 ghetto inhabitants died between May 1 and May 15 of that year, mostly from starvation, but also from other causes, such as a rapidly spreading typhus epidemic, tuberculosis and various stress-related diseases, especially heart attacks (nos. 144–147, 160–170).[26]

Socially and economically uprooted, the large contingent of refugees from Western Europe and rural Poland faced the bleakest prospect of survival. The Jewish Council and the various charitable organizations were aware of the problem, but little could be done apart from perennially insufficient food and housing allocations. "I have visited a refugee home," reports Mary Berg in her diary. "It is a desolate building. The former walls of the separate rooms have been broken down to form large halls; there are no conveniences; the plumbing has been destroyed. Near the walls are cots made of boards and covered with rags. . . . On the floor I saw half-naked, unwashed children lying listlessly."[27]

But the most unfortunate victims of the ghetto system were the thousands of orphaned or abandoned children who tried to survive from day to day by smuggling, selling small articles, begging and even stealing. In fact, young food-snatchers became a notorious part of daily street life (no. 92).[28] Again, several communal groups did their best to alleviate the problem. Relief funds were collected, orphanages built, children's kitchens opened; in addition, a "Children's Month" was declared and posters spread slogans like "Our Children Must Not Die" or "Children Are Sacred." A few weeks before the deportations began, Czerniakow even bravely launched a drive for the creation of ghetto playgrounds.[29] Little was accomplished, however, by all these efforts, and the mortality rate continued to soar among the young. According to Goldstein's account, "there were child-beggars at every step. Singly and in packs they wandered through the courtyards and the streets, singing beggars' songs, crying out their unhappiness. Imploring fingers tugged at every passerby. . . . These had once been our future, these broken little bodies, these cracked voices begging for bread" (nos. 140–151).[30]

As the children, the refugees, the poor and the sick led an increasingly futile struggle for survival, a sense of gloom and resignation spread through the ghetto. By and by, people became indifferent toward death at best, and cynical at worst. As an indication of this, corpses were left lying in the streets, hastily covered by newspapers, until they were carted away in the early morning hours to be buried naked in mass graves—clothes being too precious to be wasted. For the well-to-do the talented entrepreneur Pinkiert offered a whole range of luxurious funeral services, pallbearers included. In fact, this establishment prospered to such a degree that the ghetto wondered "who worked for whom—Pinkiert for the Germans, or the Germans for him" (nos. 175–178).[31] Ironically, special funeral privileges were available for Jewish converts, whose efforts to escape their ethnic heritage were only rewarded in death by the allocation of a lot in the Catholic cemetery on Warsaw's "Aryan" side (nos. 182, 183).[32]

What has become visible in this brief description of the ghetto streets is, of course, no more than the facade, the outward appearance of a community with a highly complex internal structure. In turning our attention to the ghetto's infrastructure we should remember L. Dawidowicz's convincing distinction between "official" and "alternative" community activities.[33]

THE OFFICIAL GHETTO COMMUNITY

As a community of half a million people physically cut off from the rest of the world, the Warsaw ghetto could not do without its own internal administration. Recognizing this need, the occupation forces ordered the institution of the Judenrat, a council of 24 prominent Jews who acted as intermediaries between the German authorities and the ghetto population. In historical times, such councils had often played a beneficial role, offering financial tribute to the authorities in return for civil privileges for their coreligionists, and thus engineering mutually advantageous compromises. Deplorably, the inhumane regime of the Nazi functionaries in the Warsaw ghetto left little latitude for such precarious give and take. Seeing most of its requests and remonstrations ignored, the Warsaw Judenrat was largely confined to the execution of German orders, and in those gray areas where the council was capable of autonomous initiative the outcome necessarily reflected in one way or another the perversion of the general political framework.

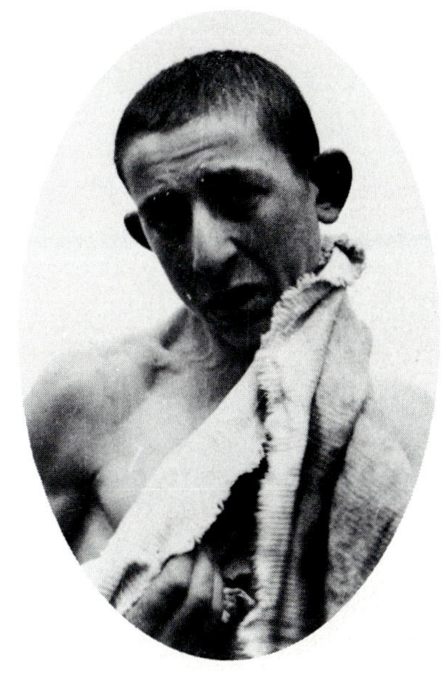

The taxation system is a case in point. In order to live up to its principal administrative duties, that is, the maintenance of a police force, labor brigades, a food-rationing system and postal and medical services, not to mention a host of welfare offices, the Jewish Council gradually established a large bureaucracy. It was a useful civil-service apparatus and it created thousands of much-needed jobs, but its financing required highly controversial measures. Of the regular communal taxes paid by the Jews, not a penny flowed back into the ghetto, which meant that the Jewish Council had to levy its own taxes. But few people had regular incomes, material resources were carefully hidden, and the real-estate and banking sectors were thrown into chaos by the German expropriation (robbery) tactics. As a result, the imposition of "just" taxes based on a family's actual net worth proved all but impossible, even though well-to-do community members did provide an irregular flow of contributions when pressured. But the bulk of the taxes had to be secured from such questionable sources as the fee the council charged for issuing food ration cards (in effect forcing the poor to finance their own welfare system) or the "ransom money" that prosperous Jews paid to be exempted from the ruinous work in the labor camps.[34]

Unjust as they were, these taxation practices directly benefited the ghetto insofar as they translated into jobs for the unemployed, bread for the starving or shelters for the refugees. Other Judenrat activities, however, primarily reflected German priorities. For example, an internal Jewish police force was created which maintained "law and order" and squelched Jewish resistance in the interest of, and at no expense to, the occupation forces (nos. 16–19). Initially, the measure was less unpopular than one might expect. Since Jews had never worn uniforms in prewar Poland, Mary Berg, for one, experienced "a strange and utterly illogical feeling of satisfaction" at the sight of policemen adorned with a Star of David, while C. Kaplan greeted the newly created Ordnungsdienst as a "godsend to the street vendors. . . . A Jewish policeman, a man of humble sensibilities—one of our own brothers would not turn over their baskets and trample their wares."[35] In the long run, however, the police force proved to be a divisive and corrupting element in the ghetto and was destined to play a particularly loathsome role during the deportations. Even earlier, Jewish police officials had been known to spend the rewards of bribery and blackmail in certain luxury restaurants and entertainment places on Leszno Street that also attracted Gestapo informers, smugglers and wealthy merchants (nos. 63–72).[36]

The Jewish Council also lent its assistance to the many German schemes aimed at extorting financial and material contributions from the ghetto, and it effectively organized the exploitation of Jewish labor both in German factories within the ghetto and in the outlying labor camps established for irrigation and land-reclamation projects along the Vistula River. How little these camps deserved the Judenrat's support can be gathered from the frightful news about them that reached Warsaw in May 1941, about the time photographs 50–62 were made. Ringelblum's diary mentions a large number of deaths due to starvation rations and cruel treatment by the Ukrainian guards; and even a German document openly states: "The treatment of the Jews in labor camps . . . can only be described as bestial."[37]

Eventually, the Jewish Council even became instrumental in the so-called "resettlement" operation, the forcible conscription of mass transports to the gas chambers of Treblinka—but only after its chairman, Adam Czerniakow, had committed suicide, posthumously winning the respect of many of his former critics.[38]

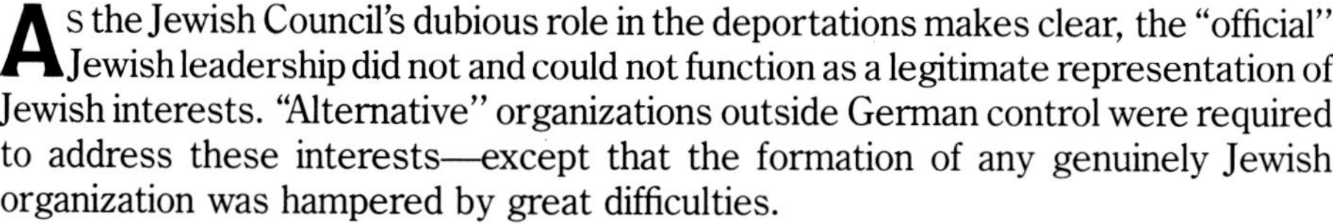

THE ALTERNATIVE GHETTO COMMUNITY

As the Jewish Council's dubious role in the deportations makes clear, the "official" Jewish leadership did not and could not function as a legitimate representation of Jewish interests. "Alternative" organizations outside German control were required to address these interests—except that the formation of any genuinely Jewish organization was hampered by great difficulties.

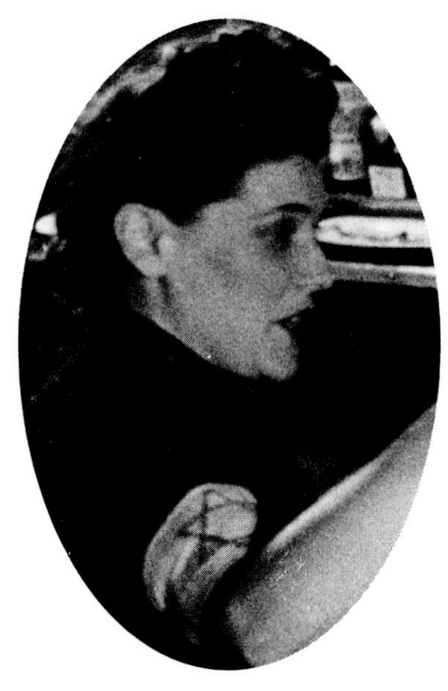

It would be naïve to assume that the relentless German terror and starvation compaign failed to demoralize the ghetto population to some degree. The extant diaries confirm this by their repeated complaints that charity and compassion wilted while corruption, blackmail and theft were on the rise; that fear and suspicion became so pervasive as to curtail social intercourse; and that constant bickering undermined family unity. After all, "even the closest family cannot get along living seven in a room," as a survivor commented.[39] Specifically Jewish values and customs were subject to the most obvious erosion. But the disappearance of traditional costumes and Yiddish and Hebrew as the principal ghetto languages was only the external symptom of a deep-reaching crisis of Jewish self-respect and identity. The sad irony of the situation was poignantly summarized in Kaplan's observation: "Our suffering is inflicted on us because we are Jews, while the real meaning of Jewishness has disappeared from our lives."[40]

Yet, in spite of the overwhelming German repression, a substantial part of the ghetto inhabitants refused to be mere victims. Using countless precautions and disguises, they proceeded to meet, to communicate, to act independently. In short, the ghetto *resisted*, but the extent and meaning of Jewish resistance can be appreciated only if one takes into account the tight prison conditions under which it occurred. Thus limited, resistance began with the simplest things: "You ask of resistance. To live one more day was resistance. Amidst the dysentery and typhus, the starvation, was resistance," noted a survivor.[41]

While resistance was rooted at the level of mere physical survival, it extended to political, cultural and economic matters as well. Most importantly, the struggle was carried out not just individually, but also socially, in the form of countless unofficial or altogether secret group activities. Nuclei of resistance sprang up everywhere, and tapped every available human and material resource. Somewhere in the recesses and beneath the surface of the official ghetto system there was room for an "alternative" ghetto community, one that bore more distinctly Jewish characteristics.

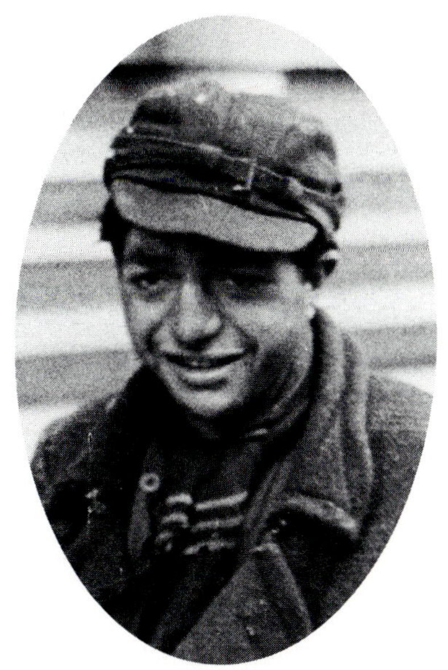

This other ghetto possessed a closely knit infrastructure in the form of Tenants' or Courtyard Committees, which originated during the siege of Warsaw and spread throughout the community as the mounting social problems called for an organized response at the grass-roots level. By September 1940, 2000 committees with 10,000 democratically elected members had come into existence. Current business lay in the hands of reporting subcommittees (for financial, sanitary, educational and political affairs, as well as housing, clothing and food), and since each of these was further divided and subdivided, most inhabitants found themselves involved to some degree or other in a vernacular political process geared toward collective survival.[42] Brought under the umbrella of the officially accredited ŻTOS (Jewish Organization for Public Care) network, the Courtyard Committees were not in and of themselves illegal, but by definition they represented the interests of the Jewish population, which automatically meant involvement in some clandestine operations, as well as habitual opposition to the policies of the Jewish Council. What made the Courtyard Committees particularly effective was their unofficially assumed authority to assess everyone's financial resources and to impose monthly contributions gradated accordingly. Obstinate tenants, or "stubborn pigs," found their hearts softened "by various means, some ethical, others coercive." The substantial funds raised in this manner were used for a variety of charitable projects, notably an increasing number of communal soup kitchens which, by May 1941, had handed out 50,000 daily portions to the needy.[43]

Jewish resistance also expressed itself by tenacious adherence to religious and cultural traditions, which were probably more durable than casual observation could reveal. Even though the Germans closed the synagogues, prohibited worship and generally harassed anyone suspected of Jewish orthodoxy, there was at all times a core of believers who continued to honor their religious heritage, clandestinely yet without compromise. From March 1941 on, prayer services were permitted again on a small scale, but to take advantage of this concession still required courage (nos. 75–82). How central such undaunted display of orthodoxy was to the ghetto's sense of identity can be gathered from the fact that it received the support of community leaders like J. Korczak and Czerniakow even though they were not personally religious. I. Milejkowski, the Judenrat member in charge of the health department, also learned to see traditional Jewish values in a more positive light: "I have realized," he said in an interview of 1941, "that the will to survive of the Jewish people, their stubbornness and persistence—'a stiff-necked people'—really come from the traditional religious approach to the problem of our survival."[44]

School education was another important front of resistance. Upon taking control of Warsaw, the Nazis not only closed the existing *yeshivot*, but also excluded Jews from public-school education. As a result, 40,000 ghetto children between seven and fourteen were legally deprived of all educational opportunities. But, keenly aware that the future of a whole generation was at stake, a coalition of welfare organizations and Jewish intellectuals set up an elaborate network of informal classes, usually disguised as children's soup kitchens, workshops and the like. "There would be five or six people in a room with a teacher," remembers G. Silkes. "And there were no books. Because suddenly if the Germans came breaking in, the children would give the teacher shoes and he became a shoemaker, or a piece of cloth and he was suddenly a tailor."[45] Adult patrons helped to provide the teaching materials as well as salaries for the teachers and food rations for the pupils.

According to another witness, "people had never shown such a ravenous appetite for books as in those days."[46] In spite of the destruction of many Jewish libraries and constant German raids, clandestine circulating libraries operated throughout the ghetto, and great value was attached to readings from Jewish literature. The textbooks for the secret school classes often had to be laboriously duplicated by typewriter.

For a long time the only legal schooling was provided by vocational courses for mechanics, electrotechnicians and the like in the community building at 26 Grzybowska Street (no. 25). Intellectually starved, young men and women registered in large numbers, but without illusions, as Mary Berg points out in her diary: "We all realize that the Germans' real intention is to train workers for their war industries, workers who will work without wages."[47]

There were no German injunctions against cultural pursuits as long as they were void of political connotations. Partially in spite of and partially because of the depressing overall situation, the ghetto took advantage of this freedom, fostering a broad spectrum of artistic activities from frivolous songs and dances to serious theater productions and literary works. The professional standards of such performances were often modest and critics denied that they offered evidence of an "original, creative ghetto culture." At the same time, however, they were invaluable as an affirmation of the Jewish will to live. Even the severe moralist Kaplan had to admit: "The more one dances, the more it is a sign of his belief in the 'eternity' of Israel. Every dance is a protest against our oppressors."[48]

As significant as these cultural activities were, the most desperate and most effective Jewish resistance was offered at the economic level. Following the occupation of Warsaw the German authorities had created a blatantly inequitable exchange system between the ghetto and the outside world. In return for the ruthless expropriation of Jewish finances, services and goods, this cunning mechanism provided only for grotesquely inadequate food supplies; its aim was the slow starvation of the ghetto. As the official food allowance sank below 200 calories per person per day, Jewish survival increasingly hinged on one dangerous recourse: smuggling.

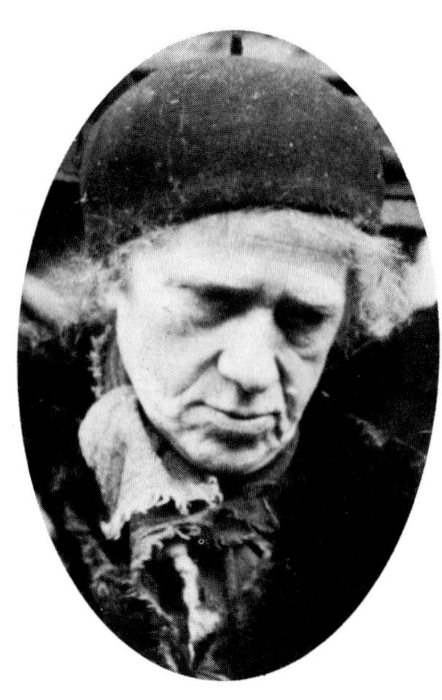

Needless to say, smuggling was a two-way business; every ounce of bread that was whisked into the ghetto had to be dearly paid for, either by personal possessions or by manufactured goods. In order to procure such payment in kind, the official, German-controlled ghetto economy was gradually supplemented by a large array of tiny underground factories, which produced "an amazing variety of things . . . including chemicals, pharmaceuticals, soap, rubber goods and electrical appliances; and Jewish resourcefulness surpassed itself in converting various and unpromising materials into finished goods."[49]

Among those specializing in the illegal transfer of the goods were many beggar children who had no other chance of survival. Clad in loose-fitting windbreakers, under which every kind of contraband could be hidden, these youngsters clustered around the ghetto gates, hoping for an opportunity to slip out. Others reached the "Aryan" side through holes in the wall concealed by loose bricks. Every day their ranks were decimated through arrests or executions on the spot; equally regularly, other desperate children filled the gaps.[50]

Obviously, though, such small individual smuggling activities could only meet a negligible fraction of the ghetto's total food demand. The rest had to be secured through well-organized smuggling rings, which involved dozens and even hundreds of collaborators on both sides of the wall and could count on the tacit tolerance of bribed guards. The schemes employed by these professional teams included the tossing of parcels from streetcars, the channeling of flour, sugar or milk through rainpipes, the use of false hearses, and so on.[51]

Smuggling was a dangerous business, pursued by courageous men constantly risking their lives. It also was a vital service without which the ghetto could not have survived for more than a few days. In view of this there may have been a grain of earnestness in the joking proposal made by the famous lawyer L. Berenson to erect a monument to the "Unknown Smuggler." At the same time, no concerned observer could deny that fundamentally smuggling was a criminal occupation that necessarily involved violence, blackmail and bribery, not to mention that the fortunes won in this manner financed the frivolous pleasures of a ghetto "elite" oblivious to the fate of the less-privileged community members. Thus one can understand Milejkowski's bitter question: "If, for a moment, we discount the utilitarian factor in smuggling

. . ., if we ponder instead on what sort of generation will grow out of these smugglers, good-for-nothing scamps—is the ghetto not a curse?"[52]

Finally, a word is in order about direct political and military resistance. The fact that half a million ghetto inhabitants failed to shake off the stranglehold of a few thousand German guards may seem strange in hindsight, but at the time no viable alternative existed. First of all, the Jewish leadership was in the dark about the ultimate Nazi intentions, the horrors of Auschwitz and Treblinka. As long as these could not be anticipated, accommodation with the German authorities seemed indeed the wisest strategy. Leftist groups such as the Bund, which refused accommodation, faced tremendous difficulties in smuggling a single handgun into the ghetto. And even if weapons had been available in quantity, it was clear that any form of armed resistance would not only have been suicidal for the fighters themselves, but also costly to the Jewish community as a whole. Even conventional nonviolent measures such as strikes and demonstrations met with such massive German reprisals that they could rarely be attempted. Under these conditions, all that could be done was to maintain a network of underground cells that observed developments and published several illegal newspapers but did not directly challenge the German occupation forces.[53] Only after the deportations of 1942 did these cells turn militant and proceed to set the example of an armed rebellion undertaken for reasons of principle, without realistic expectation of success.

READING THE PHOTOGRAPHS

BY basing the previous chapters on diaries instead of history books, we have given preference to the individual voices of Holocaust victims rather than the objective accounts of later researchers. That is, we have drawn on sources with a very immediate and "real" ring. A voice belongs to a person, it comes from within, it expresses personal views and experiences. In short, a voice is authentic; yet, wherever we hear only the voice without seeing the body to which it belongs, something essential is missing. In the case of the ghetto diaries, this deficiency is particularly noticeable. The social and architectural body of the Warsaw ghetto was so thoroughly eradicated that the ghetto's voice, as echoed on a few thousand pages of printed paper, seems uncannily homeless, divorced from any physical foundation.

In addition to the diaries, we possess a remarkable set of photographs of the Warsaw ghetto. These, too, can claim to be more "real" than the accumulation of abstract facts in history books. Photographs may not reflect the inner experiences of a person, but they offer a faithful record of his or her exterior appearance; photographs can give a face, a body to a voice, they assure us that given persons actually did exist at a certain point in time or else they could not have left their imprint on the photographic emulsion. Thus we suddenly find the floating, homeless voice of the ghetto diaries anchored in the solid ground of physical appearances; combined, the words and the pictures give us an overwhelmingly immediate sense of what it meant to live the Holocaust.

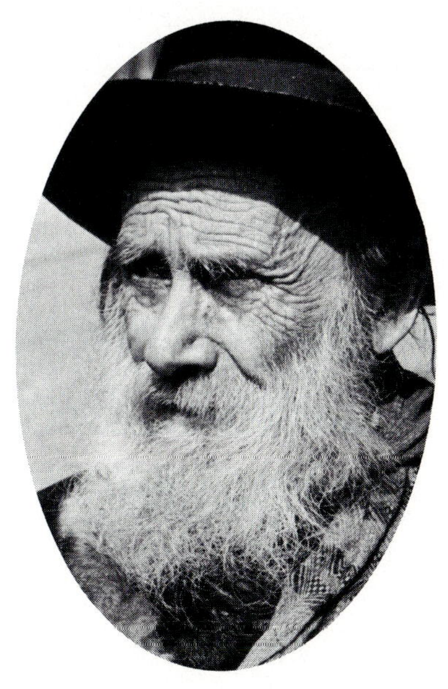

That the pictures were taken by German, rather than Jewish photographers may at first seem only a negligible flaw in the equation. As we have said before, upon cursory inspection the ghetto reportage in the present volume shows a warm, humane, sympathetic quality—A. B. Bernfes even thought it was seen through the "eyes of a Rembrandt."[54] At the very least, the photographers can be characterized as open-minded observers who made sure to record a broad variety of often intelligently selected subjects and who were able to impart to their pictures a direct and vibrant snapshot quality. No doubt we are dealing here with an aesthetically appealing and professionally accomplished photo-essay that does not have to fear comparison with the best work of contemporary *Life* or *Picture Post* photographers.

But our attempt to read and evaluate the Warsaw ghetto reportage should not end with such preliminary impressions. Too often, careful research has revealed the deceptive nature of photographs and especially news photographs—those minimal fragments lifted out of complex historical situations that remain invisible in their

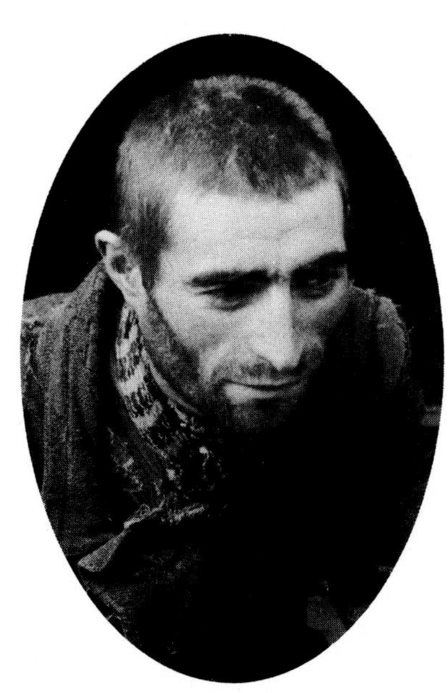

totality. In spite of all its technical accuracy, the camera renders images of much less fixed and unequivocal meaning than we commonly acknowledge. How we perceive and interpret a given photograph is largely a matter of the specific context in which we find it embedded, as well as the specific historical situation in which we are rooted ourselves, whether we are aware of it or not.[55] With regard to the images under discussion, historical and contextual factors can hardly be overestimated. Admittedly, from our modern point of view it is both natural and legitimate to read the reportage in a positive sense, as a tribute to the ghetto's courage and humanity, as a memento of the victims and as an indictment of the perpetrators. But our particular historically determined position should not blind us to the fact that a major watershed separates us from the time and the ideological climate in which the pictures were produced. We face the distinct possibility that they were originally made, read and intended to be read in principally different terms.

Even if we momentarily make the—much too generous—assumption that the photographers did not knowingly manipulate and distort the evidence, it still is difficult to doubt that they and their contemporary German audience were affected to some degree or other by a decade of massive anti-Semitic indoctrination. Consequently, what they recorded and saw in those pictures probably had a much more negative tinge than our own perceptions.[56] Specifically we can surmise that such ethnic characteristics as the white beards (remarkably often shown), curved noses, black costumes and the like were noted with reservation, if not revulsion. The same must have been true of certain behavioral patterns. For example, what may appear to us as a scene of friendly conversation may originally have been read as an instance of typically Jewish idleness or conspiratorial conduct. As difficult as it is to verify these assumptions today, it would be naïve to rule them out.

Even more relevant to the analysis of the present photographs is the circumstance that they were made by members of a German Propaganda-Kompanie and that they were put to some sort of official use. While it may be tempting to believe that Cusian and Knobloch were crusaders working in silent opposition to the Nazi regime, it is significant that they never made such a claim, nor did they like to see their names connected with the reportage in postwar years.[57] And the fact that a set of their pictures has been found mounted on the gray cardboard sheets common in German government agencies does indeed point in a different direction.[58] No doubt, the Warsaw ghetto photographs found their way into a German army or government office, presumably without raising eyebrows and clearly without getting the photographers in trouble.

Unfortunately, there are no clues to the intriguing question of which office this may have been and for what specific purpose the set was ordered and kept on file. Some general comments can safely be offered, however. Among other things, it should be well understood here that Nazi propaganda was a sophisticated undertaking which distributed many different messages to many different audiences. Prominent among the latter was the large international public composed of neutral countries like Switzerland, Sweden, Portugal and the United States, which monitored the political developments in Germany and occasionally even sent diplomatic missions to specific trouble spots. Overt, heavy-handed Nazi propaganda would have been self-defeating in such countries, and thus it is not surprising that *Signal*—with over 20 foreign-language editions and a run of 2.5 million, the National Socialists' main international propaganda magazine—followed an ideologically "soft" editorial policy designed to appeal even to critics of the regime. Since *Signal* was the main outlet for the photographic production of the Propaganda-Kompanien, this policy must have exerted a moderating influence on the cameramen at the front.[59]

Cusian's and Knobloch's photo-essay seems to be a case in point, even though it was apparently never published in *Signal* or any other Nazi magazine. That the pictures lack overtly propagandistic overtones does not mean, at any rate, that they were unusable for official German publication channels, nor does it point to subversive intentions on the part of the photographers. In fact, blatant instances of ideological bias and factual distortion seem surprisingly rare in the work of Nazi photographers, perhaps because the camera did not provide the best means to such devious ends. This is confirmed by the observation that in heavily prejudiced picture reportages it usually is the poisonous captions, rather than the more or less neutral pictures, that manipulate the viewer's perception.

All questions of propagandistic "processing" aside, we must acknowledge that, in spite of its seemingly sympathetic tone, Cusian's and Knobloch's ghetto documentation already reveals a subtle, but nevertheless distinct, anti-Jewish bias at the very level of making the pictures: the selection, the framing and the staging.

To begin with the photographers' choice of subject: according to the historical sources, the Gestapo, SS and regular German troops made frequent forays into the ghetto, indiscriminately harassing, plundering, interrogating, arresting, beating and shooting the population. Even when they refrained from such incursions, they still were busy sealing off and starving the ghetto. For reasons that do not speak in their favor, Cusian and Knobloch chose not to record any of these criminal activities. Among hundreds of photographs showing myriads of people, only a handful of German soldiers can be made out, and none of these are engaged in more incriminating pursuits than shouting a command at a group of camp workers or judging the complaint of a Jewish policeman (nos. 23, 49). If these photographs were our only extant documents, we could never guess that the Warsaw ghetto was a prison city held down by German boots. Similarly, the labor-camp views in photographs 50–62 create the deceptive impression that the inmates were treated correctly and received sufficient nourishment.

Bias of another kind is reflected in the extensive coverage of the Jewish police force, the internal Jewish postal service, communal disinfection facilities, vocational courses, religious worship, factory work, streetcar traffic and the like. These pictures unmistakably suggest to the viewer that the German authorities not only kept out of the ghetto but even encouraged the Jews to set up an autonomous communal structure of their own. As we have seen earlier, the semblance of such a structure did exist, except that it was far from autonomous, primarily serving to camouflage the true intentions of the Nazis. Whether Cusian and Knobloch innocently accepted this camouflage as real, or whether they looked through the ruse and opted not to expose it, is impossible to say. Either way, it is clear that their reportage provided the German authorities with an alibi. Had the pictures ever been published in *Signal* or a similar propaganda organ, they would have helped to assure the world that—certain problems with hunger and typhus notwithstanding—the Warsaw Jews were permitted to lead a reasonably secure and orderly life.

Independent Jewish agencies were a different matter. Even though legal and visible, the courtyard committees, soup kitchens, clothes collections and similar projects sponsored by the "alternative" ghetto community did not fit the official German view of the ghetto. It was certainly no accident that Kommissar Auerswald (Czerniakow's immediate superior), while taking great interest in the Jewish police force, mail service and factory system, never inquired about the Jewish charities. Cusian and Knobloch did not inquire, either. In keeping with prevailing Nazi attitudes, they neglected to record orphanages, soup kitchens and related forms of genuine Jewish self-help.

In some cases the two army photographers even came dangerously close to Goebbels' movie teams, who dwelt so gleefully on the scandalous aspects of ghetto life—without explaining, of course, that these conditions were the result of German cunning, rather than Jewish "decadence." Knobloch, for one, devoted an unnecessarily extensive picture sequence to the disinfection procedures which show Jews in humiliating situations and may well have been meant as indirect proof of the filthiness commonly ascribed by Nazi authorities to their Jewish victims (nos. 7–15). The amusements of the ghetto "elite" receive equally comprehensive exposure, and in view of the overall misery these amusements automatically assume a frivolous and irresponsible character.

Knobloch's and Cusian's intense interest in Pinkiert's funeral operations and burial scenes also seems to be motivated by less than innocent reportorial intentions. The obvious disregard for the feelings of the bereaved families; the macabre close ups of naked bodies carelessly stacked in heaps and sometimes identified by tags around the ankles; the emphasis on the employees' indifference in registering

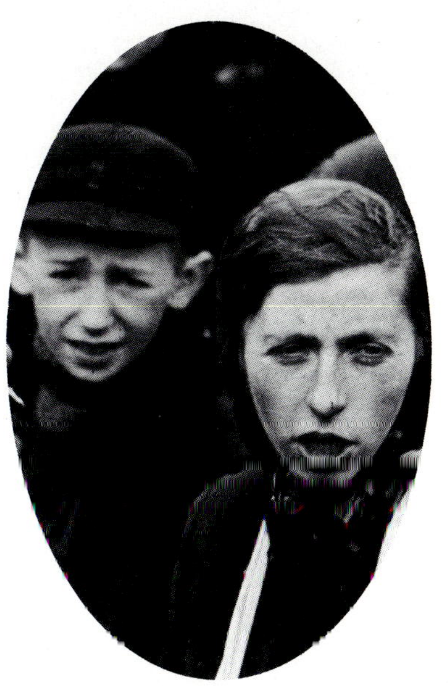

and handling the corpses—all this suggests at best a lack of compassion on the photographers' part, at worst a tendency to blame the Jews for moral shortcomings which—if they existed at all—were ultimately the product of German repression (nos. 175–188).

In this context even Knobloch's and Cusian's numerous snapshots of starving and dying Jews in the streets take on a different complexion. That most of these pictures express a measure of compassion with the victims can hardly be denied. But upon a closer examination the photographers appear to make a point of contrasting such suffering with the indifference of pedestrians who pass without taking notice, with the abundance of food in delicatessen windows or with the merriness of cabaret posters (nos. 1, 96, 139, 150, 163, 166).

In one instance Albert Cusian even seems to have *staged* a street scene in order to make his point. Photograph 165 can be considered as a rather candid snapshot of a young man who has just collapsed in the middle of a busy street. In a second picture, taken a few minutes later (no. 166), a crowd has gathered in a circle around the victim. Three policemen make sure that the bystanders keep at a certain distance, leaving enough space for a mother and child to stroll by casually. But there is something strange about these casual passersby. Since street life has come to a complete standstill and everyone is aware of, if not directly looking at the German photographer, who clearly has taken control of the situation, it appears highly improbable that anyone could just "happen" to stroll by the spot of the accident, not to mention that the crowd is too densely packed to permit free movement. We must conclude that the photographer had a hand in this; most likely he picked the mother and child from among the bystanders and positioned them *as if* they were passing by fortuitously. The elegant, well-to-do appearance of the two gives us the clue to the whole fabricated scene: once more the photographer aims at exposing the indifference of the wealthy toward the sufferings of the poor—never mind the employment of less than candid photojournalistic techniques.

Bernfes erred: these pictures were seen through the eyes of German army photographers rather than the eyes of a Rembrandt. As vivid and persuasive as many of them are, they essentially amount to an *outside* view of the Warsaw ghetto. The faces that have inscribed themselves on the photographic emulsion are Jewish, but the angle under which they are seen is not.

What it was like to use the camera for an *inside* documentation of the ghetto can be gathered from Mendel Grossman's recently published Lodz photographs.[60] In subject and tone these have surprisingly little in common with the German army reportage in the present volume. Grossman was not interested in dignified old Jews with long white beards, he showed no fascination with the hustle and bustle of street life, he did not encourage young street vendors to smile into his camera, he had no time for aesthetically pleasing composition, and the technical quality of his prints was inferior. Grossman worked hurriedly and secretly, with an old, patched-up camera, from the corner of a remote window or through a slit in his coat, and for the most part he captured what German cameramen did not see or did not want to see: the change of the German guards, the distribution of bread loaves and relief funds, the secret meeting of an underground organization, carts collecting corpses in the streets, women scrambling for scraps of food around a public kitchen, children digging in the ground for fuel, relatives kissing each other through a chain fence before being deported, someone writing a letter before boarding a train to the gas chambers, and the faces of hundreds of murdered Jews, photographed for identification by their families. Instead of the exterior, Grossman described the inner workings of the ghetto. He became the eye and the agent of the Jewish community; subject and object, the photographer and the photographed converge in his pictures.

The fact remains that, even though the photo reportage in this volume was compiled by members of a German Propaganda-Kompanie, it is not a propaganda product in itself. True, some important ghetto aspects were ignored by the photographers, and there are instances where the subject was manipulated with dubious intentions. But the large majority of the pictures is either neutral in tone or directly sympathetic to the ghetto population. While this makes them eminently readable

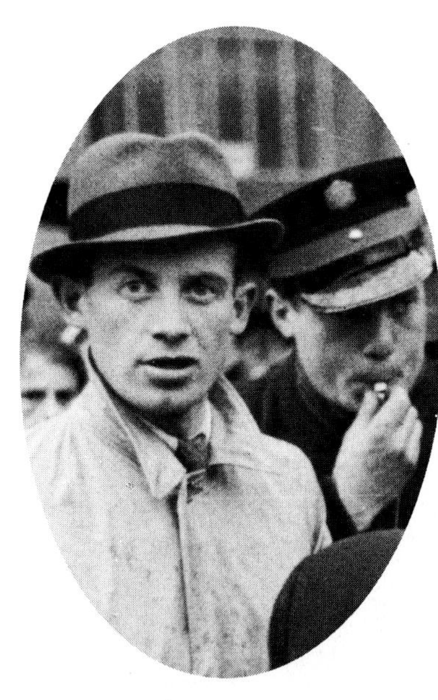

and acceptable for present-day viewers, however, it does not reflect too positively on the makers of the pictures. Undeniably their benevolent attitude toward the terrorized, starving people before their camera was a cheap gesture as long as it did not lead to protest and opposition against the crime in progress. Sympathy alone was a self-serving strategy designed to certify the photographers' sensibility and to offer them an illusionary moral indemnity from the horrors they witnessed. The photographers could feel superior to the brutal SS guards and the indifferent ghetto "elite." They could feel good about their pictures, so good, in fact, that they could consider themselves absolved from doing anything about the photographed situation. While thousands starved to death in the streets of Warsaw and millions were annihilated in the death camps, the photographers could continue to wear their uniforms and to do their photographic duty; and thirty years after the fact one of them could reminisce with surrealistic naïveté:

> I photographed everything in sight in the Warsaw ghetto. The subject
> matter was so interesting. I took pictures in the morgue and at the Jewish
> cemetery. Bodies of Jews who had died during the night were laid out on
> the pavements for collection in the morning. I'd wait until the collectors
> came and then take pictures of them.[61]

Absorbed by the interesting subject matter, Cusian never seems to have been troubled by the question *why* there were so many deaths in the ghetto.

But we have been sidetracked. We need to remember: whatever the photographers felt and intended while taking their pictures is comparatively irrelevant in view of the actual picture content. The old truism that the camera sees much more than its operator may realize is certainly applicable in the present case. The Warsaw ghetto reportage does represent an indelible and inexhaustible document of the crime of the Holocaust, even if the cameramen failed to realize that they were witnessing a crime, and that they themselves were part of the complex state and military apparatus which committed it.

HISTORY

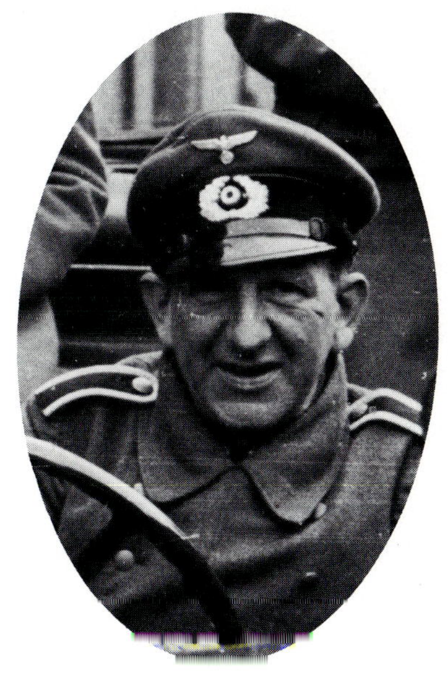

THE labelling of 500,000 men, women and children as "Jews," their imprisonment in one and a half square miles of half-ruined city streets, their forced chaotic, desperate coexistence have long "become history," to use a common figure of speech. But while history usually means continuity in change, the history of European Jewry is different in a disturbing way. As Davidowicz pointed out, all other countries and peoples ravaged by the Second World War "eventually returned to their normal existence." Sons took the place of their fathers, new buildings rose out of the ruins. "But the annihilation of the six million European Jews brought an end with irrevocable finality to the thousand-year-old culture and civilization of Ashkenazic Jewry, destroying the continuity of Jewish history."[62] Nobody can ever live this culture again, and since it left behind fewer material remainders than many civilizations that perished thousands of years ago, memory itself is a precarious project, having to feed upon woefully inadequate sources. Nevertheless, it is an indispensable project. Memory, too, is a historical agent and offers the only substitute for the lost continuity of Jewish history.

During the Holocaust itself this was already clearly understood. When the hope for personal survival ceased, when the destruction of the Jewish people loomed large and at last became certain, one undertaking remained meaningful: to leave a trace in human memory. Thus, collecting documents, writing memoirs, committing pieces of the overwhelming events to paper became the last line of resistance to many ghetto inhabitants, not only intellectuals, journalists and writers, but housewives and children as well.[63]

On a merely personal, psychological level such literary activity was comforting. It constituted an act of self-assertion and permitted thoughts to be clarified, anxieties to be released. As Kaplan noted on November 13, 1941, nine months

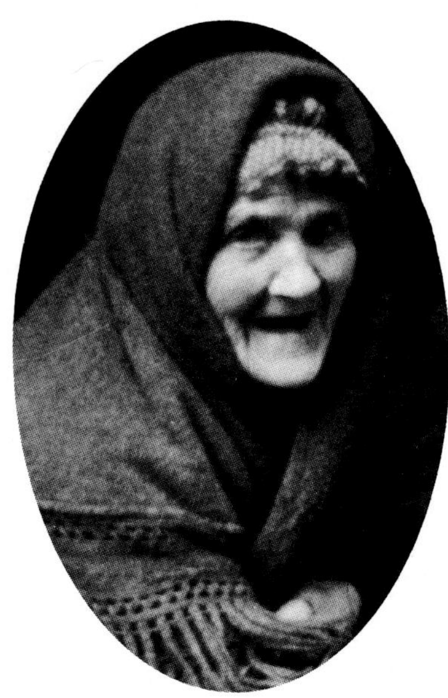

before his death: "This journal is my life, my friend and ally. I would be lost without it." [64]

However, the main purpose of these memoirs was not soliloquy, but a dialogue of sorts, the posthumous communication with the outside world and other generations. Nobody understood this better than E. Ringelblum, who turned the writing of contemporary history into an organized underground activity. Under the intentionally misleading name Oneg Shabbath (Pleasures of the Sabbath), Ringelblum's association not only collected a broad variety of documents related to the Polish ghettos under Nazi rule, but also encouraged writers to produce manuscripts for regular fees. In March 1944, Ringelblum was arrested in Warsaw's Aryan district, brought to Pawiak prison and shot. But, packed in metal cans and buried in a basement, his historical archive survived the war largely undamaged and has since spoken of and for the millions who did not live to speak for themselves. [65]

Even during the war, several Ringelblum dossiers were smuggled through German lines, supplying the British radio service with solid information about the wholesale massacres of Jews in the German extermination camps. When Ringelblum overheard one of these broadcasts in June 1942, he was hopeful that the revelation would lead to the rescue of hundreds of thousands of Polish Jews threatened by destruction. Unfortunately, the indifference of the Allied governments proved to be too solid to be shaken by a scant trickle of horrible information. Ringelblum's work may have saved few lives, but to the extent that it preserved the memory of something that must never be forgotten he had a right to conclude that Oneg Shabbath had "fulfilled its great historical task." [66]

In the body of records constituting the martyrology of European Jewry the photographs presented in this volume can claim a distinct place of their own. In studying them it would be unwise to forget that, in contrast to Ringelblum's manuscripts or Grossman's pictures, they were never buried in the ground, but came down to us as part of the official propaganda legacy of the Third Reich. Still, even if these are outside views produced by German cameramen, it remains true that the camera's glass eye is less docile than a brush or pen. In spite of all avenues of manipulation that a century of technical improvements had opened to World War II photographers, there was still some validity in H. F. Talbot's claim that photography allowed the objects to inscribe *themselves* on the picture surface. In a manner characteristic of the photographic medium, the present pictures oscillate between factual recording and personal interpretation; they represent a complex blend of what the photographer wanted to record and what the camera happened to capture. However ambiguous, this photo reportage can help, if not to understand, at least to remember, one of the most critical chapters of twentieth-century history.

Perhaps the paradox of the Jewish Holocaust, seen through the sympathetic eyes of the perpetrators, can become more intelligible with reference to the bitter joke about a German soldier's glass eye related in Donat's ghetto memoirs. [67] According to that story, the soldier "came to take a Jewish child from its mother. When she pleaded for its life, he said, 'If you can guess which of my eyes is artificial, I'll give you the child.' She looked intently at him and said, 'The right one.' Astonished, the Nazi asked, 'That's so, but how could you tell?' After hesitating for a moment, she replied, 'It looks more human than the other.' "

ULRICH KELLER

NOTES

[1]*Faschismus—Getto—Massenmord. Dokumentation über Ausrottung und Widerstand der Juden in Polen während des 2. Weltkriegs*, ed. by Żydowski Instytut Historyczny (Warsaw), Frankfurt/M, 1962, p. 112.

[2]S. L. Shneiderman, *Between Fear and Hope*, Arco Publishing Co., New York, 1947, p. 53.

[3]Among the numerous historical studies of the Holocaust I have found the following especially useful: L. S. Dawidowicz, *The War Against the Jews 1933–1945*, Holt, Rinehart and Winston, New York, 1975; I. Trunk, *Judenrat. The Jewish Councils in Eastern Europe under Nazi Occupation*, Macmillan, New York, 1972; K. D. Bracher, *The German Dictatorship: The Origins, Structures and Effects of National Socialism*, Praeger, New York, 1970.

[4]For the history of the Warsaw ghetto compare: *Martyrs and Fighters, The Epic of the Warsaw Ghetto*, ed. by P. Friedman, Praeger, New York, 1954; *The Warsaw Ghetto*, ed. by C. Z. Banasiewicz, Yoseloff, New York, 1968; R. Ainsztein, *The Warsaw Ghetto Revolt*, Holocaust Library, New York, 1979; A. Katz, *Poland's Ghettos at War*, Twayne, New York, 1970.

[5]*The Stroop Report: The Jewish Quarter of Warsaw Is No More*, translated and annotated by S. Milton, Pantheon, New York, 1979.

[6]That this is more than a convenient figure of speech is confirmed by almost all noted Holocaust historians. For example, Dawidowicz stated recently: "Despite the recent outpouring of popular and scholarly books on Hitler, no work has yet been produced that satisfactorily explains Hitler's obsessive ideas about the Jews, the readiness of the German people to accept those ideas, and Hitler's ability to harness an enormous apparatus of men, institutions, and facilities just in order to murder the Jews" (L. S. Dawidowicz, *The Holocaust and the Historians*, Harvard University Press, Cambridge, Mass., 1981, p. 34). Compare similar statements by N. Levin, *The Holocaust. The Destruction of European Jewry 1933–1945*, Thomas Y. Crowell, New York, 1968, p. xi; and D. Weinberg, "The Holocaust in Historical Perspective," in: *Encountering the Holocaust. An Interdisciplinary Survey*, ed. by B. L. Sherwin and S. G. Ament, Impact Press, Chicago, 1979, p. 53.

[7]K. Jaspers, *The Origin and Goal of History*, Yale University Press, New Haven, 1953, p. 149.

[8]For the lively debate that followed the broadcast of *Holocaust* in America compare the reviews by J. J. O'Connor, E. Wiesel, G. Green and W. Safire, published by the *New York Times* on April 14, 16, 23 and 24, 1978. An excellent summary of the film's impact in West Germany will be found in: *Im Kreuzfeuer: Der Fernsehfilm 'Holocaust'. Eine Nation ist betroffen*, ed. by P. Marthesheimer and I. Frenzel, S. Fischer, Frankfurt/M, 1979. For the book version of *Holocaust* see G. Green, *Holocaust*, Bantam Books, New York, 1978. I. Schwartz reviewed *The Wall* in the *New York Times* on February 10, 1982; the film is based on John Hersey's novel *The Wall*, Knopf, New York, 1950.

[9]A broad variety of documentary photographs of the Warsaw ghetto, taken by German as well as Jewish cameramen, is presented in the following publications: *The Warsaw Ghetto in Pictures. Illustrated Catalogue*, YIVO, New York, 1970; Z. Szajkowski, *An Illustrated Sourcebook of the Holocaust*, 3 volumes, KTAV Publishing House, New York, 1977; *Archives of the Destruction. A Photographic Record of the Holocaust*, Yad Vashem, Jerusalem, 1981. (The latter is a microfiche edition with over 3200 images, including many which are also reproduced in the present volume; unfortunately, no serious effort was made to identify the precise subjects, locations and dates of these invaluable picture documents.)

[10]Compare *Scroll of Agony. The Warsaw Diary of Chaim A. Kaplan*, translated and edited by A. I. Katsh, Collier Books, New York, 1973, pp. 243, 300; M. Zylberberg, *A Warsaw Diary 1939–1945*, Hartmore, London, 1969, p. 31; *Notes from the Warsaw Ghetto. The Journal of Emmanuel Ringelblum*, edited and translated by J. Sloan, Schocken Books, New York, 1974, pp. 168, 181; *The Warsaw Diary of Adam Czerniakow. Prelude to Doom*, ed. by R. Hilberg, S. Staron and J. Kermisz, Stein and Day, New York, 1979, pp. 228, 348 ff.

[11]Zylberberg, *loc. cit.*, p. 31.

[12]Compare Czerniakow's repeated diary entries, *loc. cit.*, pp. 348 ff.

[13]Czerniakow, *loc. cit.*, p. 353. (By 1942 some Jewish schools had been legalized.)

[14]Czerniakow, *loc. cit.*, pp. 349, 353.

[15]Compare *Martyrs and Fighters*, p. 43.

[16]Interesting comments on the organization and role of the German Propaganda-Kompanien are offered by P. Knightley, *The First Casualty. From the Crimean War to Vietnam: The War Correspondent as Hero, Propagandist, and Myth Maker*, Harcourt Brace Jovanovich, New York, 1975, pp. 220 ff. More detailed information can be found in: O. Buchbender/H. Schuh, *Heil Beil. Flugblattpropaganda im II. Weltkrieg*, Stuttgart, 1974, pp. 13 ff. According to Buchbender/Schuh, a Propaganda-Kompanie comprised two "light" reportage teams with two to three writers and one or two photographers each, and one "heavy" reportage team with additional movie and radio personnel. For further information see: H. von Wedel, *Die Propagandatruppen der deutschen Wehrmacht* (series *Die Wehrmacht im Kampf*, vol. 34), Neckargemünd, 1962; and *Die Wildente*, the bulletin of former Propaganda-Kompanie members, published in 28 issues between 1952 and 1965.

[17]*The Black Book of Polish Jewry. An Account of the Martyrdom of Polish Jewry under the Nazi Occupation*, ed. by J. Apenszlak, American Federation for Polish Jews, no loc., 1943, p. 57.

[18]G. Deschner, *Menschen im Ghetto*, Bertelsmann, Gütersloh, 1969, *passim*. It appears that the PK 689 photographers did, in fact, document the Warsaw ghetto over an extended period of time, but the greater part of their pictures seems lost, leaving only a few film rolls which were clearly exposed during a few weeks in the spring of 1941 (see the following note). According to his own recollection (quoted by Knightley, *loc. cit*, p. 221), Cusian stayed in Warsaw for some time, specializing in burial operations. However, of his substantial documentary work only four film rolls are extant at the Bundesarchiv, Koblenz, and few of these images have to do with burials. Deschner failed to recognize that the extant picture material is only a small fragment. As a result, he incorrectly dated the pictures between 1939 and 1941 and misinterpreted some of the subjects. Furthermore, Deschner mistakenly assumed that all!

photographs were taken in the Warsaw ghetto. However, careful comparison with other historical ghetto photographs (especially those published in: *With a Camera in the Ghetto. Mendel Grossman,* ed. by Z. Szner and A. Sened, Schocken Books, New York, 1977) proves beyond a doubt that some photographs represent scenes from the Lodz ghetto.

[19]The following historical circumstances are helpful in establishing a *terminus post quem* for the photographs. The Warsaw ghetto was not enclosed by walls until the fall of 1940; the police force, the post office and the vocational courses were instituted between December 1940 and February 1941. In the same winter months the horses disappeared, to be replaced by carts and rickshaws, and the streetcar service was cut down to the one line with the big Star of David emblem that is visible in some of the photographs. In March 1941, Jewish worship was legalized and the labor camps were reopened. The winter of 1941/42, on the other hand, can be considered as a *terminus ante quem* because by that time the ghetto conditions had deteriorated far beyond the point documented in the photographs. Indisputable evidence is provided by no. 96, which represents a theater poster dated "Saturday, May 17"; a check of the calendar shows that May 17th fell on a Saturday in 1941. Ringelblum's mention of the German camera team is in *loc. cit.,* p. 168; Czerniakow's in *loc. cit.,* p. 228.

[20]The following bibliographies were useful in locating the sources: *The Holocaust and After. Sources and Literature in English,* ed. by J. Robinson, Israel University Press, Jerusalem, 1973, pp. 71 ff.; *The Holocaust. An Annotated Bibliography,* ed. by H. J. Cargas, Catholic Library Association, Haverford, Pa., 1977, pp. 33 ff.

[21]B. Goldstein, *The Stars Bear Witness,* translated and edited by L. Shatzkin, Viking Press, New York, 1949, p. 90. Information not credited to diary sources has been derived from Trunk, *loc. cit.,* and Dawidowicz, *The War Against the Jews.*

[22]Kaplan, *loc. cit.,* p. 86; also see Ringelblum, *loc. cit.,* p. 83.

[23]Ringelblum, *loc. cit.,* p. 182.

[24]*Warsaw Ghetto. A Diary by Mary Berg,* ed. by S. L. Shneiderman, L. B. Fisher, New York, 1945, p. 88.

[25]A. Donat, *The Holocaust Kingdom. A Memoir,* Holt, Rinehart and Winston, New York, 1965, p. 45. A raid on such luxury stores, ordered by the Jewish Council in order to procure food for orphans, is recorded by Czerniakow, *loc. cit.,* p. 345.

[26]Czerniakow, *loc. cit.,* p. 237. The ubiquity of death and the growing indifference toward the dying and dead were noted by Goldstein, *loc. cit.,* p. 80; Zylberberg, *loc. cit.,* p. 50; Ringelblum, *loc. cit.,* p. 165; and Noemi Szac-Wajnkranc, in: *Im Feuer vergangen. Tagebücher aus dem Getto,* Rütten und Loening, Berlin, 1961, p. 371.

[27]Berg, *loc. cit.,* pp. 68 f.; for a ŻTOS report on refugee care in the Warsaw ghetto see: *A Holocaust Reader,* ed. with an introduction and notes by L. S. Dawidowicz, Behrman House, New York, 1976, pp. 179 ff. Also compare Prof. Hirszfeld's description in *Martyrs and Fighters,* pp. 47 f.

[28]Compare Szac-Wajnkranc, *loc. cit.,* pp. 372 f.; Goldstein, *loc. cit.,* pp. 80 f.

[29]Donat, *loc. cit.,* p. 48; Zylberberg, *loc. cit.,* p. 52.

[30]Goldstein, *loc. cit.,* p. 82.

[31]Ringelblum, *loc. cit.,* p. 138; Szac-Wajnkranc, *loc. cit.,* p. 379.

[32]For the situation of the converted Jews see Zylberberg, *loc. cit.,* p. 49; Donat, *loc. cit.,* pp. 28 f.

[33]Dawidowicz, *The War Against the Jews,* pp. 223 ff., 242 ff.

[34]*Martyrs and Fighters,* pp. 71 f.; Donat, *loc. cit.,* pp. 18 f.

[35]Berg, *loc. cit.* p. 42; Kaplan, *loc. cit.,* p. 234.

[36]For the amusements of this corrupt ghetto "elite" see Kaplan, *loc. cit.,* p. 291; Berg, *loc. cit.,* p. 60; Goldstein, *loc. cit.,* p. 91; Donat, *loc. cit.,* p. 89; Szac-Wajnkranc, *loc. cit.,* p. 381.

[37]*Documents of Destruction. Germany and Jewry 1933–1945,* ed.

with commentary by R. Hilberg, Quadrangle Books, Chicago, 1971, p. 40. For another German document cautiously criticizing the bad camp conditions, *ibid.,* pp. 43 ff.; see also Ringelblum, *loc. cit.,* pp. 170 f.

[38]Compare J. Kermisz's introduction to Czerniakow's diary, *loc. cit.,* pp. 23 f.

[39]L. Zuker-Bujanowska, *Liliana's Journal: Warsaw 1939–1945,* Dial Press, New York, 1980, p. 30. According to Kaplan's diary entry of February 2, 1940, "social visits have ceased," *loc. cit.,* p. 114.

[40]Kaplan, *loc. cit.,* p. 289; also compare H. Zeitlin's remarks in *Holocaust Reader,* pp. 219 f.

[41]Gensia Silkes in: *Amcha: An Oral Testament of the Holocaust,* ed. by S. S. Friedman, University Press of America, Washington, D.C., p. 137.

[42]Donat, *loc. cit.,* pp. 8 ff.; Kaplan, *loc. cit.,* pp. 227 f., 259.

[43]"Stubborn pigs": Kaplan, *loc. cit.,* p. 259; soup-kitchen statistics: *Black Book of Polish Jewry,* p. 49, and the German Biennial Report of 1941 in Czerniakow, *loc. cit.,* p. 397.

[44]*Holocaust Reader, p. 225.*

[45]G. Silkes in: *Amcha,* p. 137; also see Kaplan, *loc. cit.,* pp. 86, 242.

[46]*Witness to the Holocaust,* ed. by A. Eisenberg, Pilgrim Press, New York, 1981, p. 162.

[47]Berg, *loc. cit.,* p. 50.

[48]"Original ghetto culture": I. Milejkowski in: *Holocaust Reader,* p. 223; "The more one dances": Kaplan, *loc. cit.,* p. 245; also compare Goldstein, *loc. cit.,* p. 83. Such entertainments were still more legitimate when linked to charitable fund-raising purposes; compare Donat, *loc. cit.,* p. 44.

[49]Donat, *loc. cit.,* p. 37; also see Szac-Wajnkranc, *loc. cit.,* p. 380.

[50]Compare Donat, *loc. cit.,* p. 36; Berg, *loc. cit.,* pp. 72 f.

[51]For organized, large-scale smuggling compare M. Gray's memoirs (*For Those I Loved,* Little Brown, Boston, 1972) and P. Opoczynski's description in *Holocaust Reader,* pp. 197 ff. See also Szac-Wajnkranc, *loc. cit.,* pp. 382 ff.; Donat, *loc. cit.,* pp. 33, 36 f.

[52]*Holocaust Reader,* p. 224.

[53]For a picture of the Warsaw ghetto from an underground perspective see Goldstein, *loc. cit., passim.*

[54]Quoted from: "Warschauer Ghetto: Graue Albumblätter," in: *Der Spiegel,* January 1, 1968 (vol. 22, no. 1), p. 66. According to the article, A. B. Bernfes found and acquired after the war several sets of Warsaw ghetto photographs that later turned out to be prints from Cusian's and Knobloch's negatives in the Bundesarchiv, Koblenz. Bernfes put the pictures at the disposal of the BBC for a 1967 broadcast.

[55]For a general discussion of the problem, without reference to the Warsaw ghetto, see: A. Sekula, "On the Invention of Photographic Meaning," in: *Photography in Print. Writings from 1816 to the Present,* ed. by V. Goldberg, New York, 1981, pp. 452 ff.; U. Keller, "Photographs in Context," in: *Image,* vol. 19, no. 4, December 1976, pp. 1 ff.

[56]In this context it is interesting to read C. Meckel's inquiry into his father's past, based on the latter's posthumously discovered diaries. Eberhard Meckel was not a Nazi; even in uniform he remained a cultivated man, a poet. But as a soldier in Poland he, too, automatically assumed a "Herrenmensch" attitude toward native Poles and Jews. According to his son, Eberhard Meckel was quite familiar with the slums and ghettos of the Polish cities, especially Lodz, where he was stationed. But he looked upon these places from the "prescribed viewpoint of the military: this was the decadence of an ancient era; the new era would eliminate such remnants. It would take some time until the Pole would be equal to the German, a lot would have to be done in this direction. Meanwhile, Eastern humanity had to suffer . . ." (C. Meckel,

Suchbild. Über meinen Vater, Claassen, Düsseldorf, 1980, p. 68).

[57]Deschner, for example, was in personal contact with one of the photographers, but—presumably upon request—he gave no name in his ghetto book. My own efforts to interview one of the photographers were coldly received.

[58]The pictures found by A. B. Bernfes were mounted on gray cardboard; compare the article in *Der Spiegel*, quoted above.

[59]For *Signal* and its relation to the Propaganda-Kompanien, see J. Kasper, *Belichtung und Wahrheit. Bildreportage von der Gartenlaube bis zum Stern*, Campus, Frankfurt/M, 1979, pp. 53 ff.; *Swastika at War. A Photographic Record of the War in Europe as Seen by the Cameramen of the German Magazine* Signal, ed. by R. Hunt and T. Hartman, Futura, London, 1975 (with an informative preface by G. Heysing, former Deputy Editor of *Signal*).

[60]*With a Camera in the Ghetto*; see note 18.

[61]As quoted by Knightley, *loc. cit.*, p. 221.

[62]L. S. Dawidowicz, *The Holocaust and the Historians*, p. 14.

[63]Compare I. Halperin, *Messengers from the Dead. Literature of the Holocaust*, Westminster Press, Philadelphia, 1970, p. 46.

[64]Kaplan, *loc. cit.*, p. 278. Donat, on the other hand, ironically refers to his diary writing as the characteristic pastime of a "superfluous man" (*loc. cit.*, p. 20).

[65]Compare J. Sloan's introduction to Ringelblum's *Notes, loc. cit.*, pp. xvi ff.; L. Dawidowicz's introduction to *Holocaust Reader*, pp. 5 ff.; and Shneiderman, *loc. cit.*, pp. 66 f.

[66]Ringelblum, as quoted in: J. Wulf, *Von Leben, Kampf und Tod im Ghetto Warschau*, Bonn, 1958, p. 12. The failure of the Allied governments to intervene in behalf of the Jews is documented in: A. D. Morse, *While Six Million Died. A Chronicle of American Apathy*, Random House, New York, 1968; B. Wasserstein, *Britain and the Jews of Europe, 1939–1945*, Oxford University Press, London, 1979; *Zygelboym-bukh*, ed. by S. Hertz, New York, 1947.

[67]Donat, *loc. cit.*, pp. 102 f.

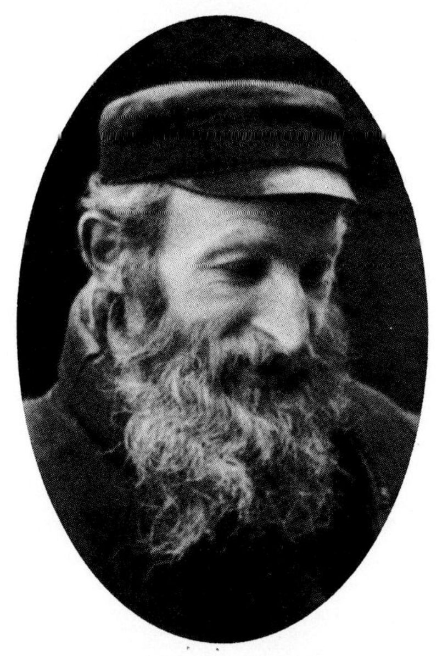

THE WARSAW GHETTO
IN PHOTOGRAPHS

INTERNAL GHETTO ADMINISTRATION
Medical, Postal, Food Stamps
(Nos. 1–15)

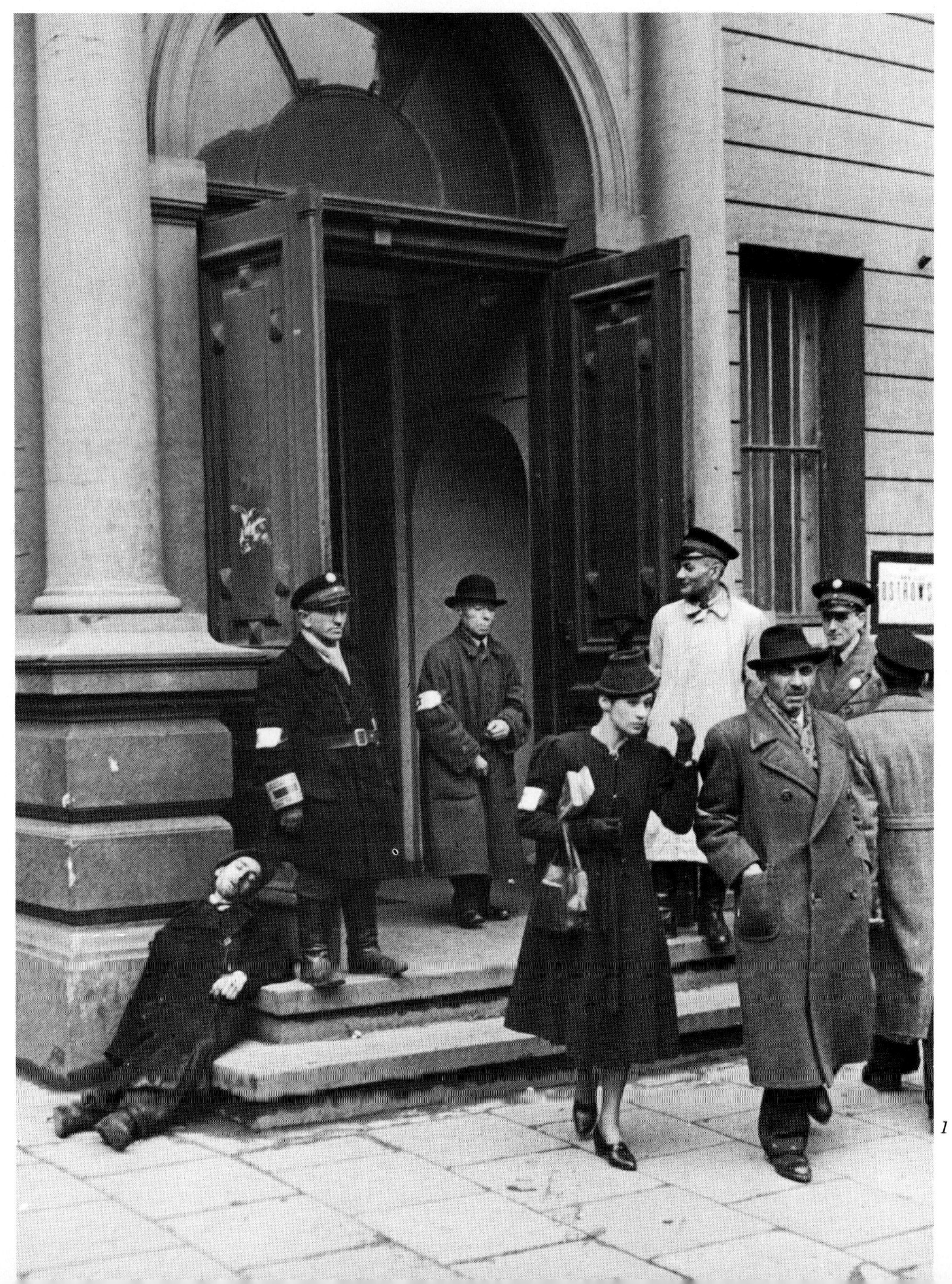

1

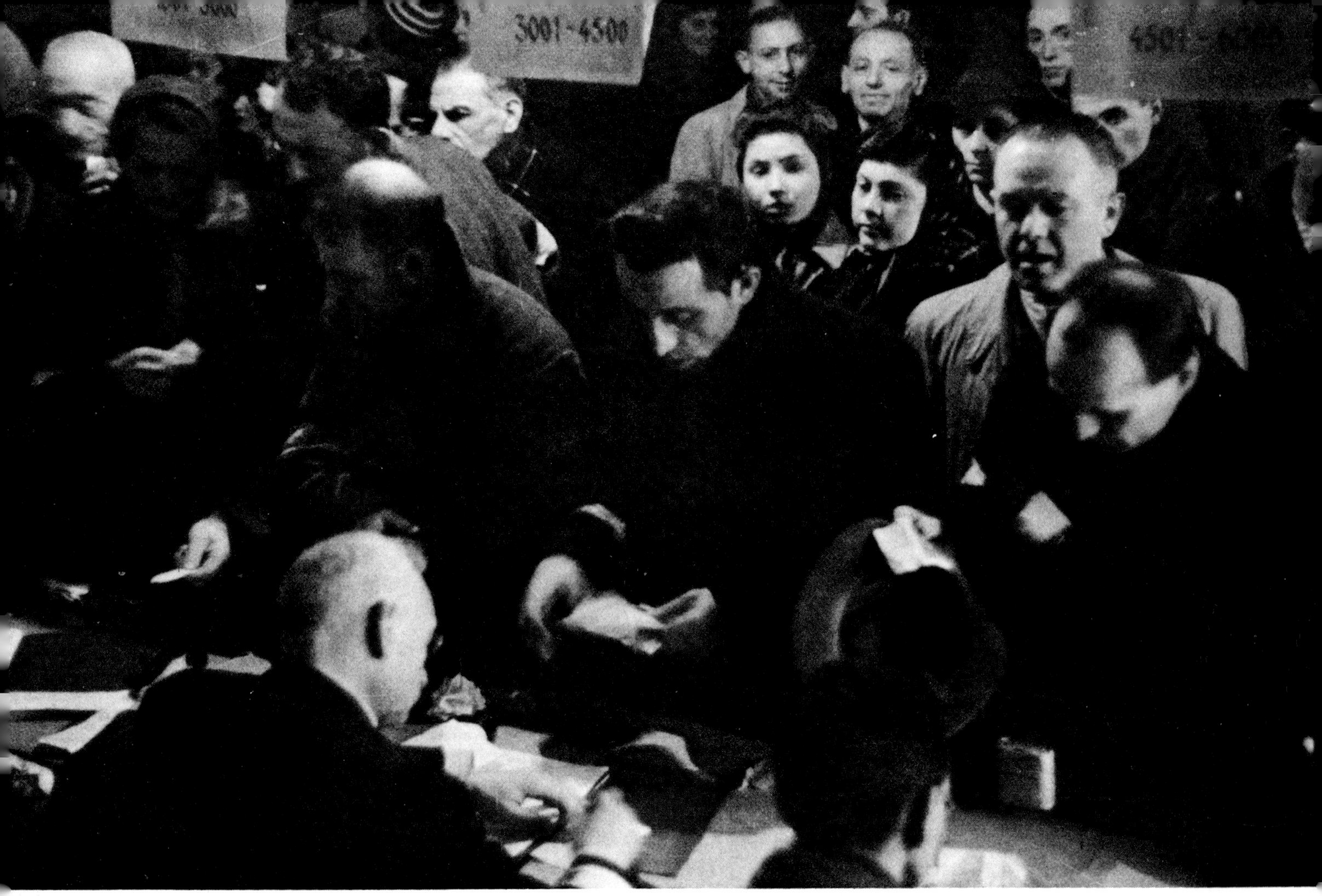

3001-4500

4501-6000

2

3

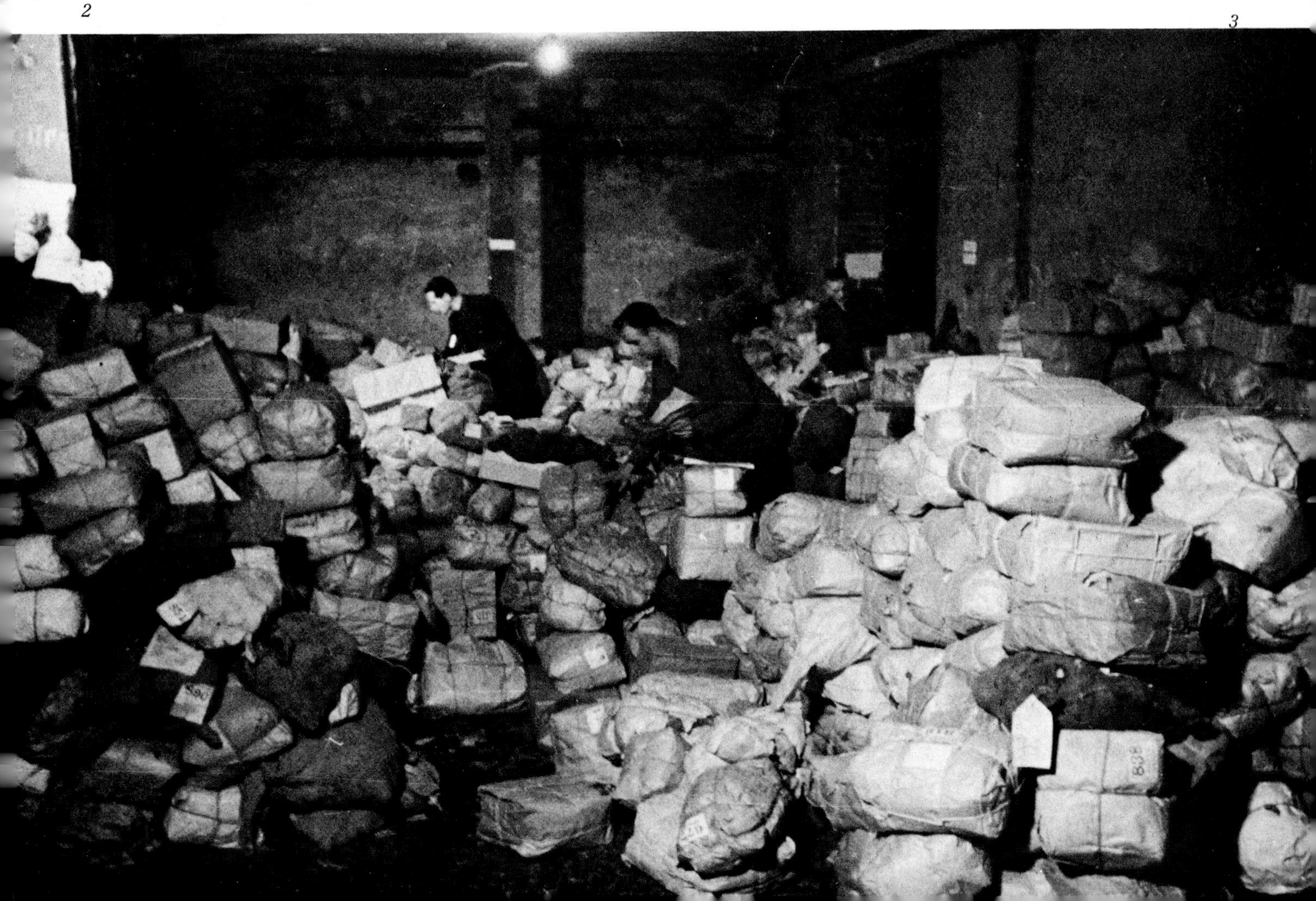

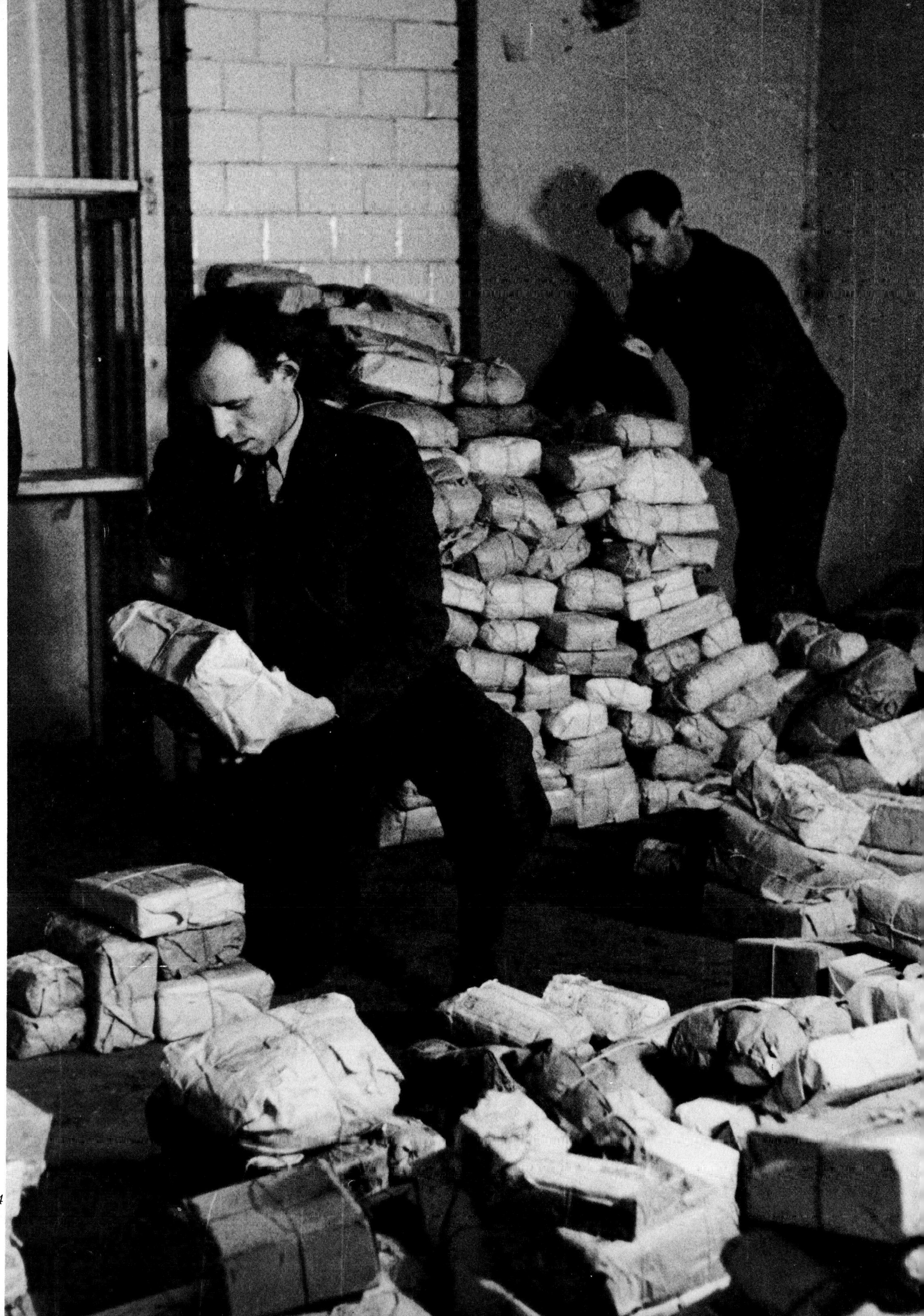

4

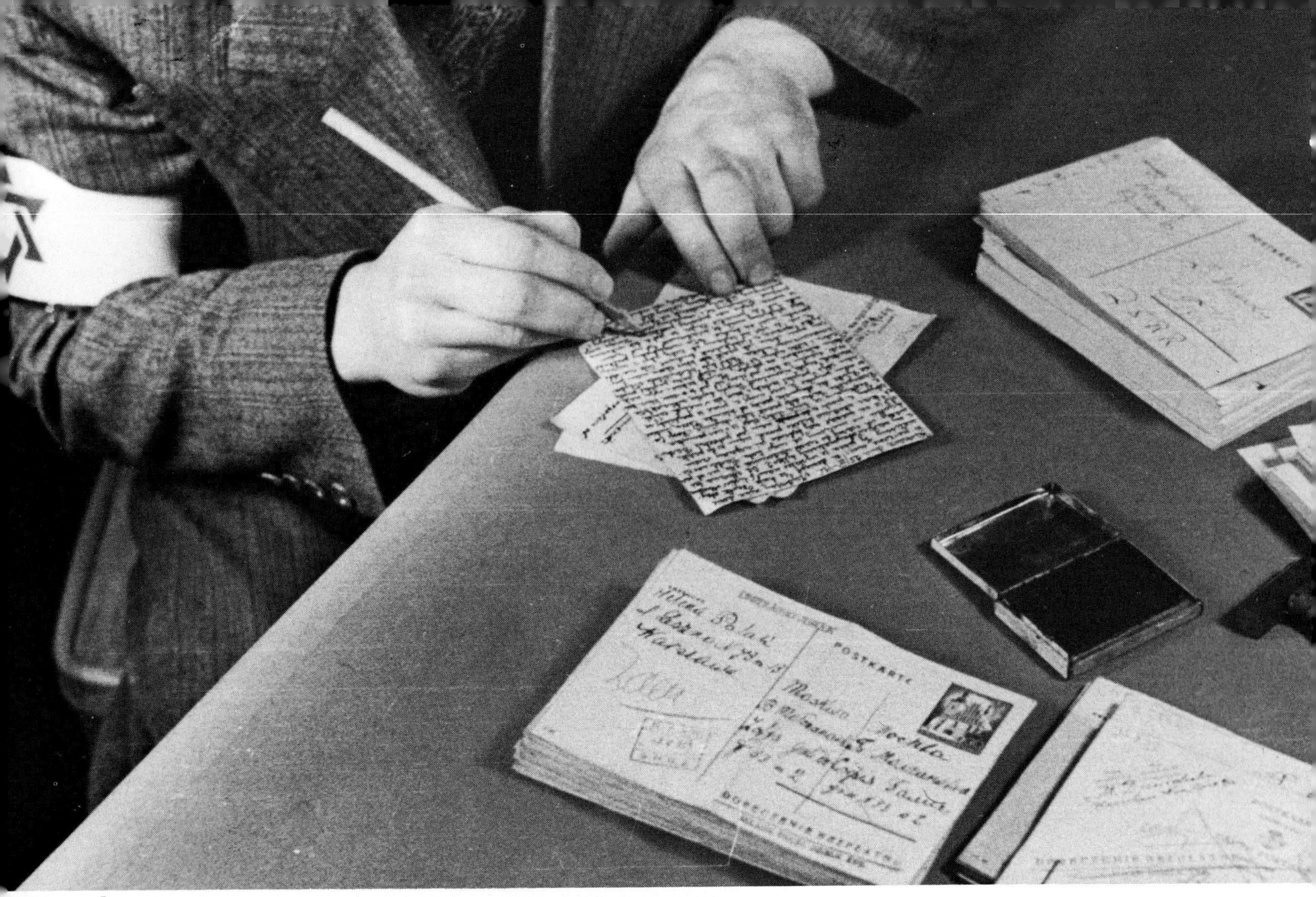

5

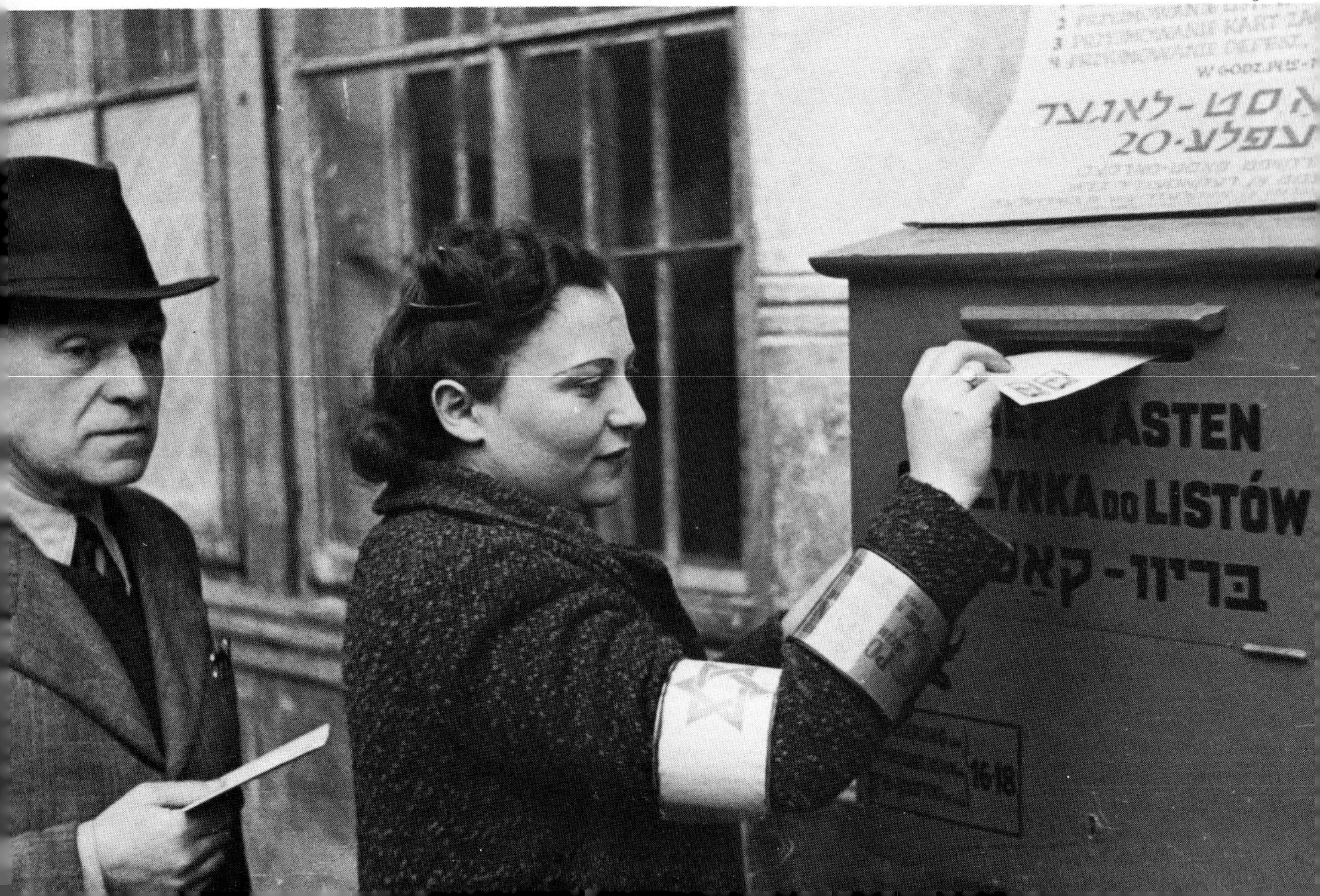

6

BRIEFKASTEN
SKRZYNKA DO LISTÓW
בריוו-קאסטן

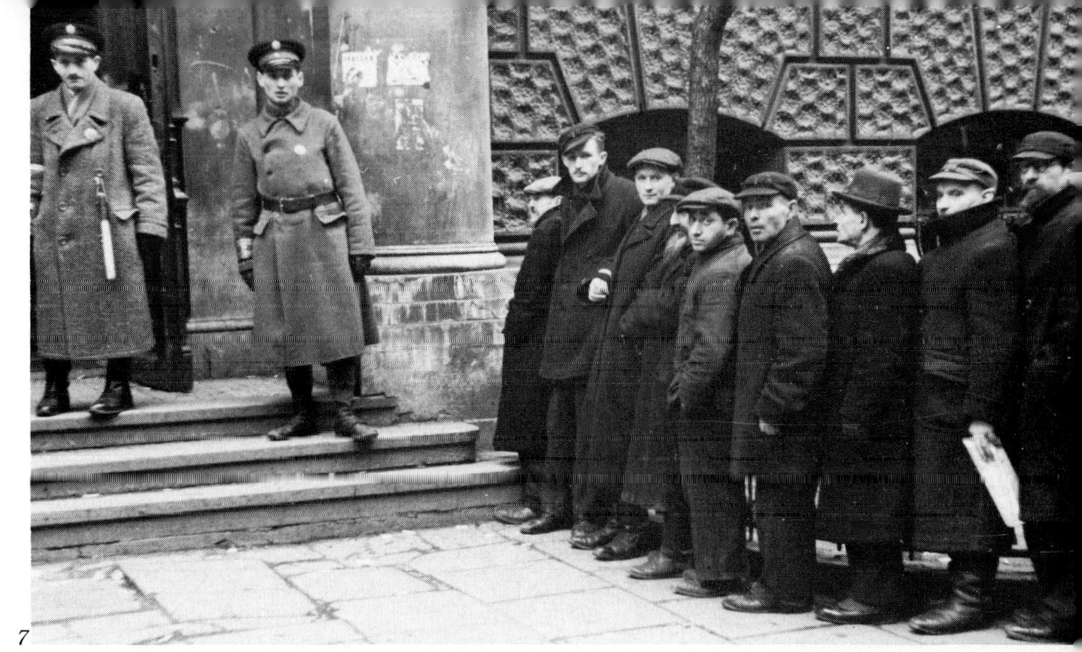

7

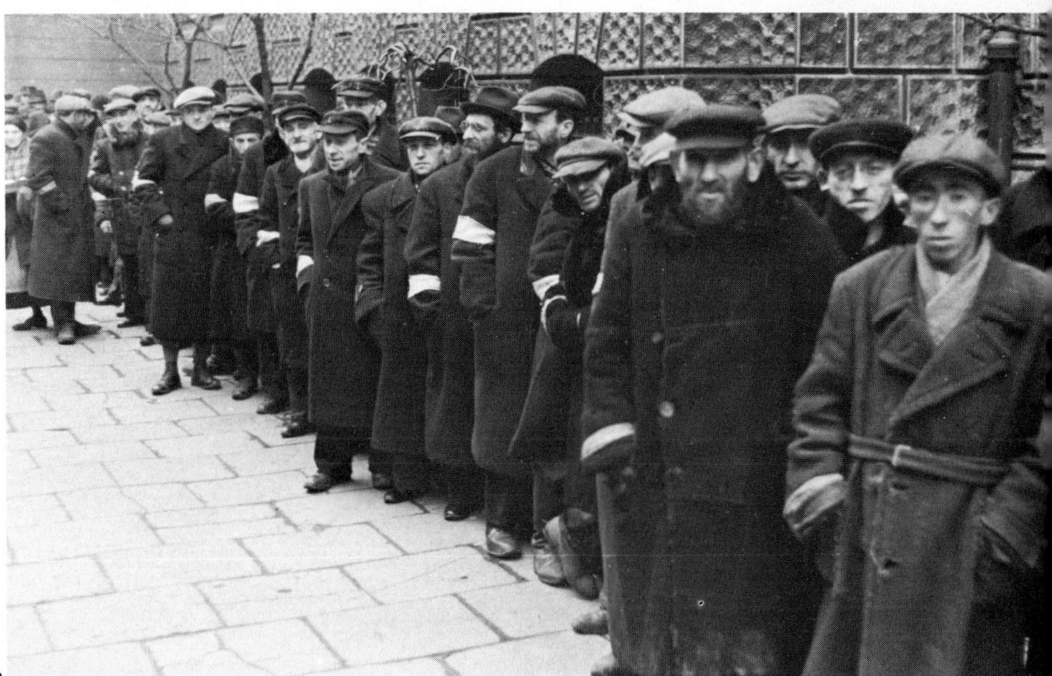

8

9

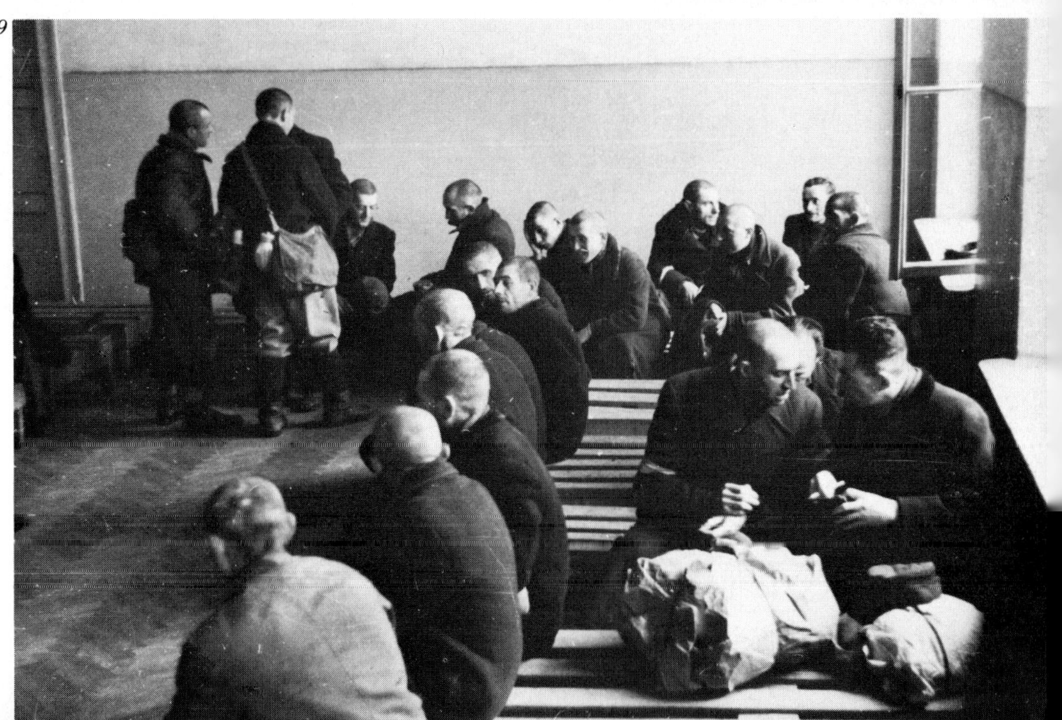

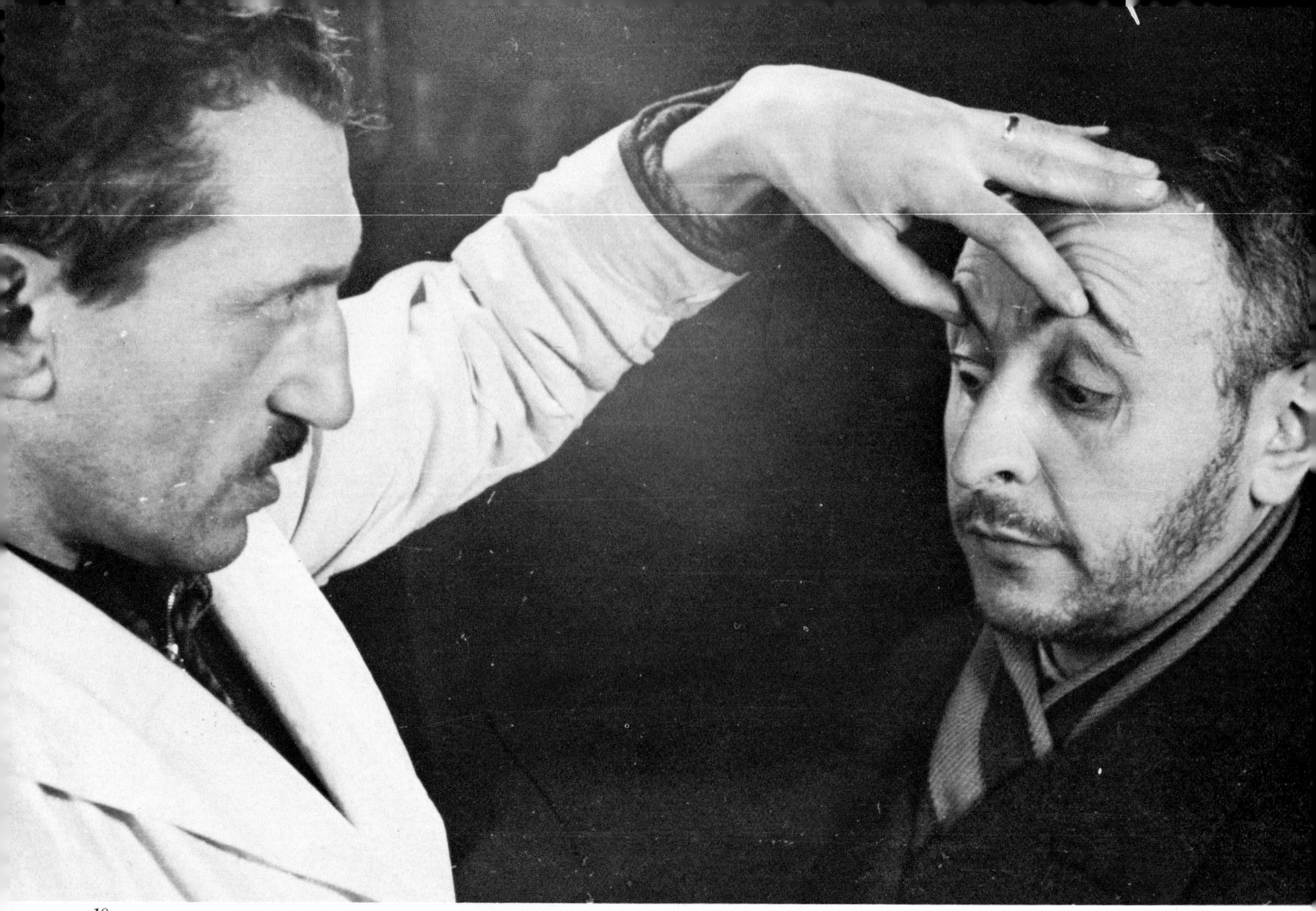

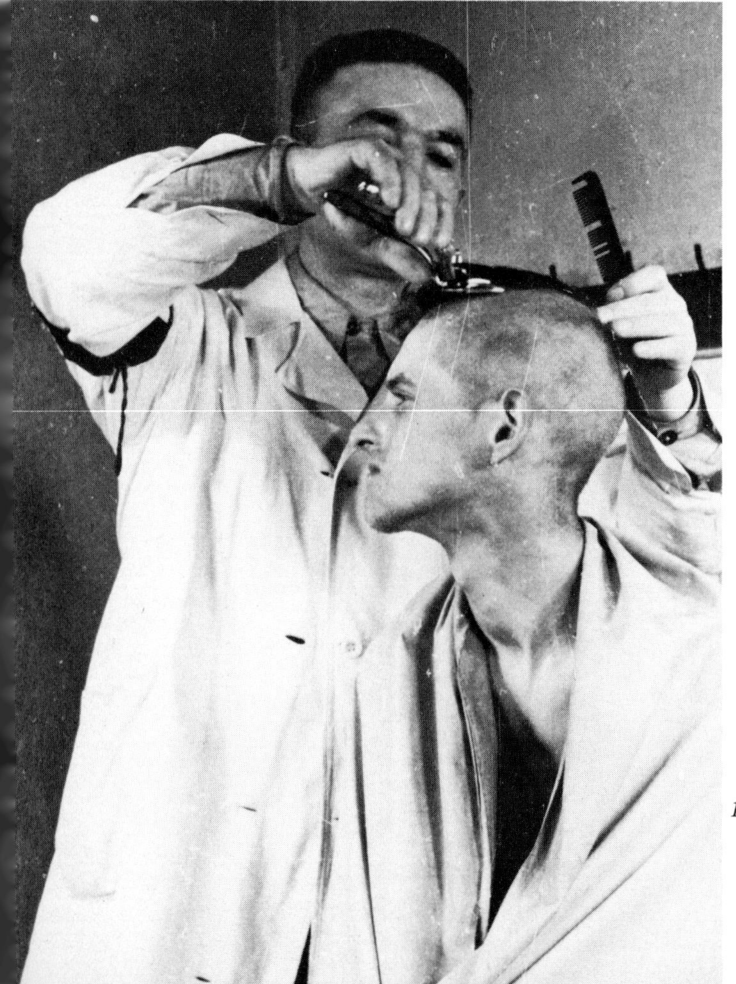

10

11

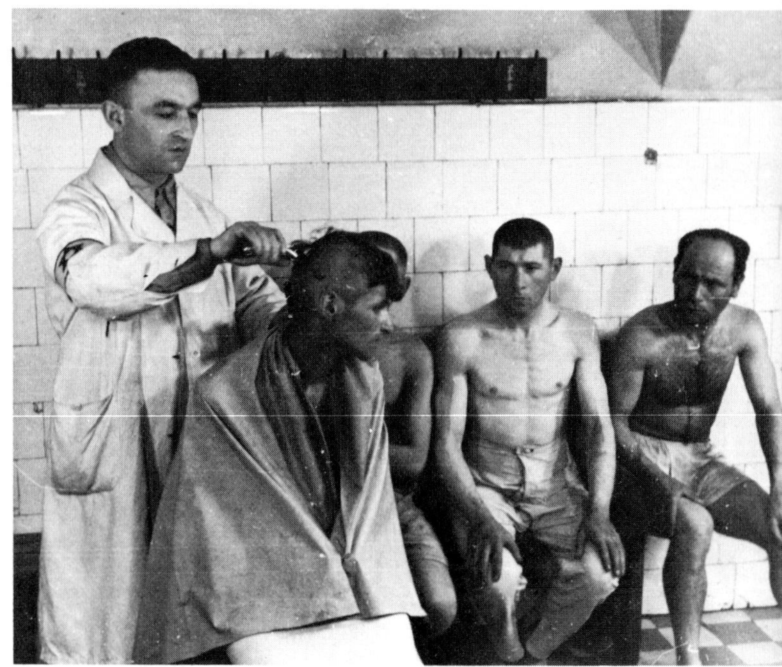

12

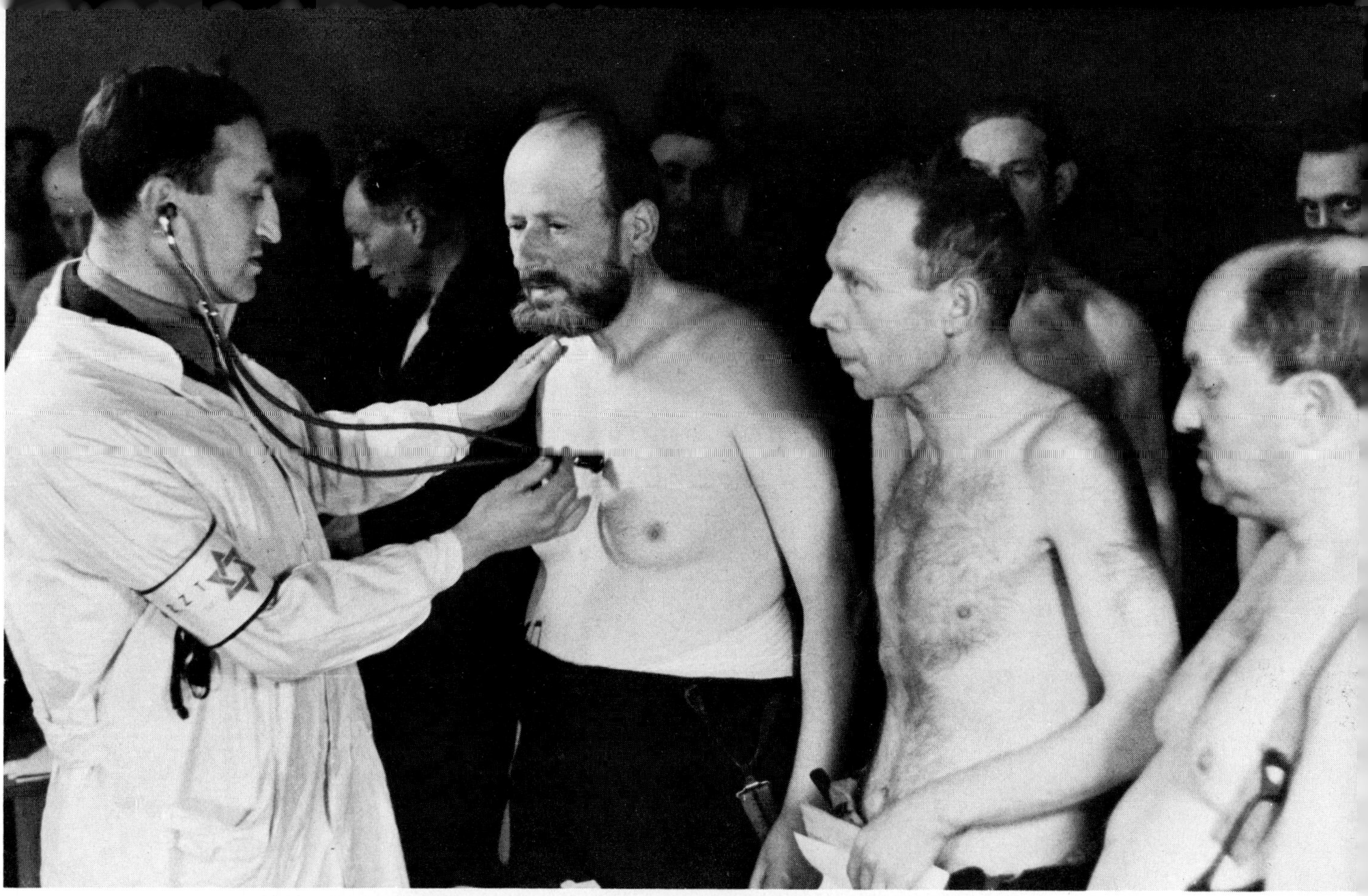

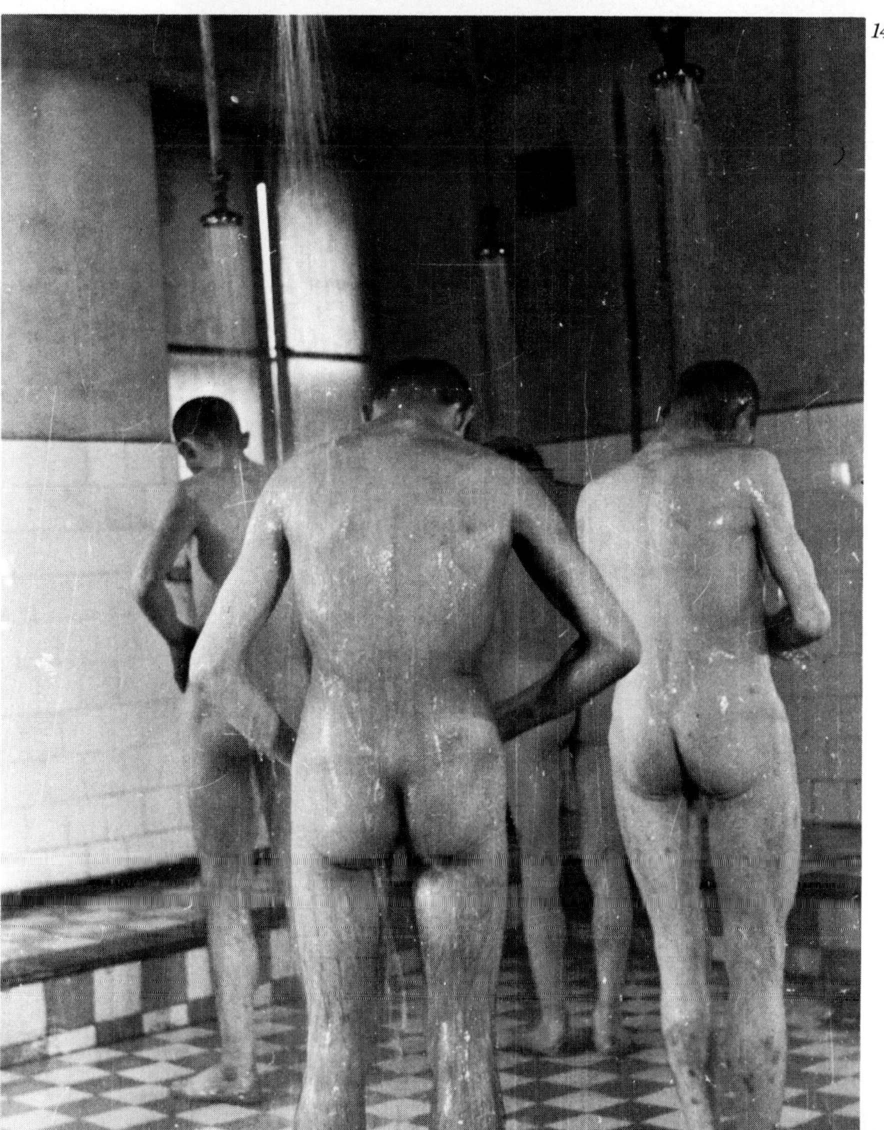

13
14

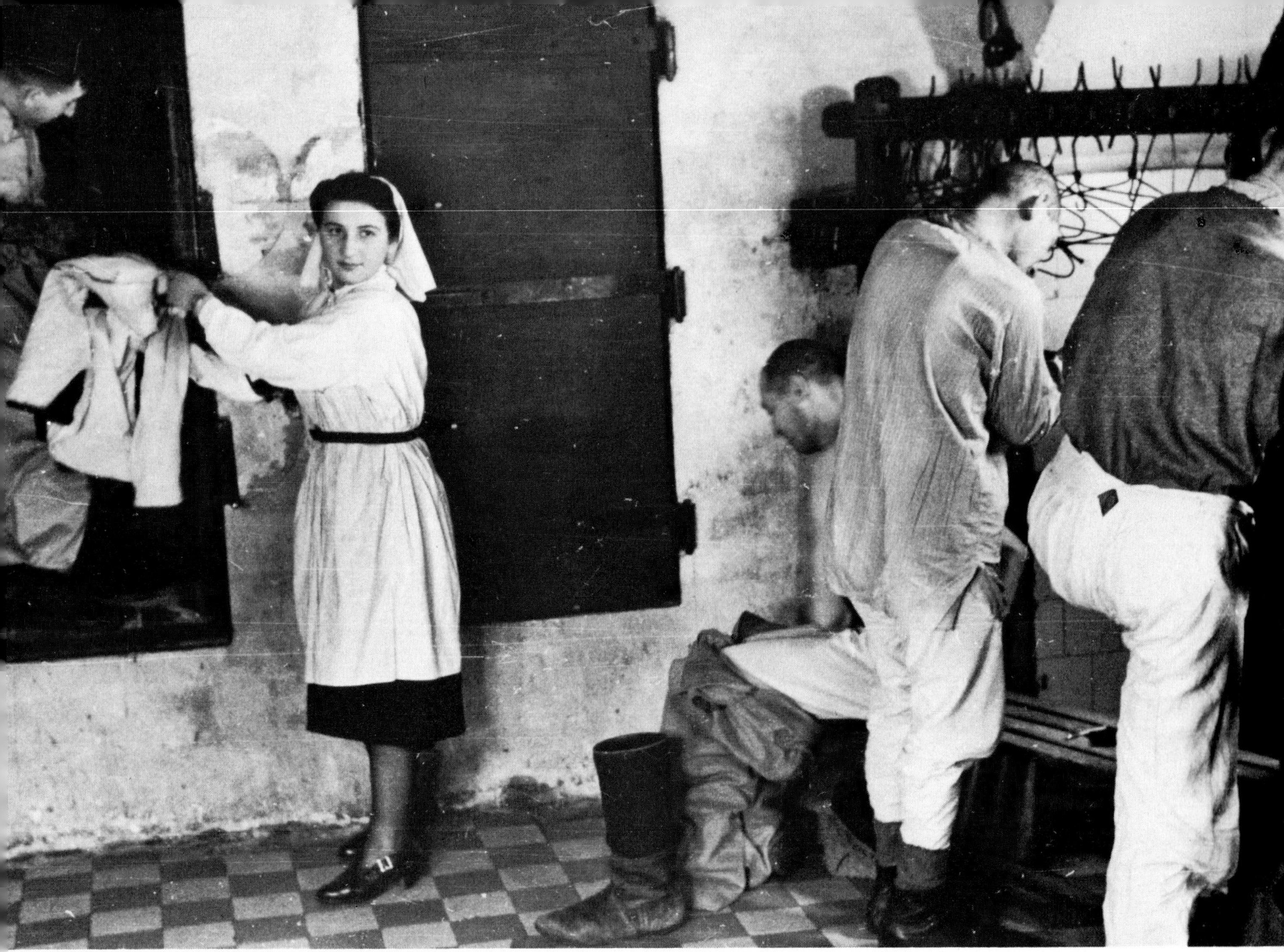

15

INTERNAL GHETTO POLICE
(Nos. 16–24)

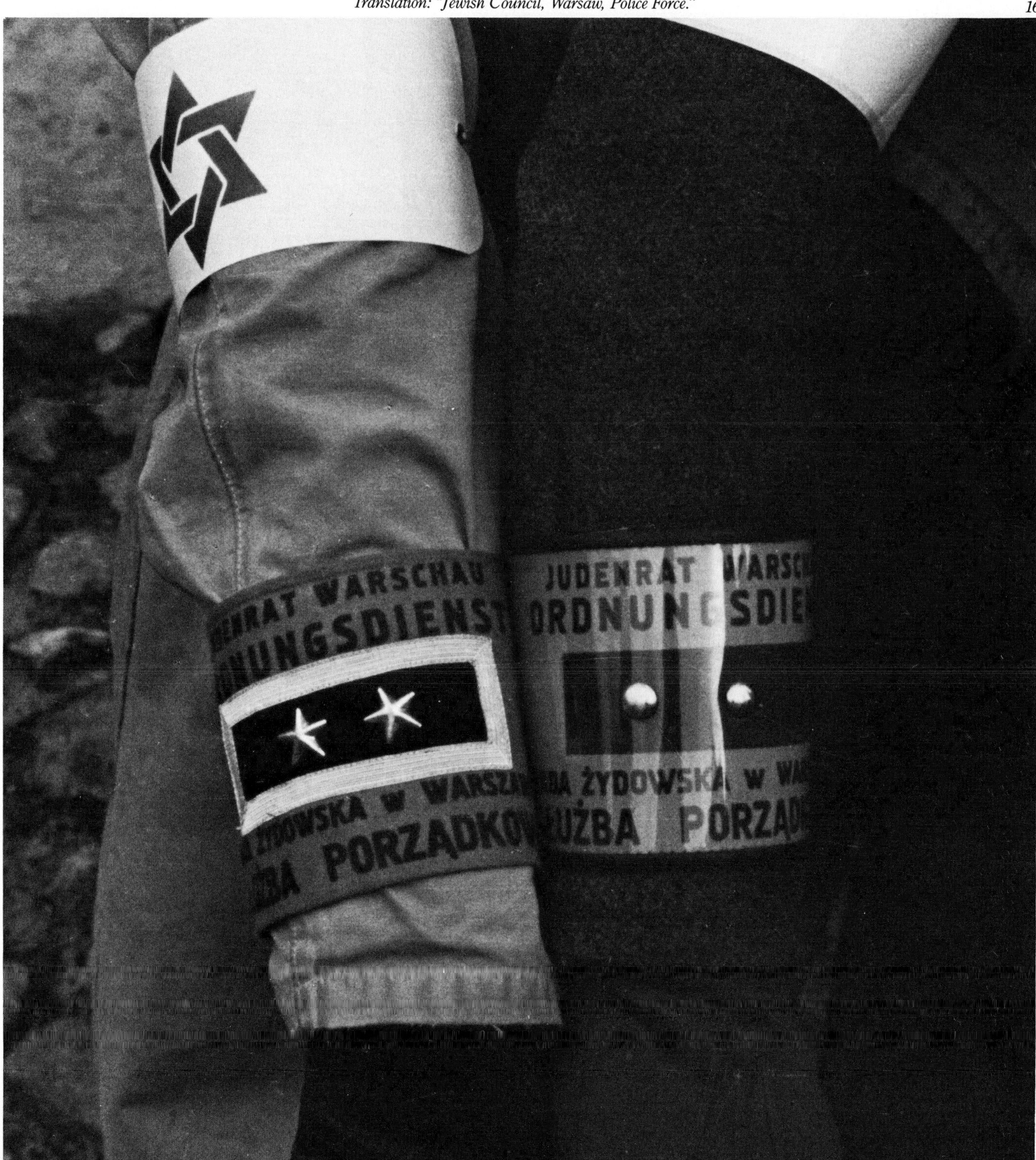

Translation: "Jewish Council, Warsaw, Police Force."

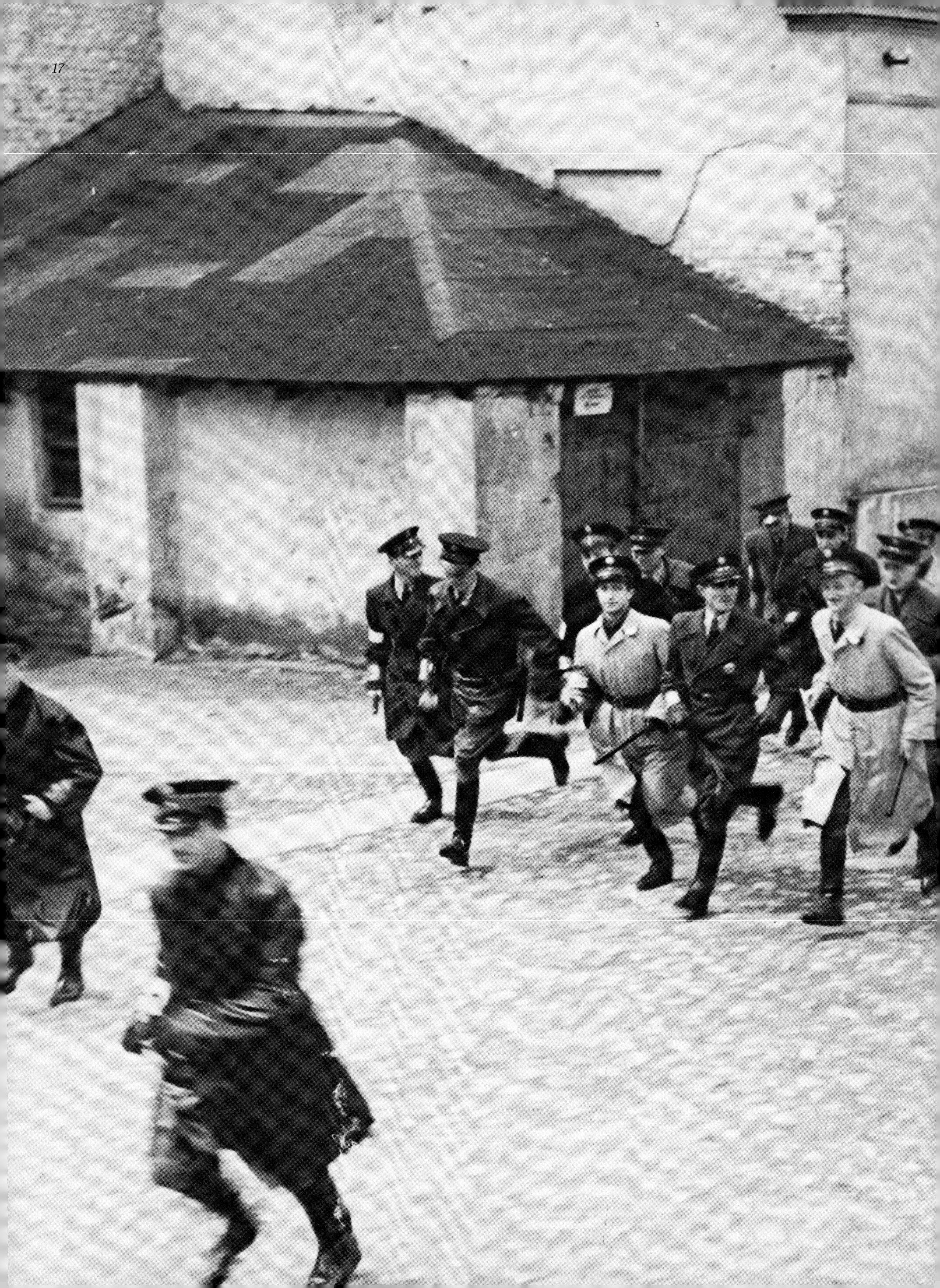

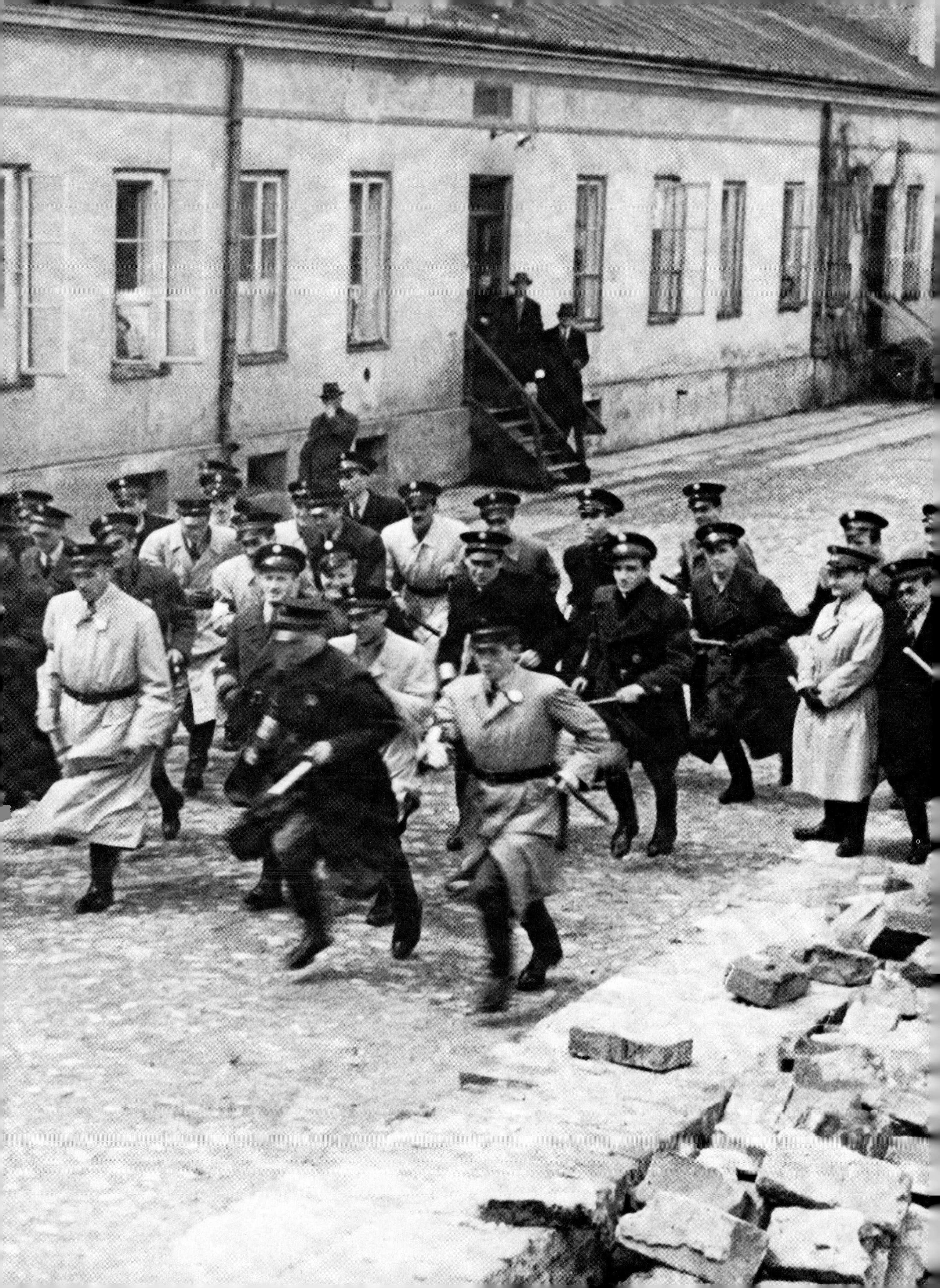

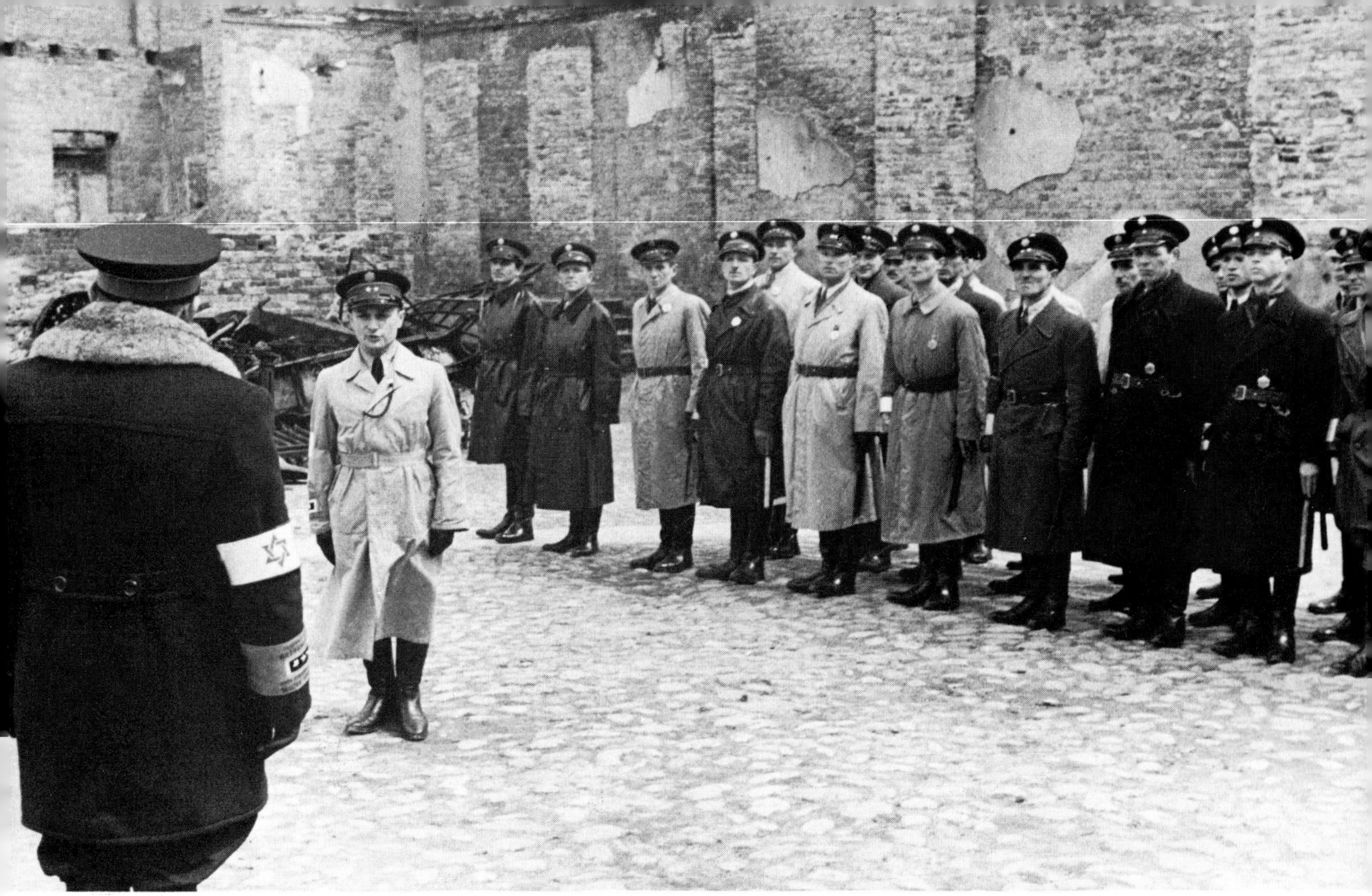

18

19

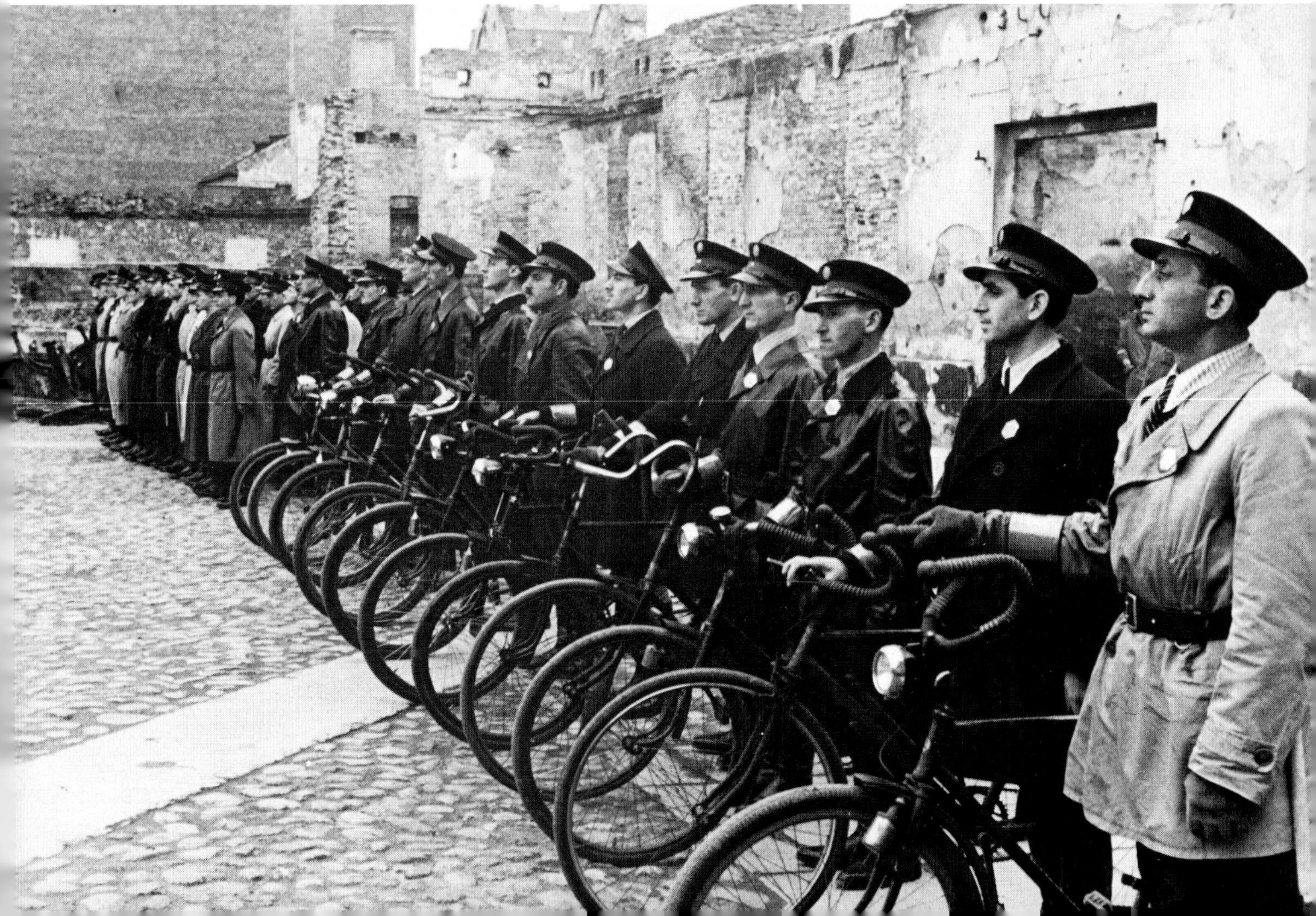

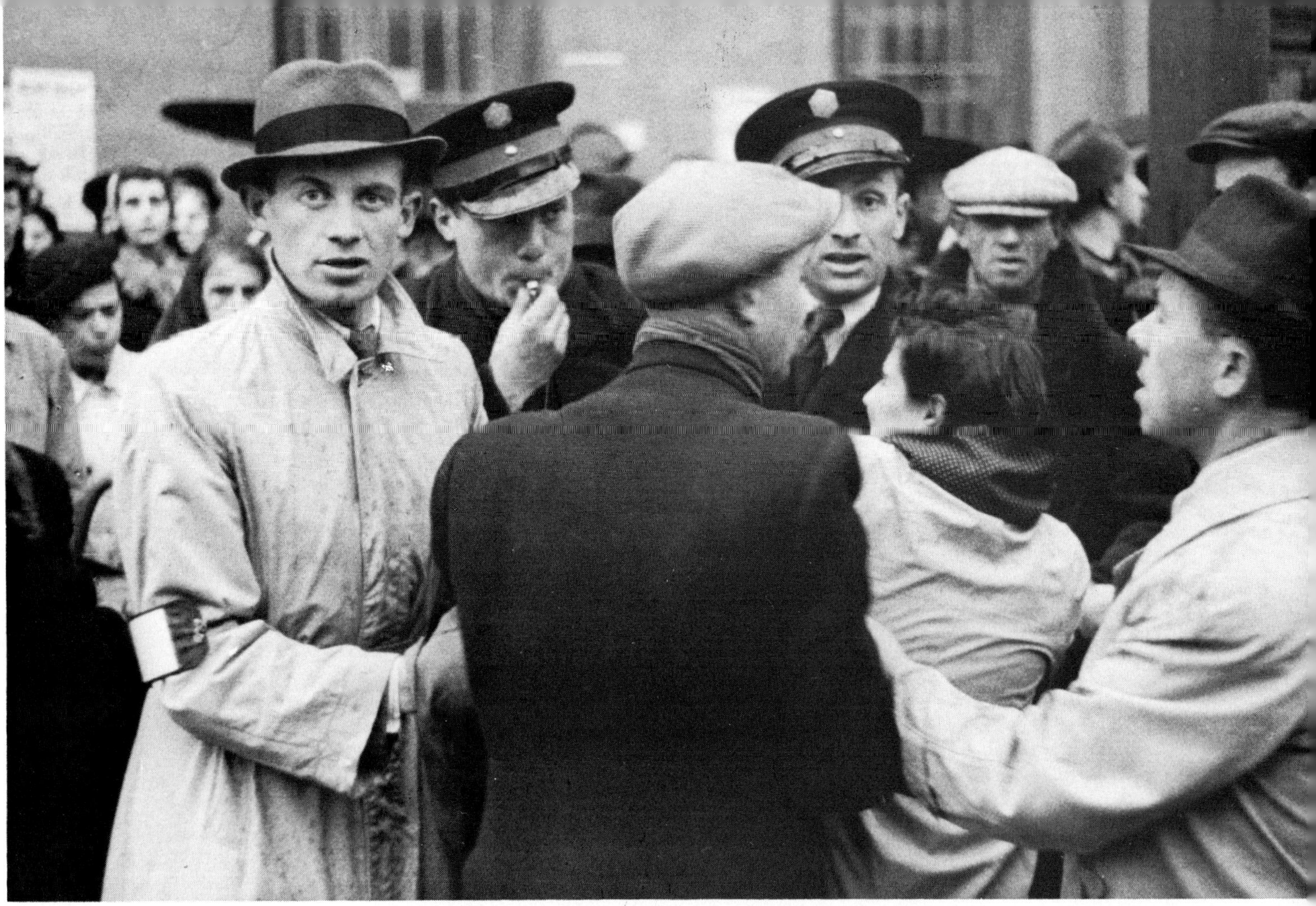

PRADNICA
FOTOGR
VIII

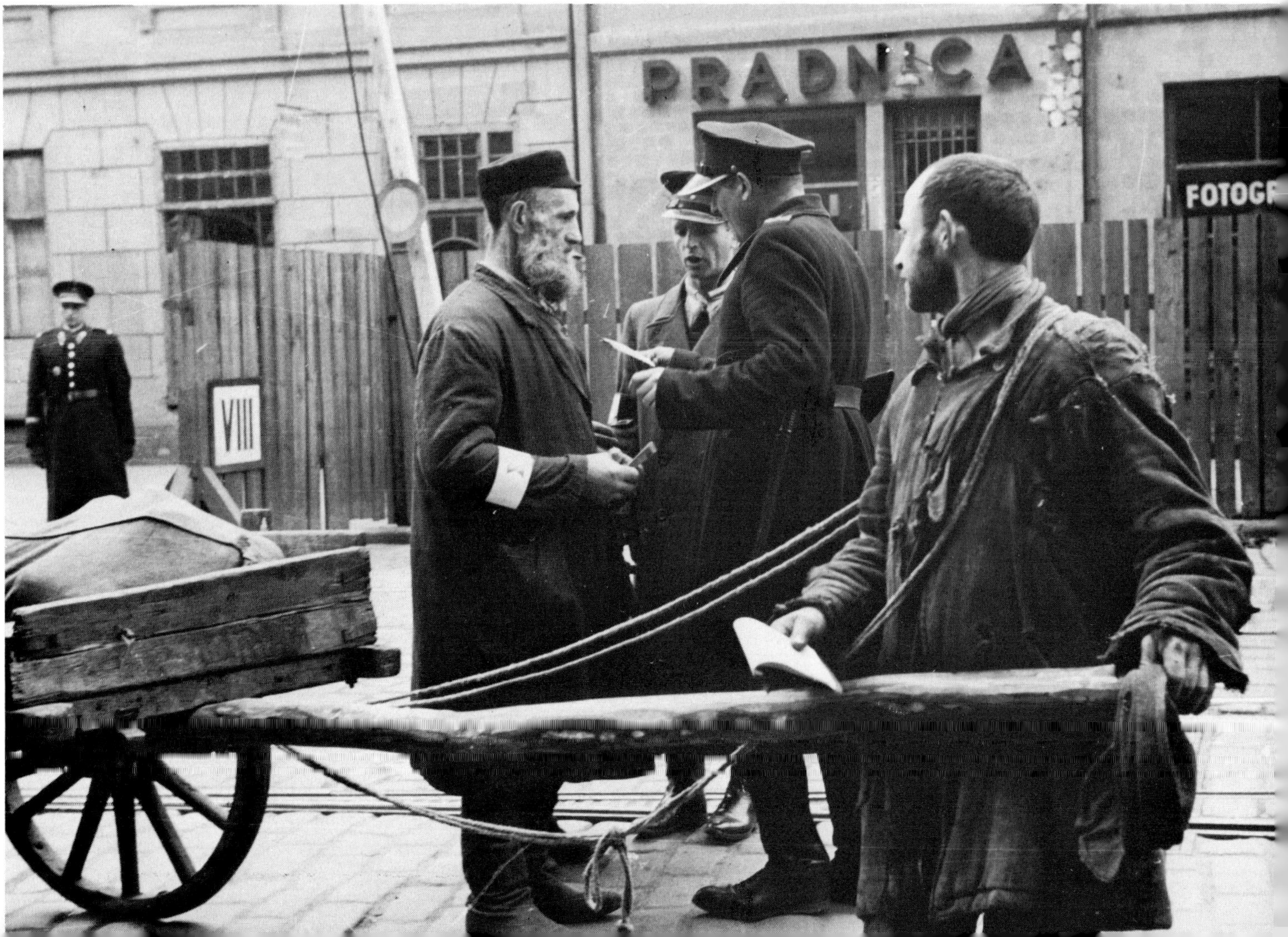

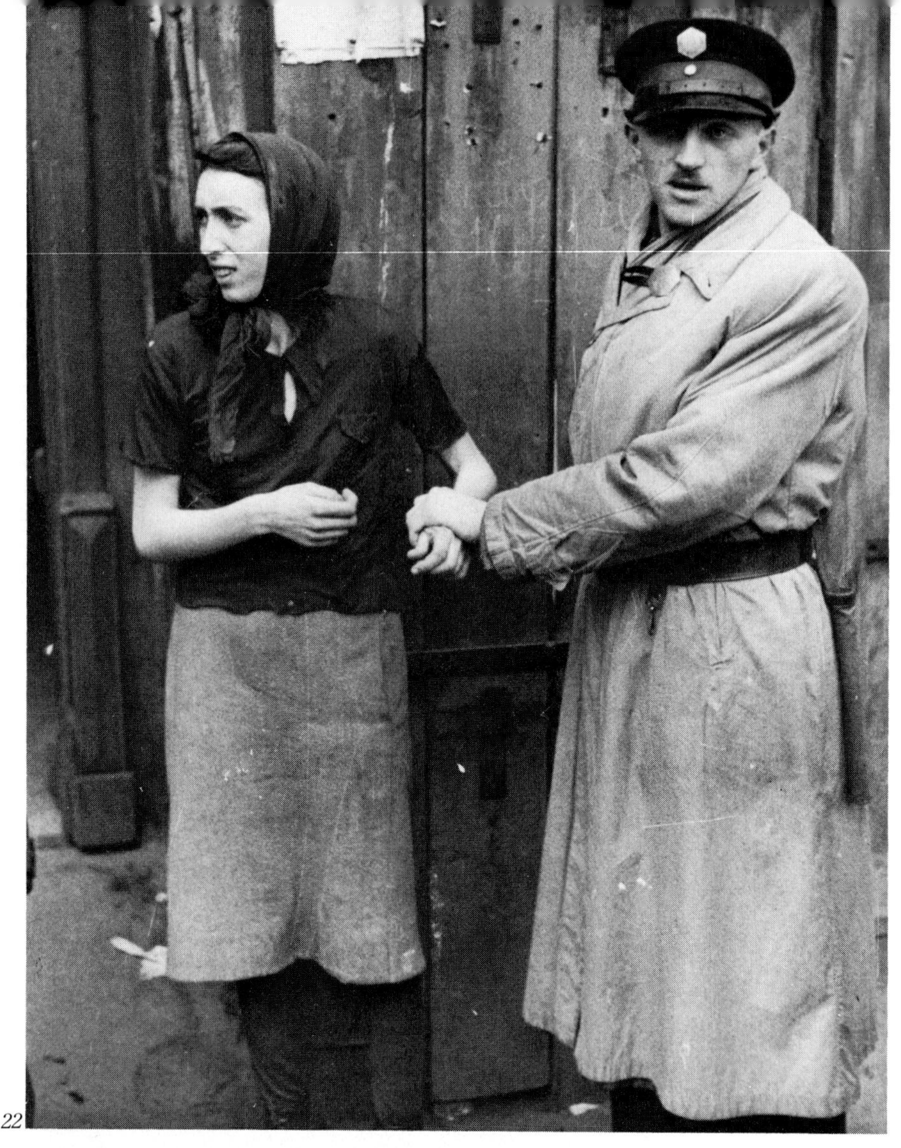

22

23

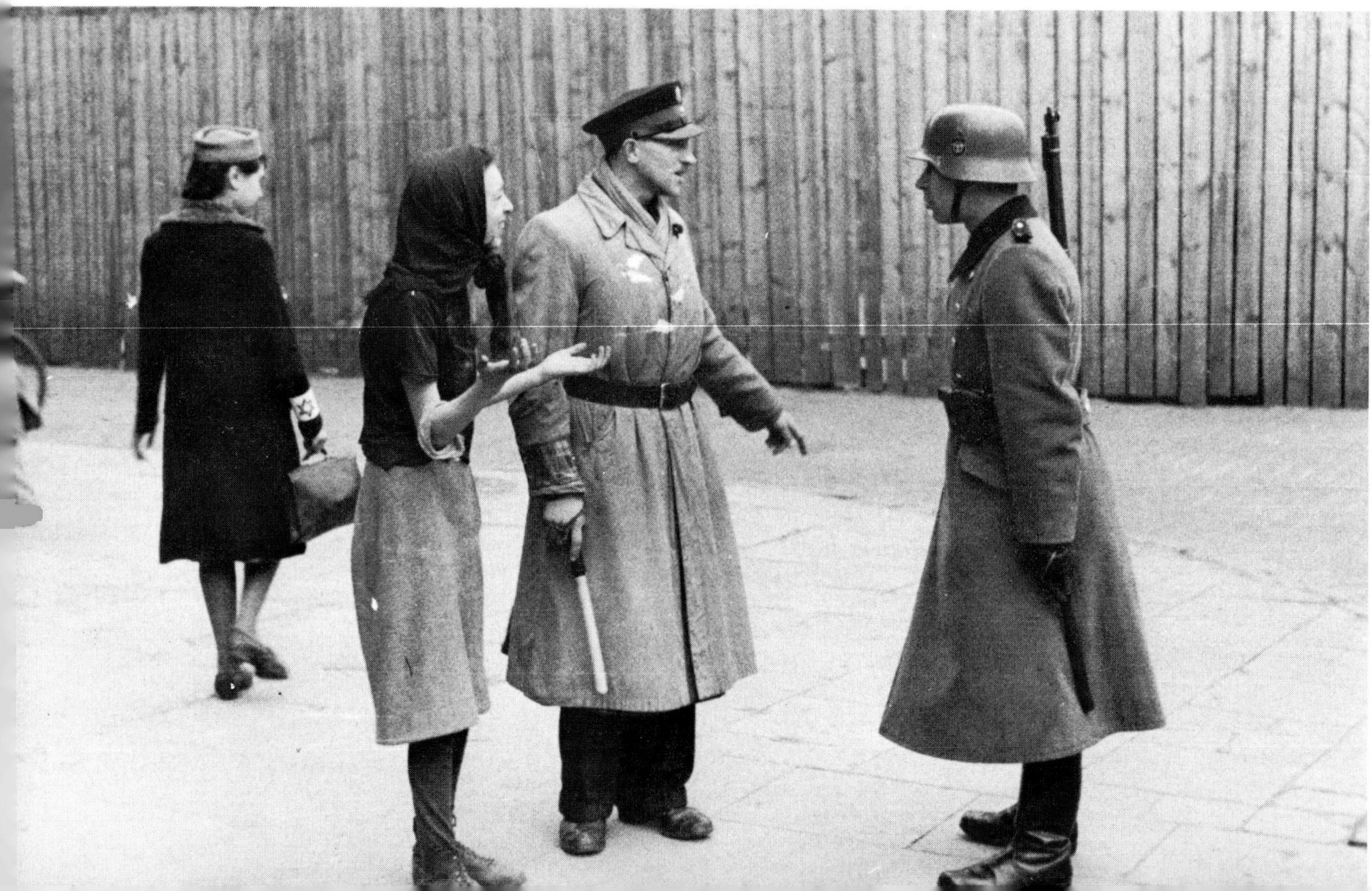

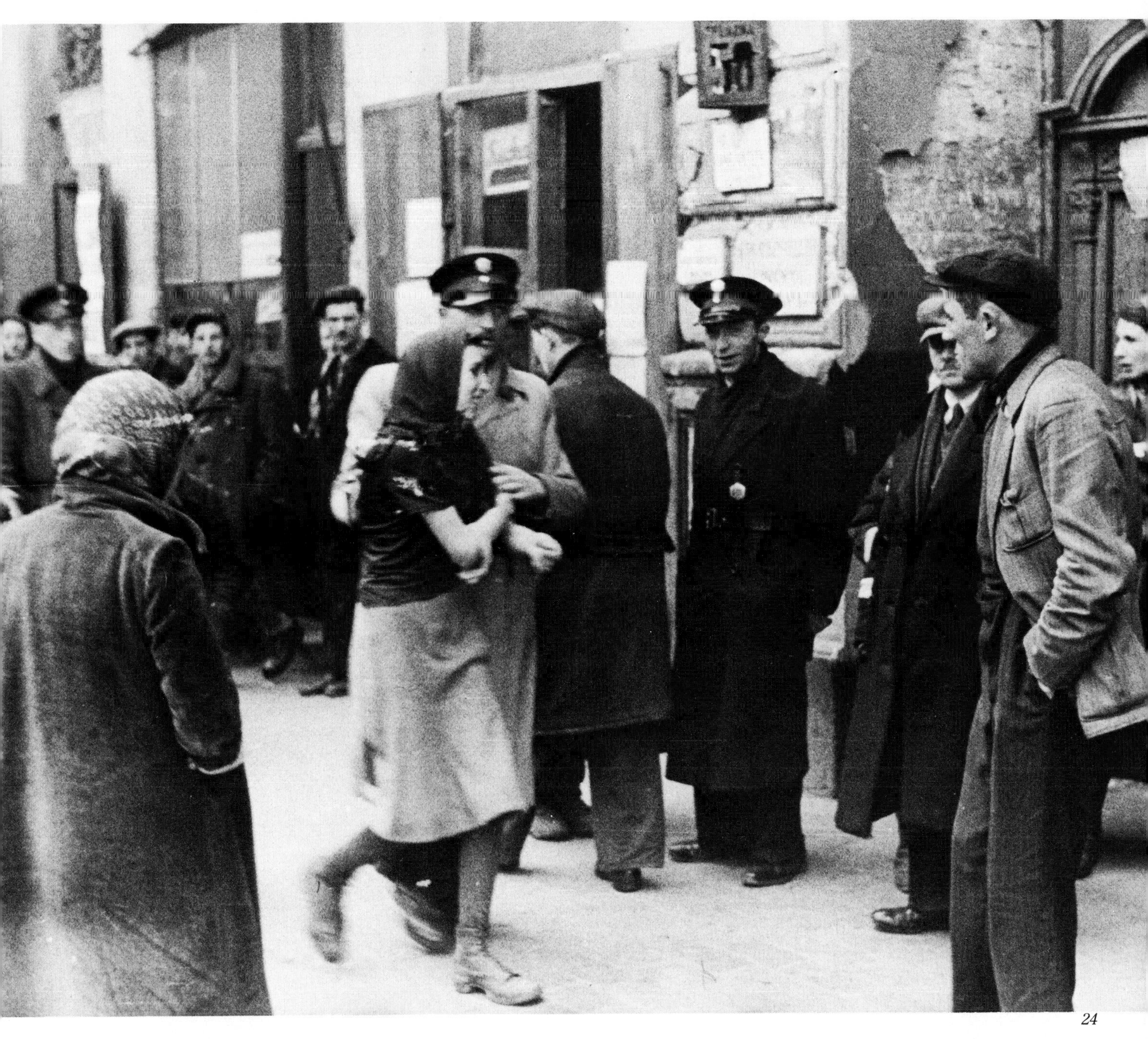

24

GHETTO LABOR
"Professional Training Courses"
(Nos. 25—47)

Sign is in German, Polish and Yiddish. Translation: "Professional training courses: metalwork, electrical work, carpentry, tailoring, laundering, millinery."

25

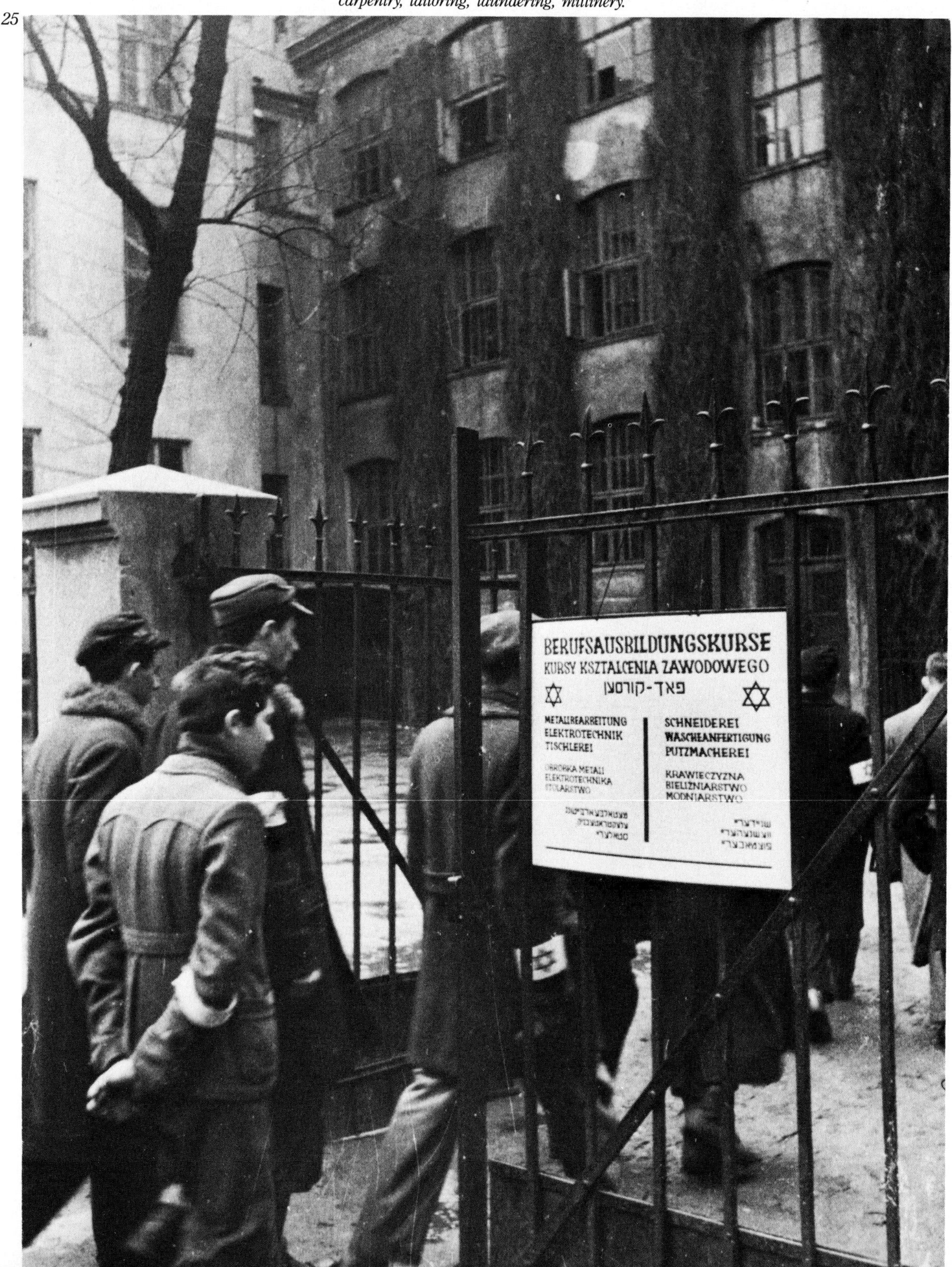

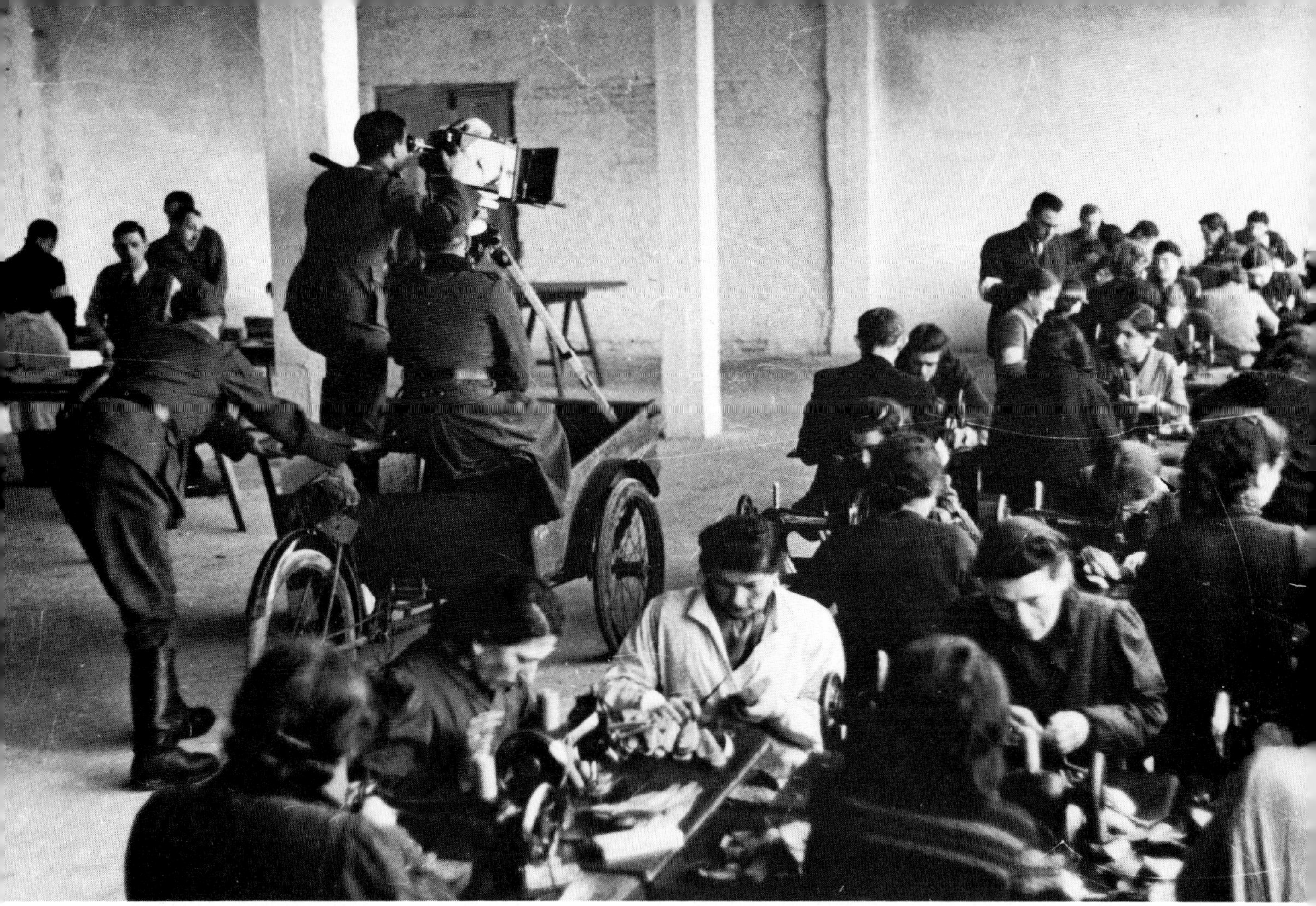

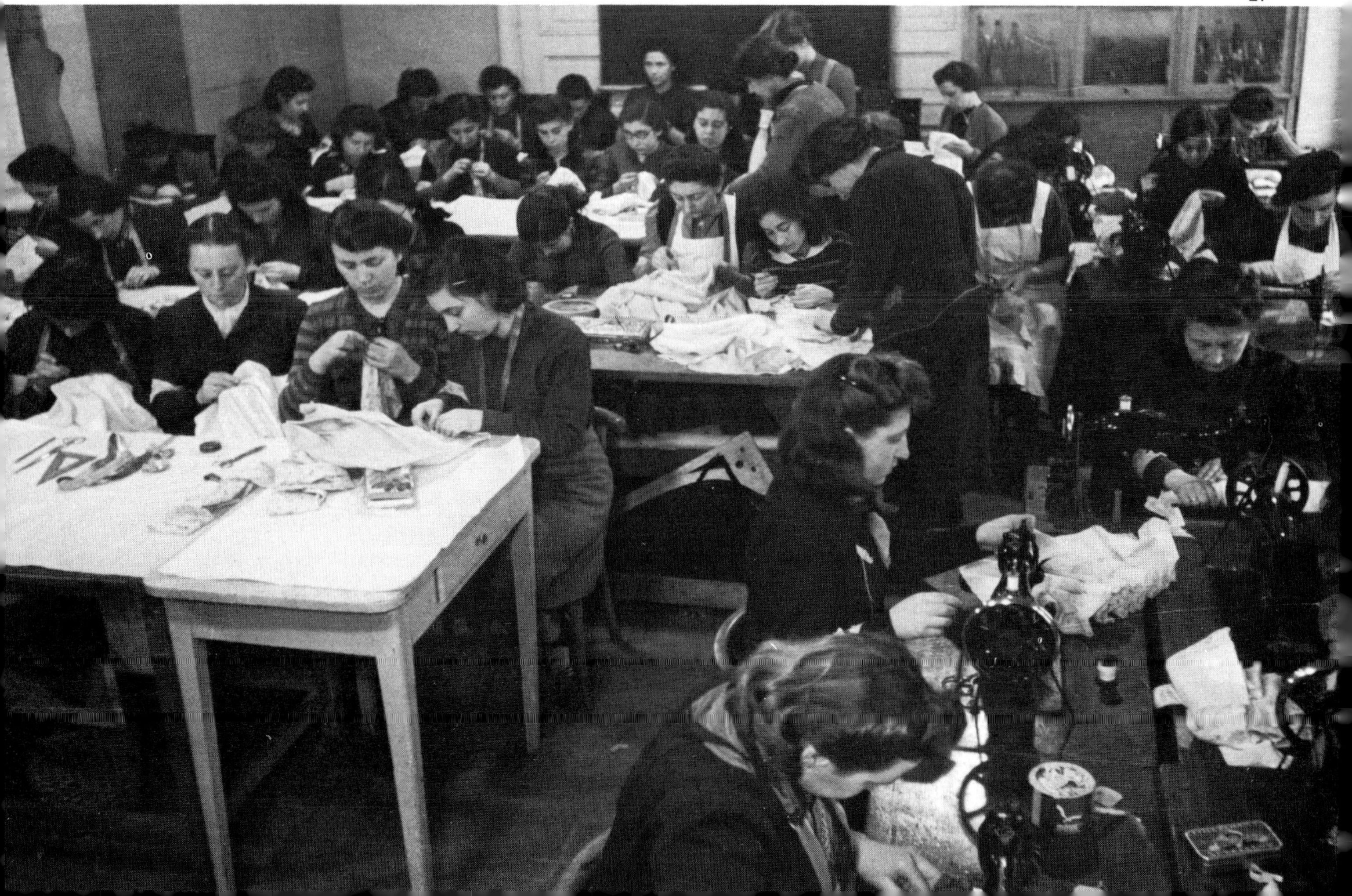

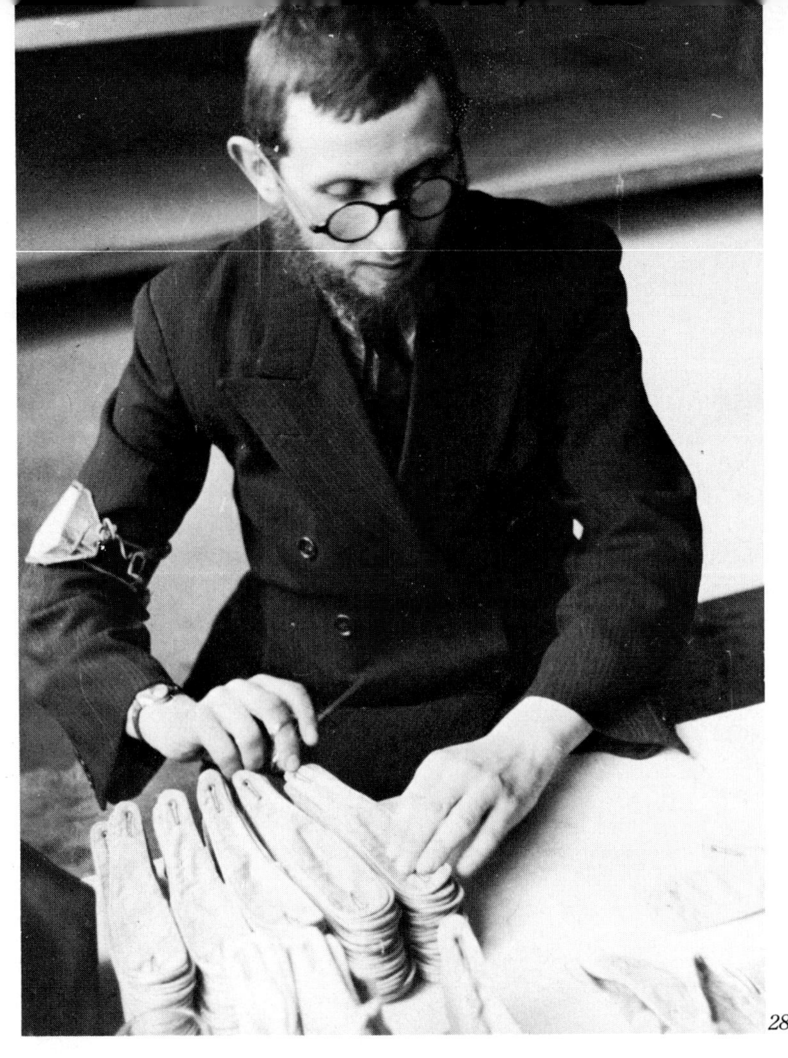

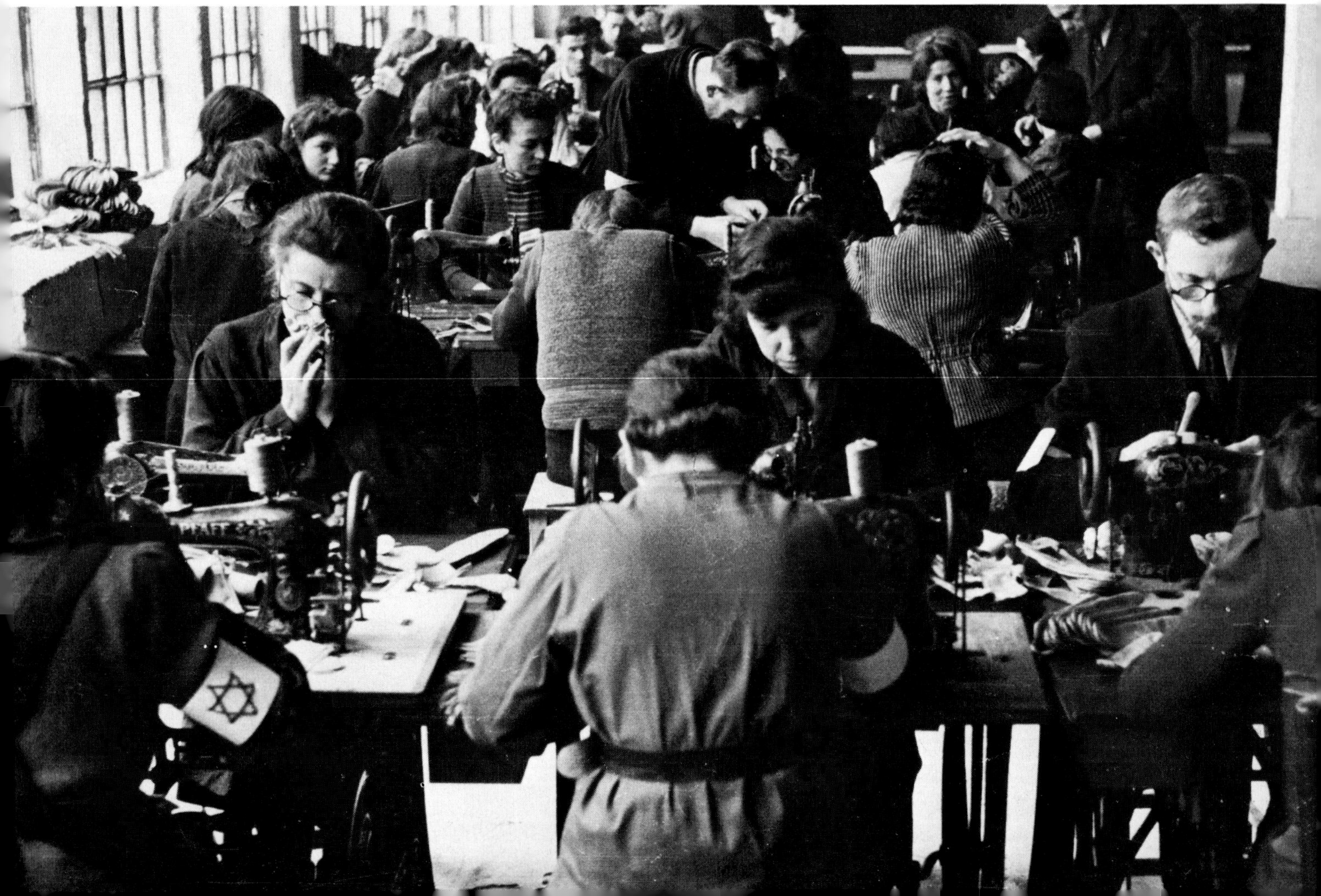

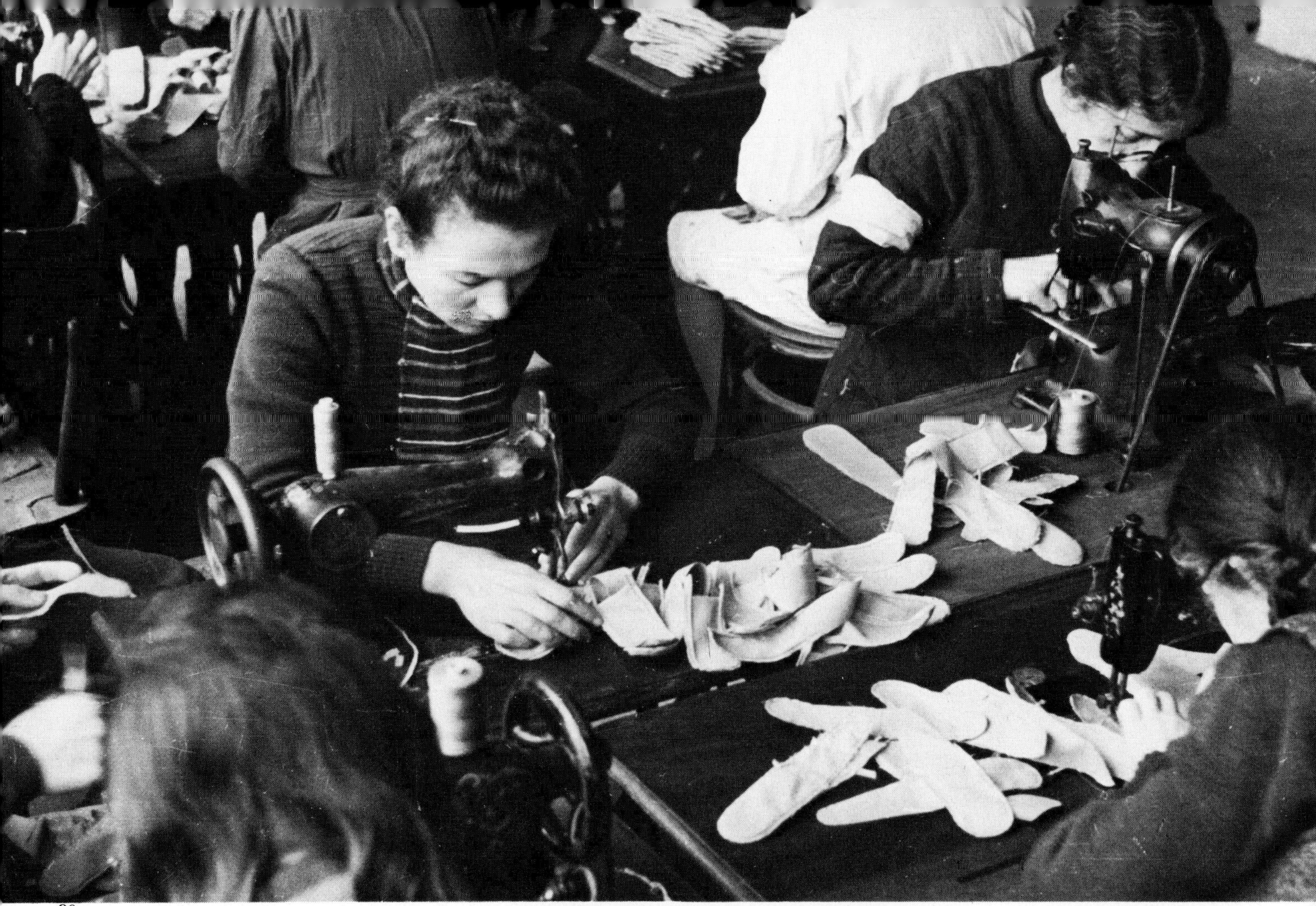

30

31

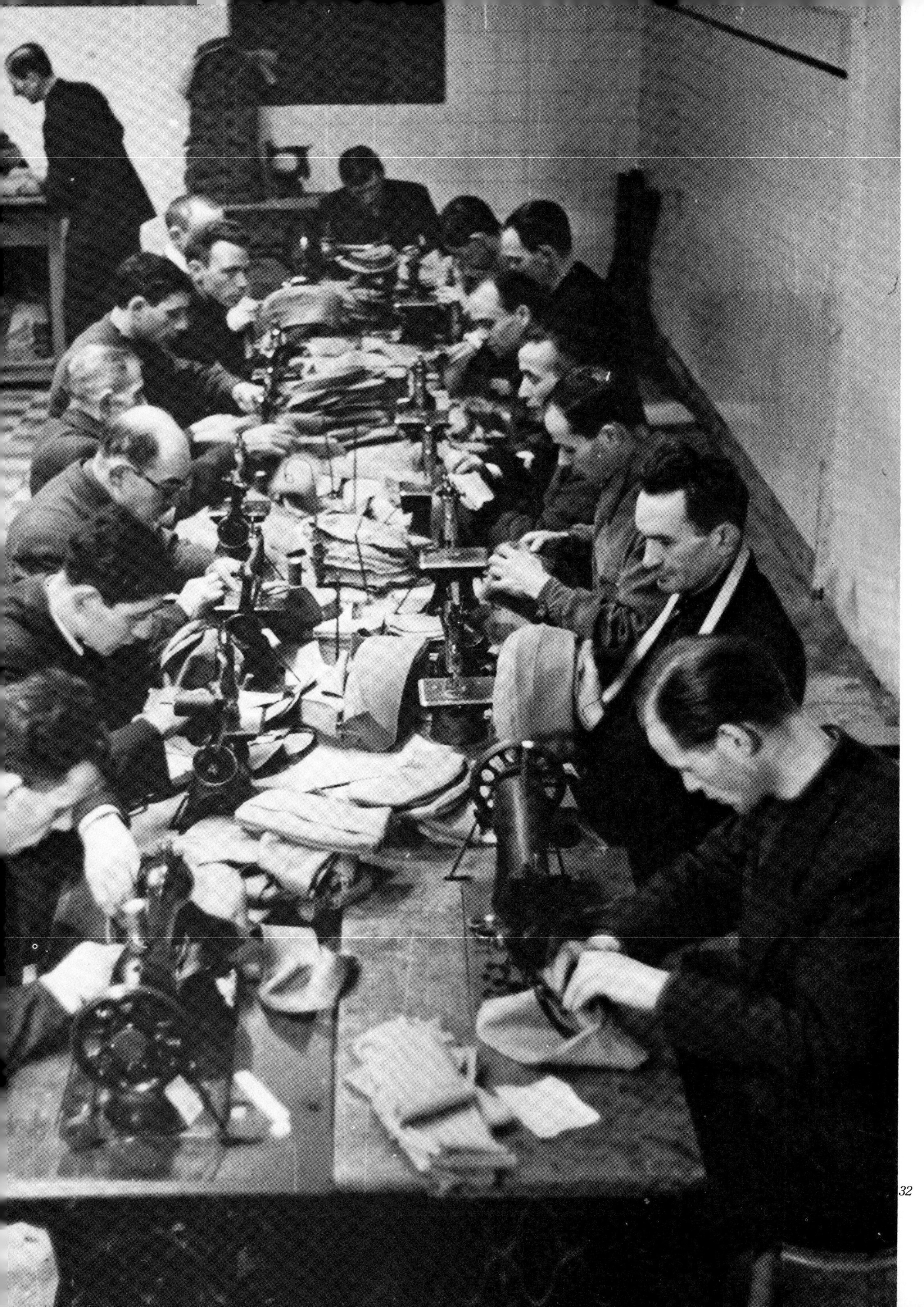

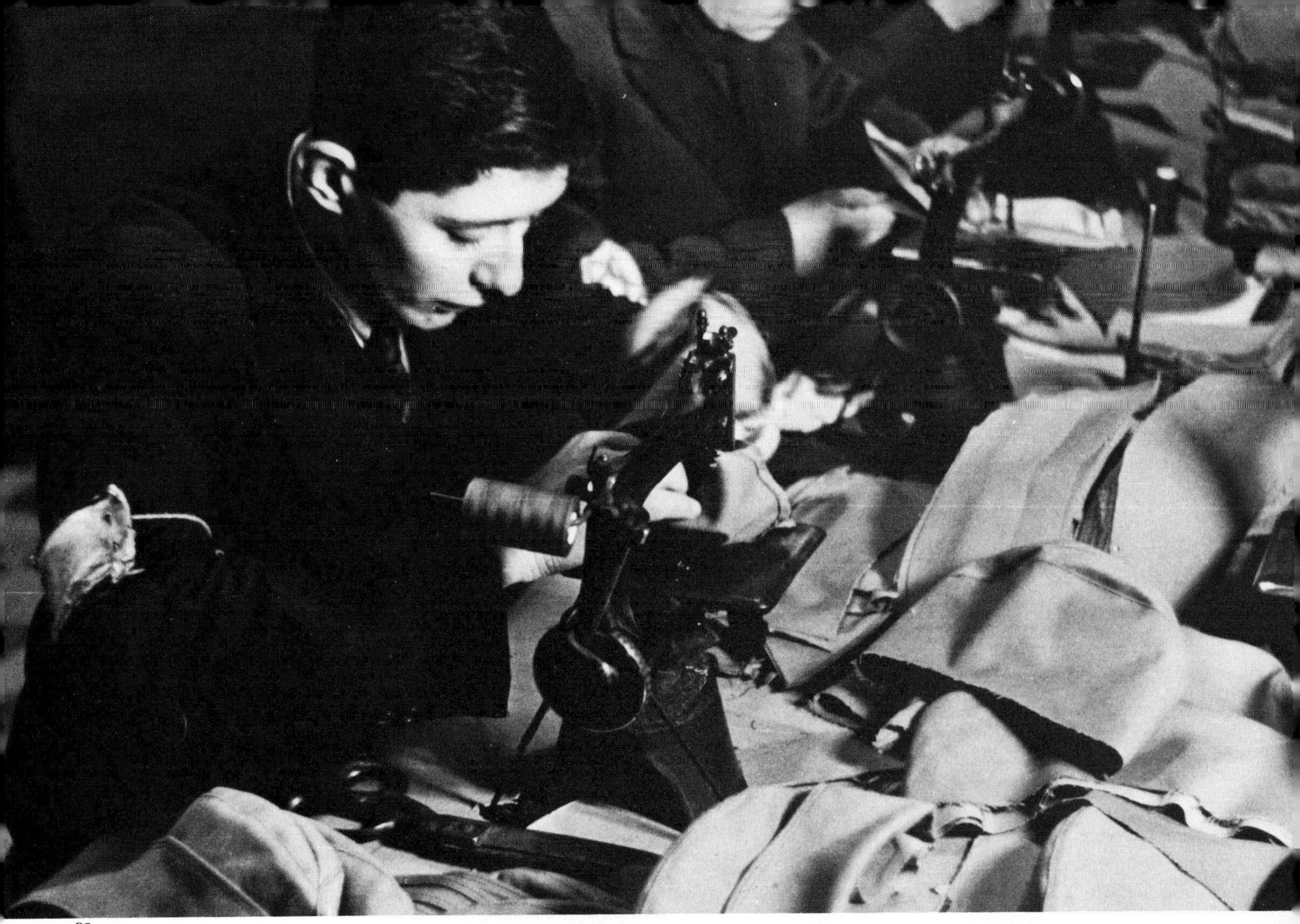

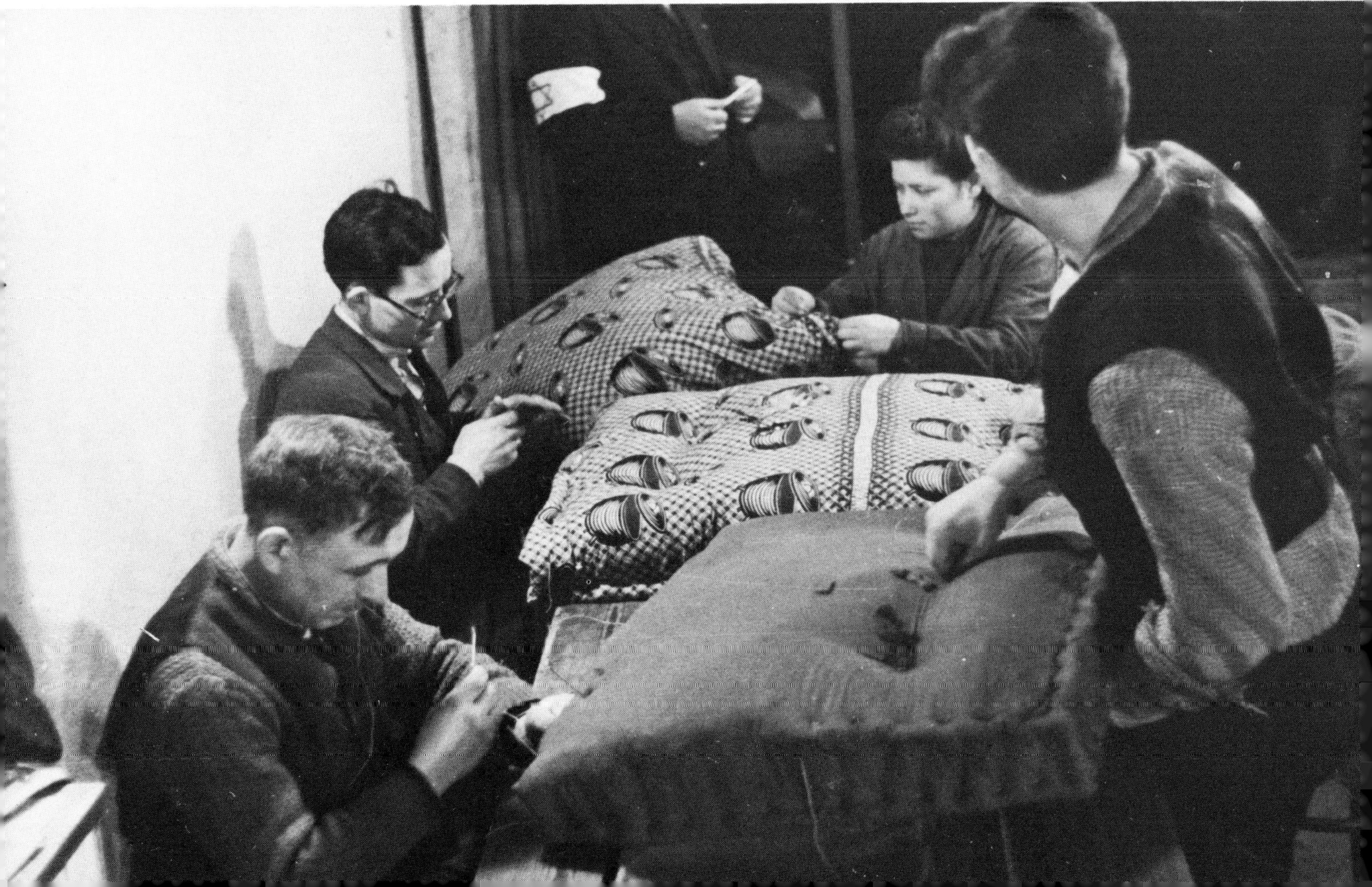

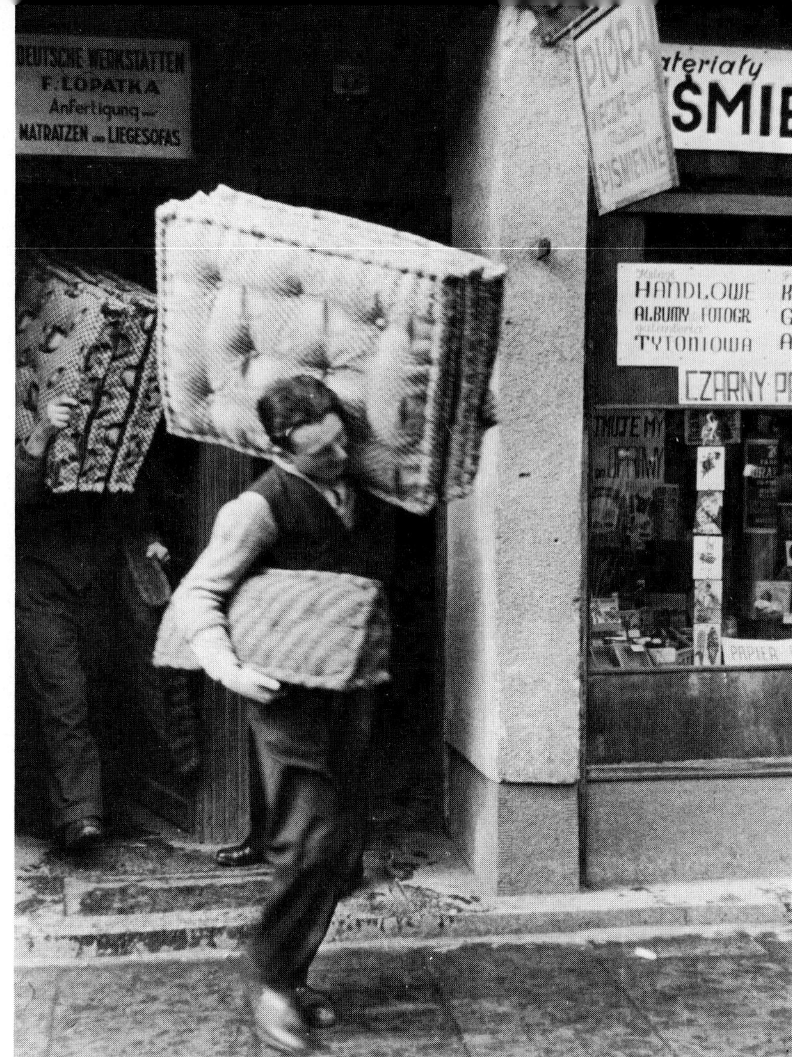

Sign over entrance: "German workshop, F. Lopatka,
manufacture of mattresses and daybeds."

35

36

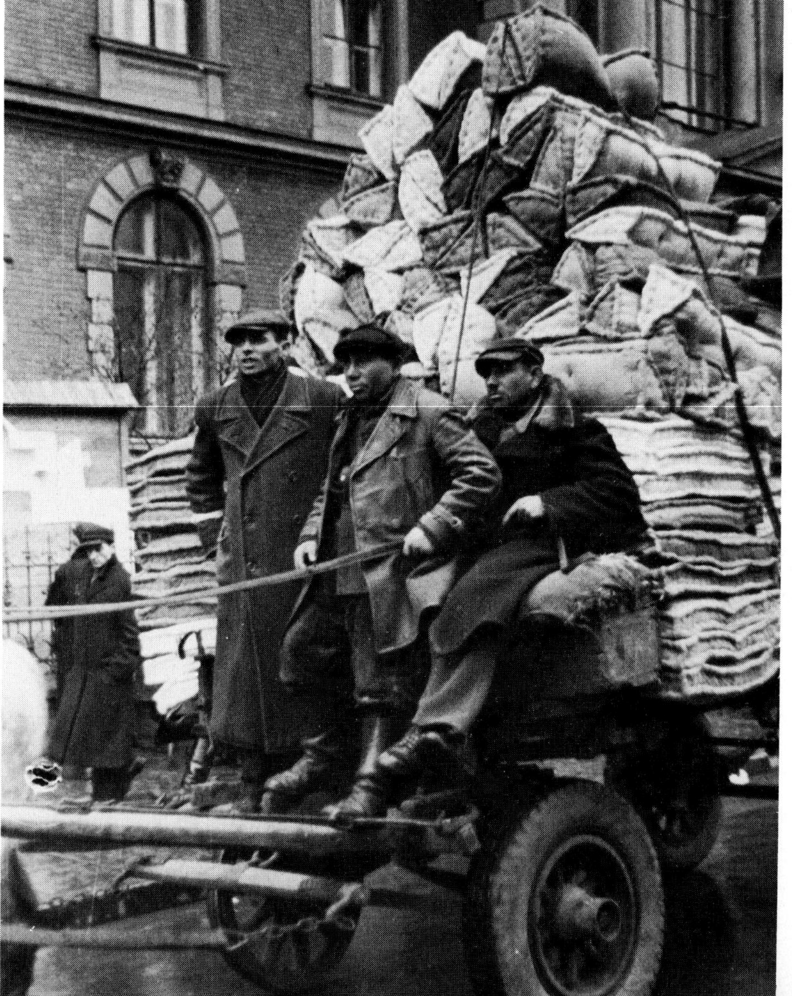

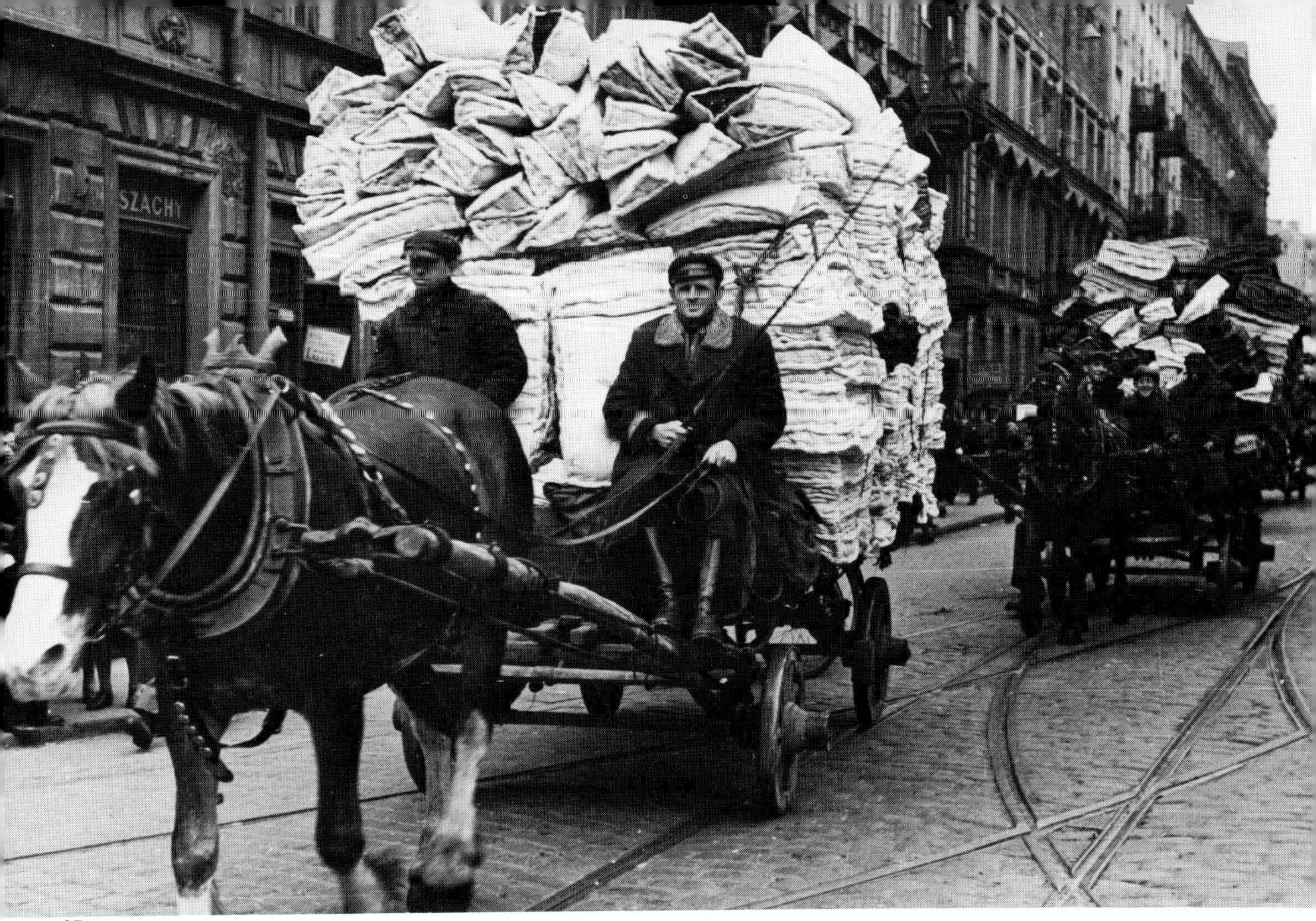

SZACHY

SZACHY

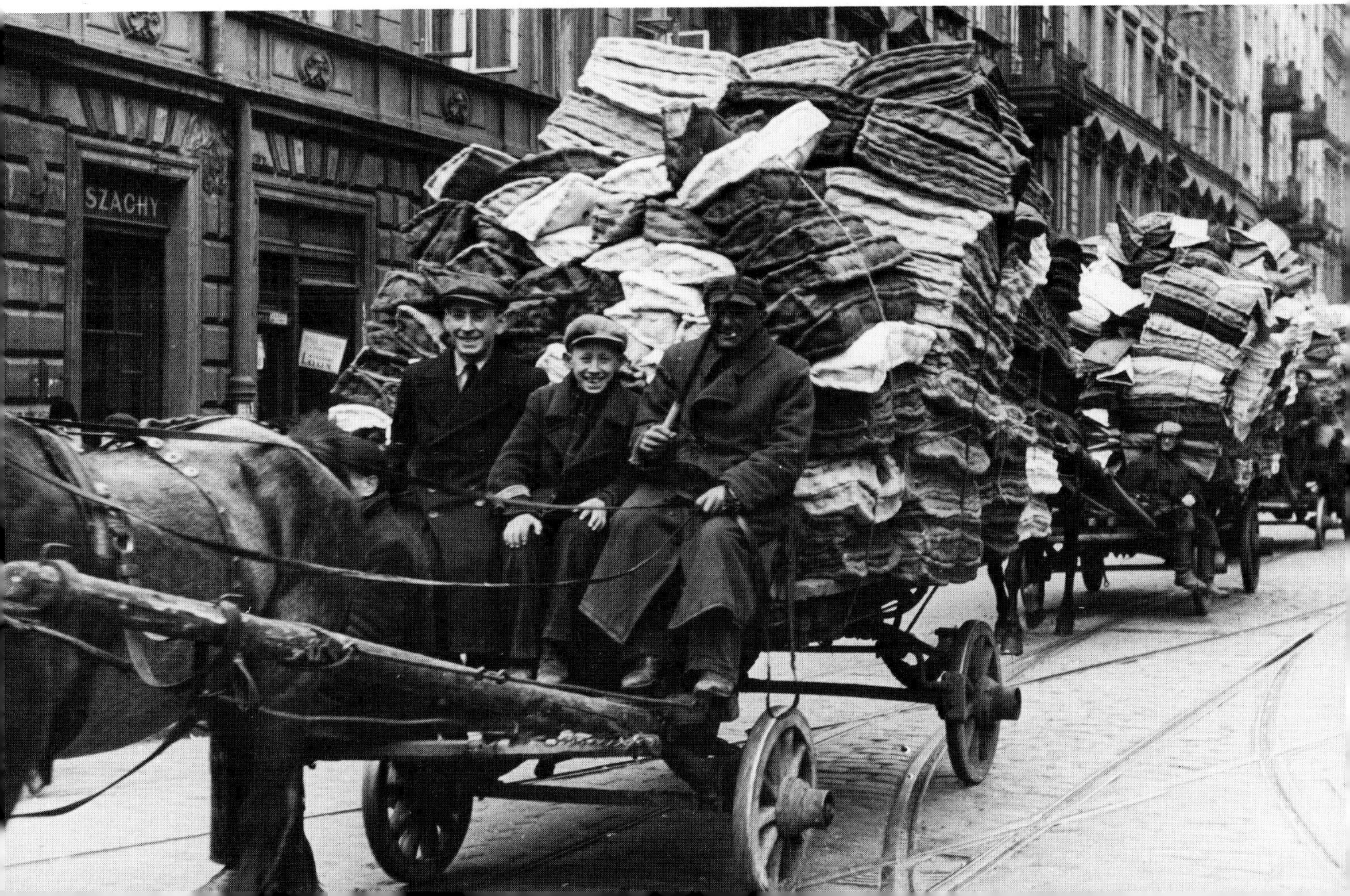

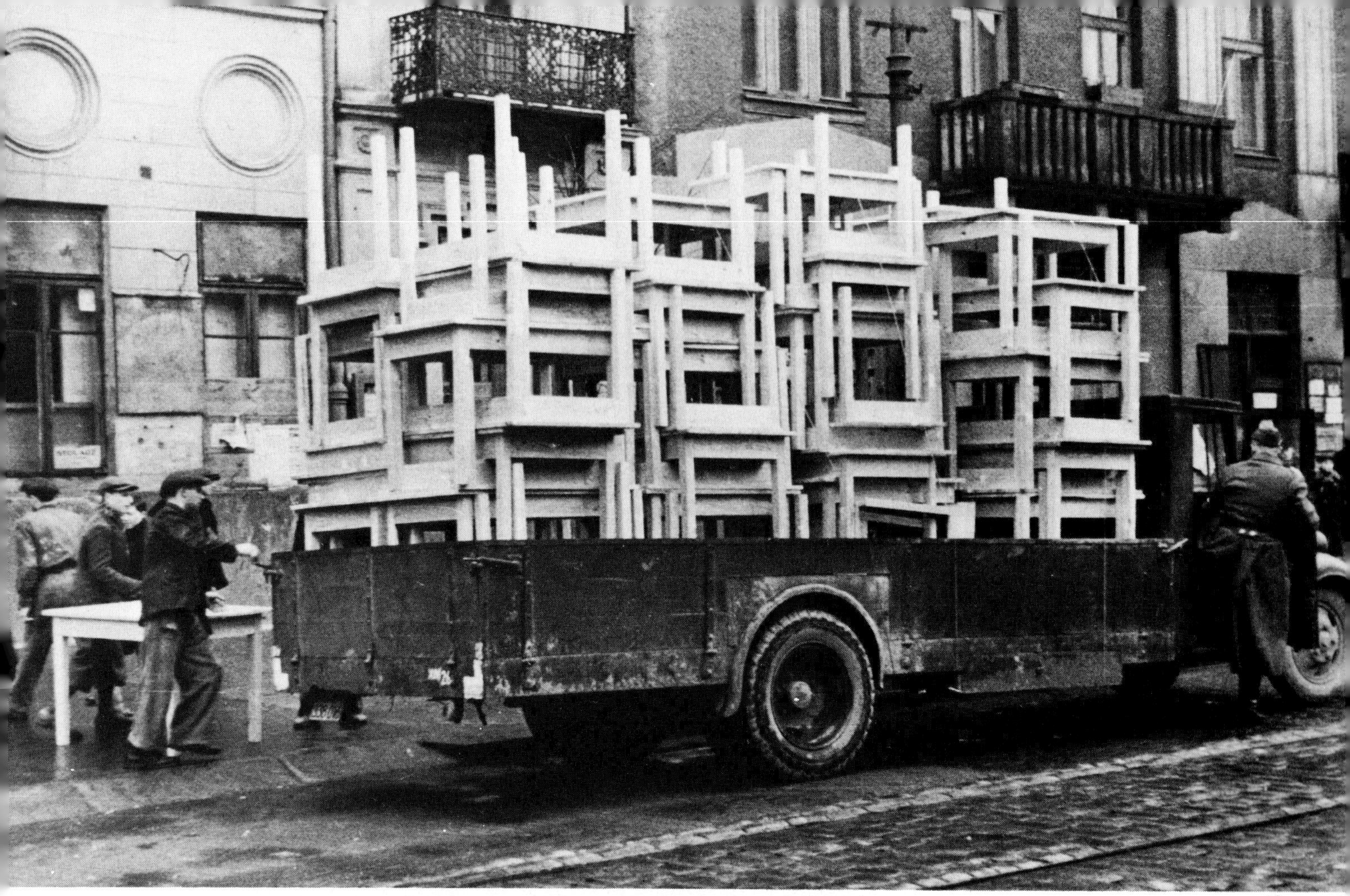

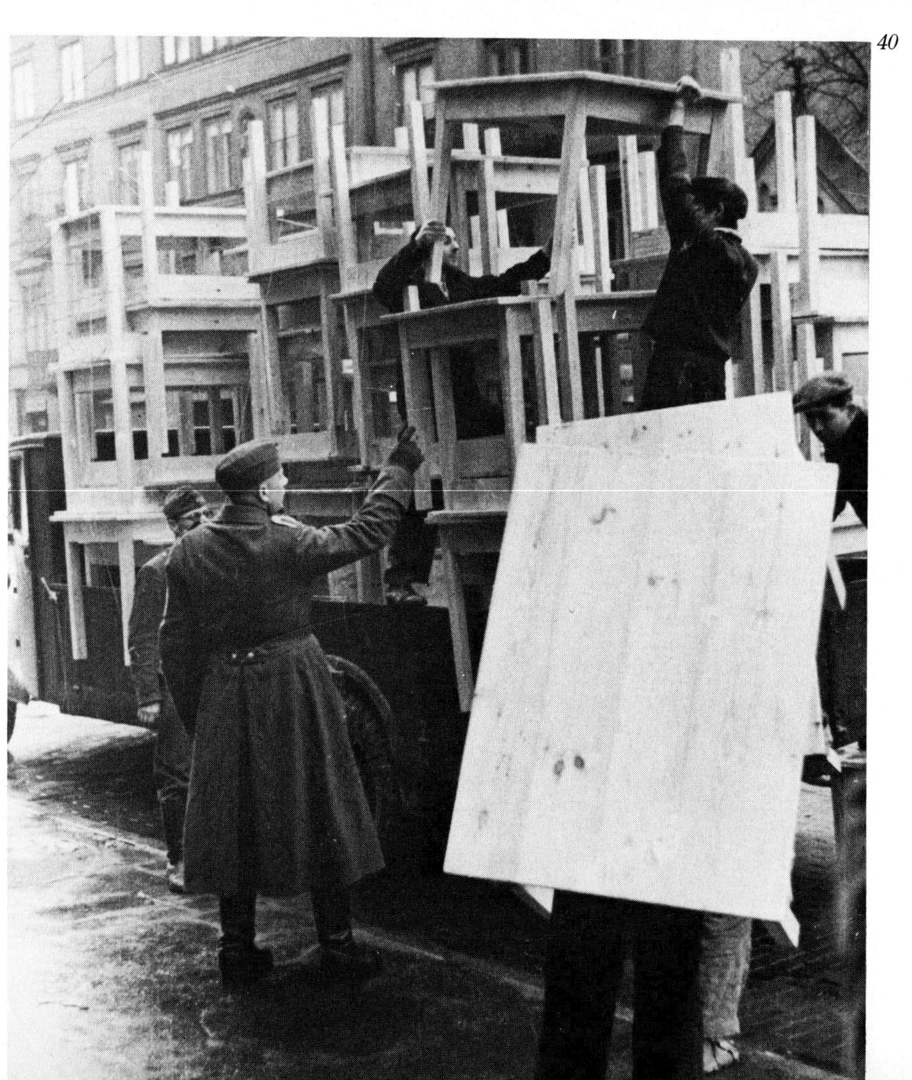

39

40

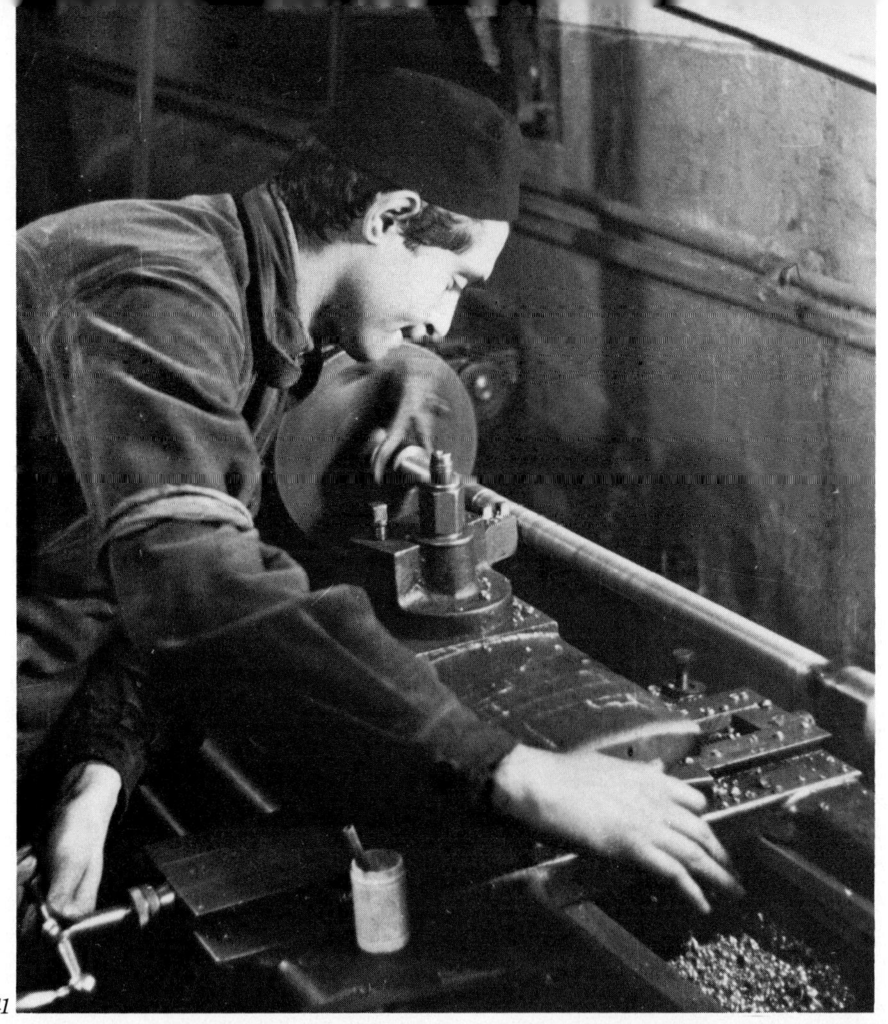

41

42

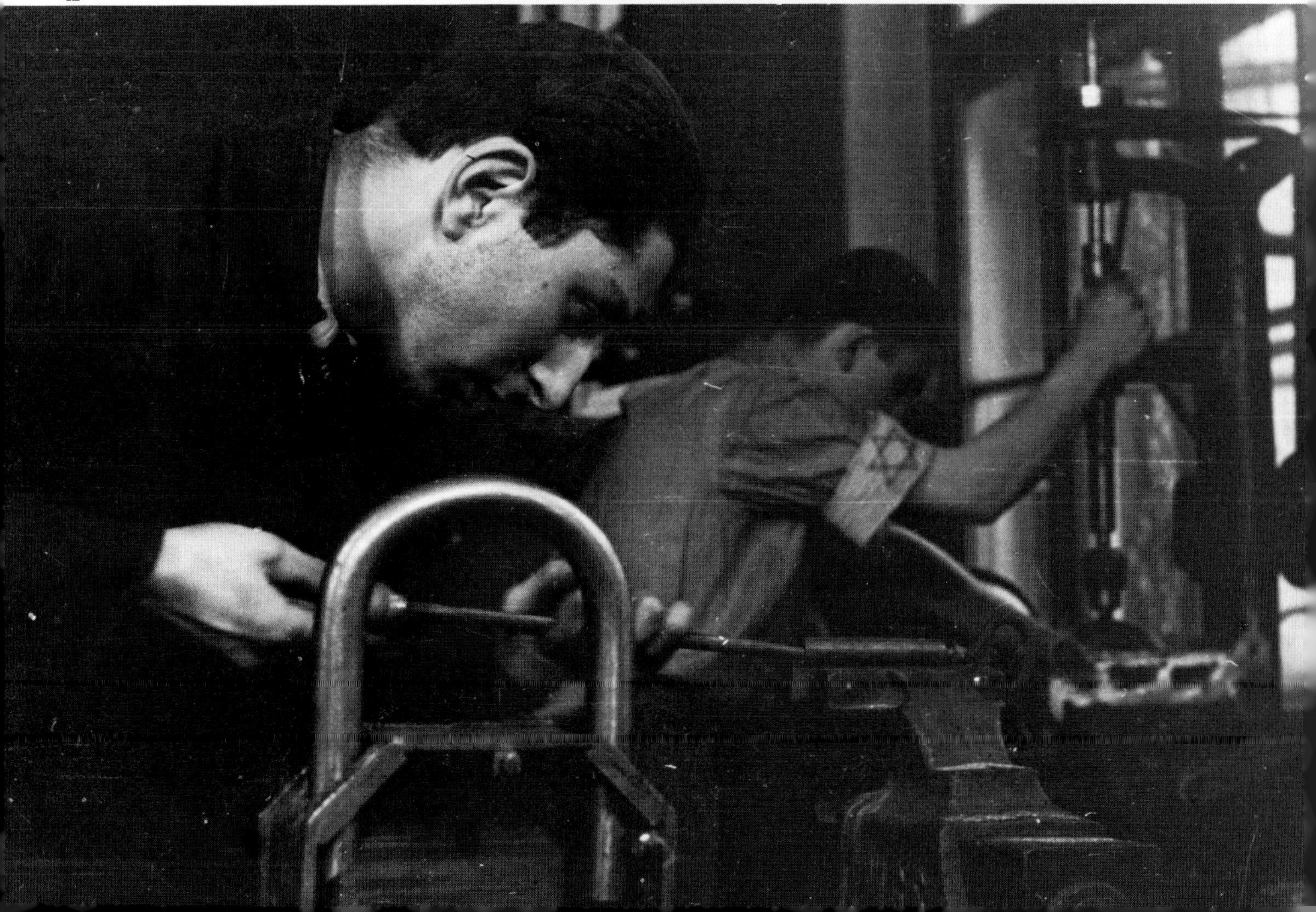

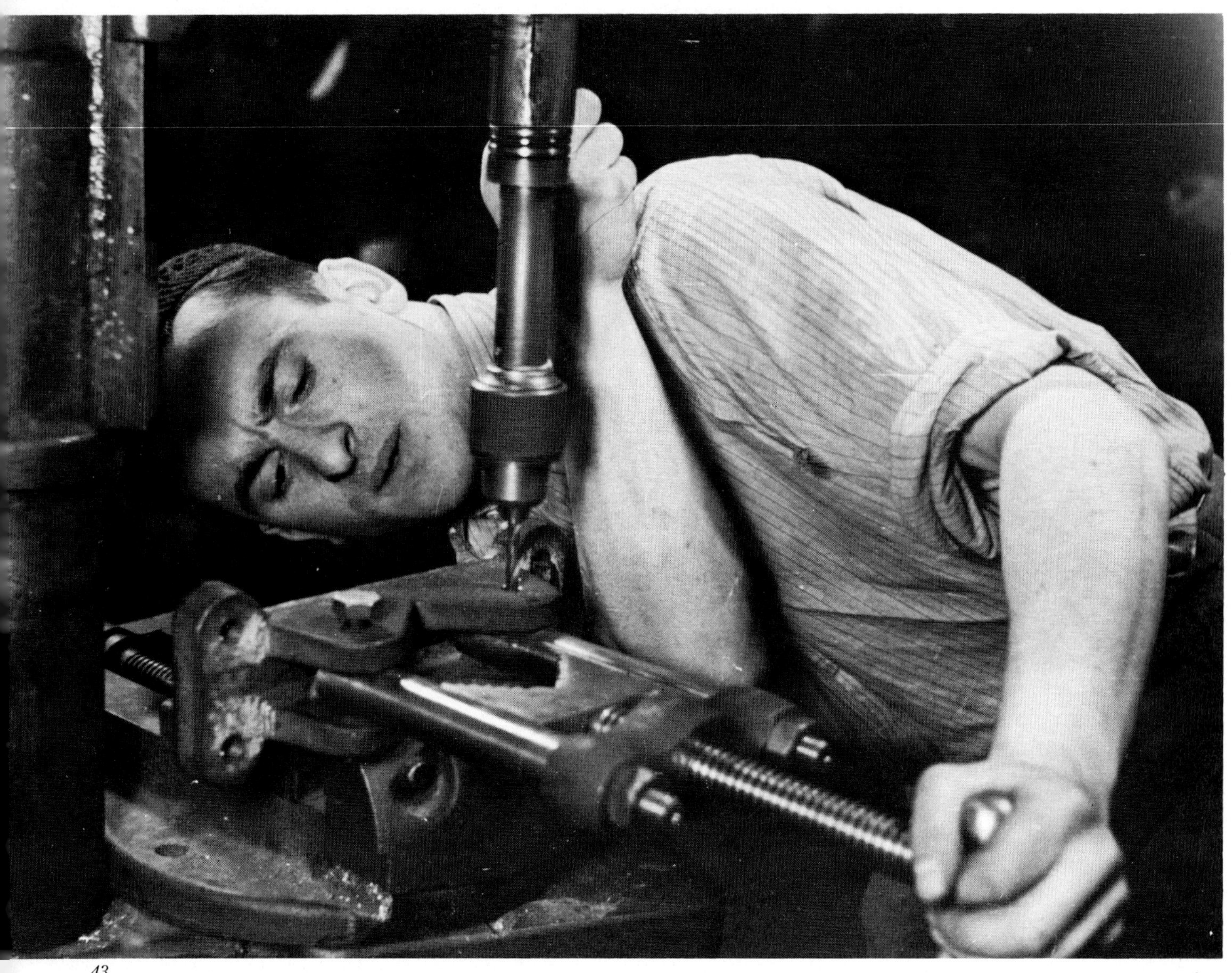

43

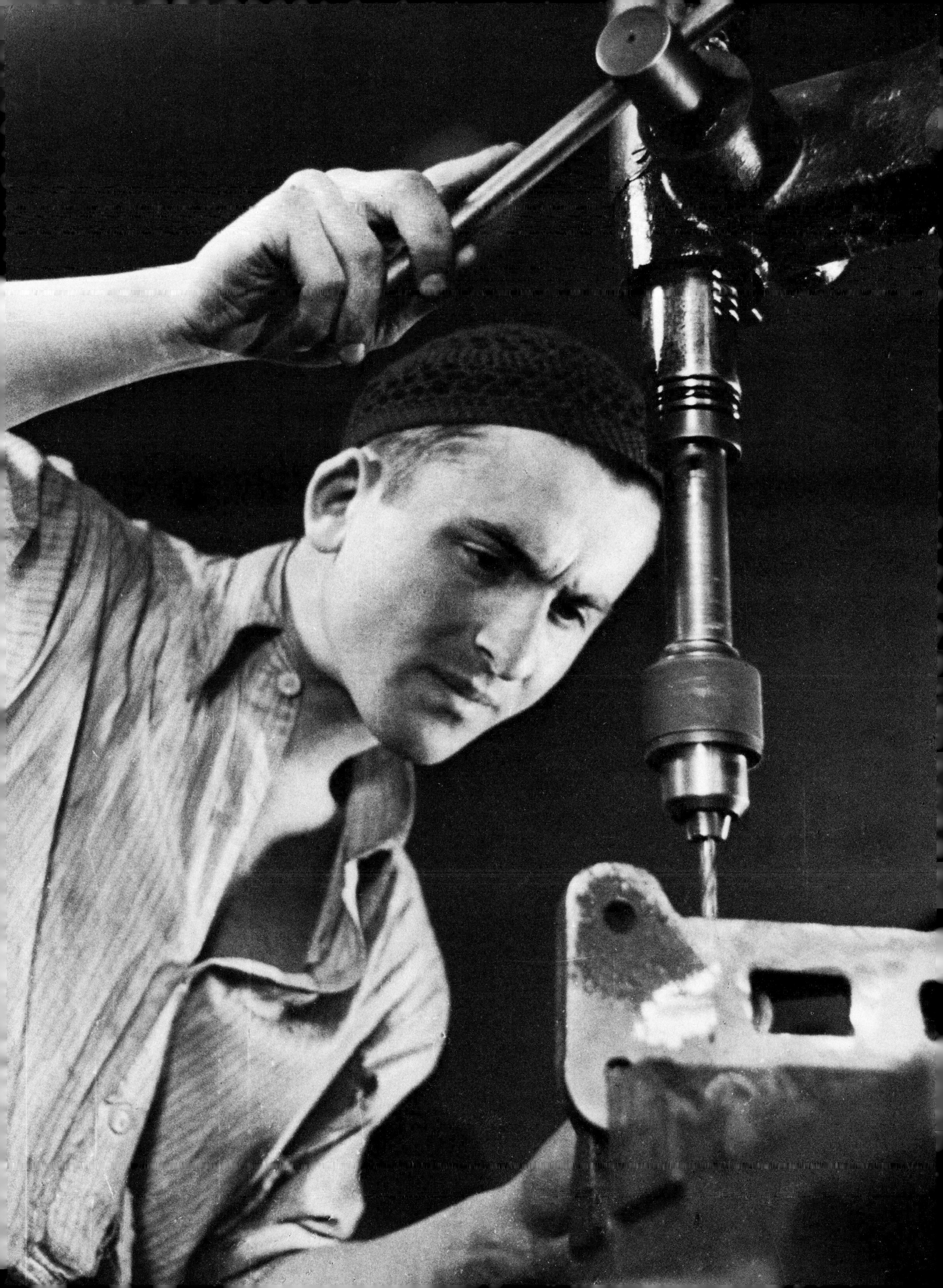

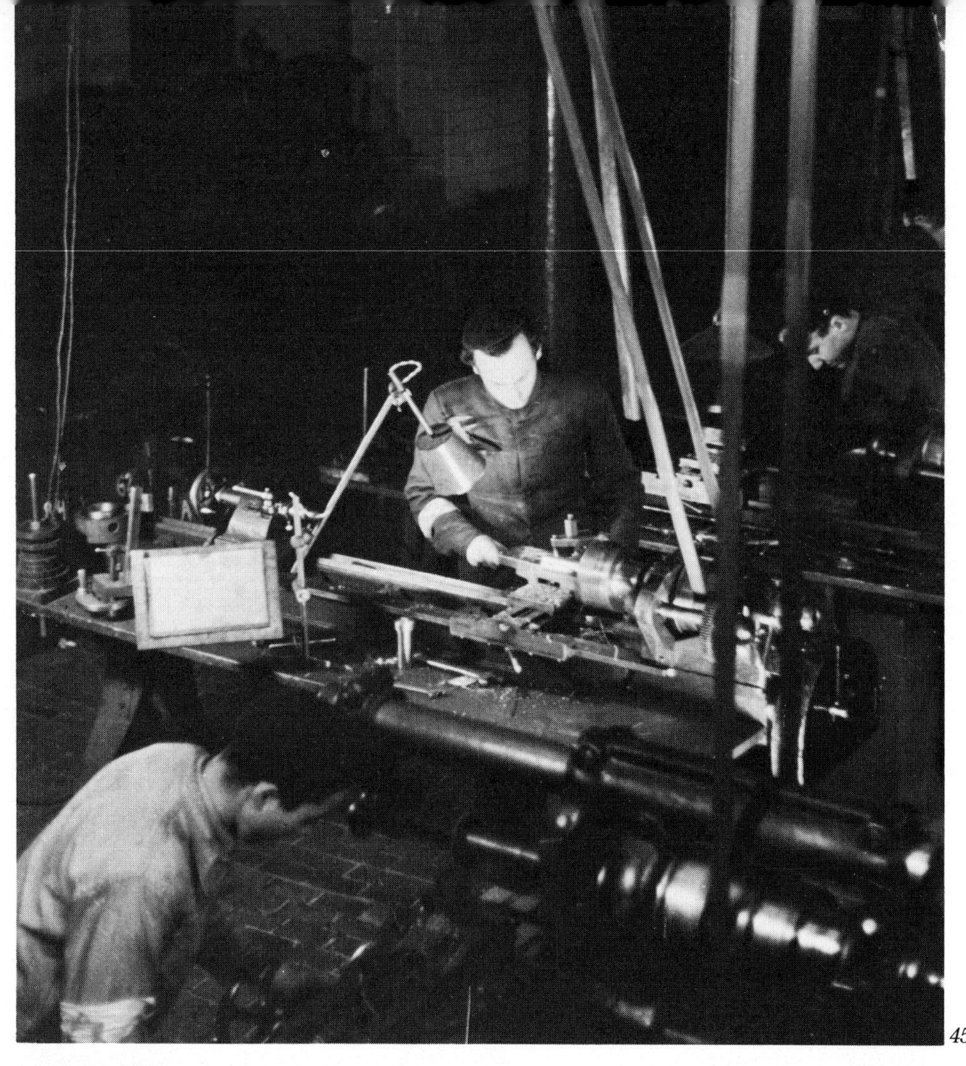

45

46

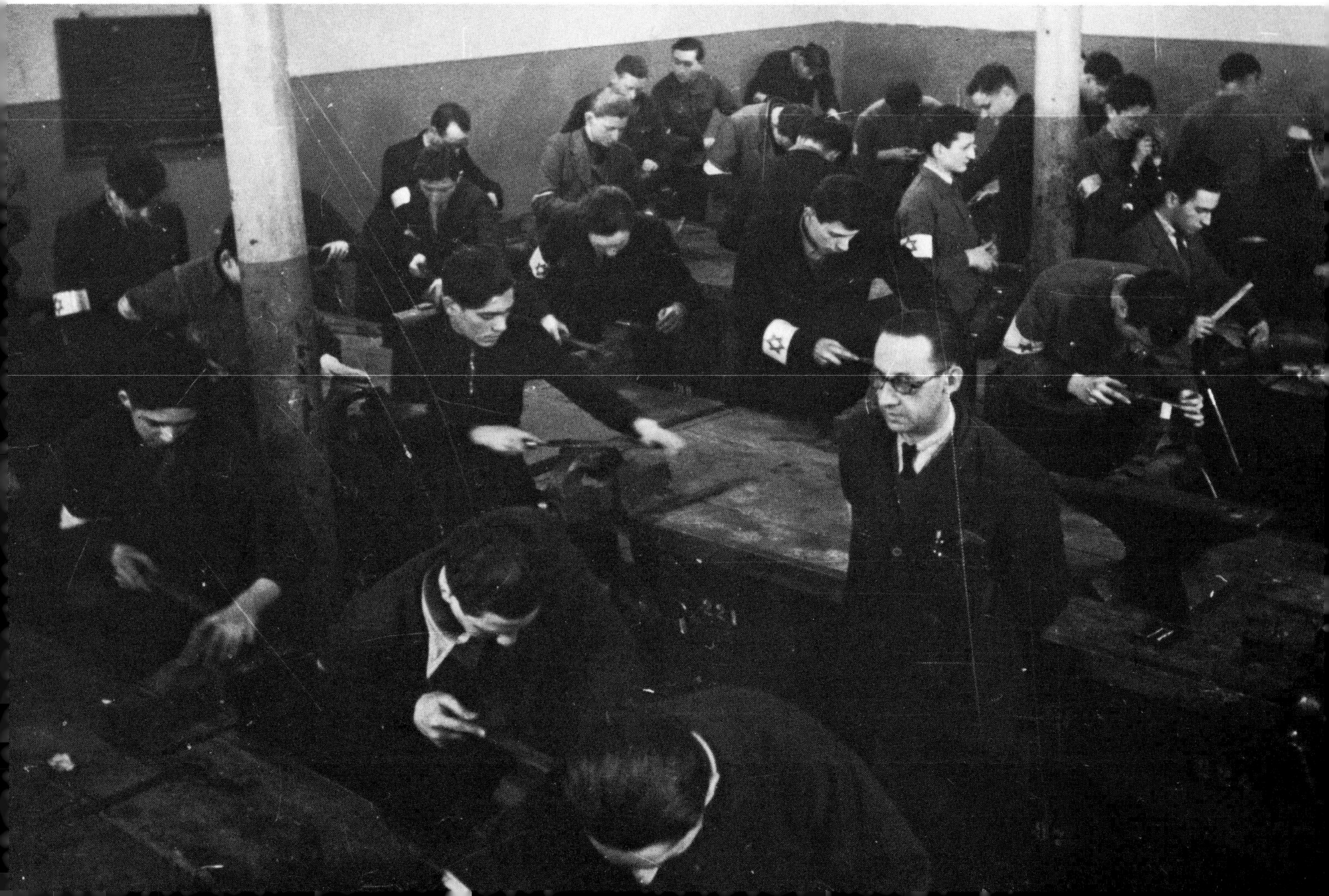

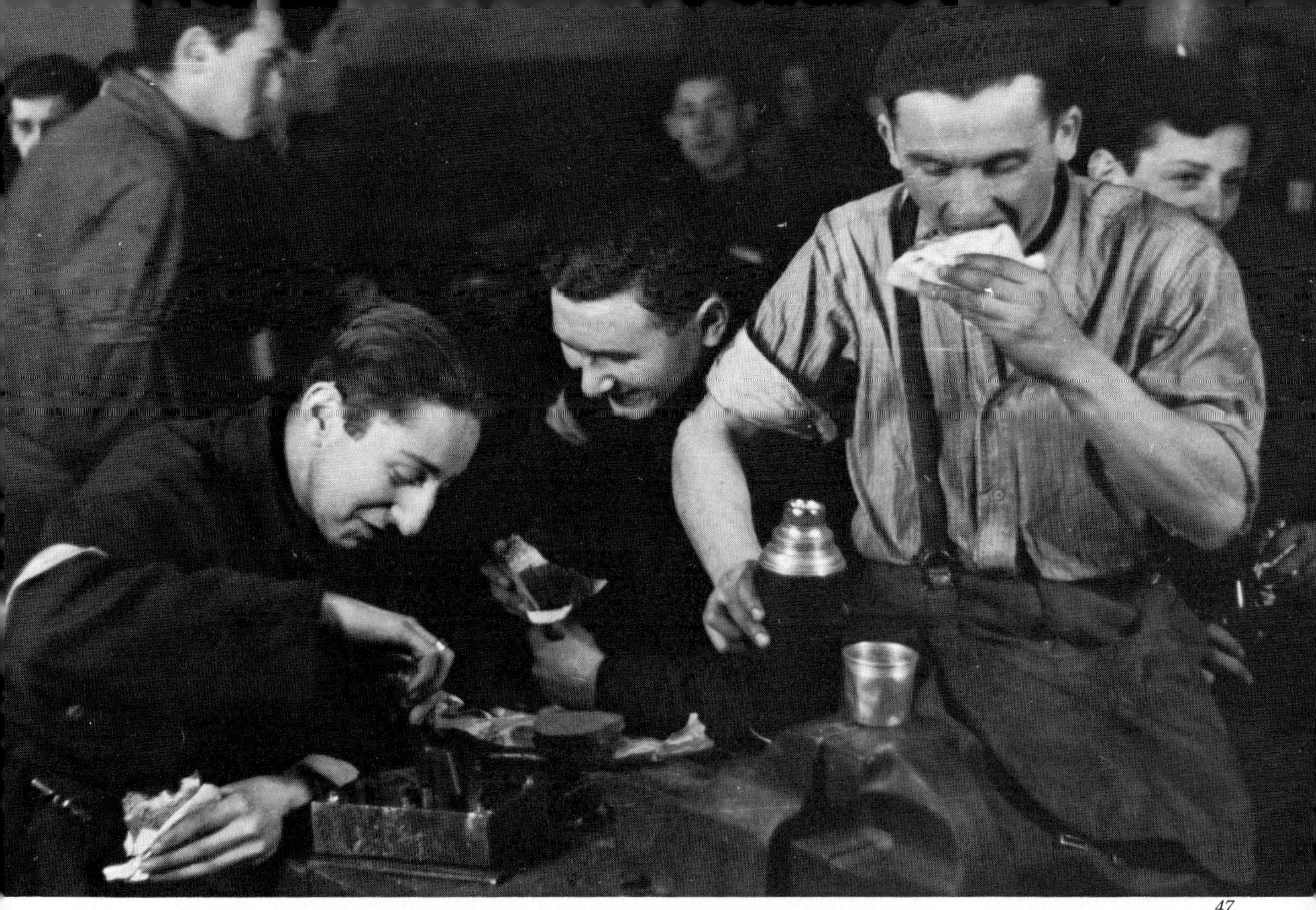

47

FORCED LABOR OUTSIDE THE GHETTO

(Nos. 48–62)

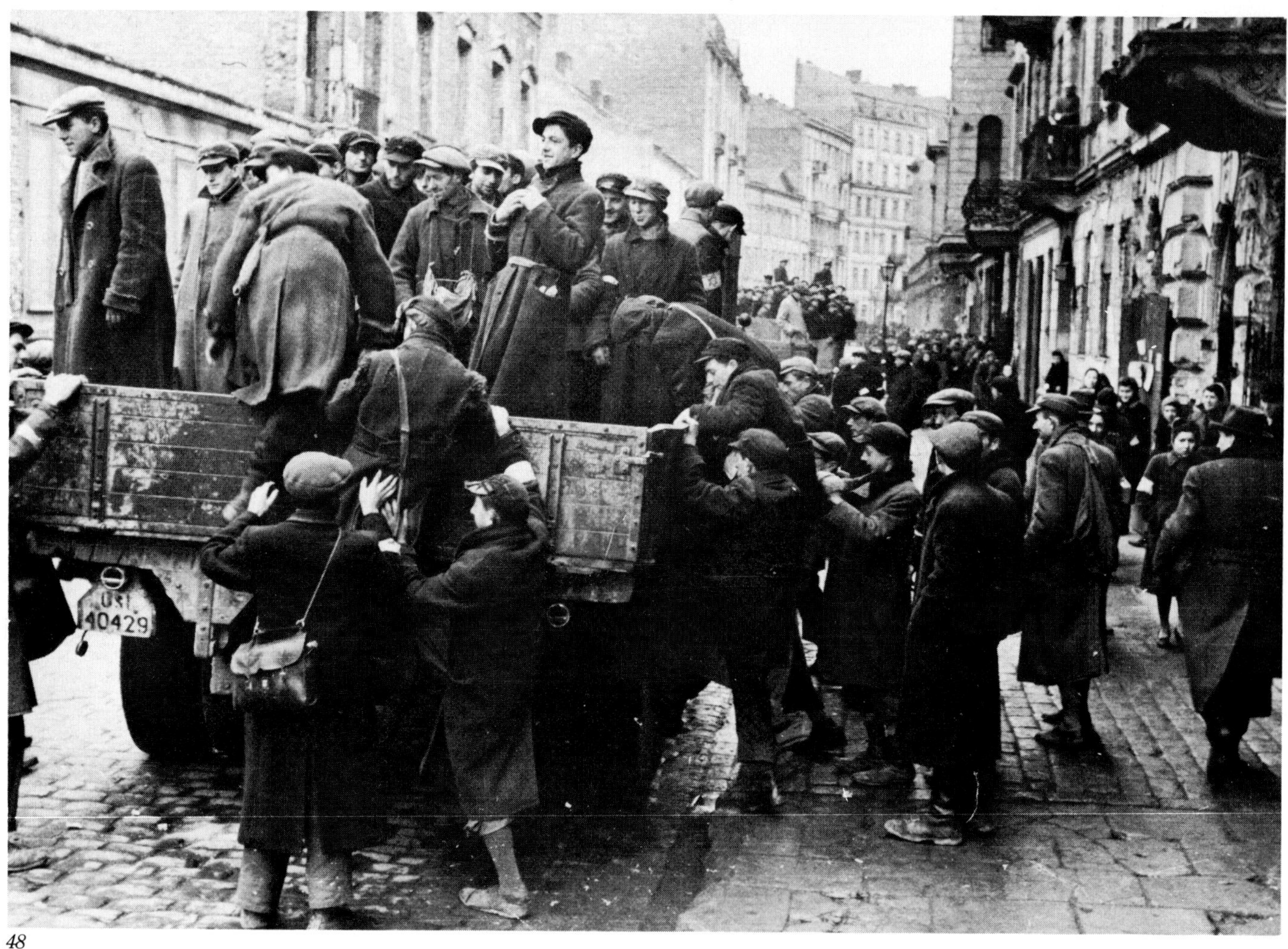

48

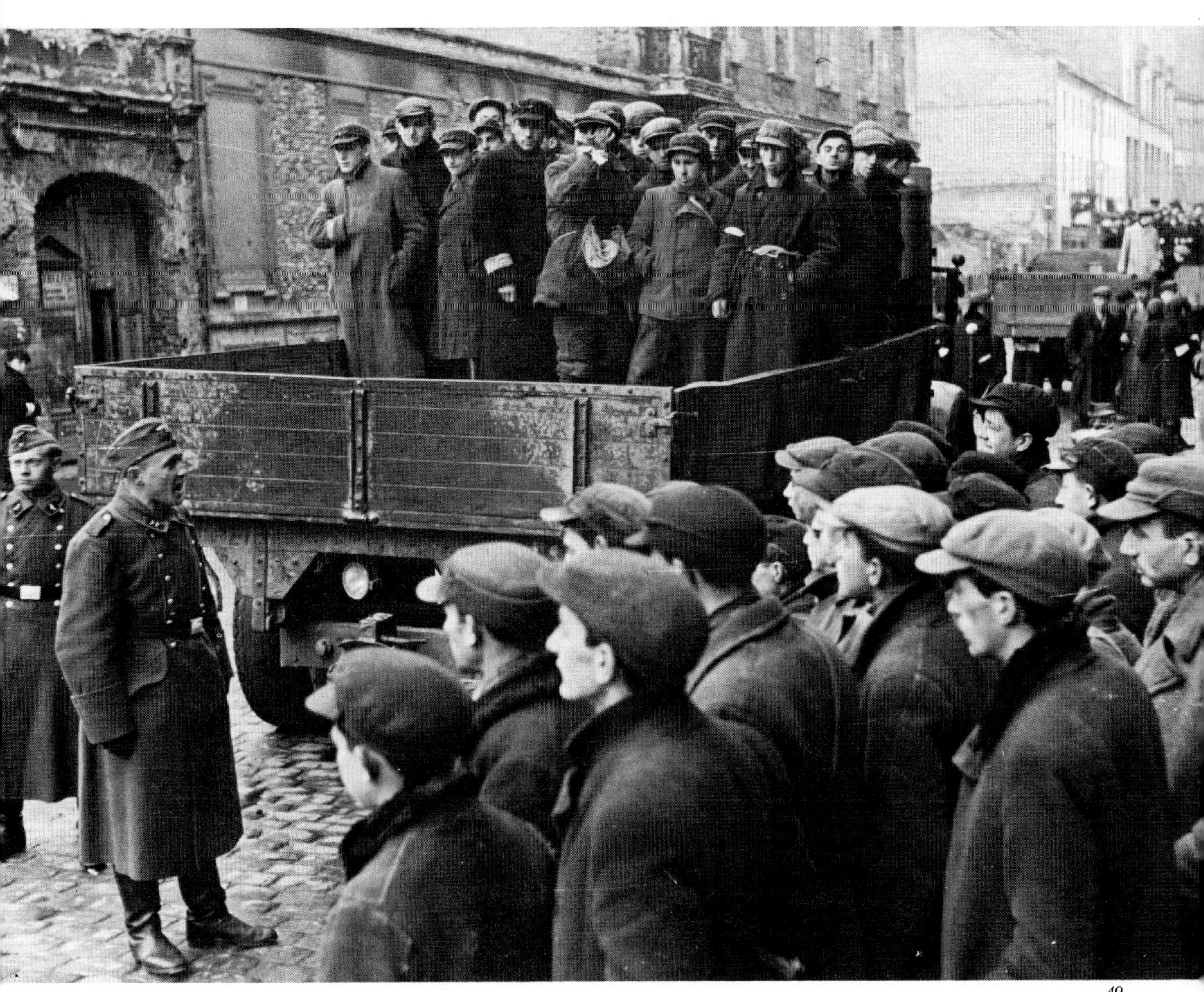

Forced Labor Outside the Ghetto   31

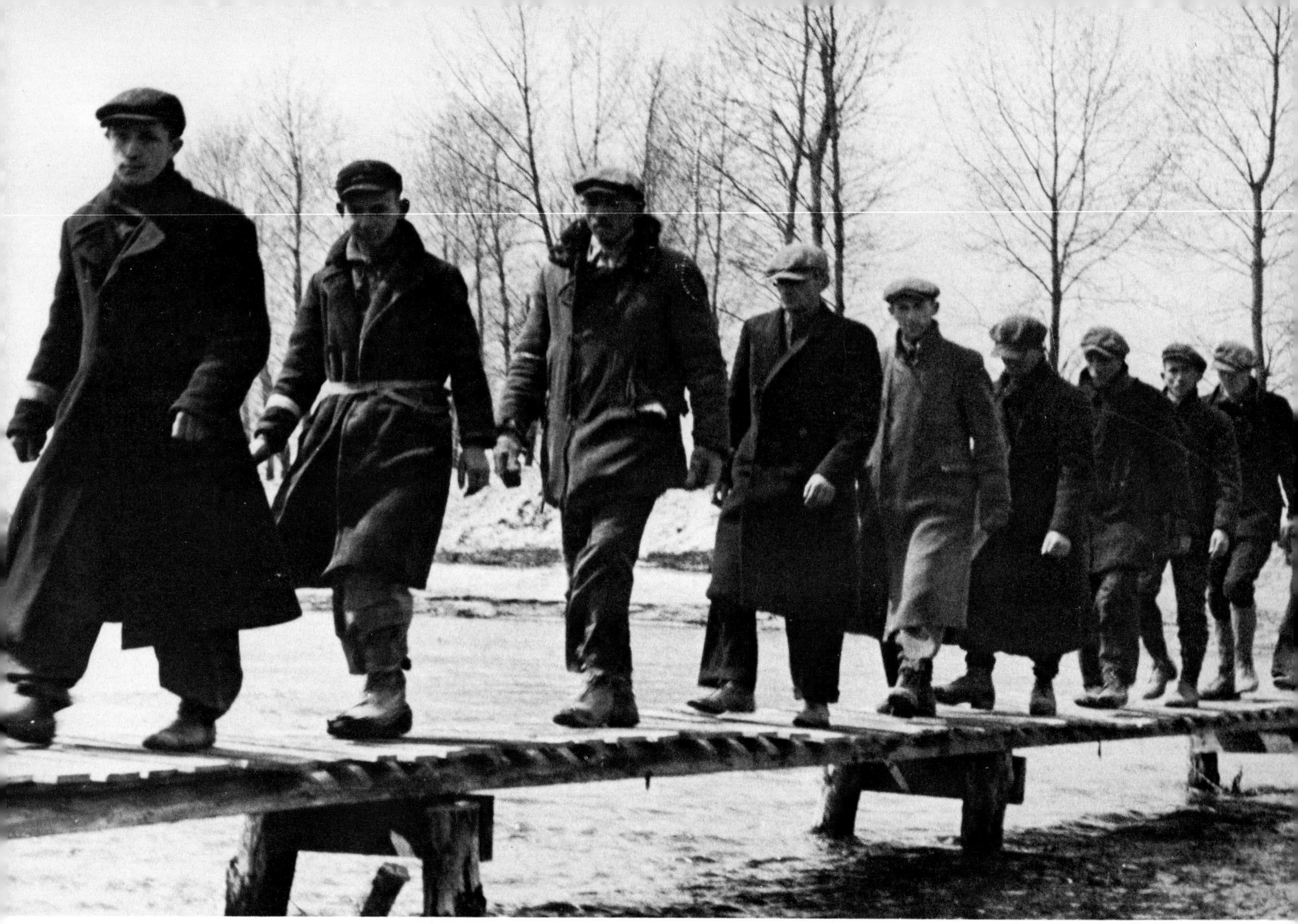

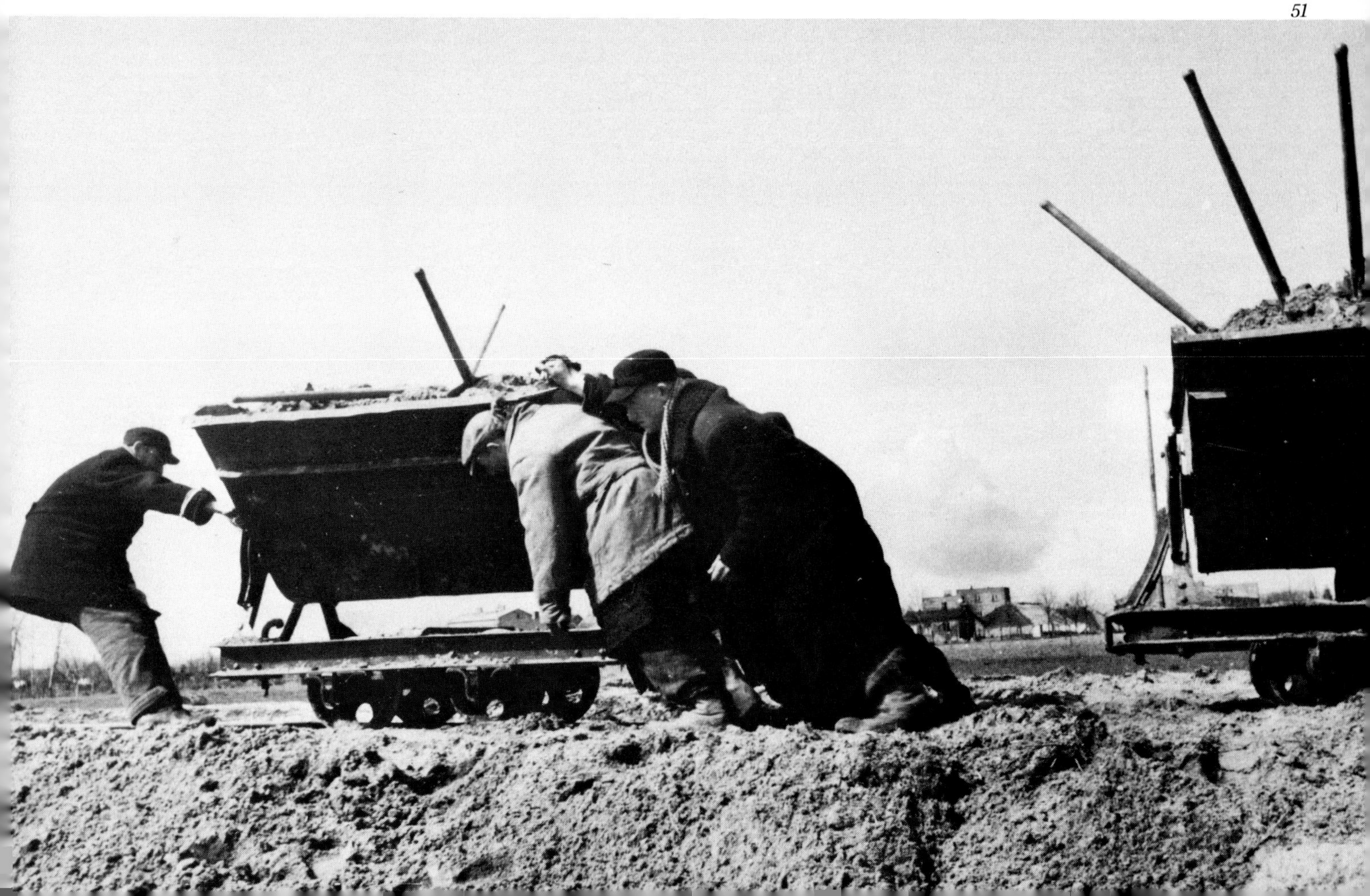

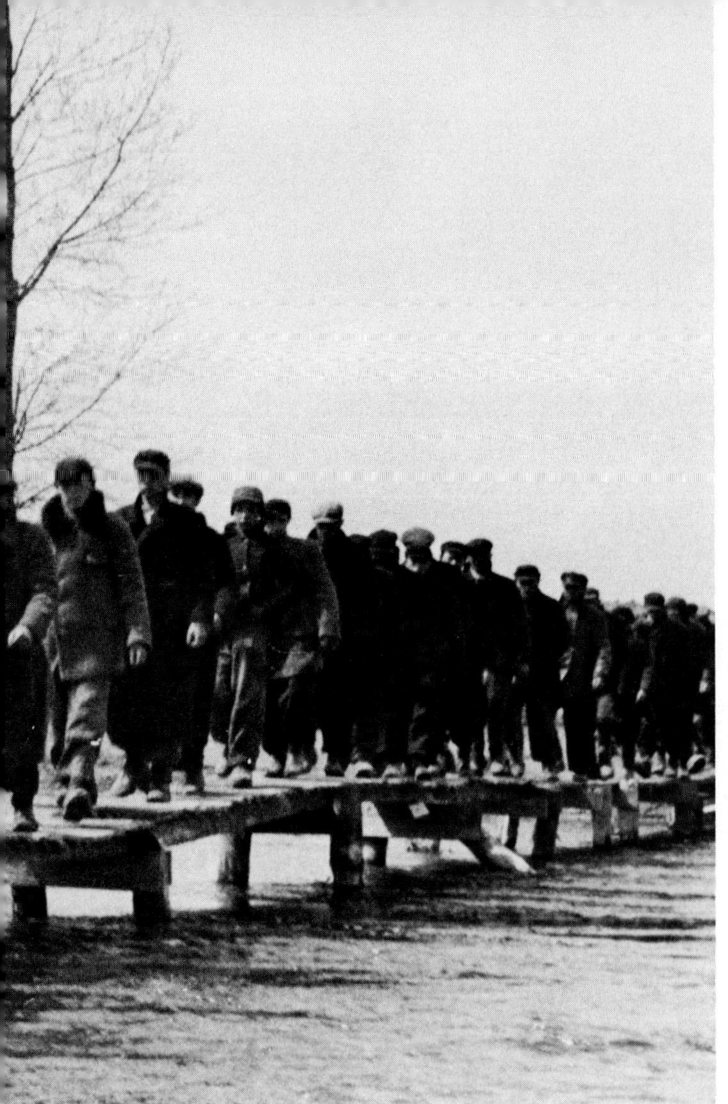

50

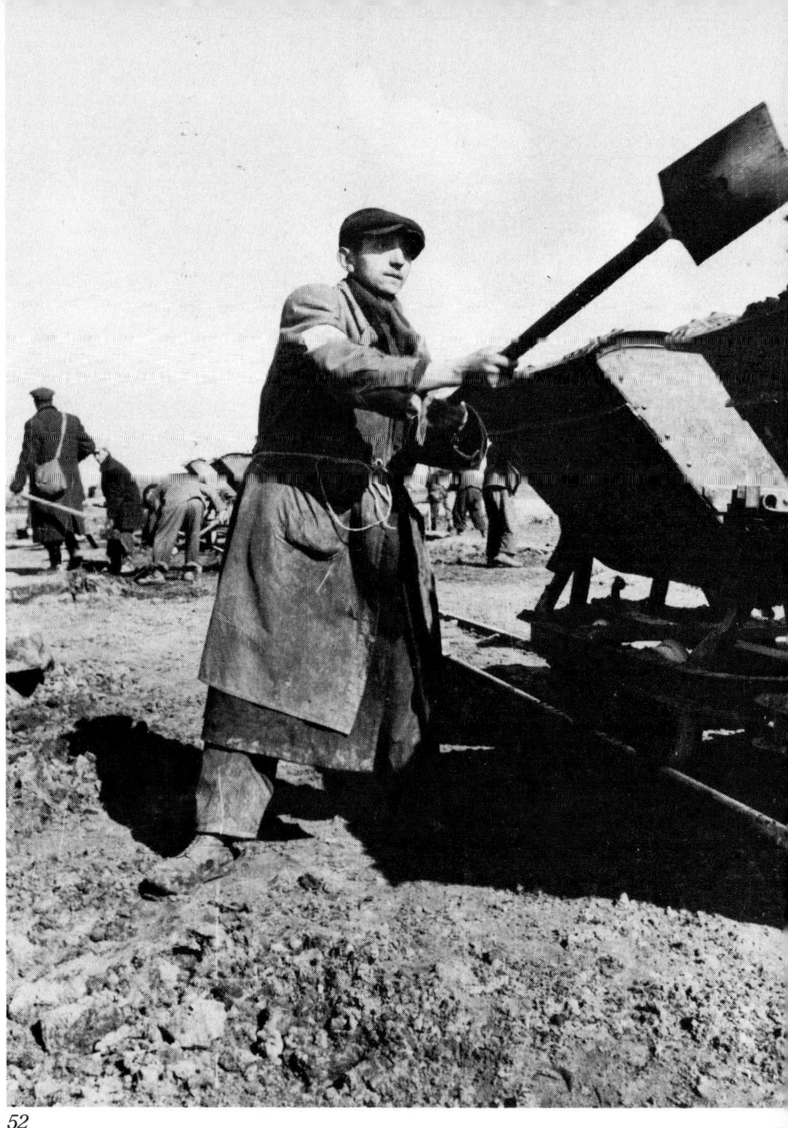

52

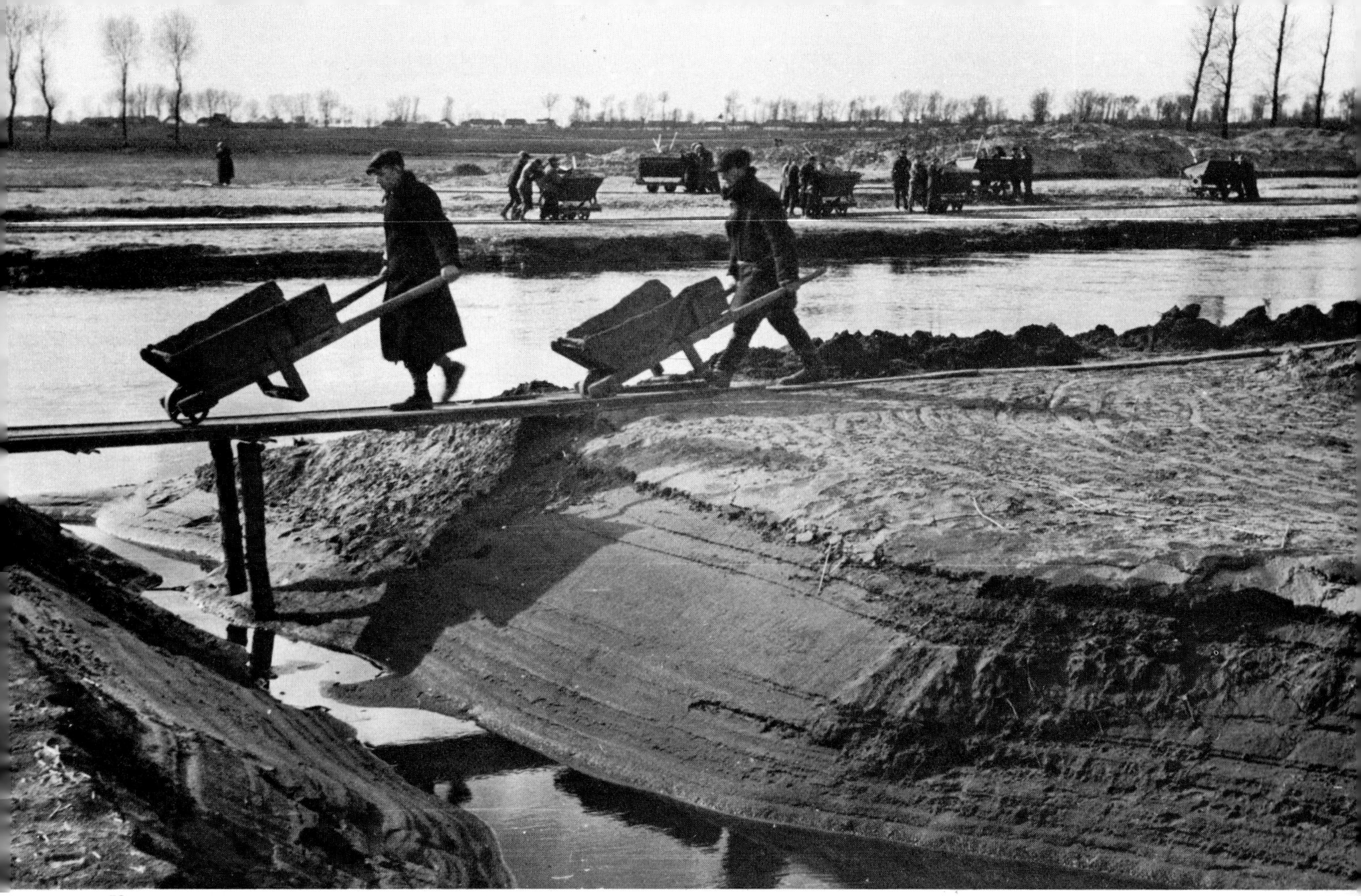

53

54

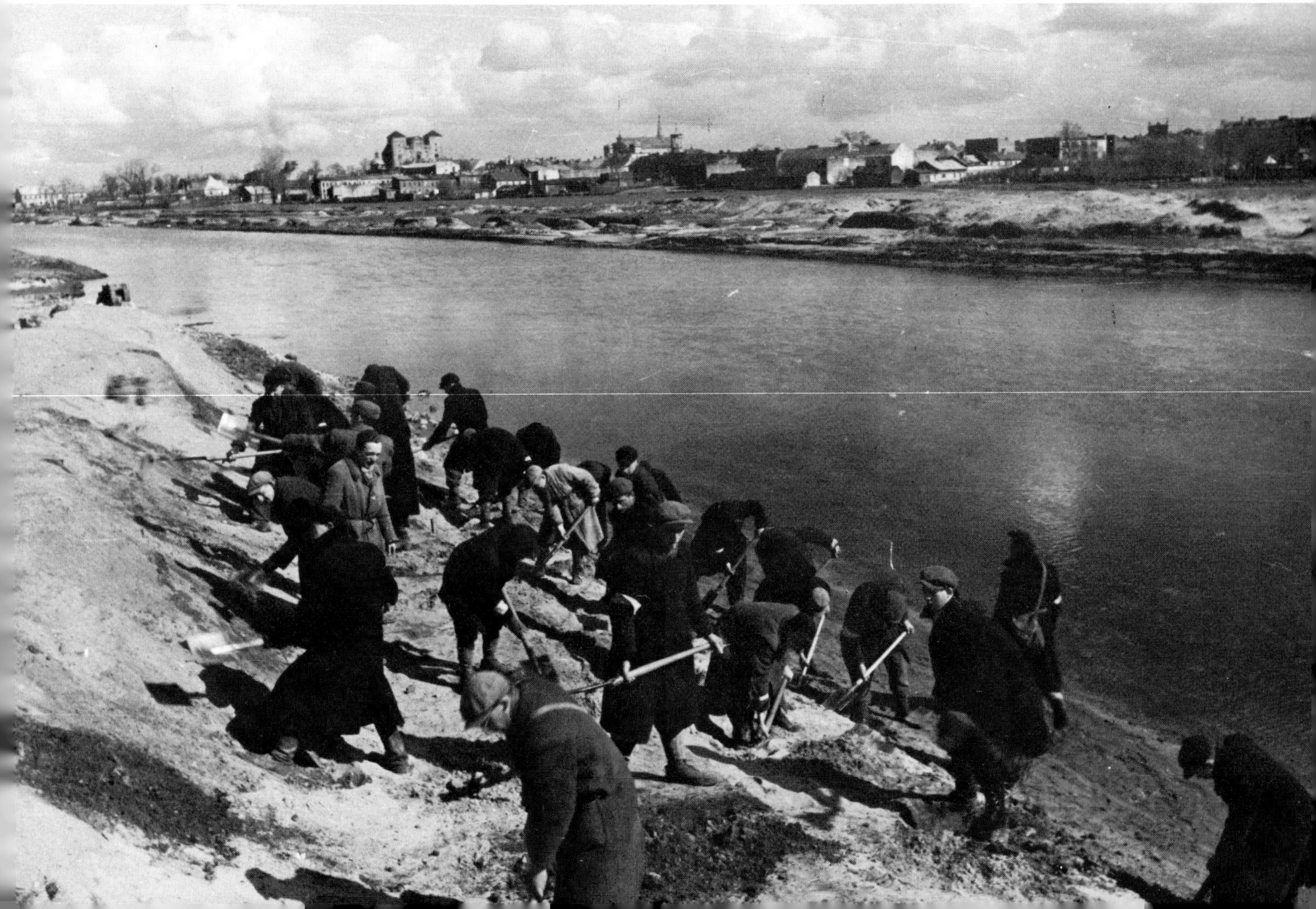

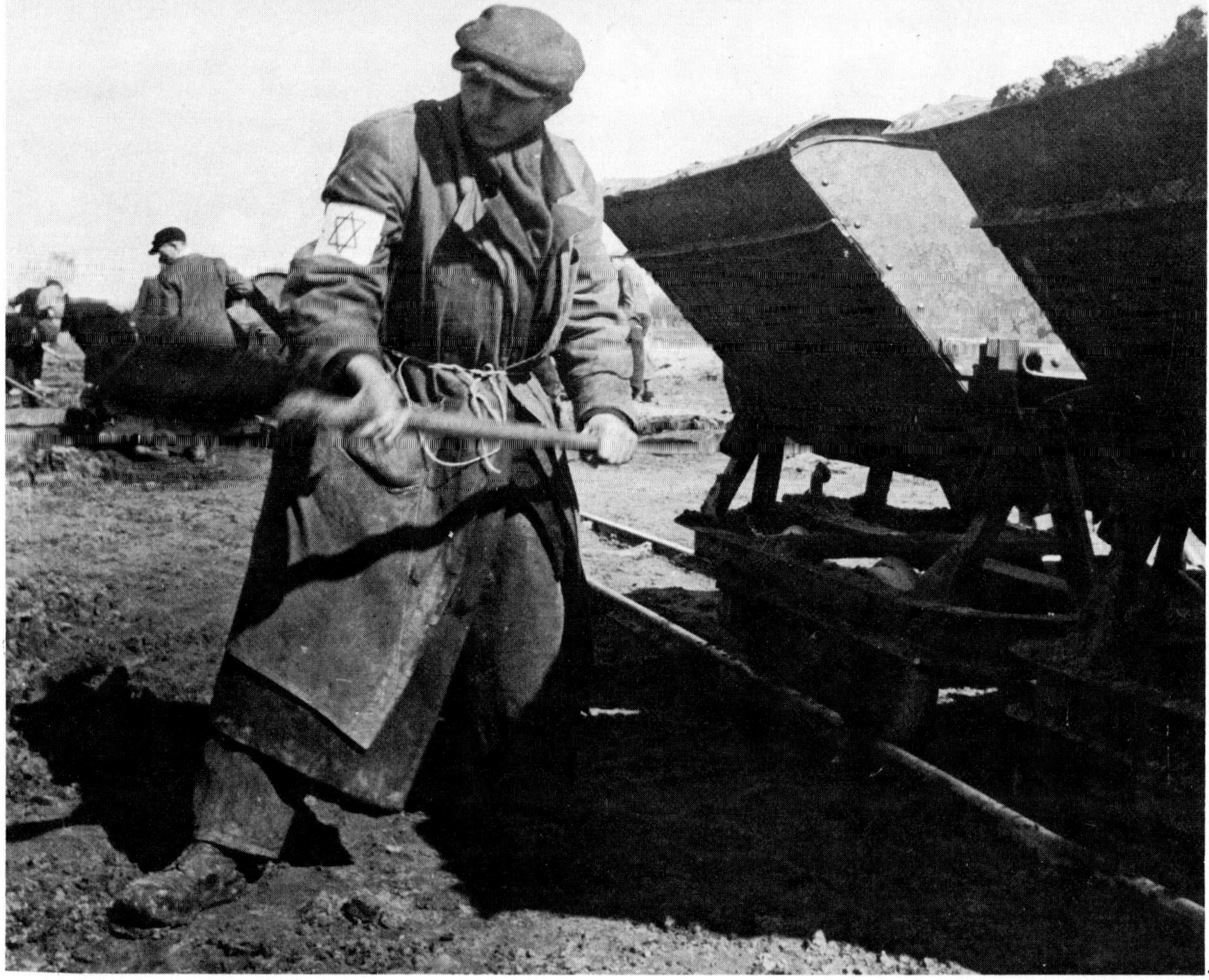

55

56

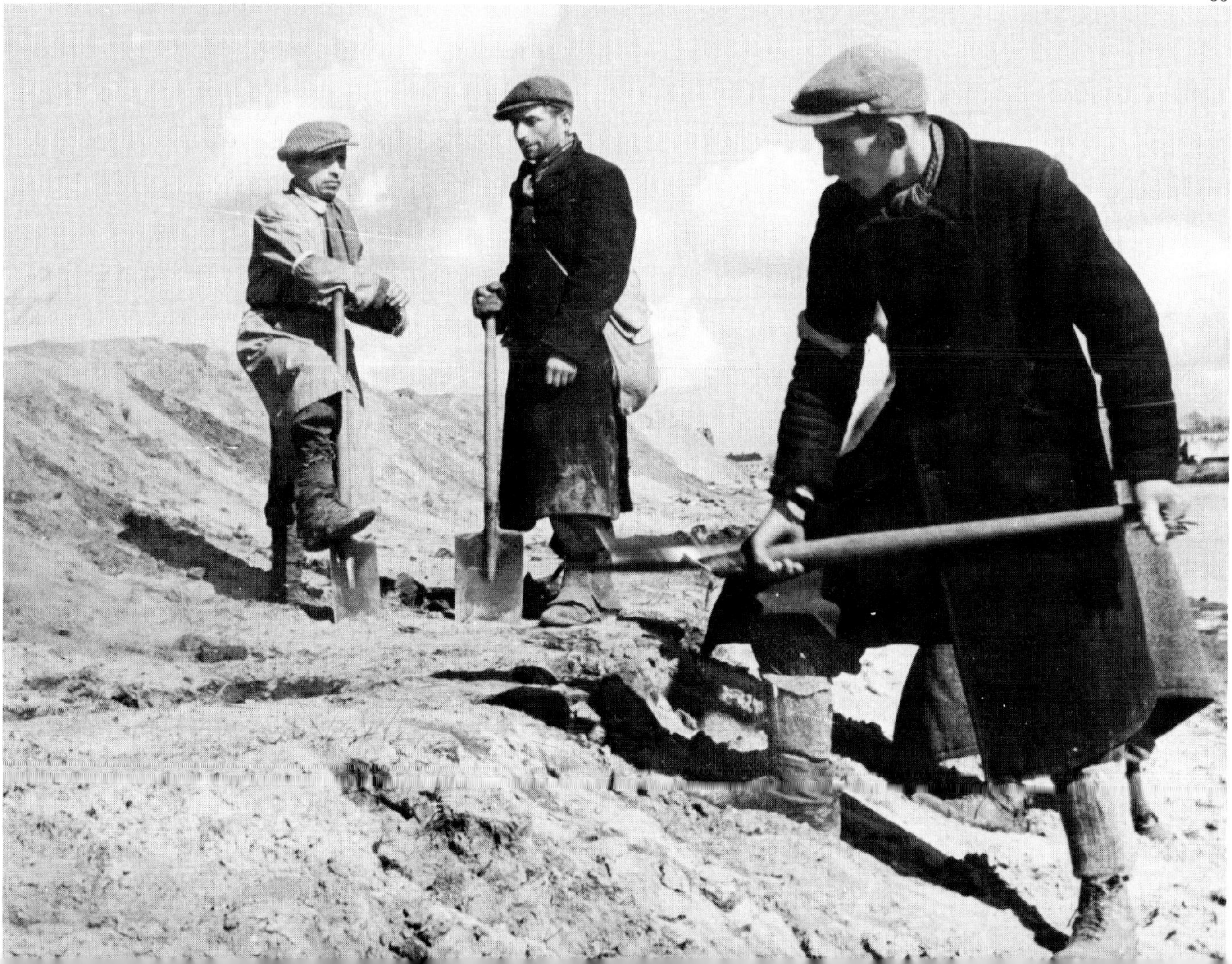

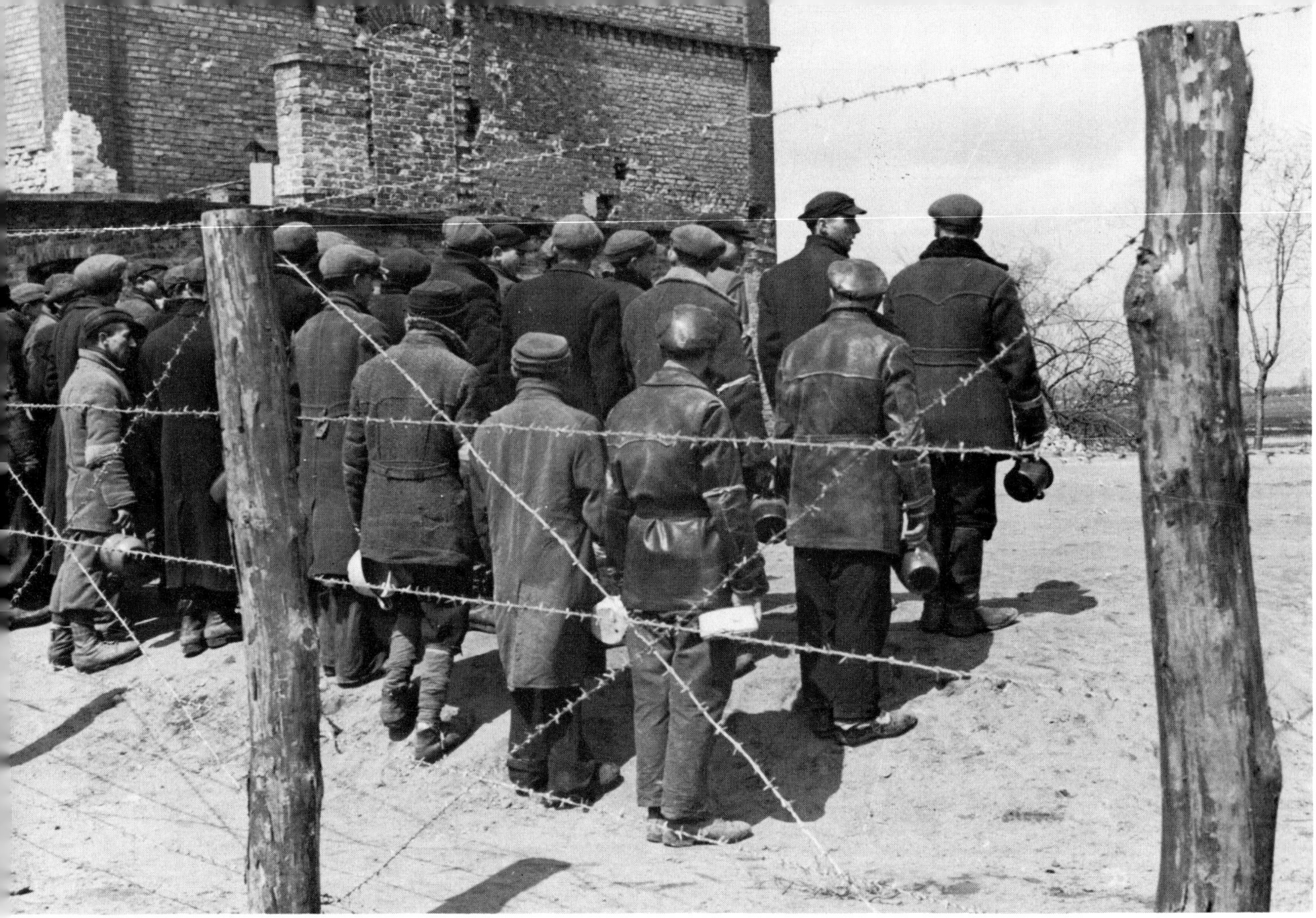

57

58

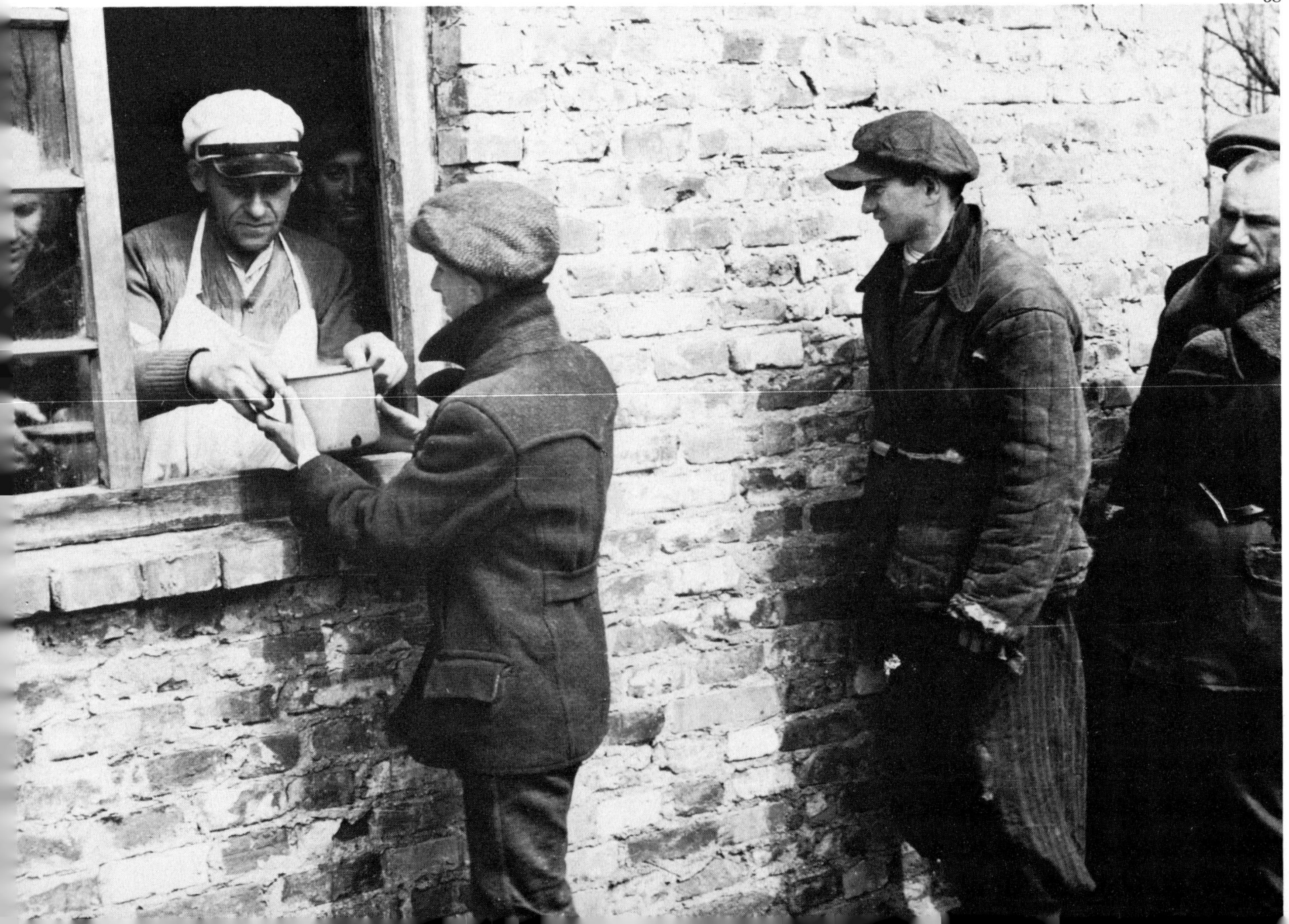

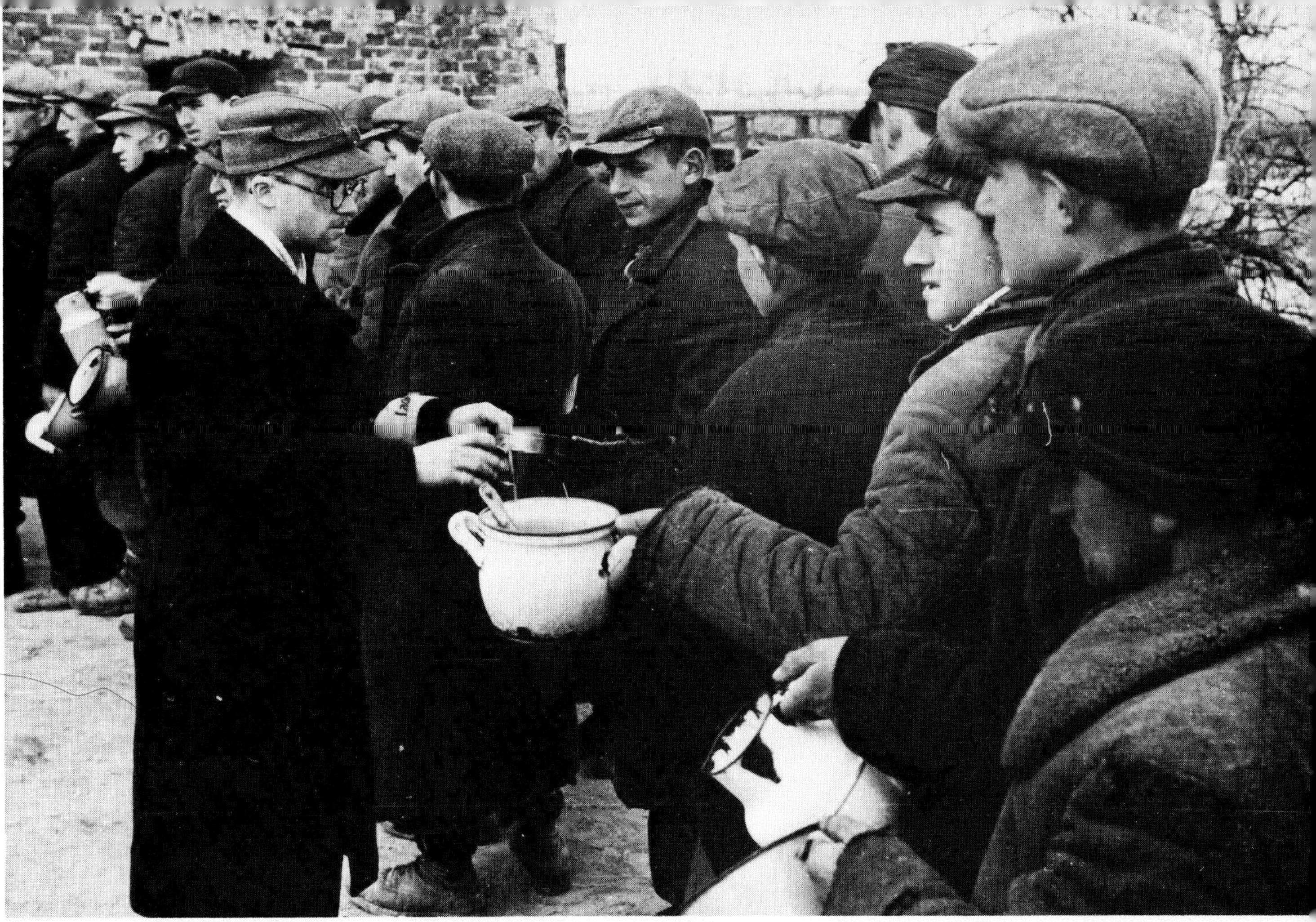

59

60

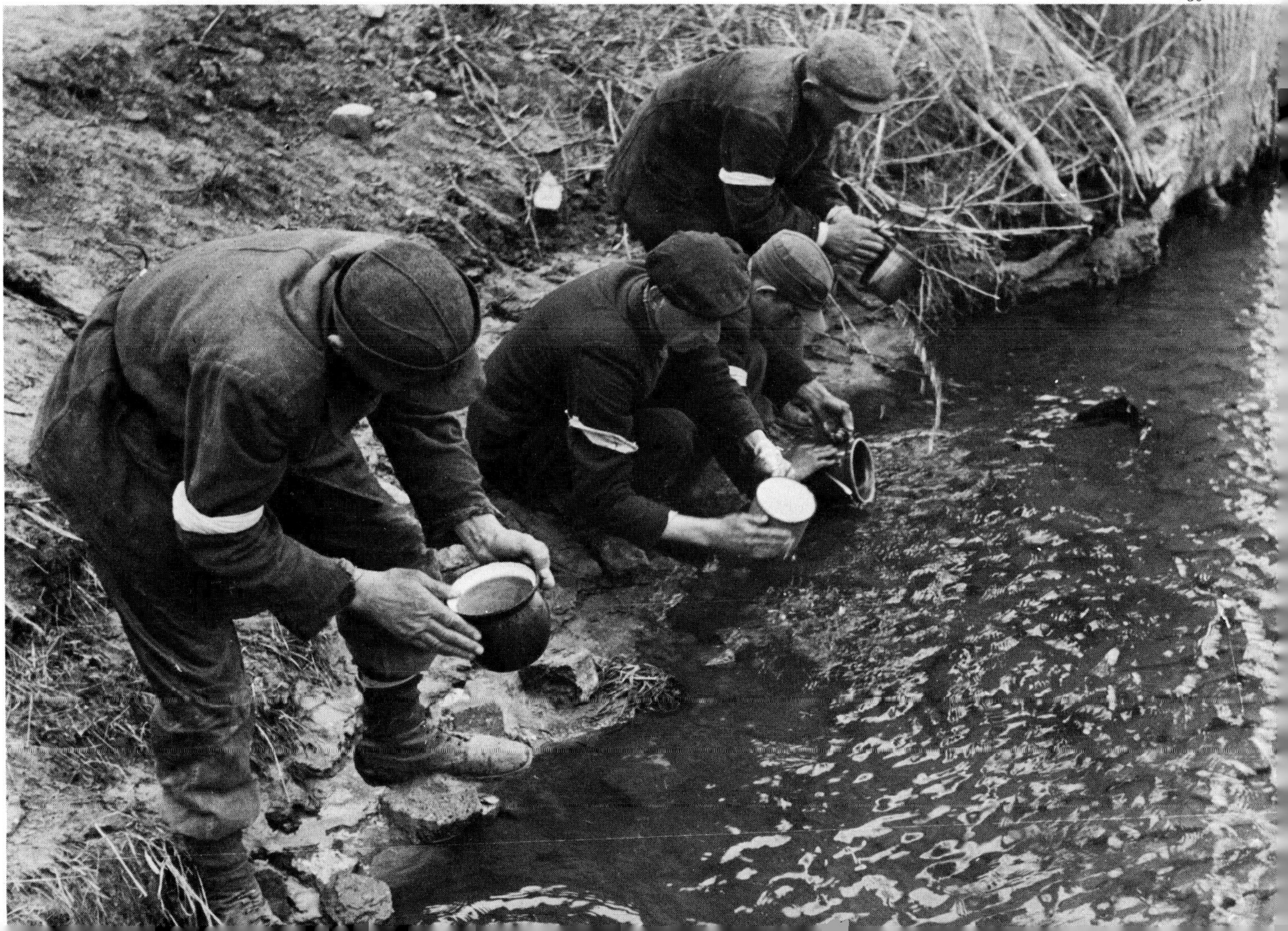

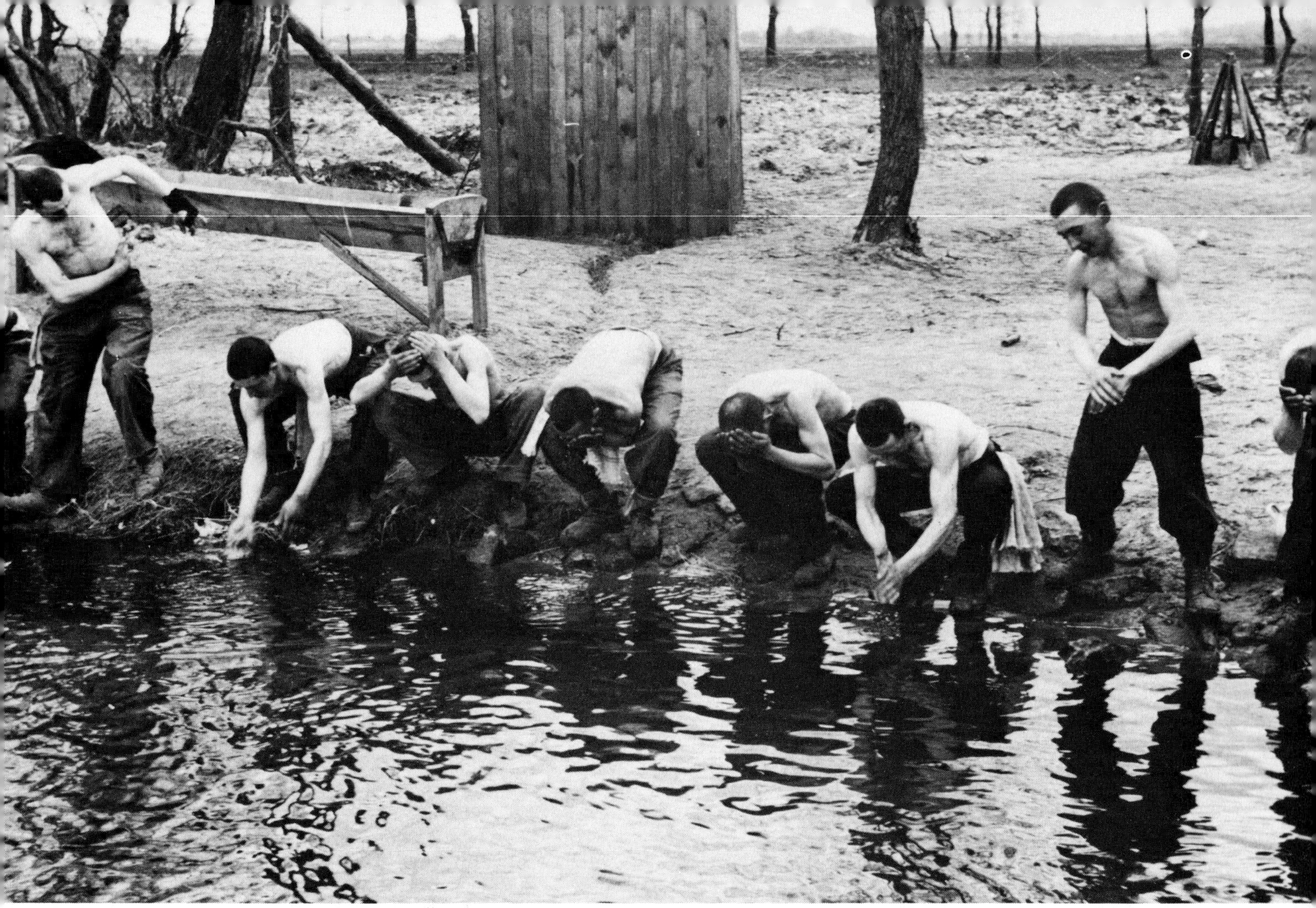

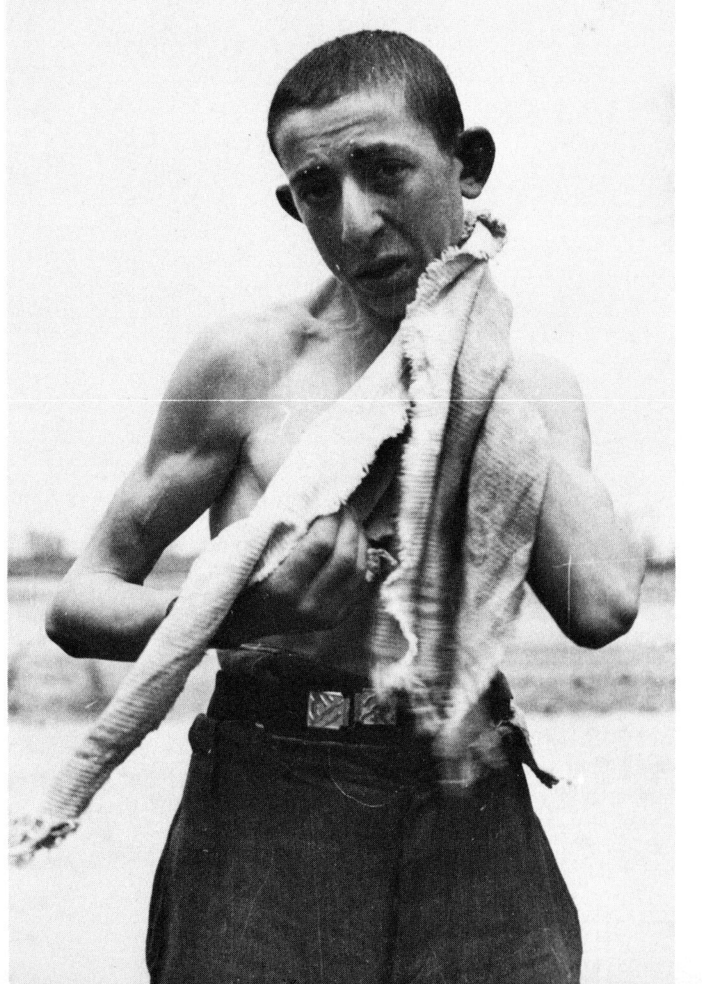

61

62

AMUSEMENTS OF THE GHETTO ELITE
(Nos. 63–74)

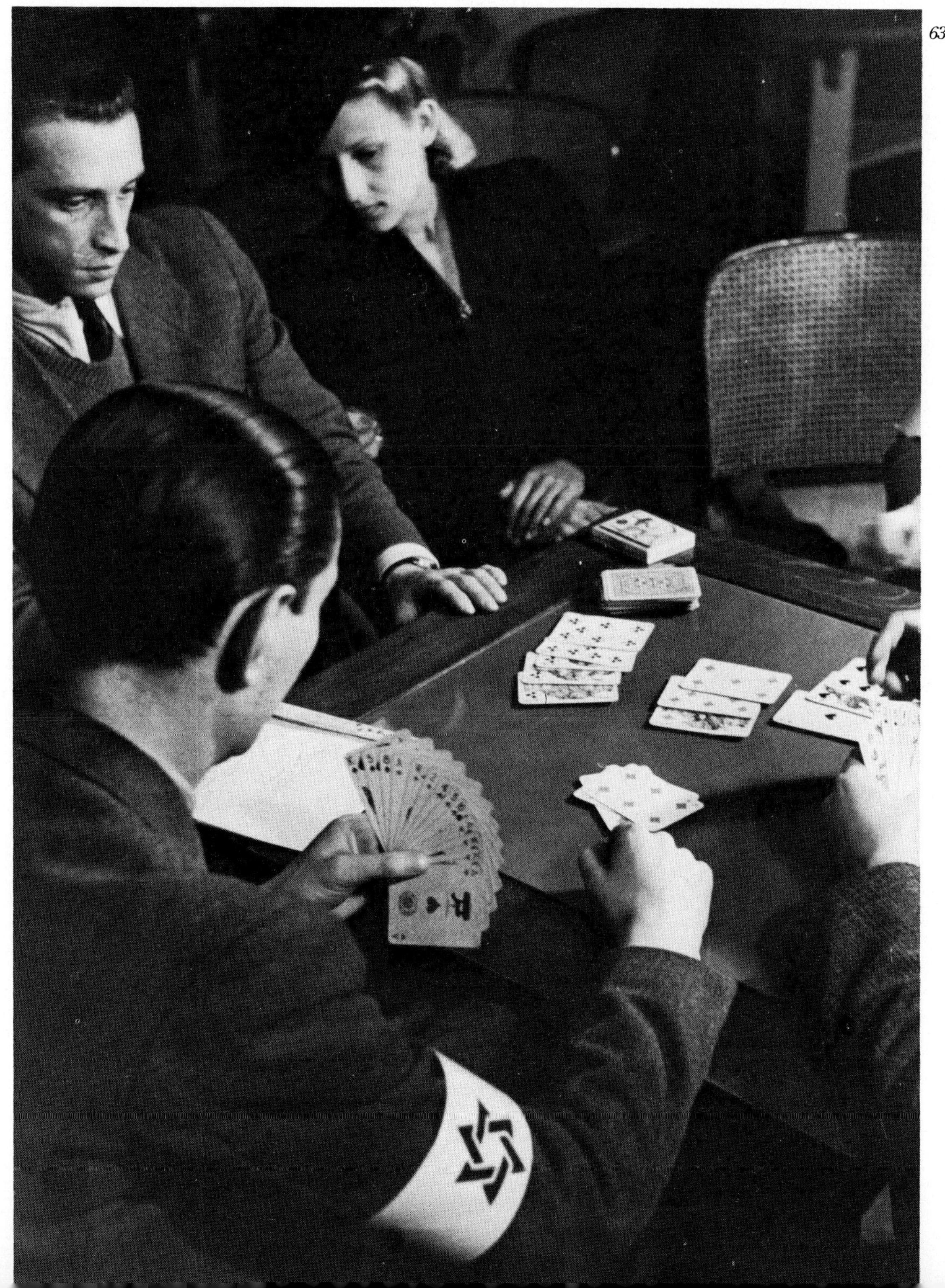

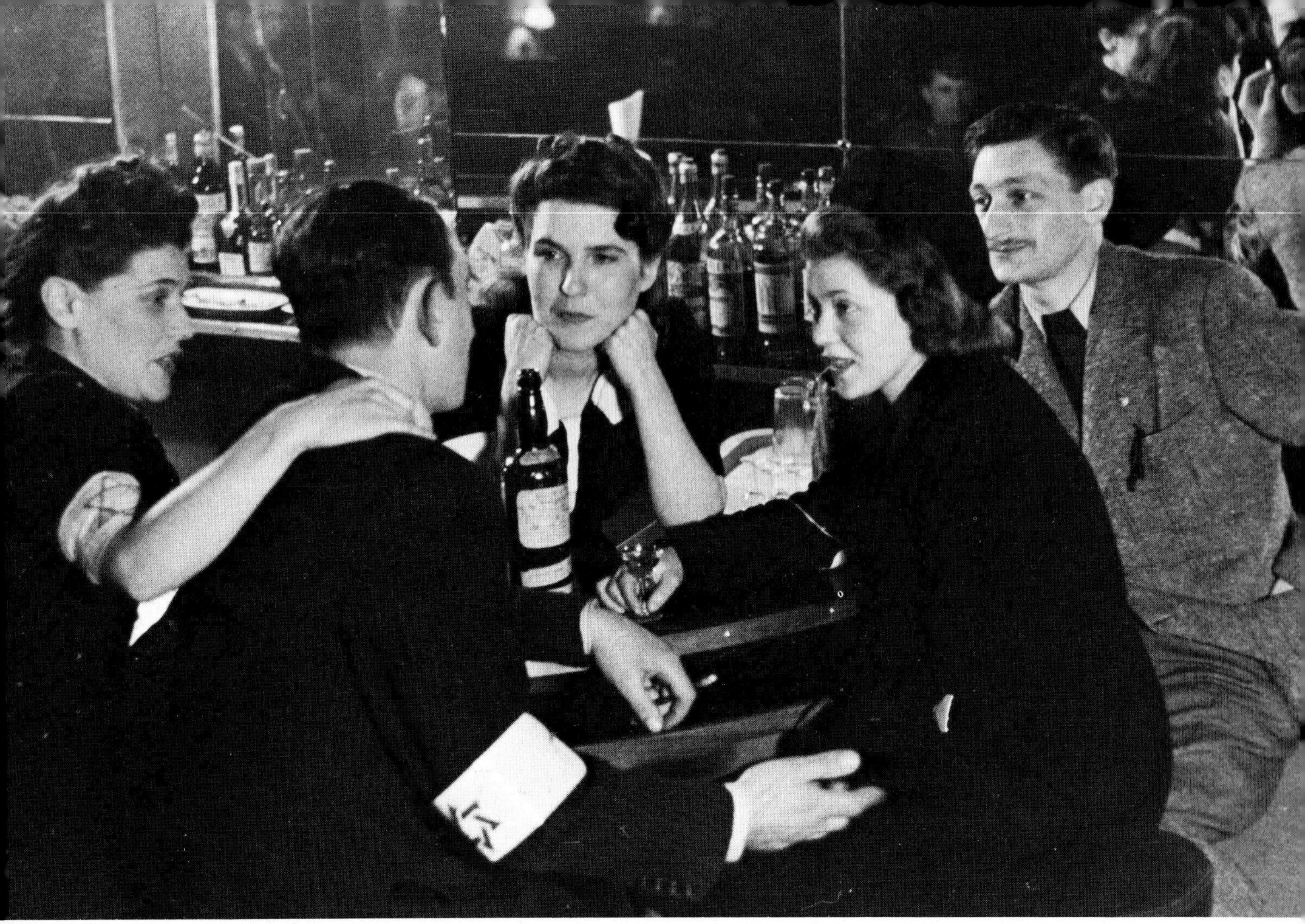

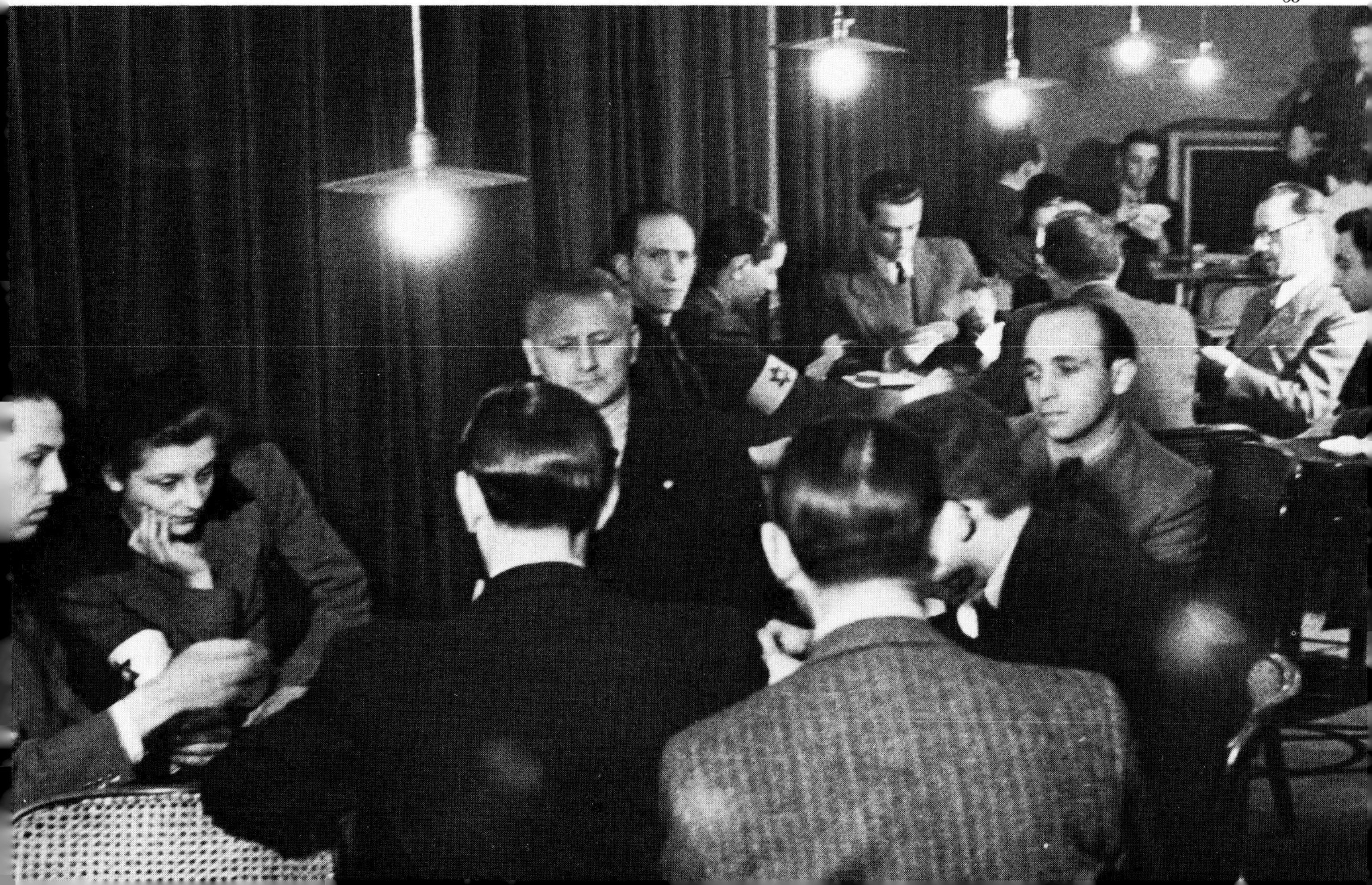

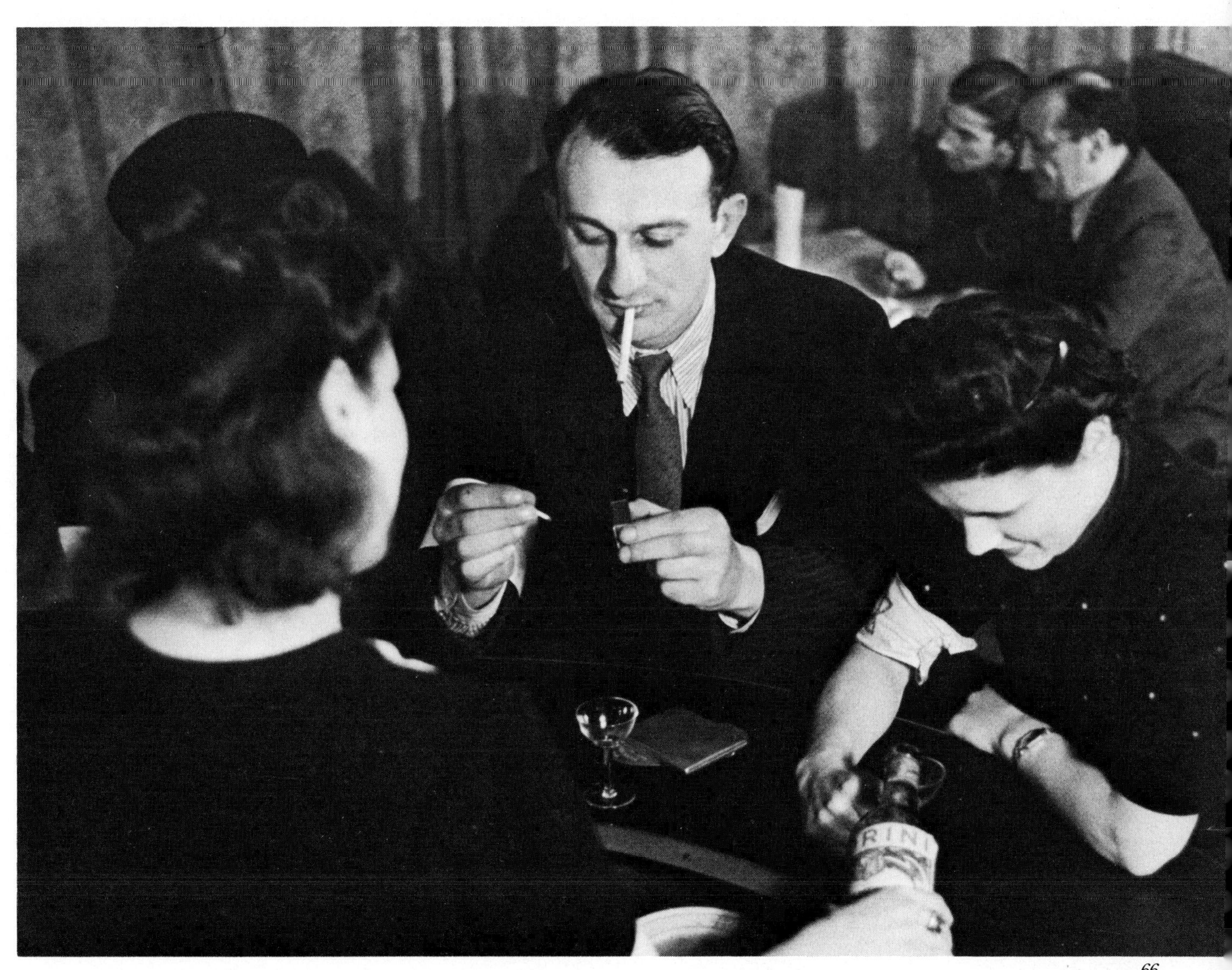

66

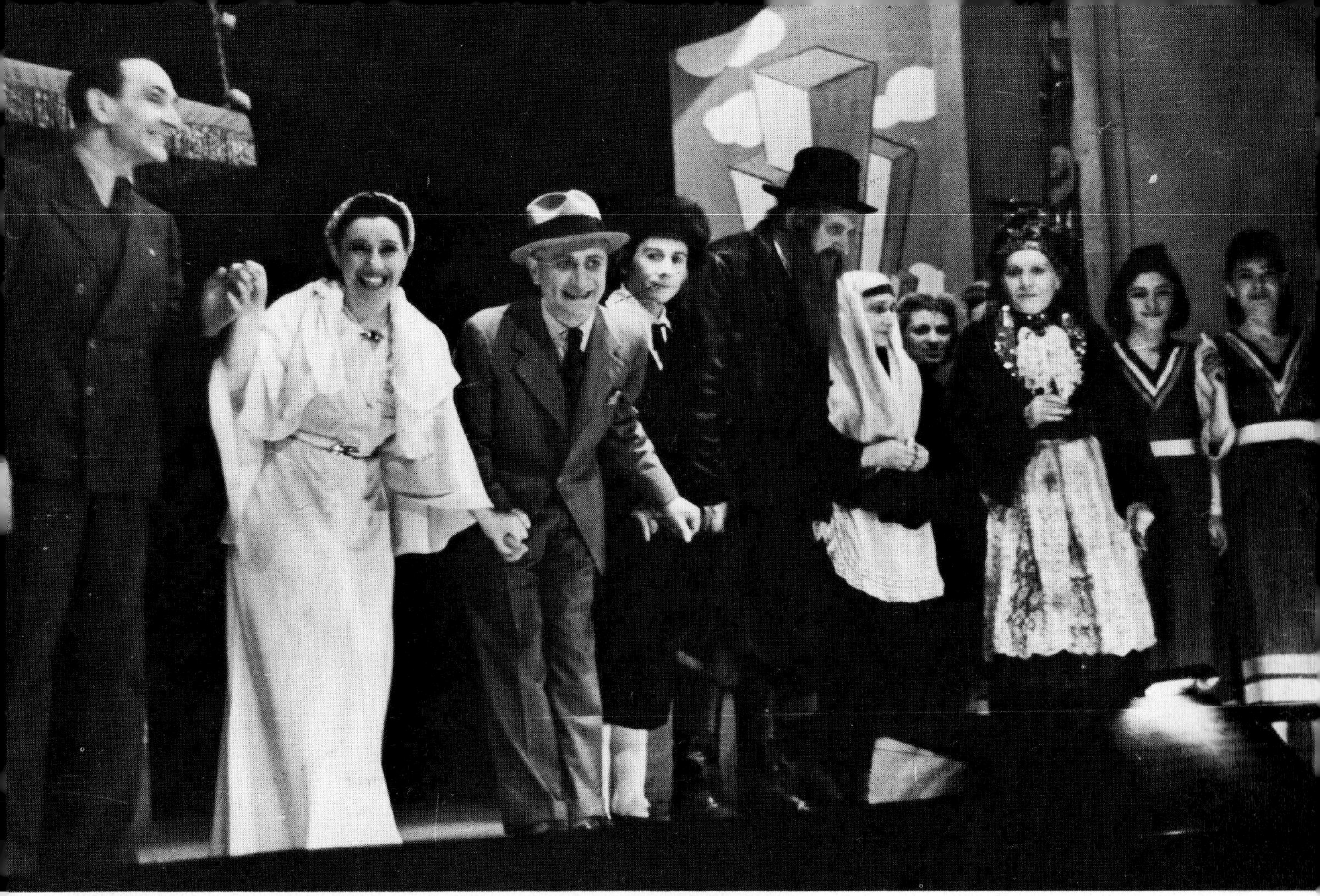

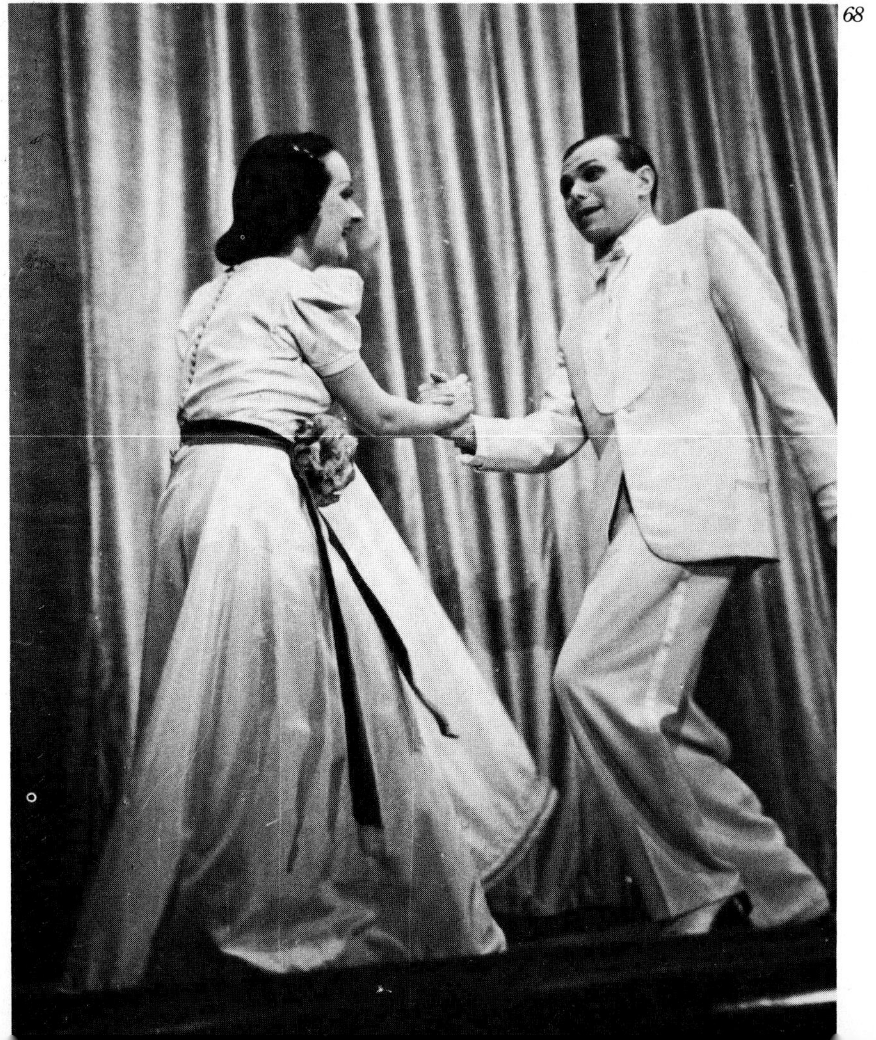

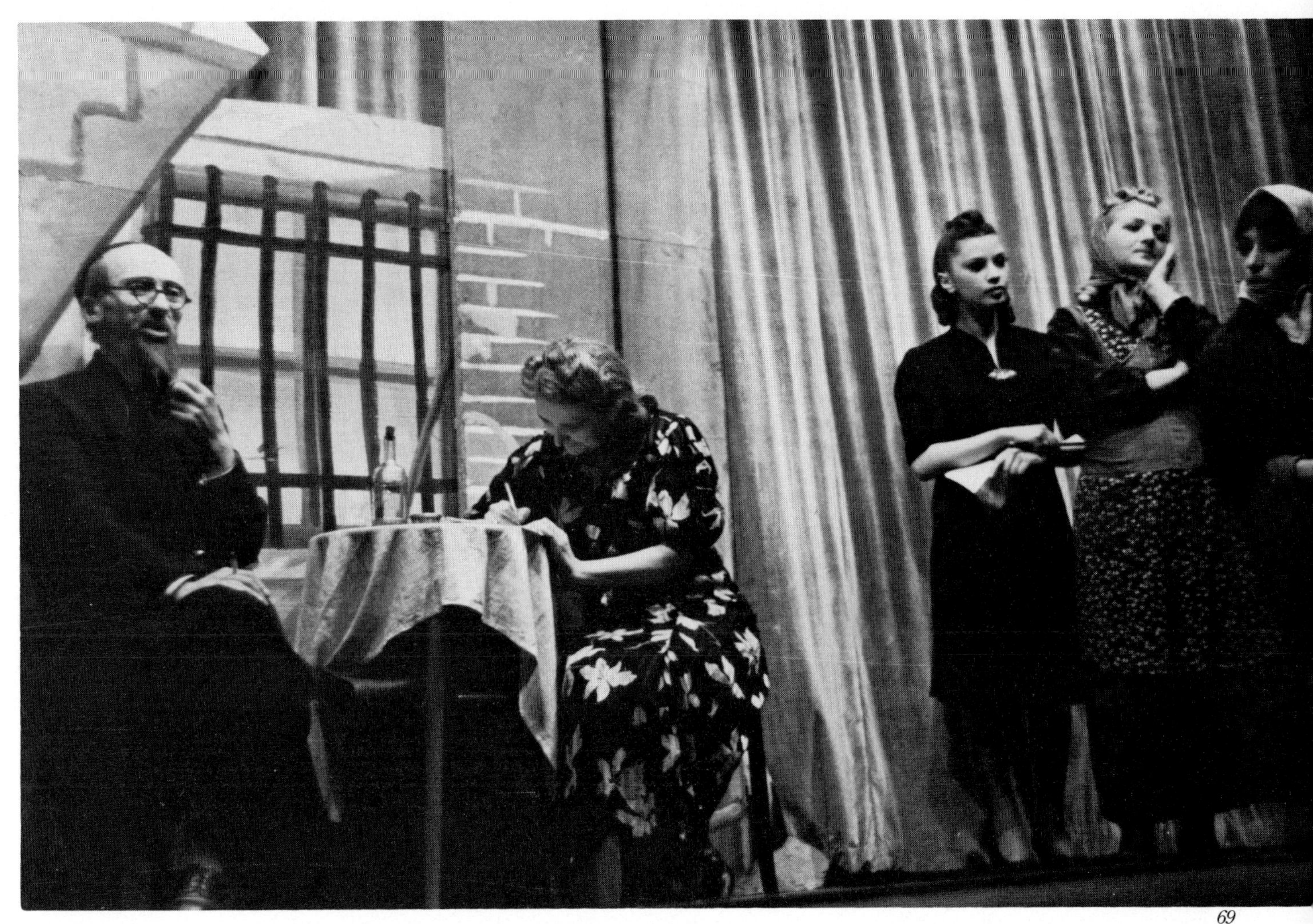

69

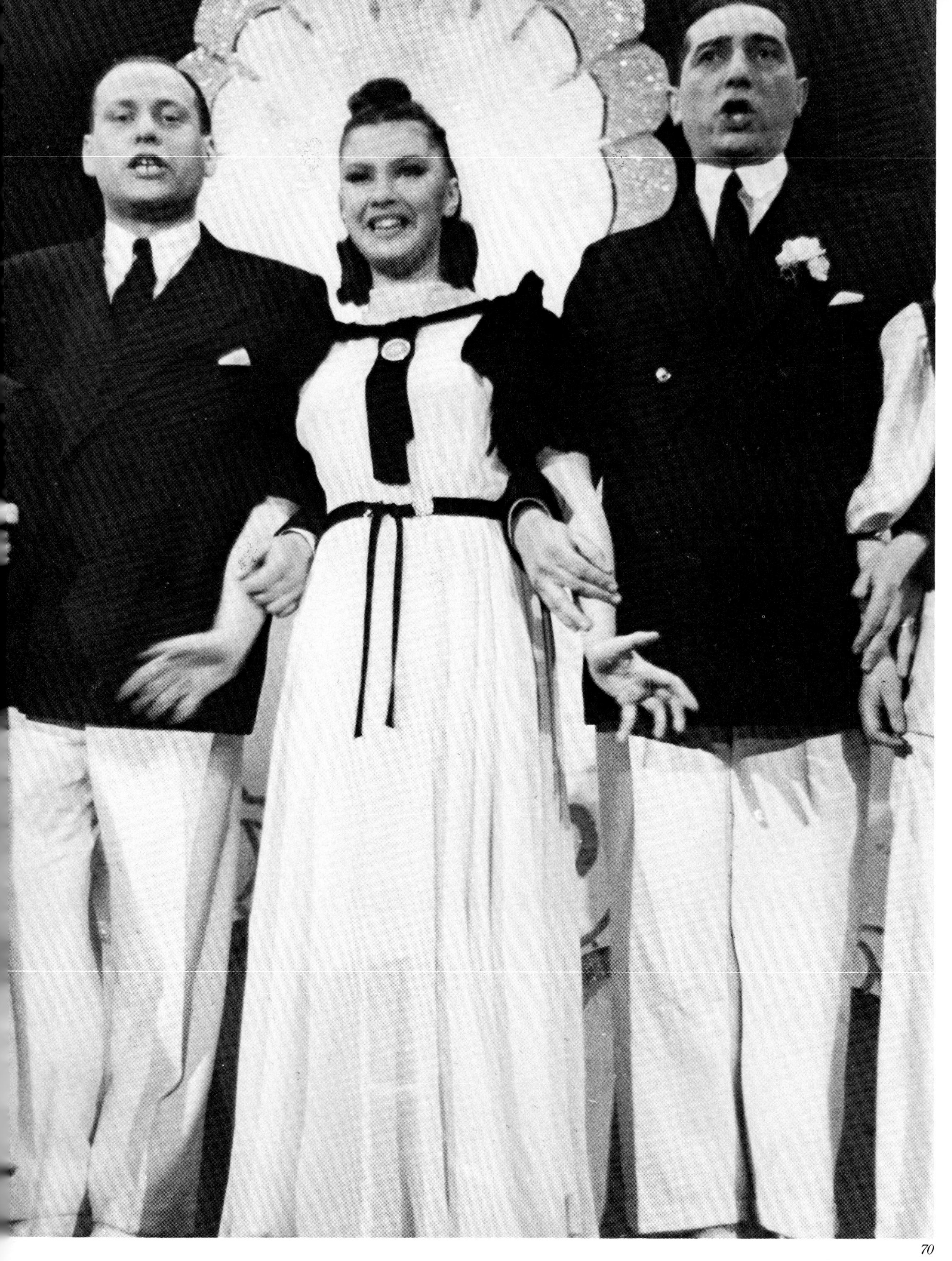

44 Amusements of the Ghetto Elite

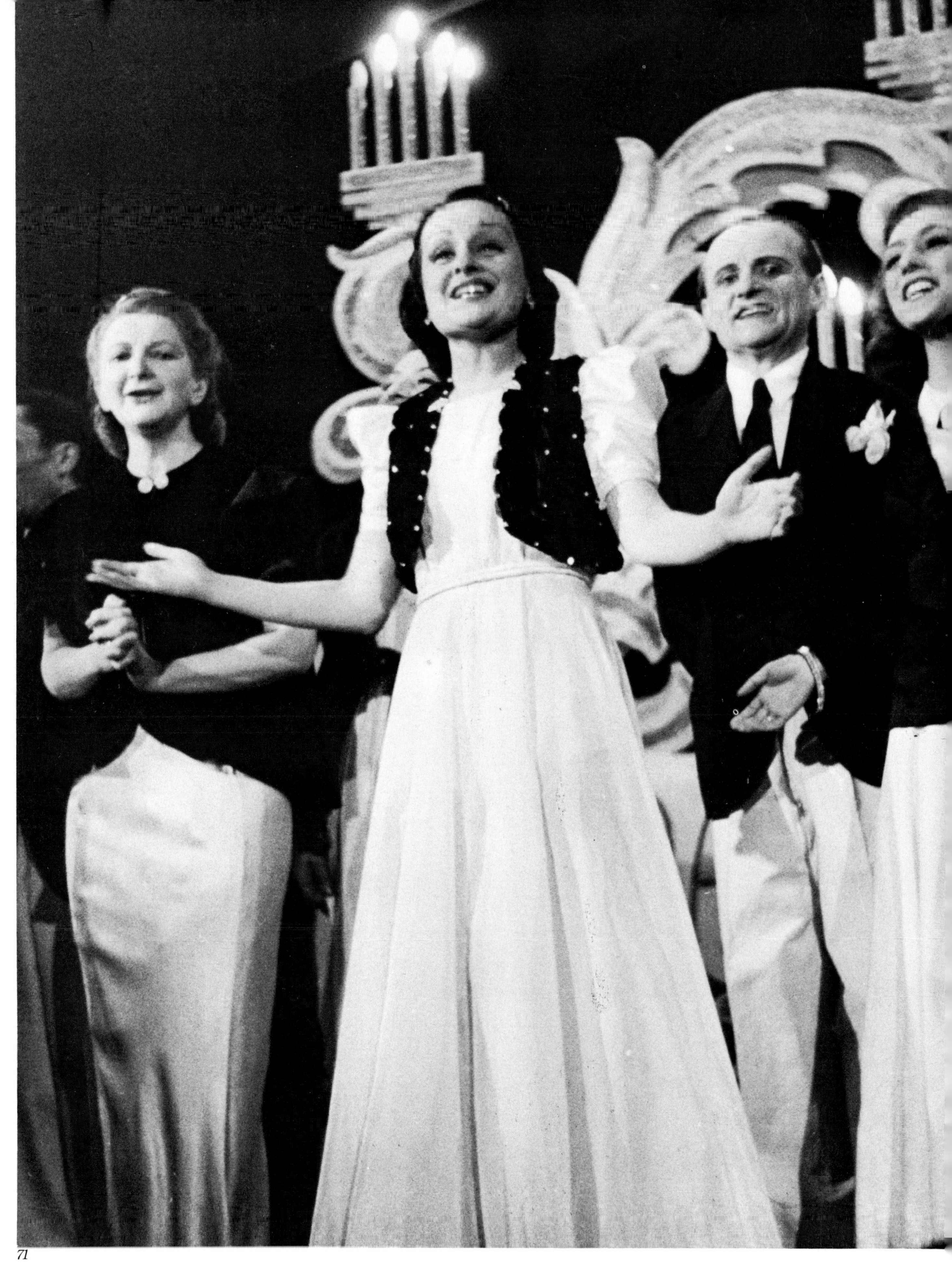

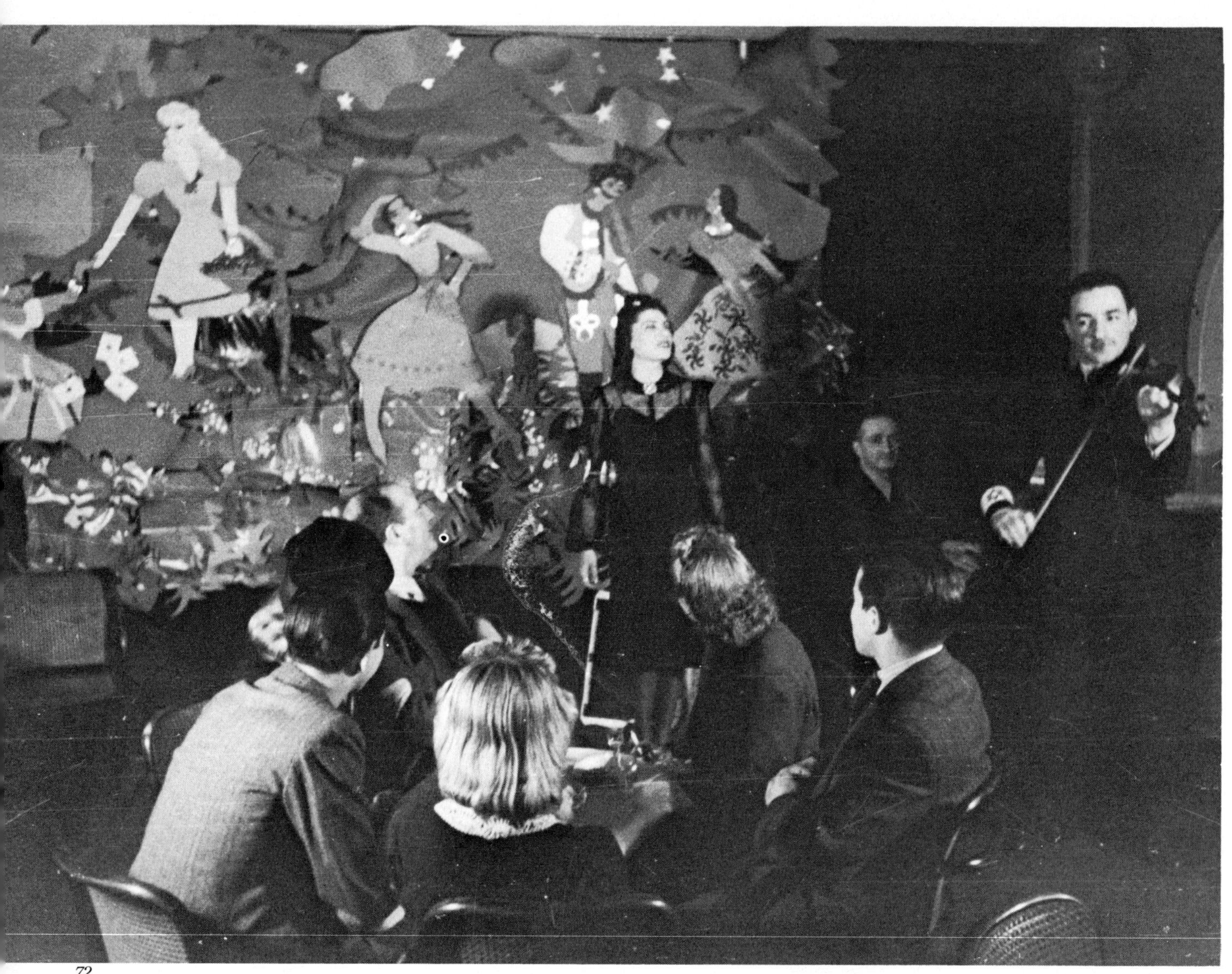

72

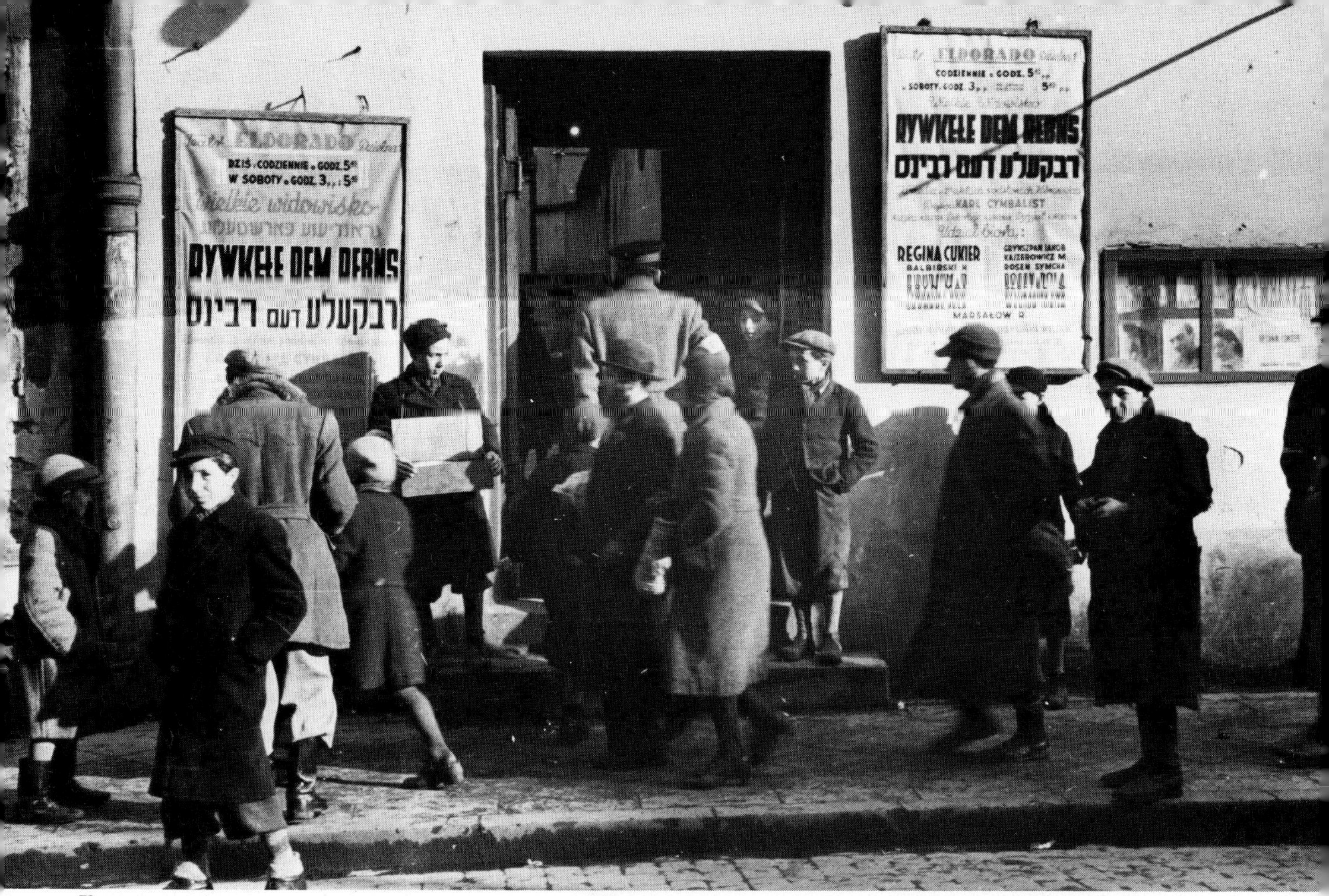

73

The name of the musical comedy is "The Rabbi's Little
Rebecca," with Regina Cukier heading a cast of 30.

74

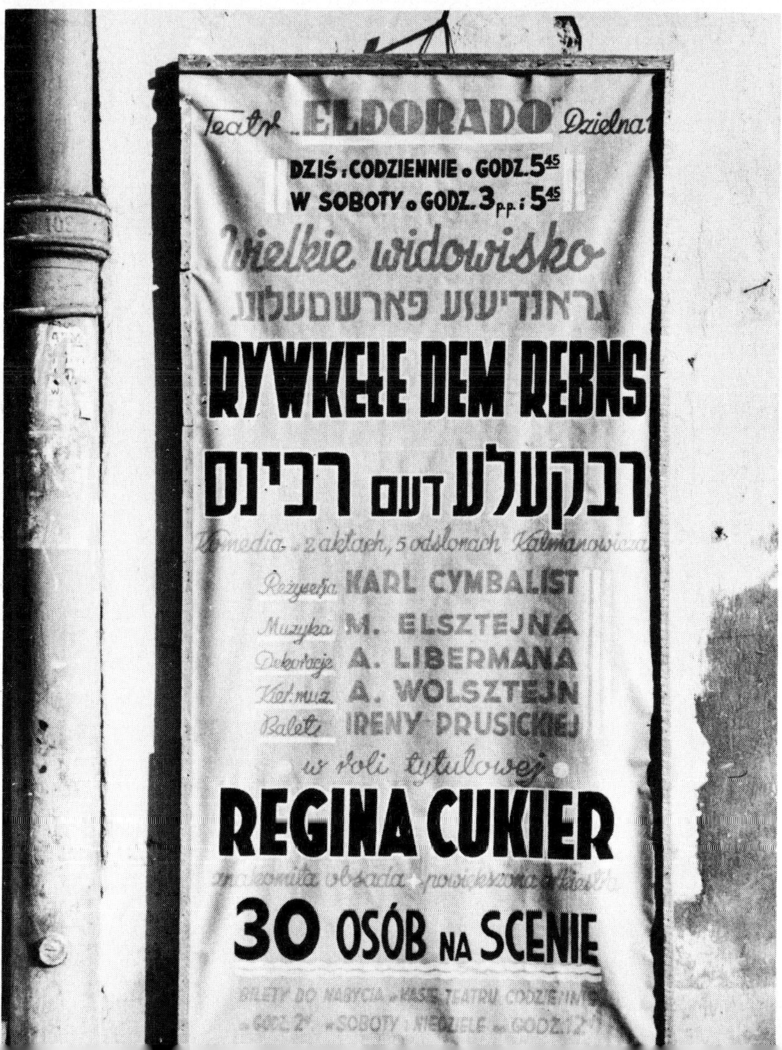

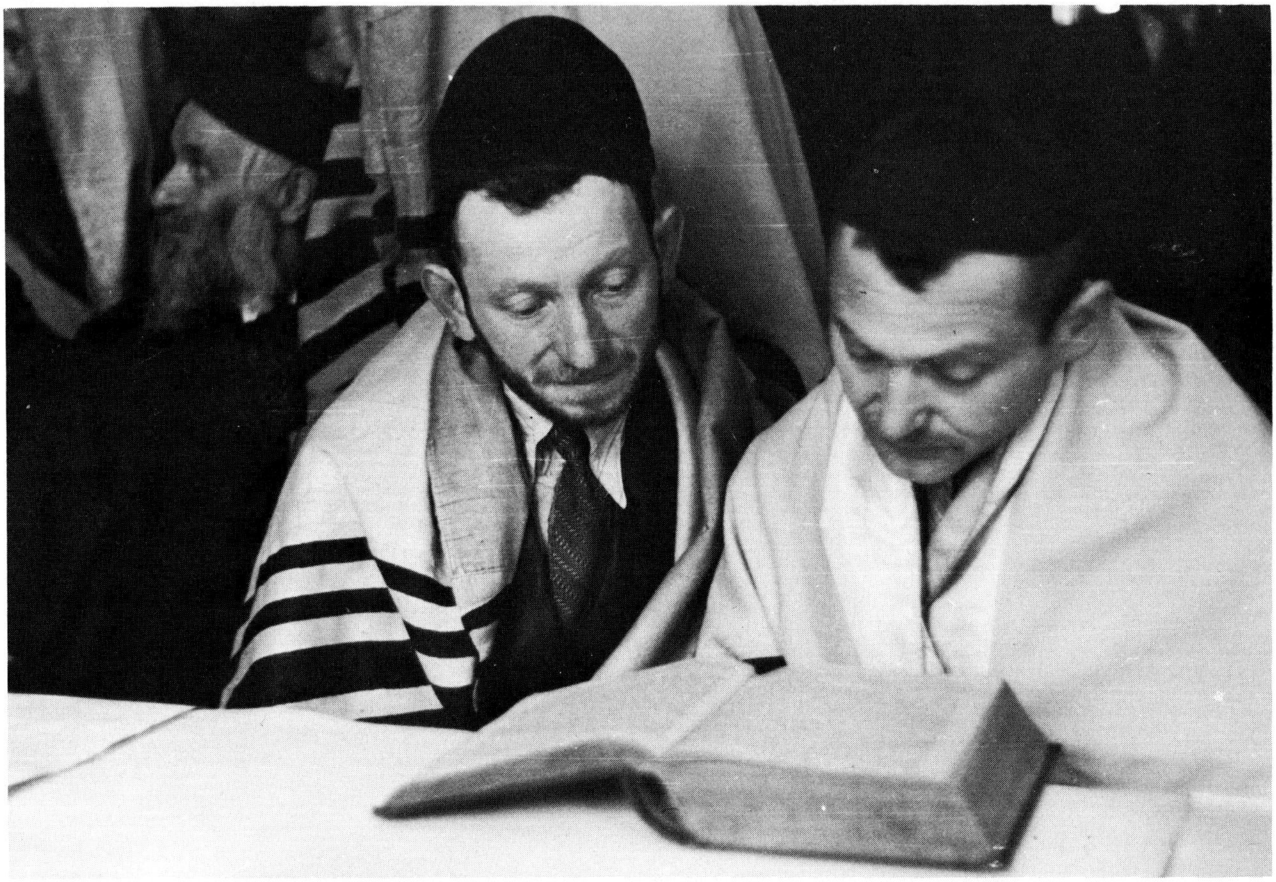

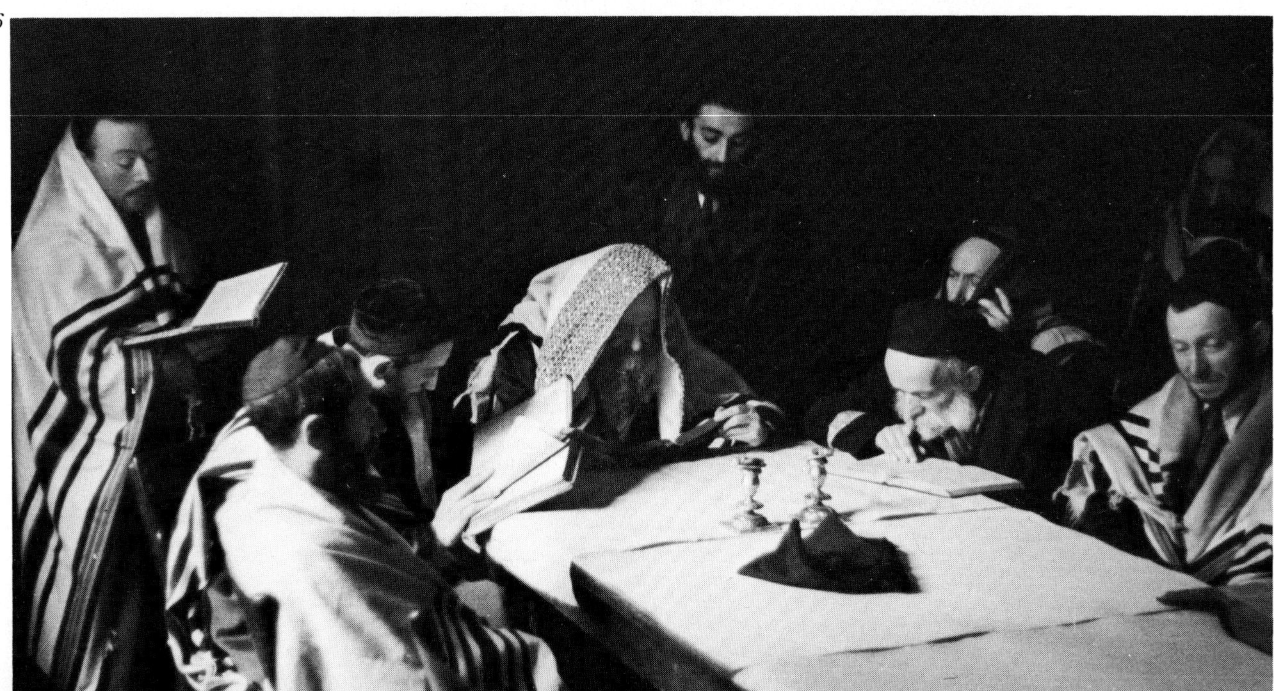

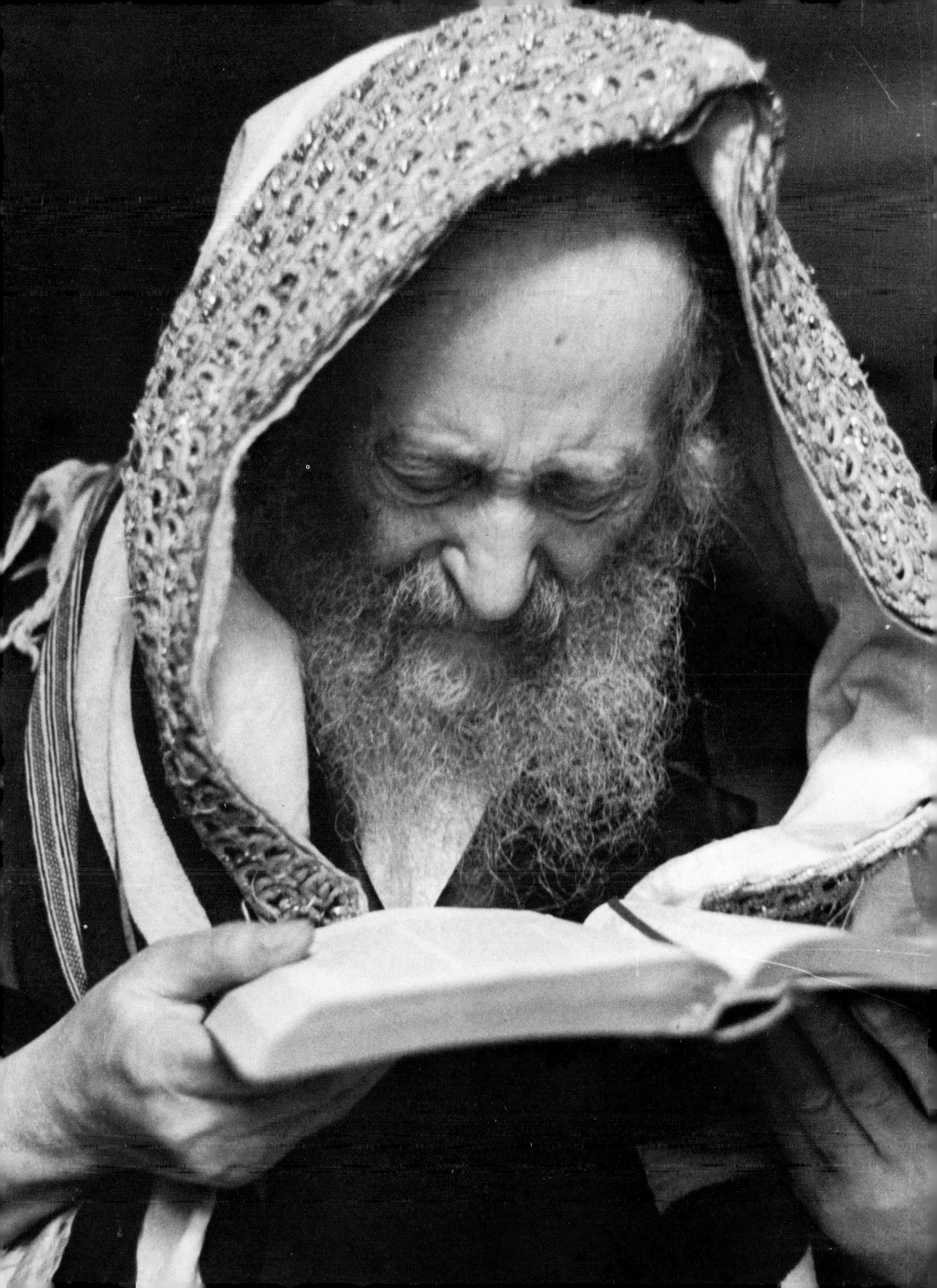

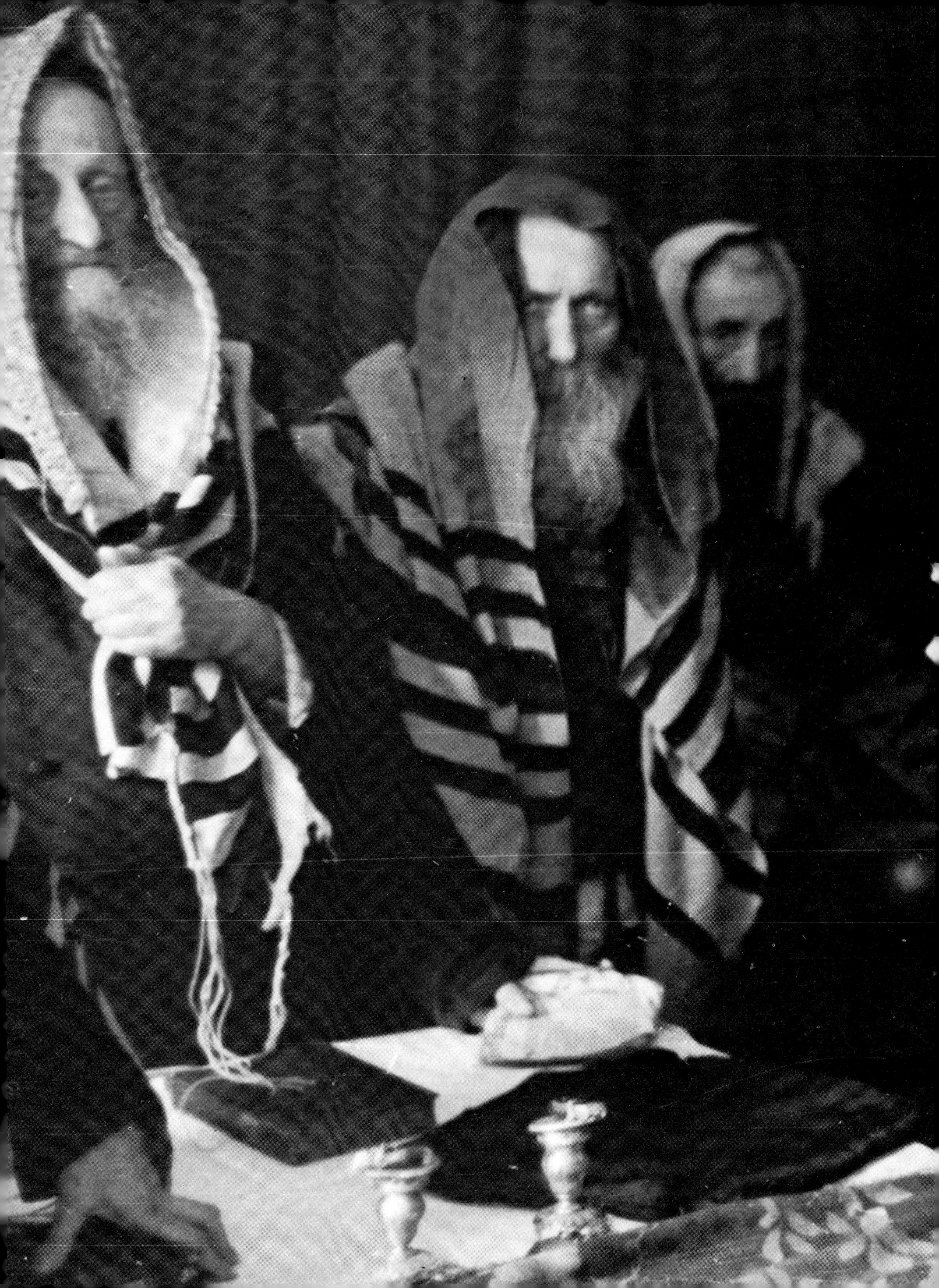

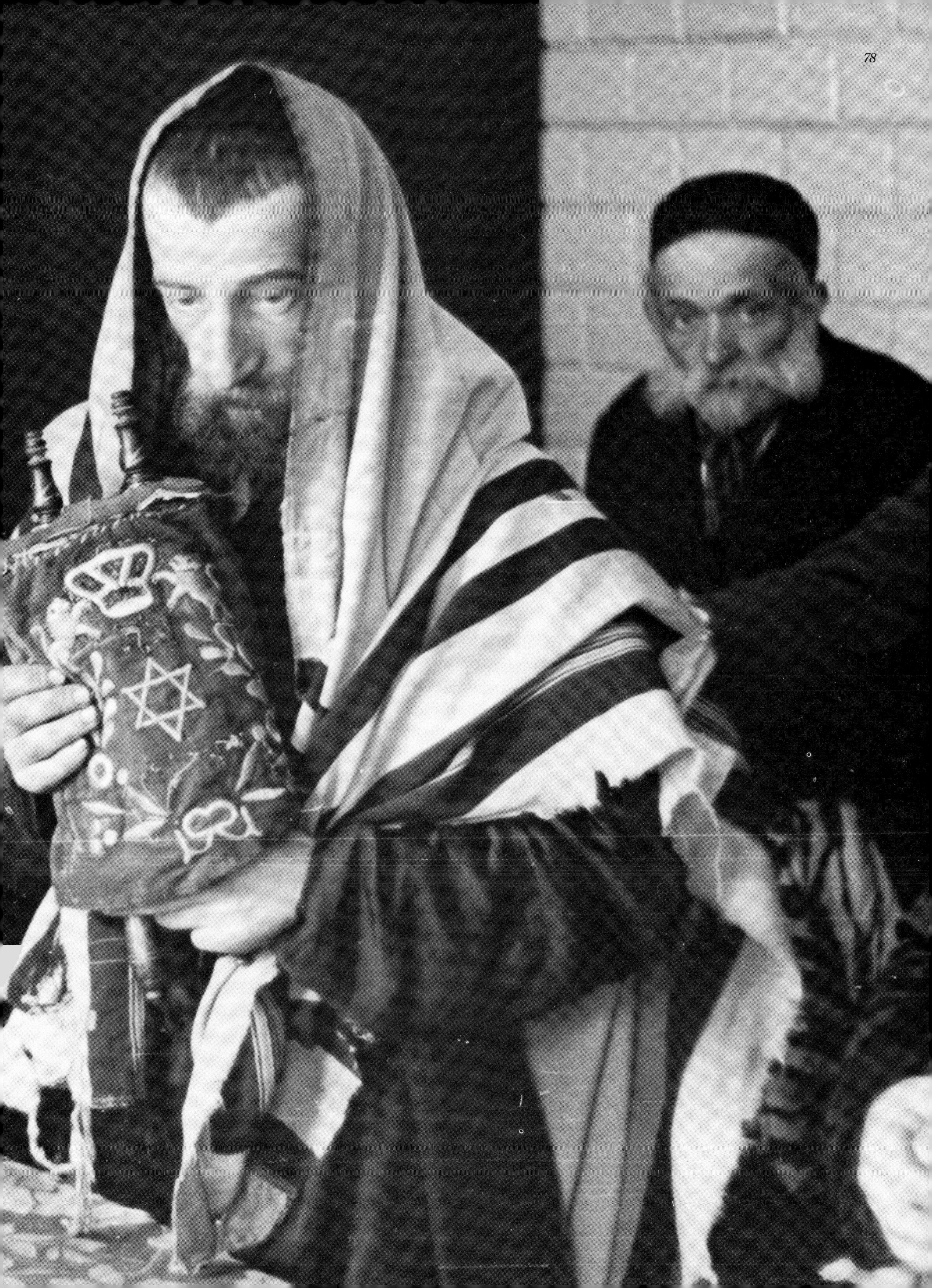

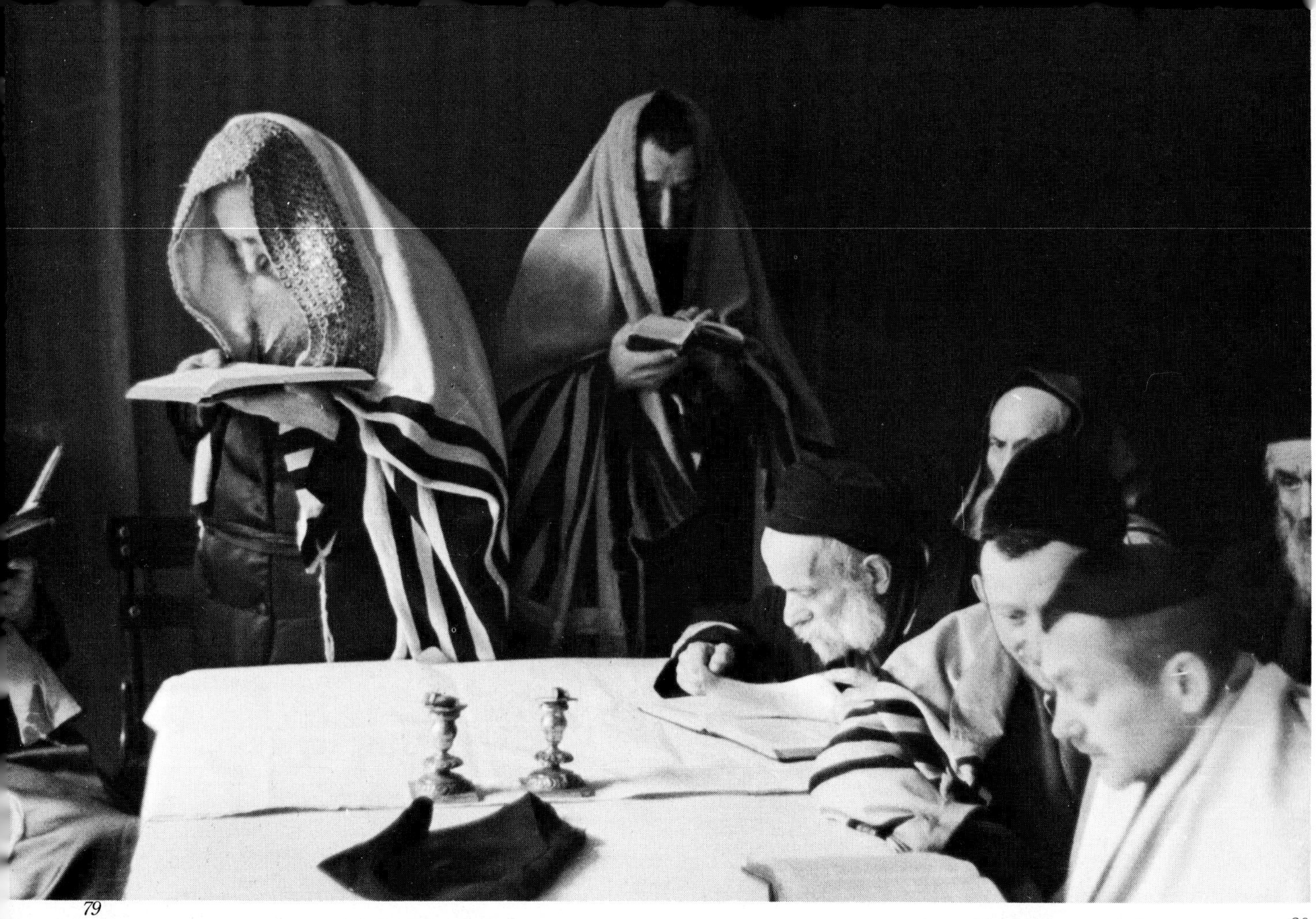

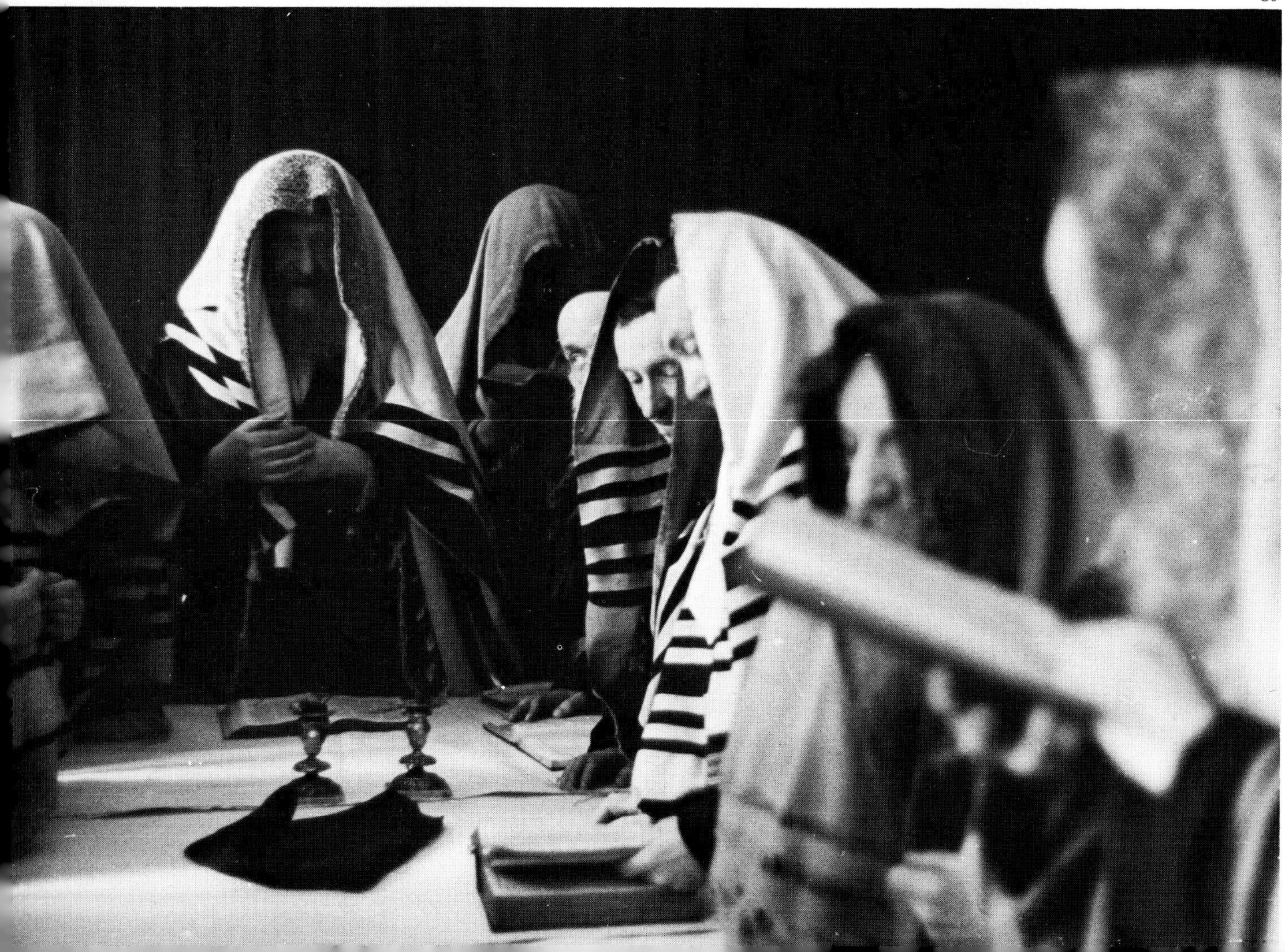

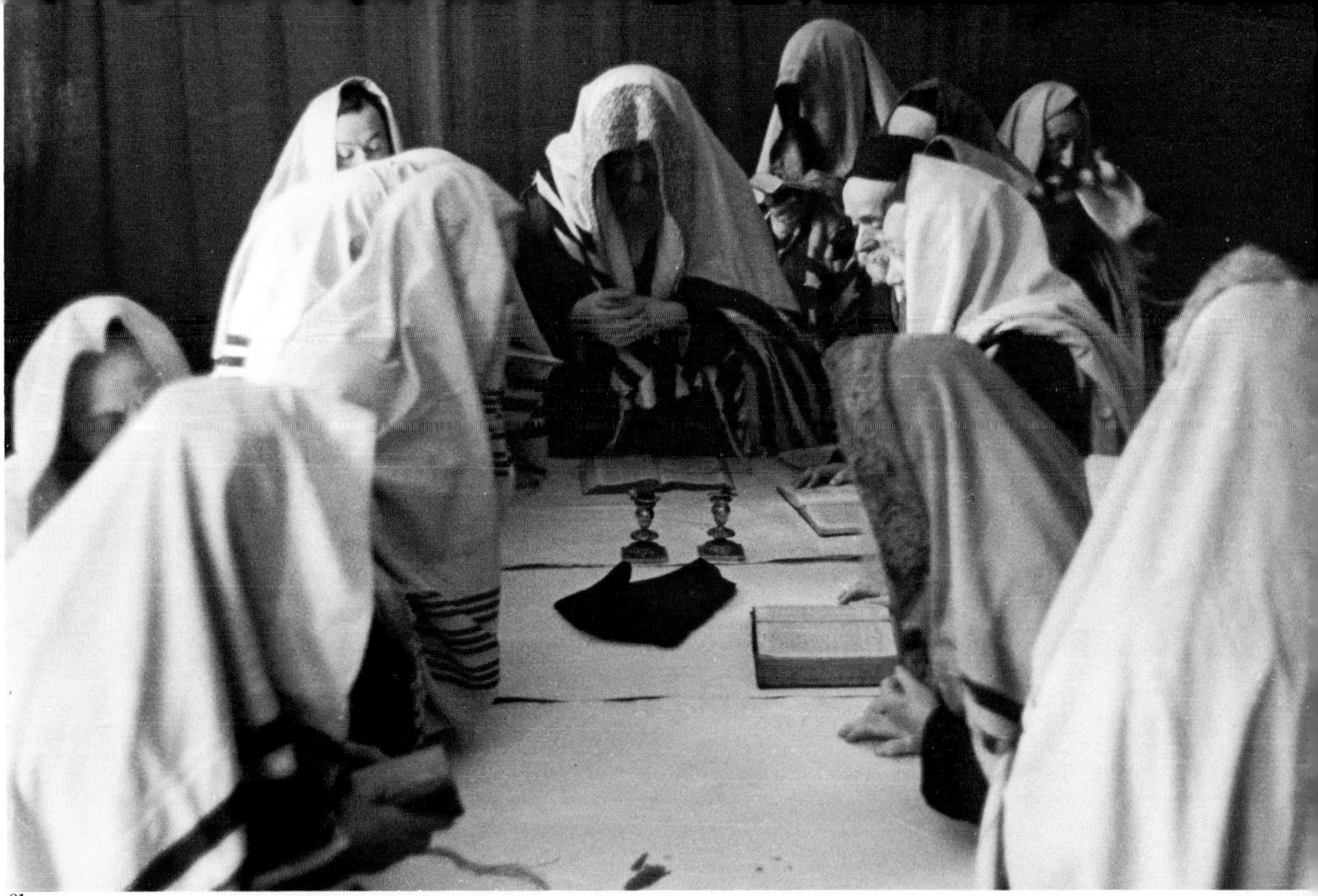

81

82

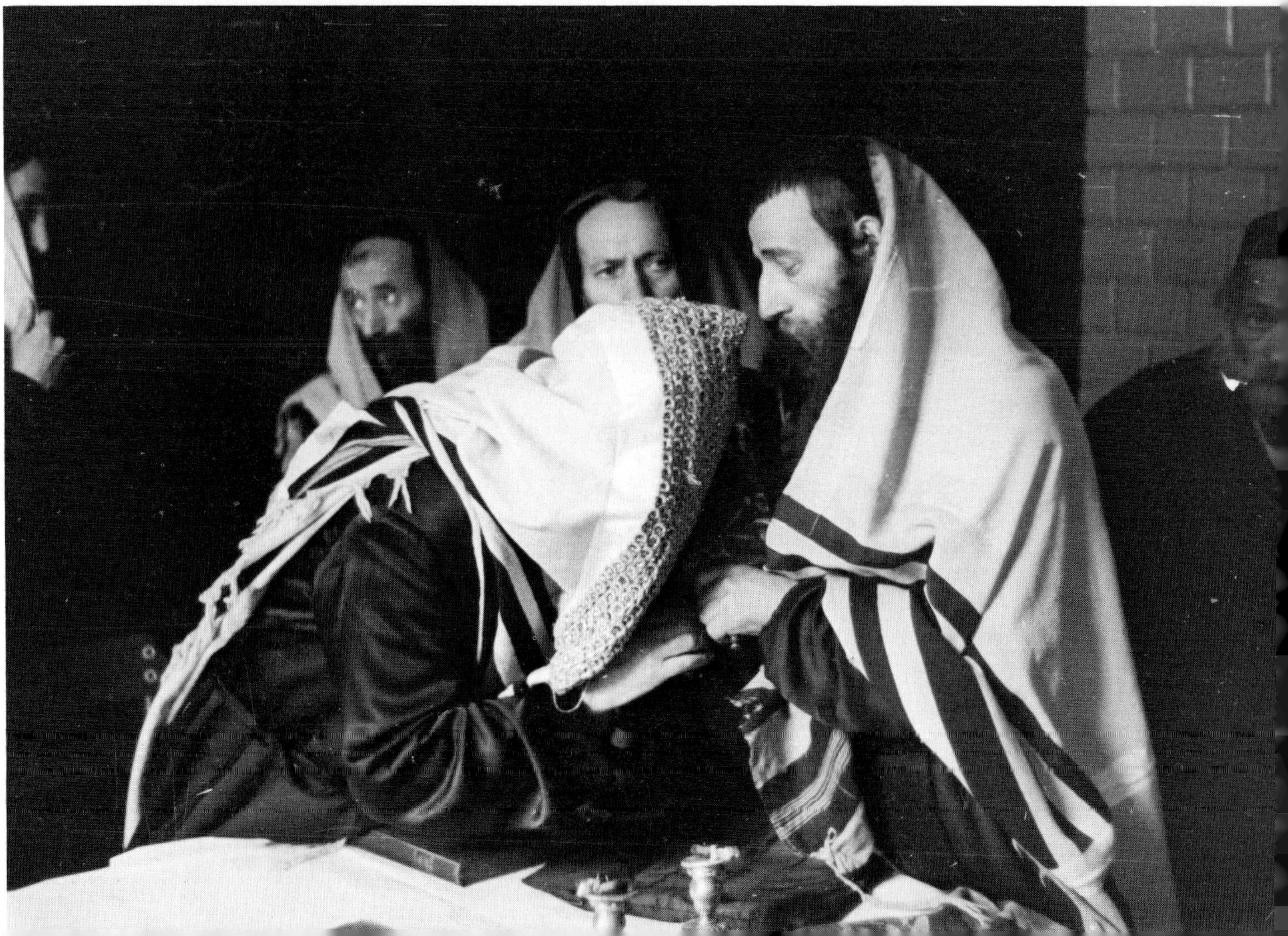

STREET SCENES

(Nos. 83–92)

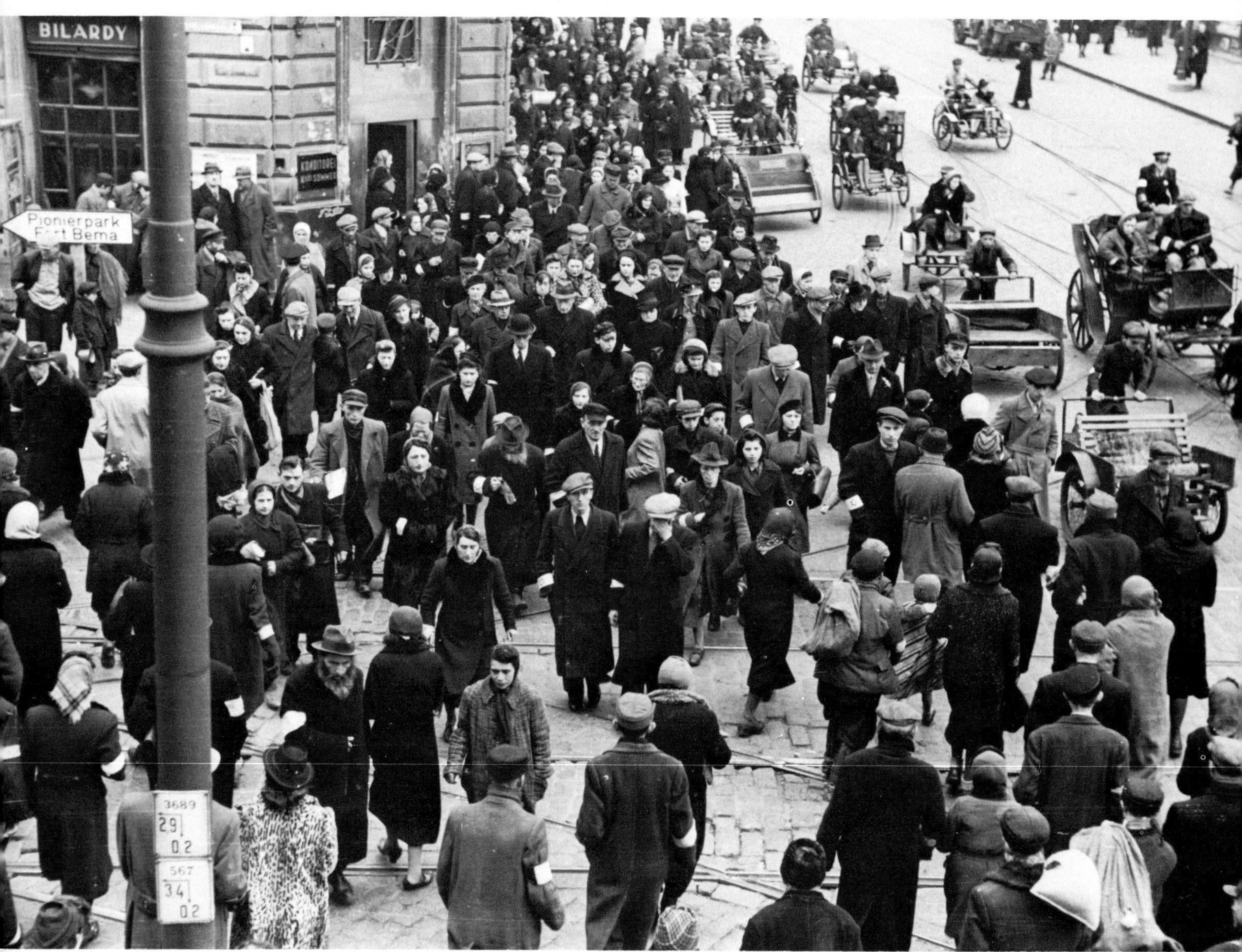

83

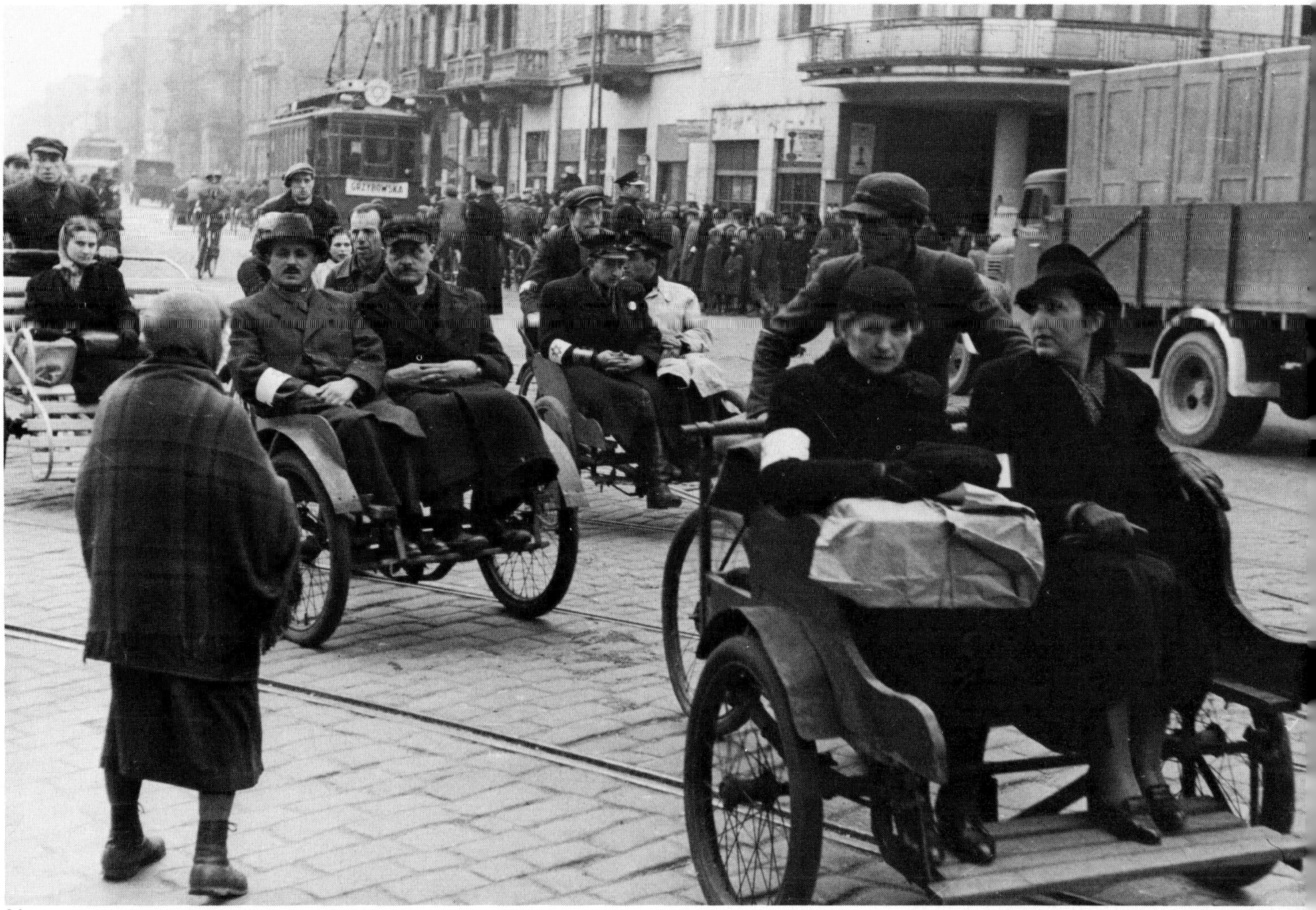

84

85

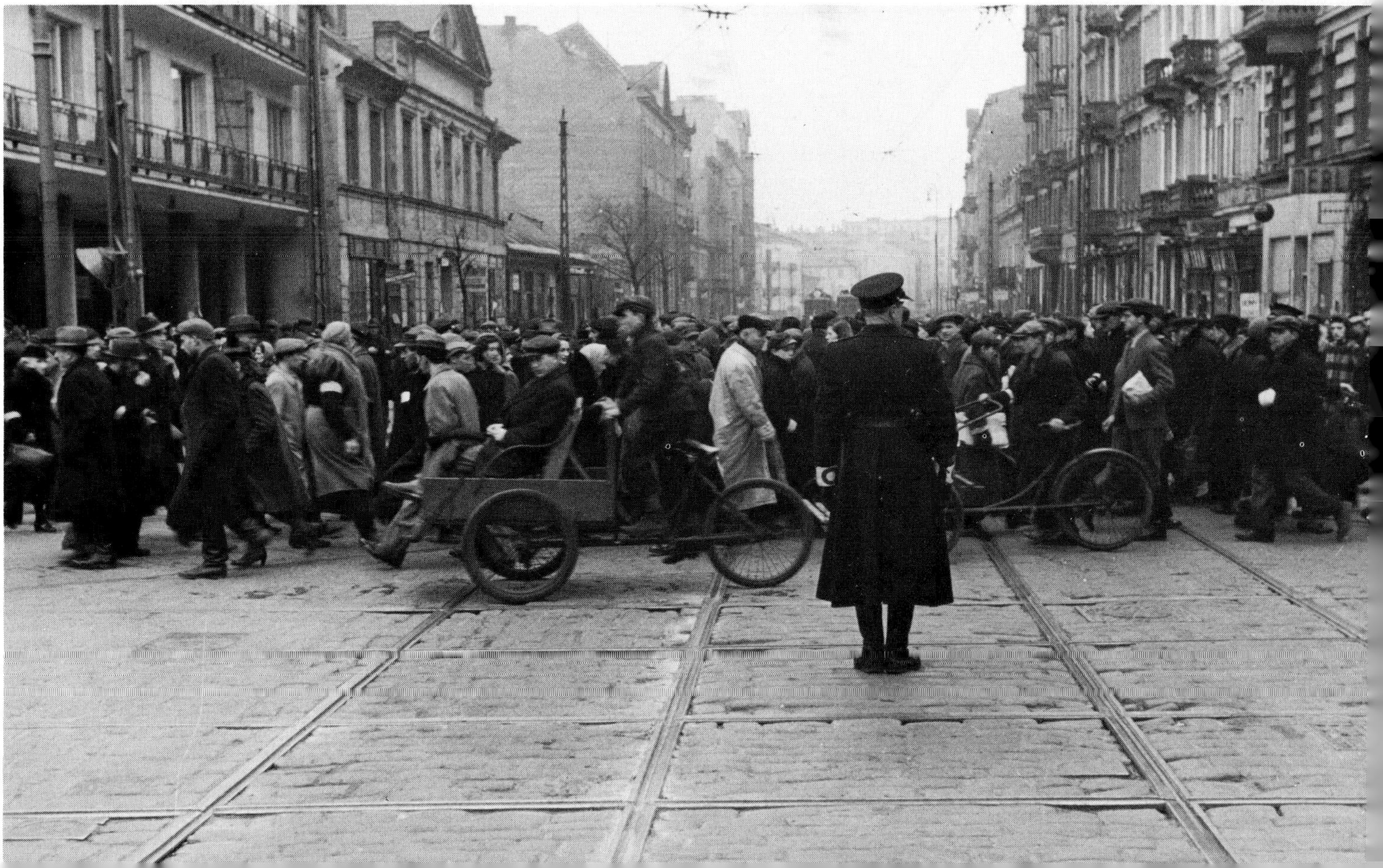

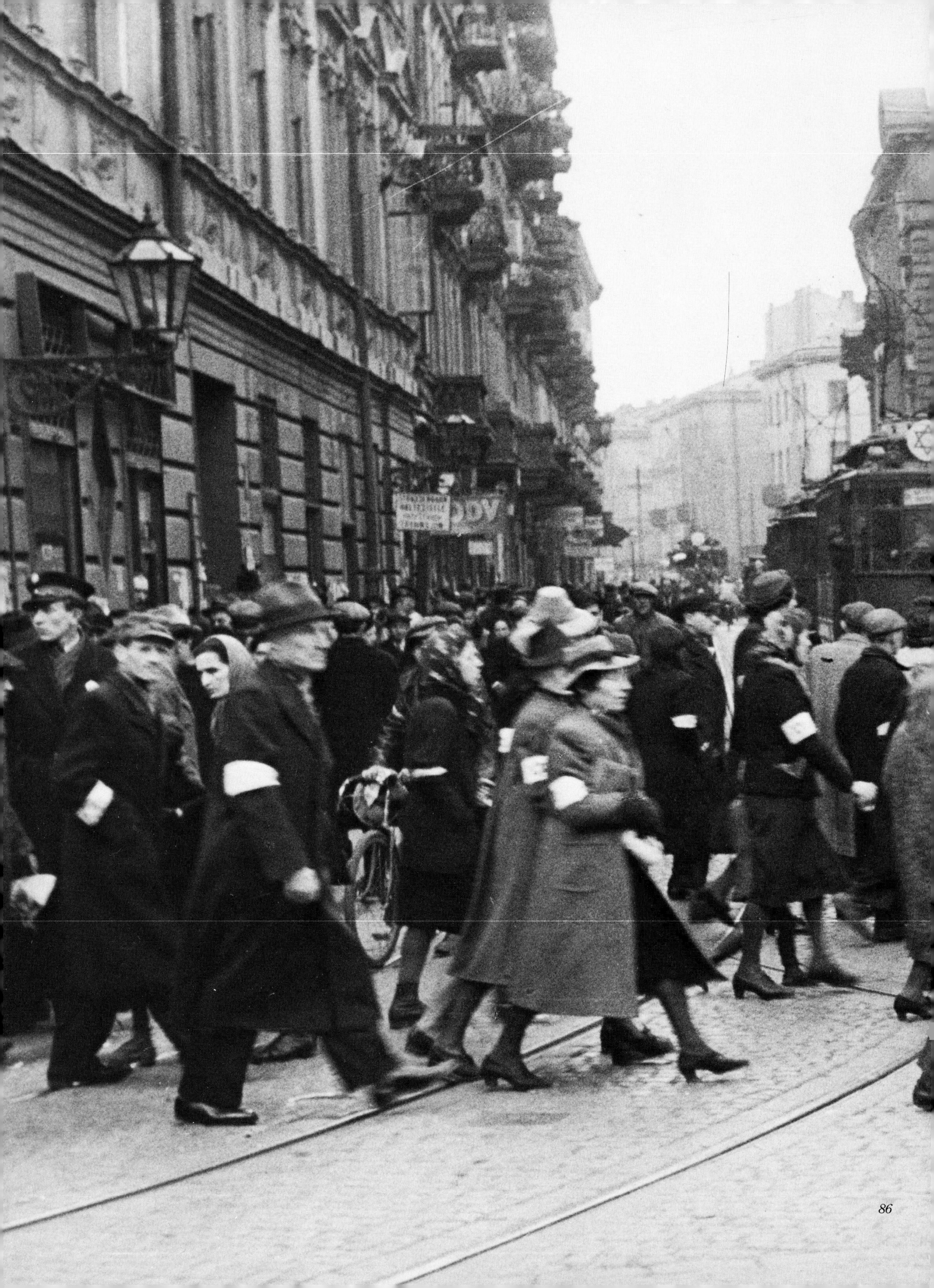

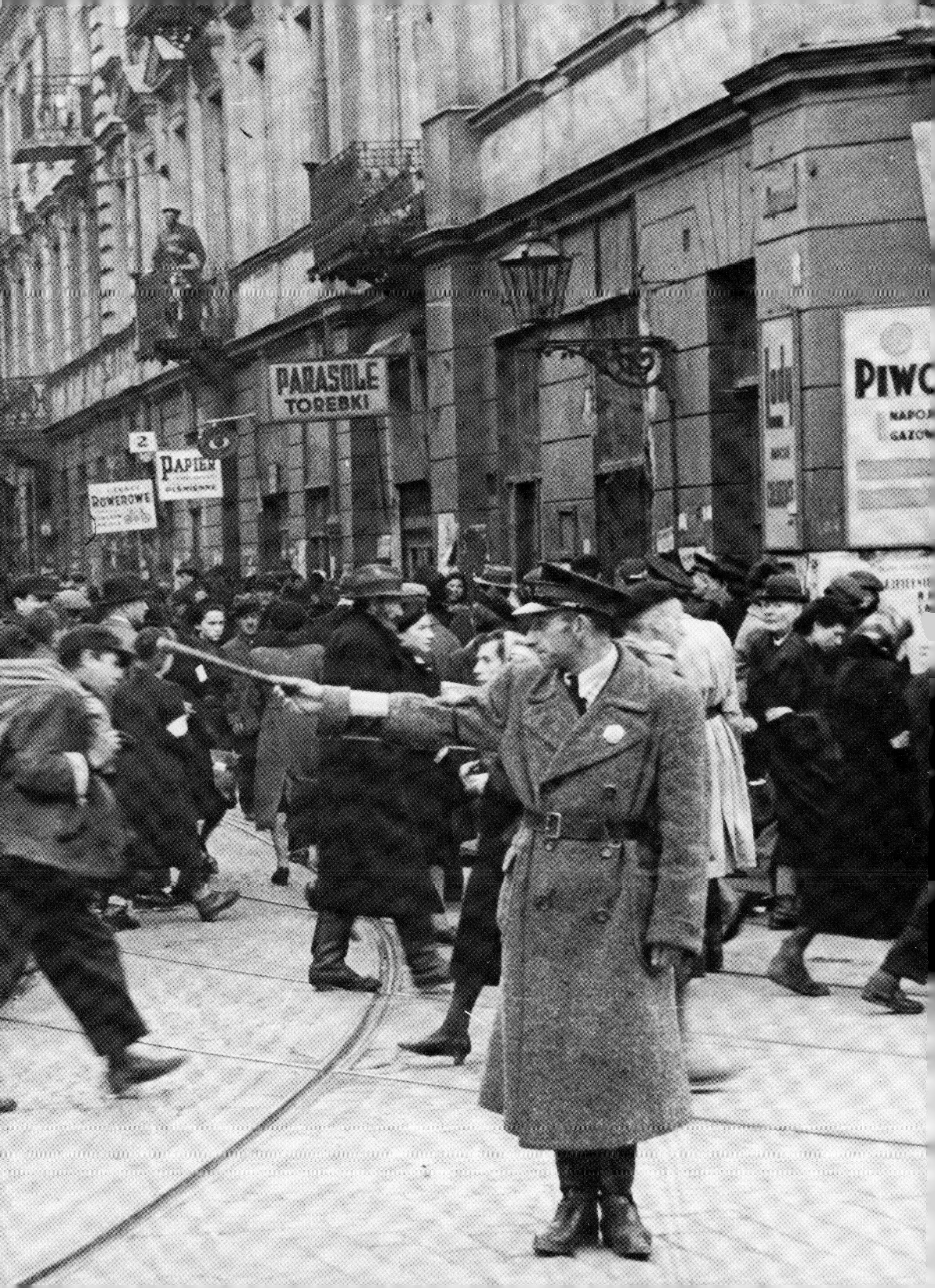

PARASOLE
TOREBKI
2
PAPIER
PIŚMIENNE
ROWEROWE
PIWO
NAPOJE
GAZOWANE
Lody

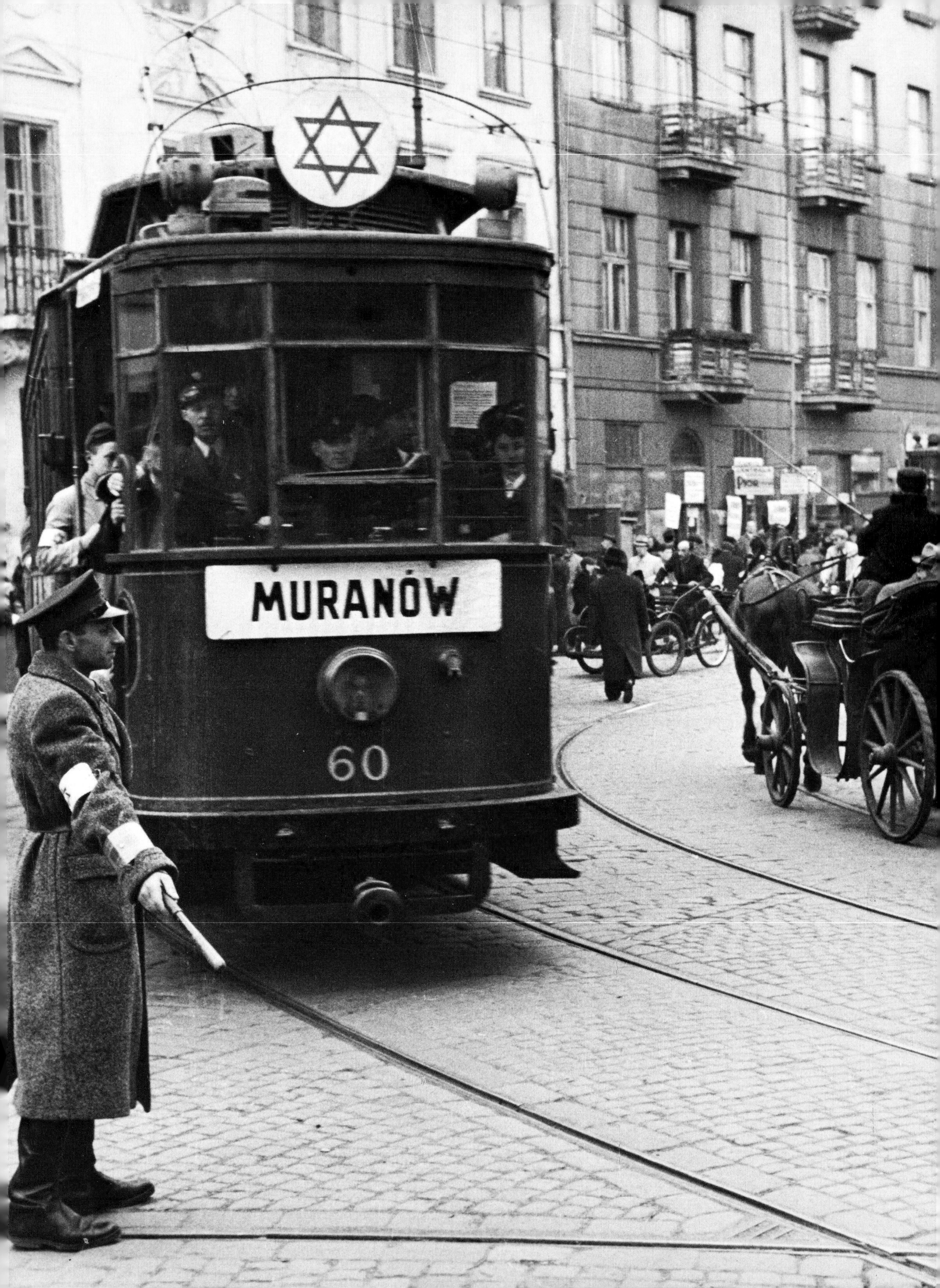

MURANÓW
60

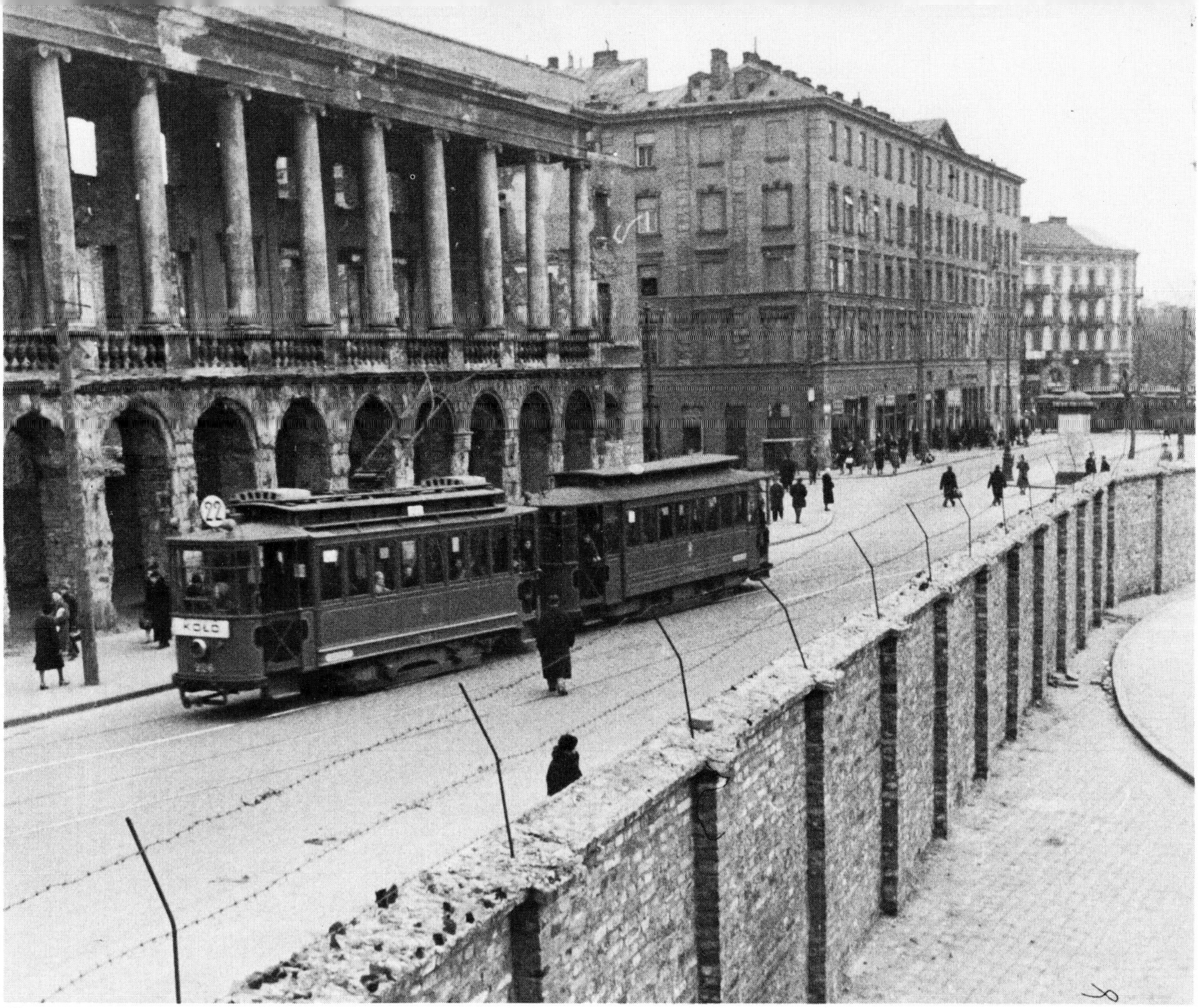

22
KOLO

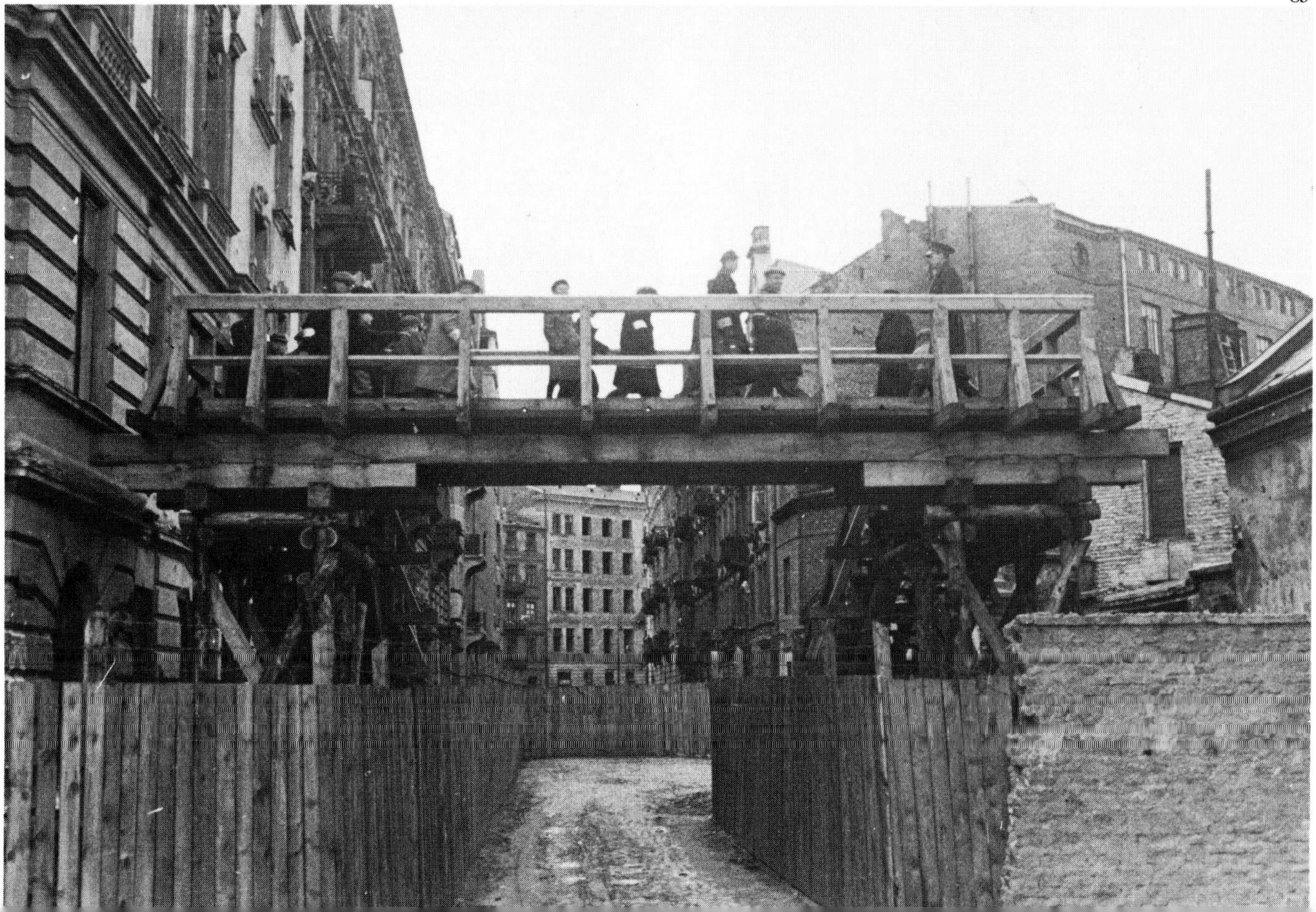

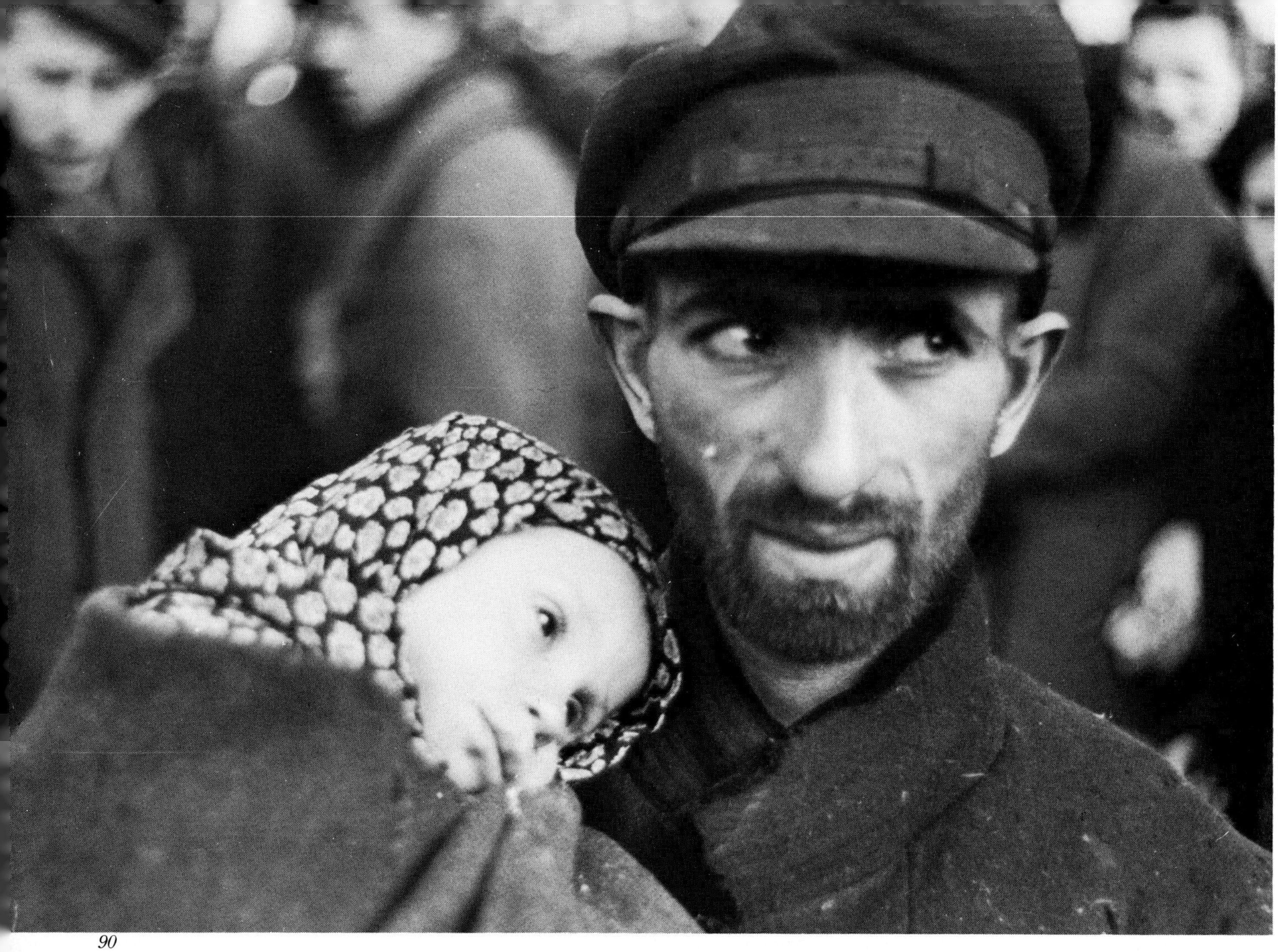

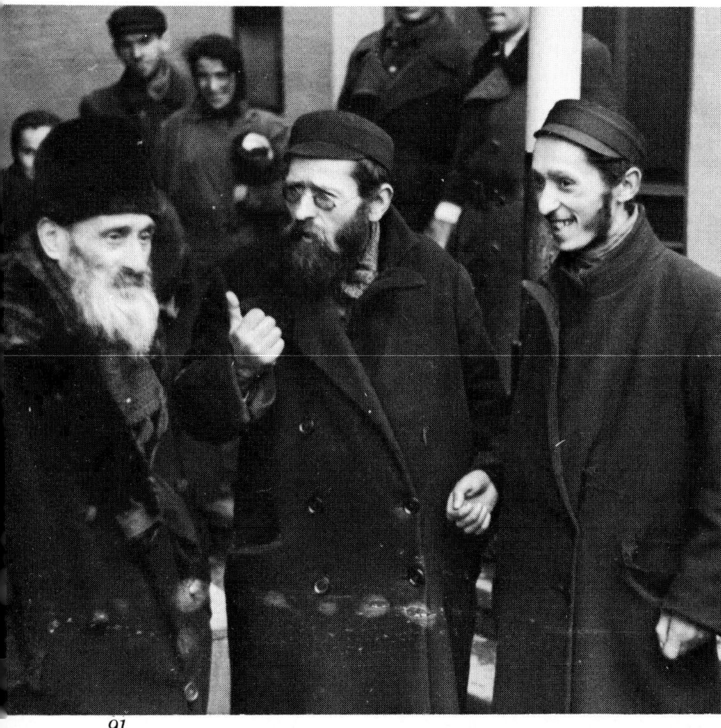

90

91

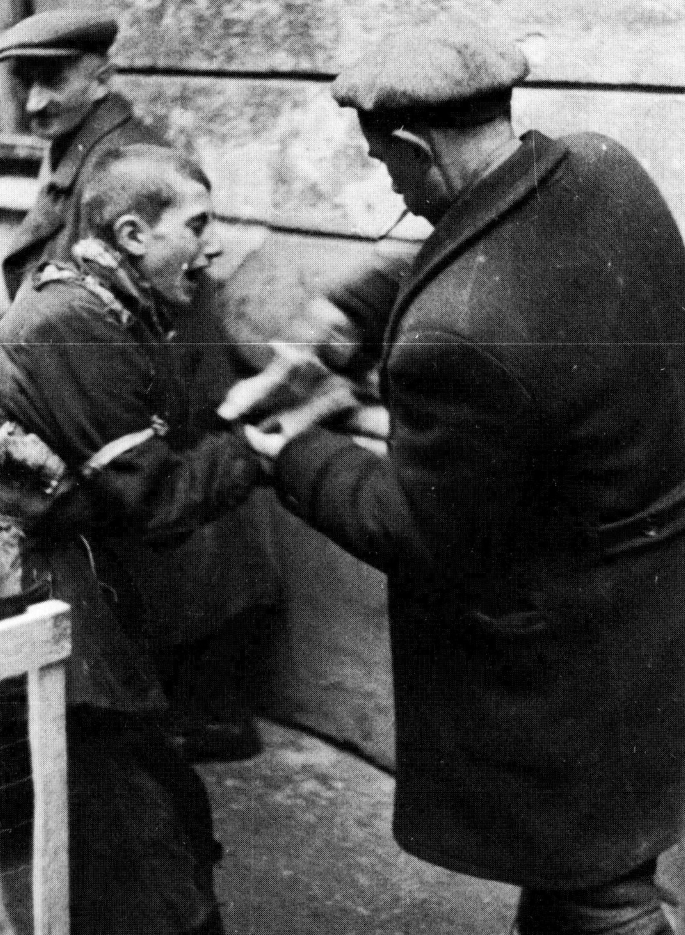

92

60   Street Scenes

STREET VENDORS
(Nos. 93–115)

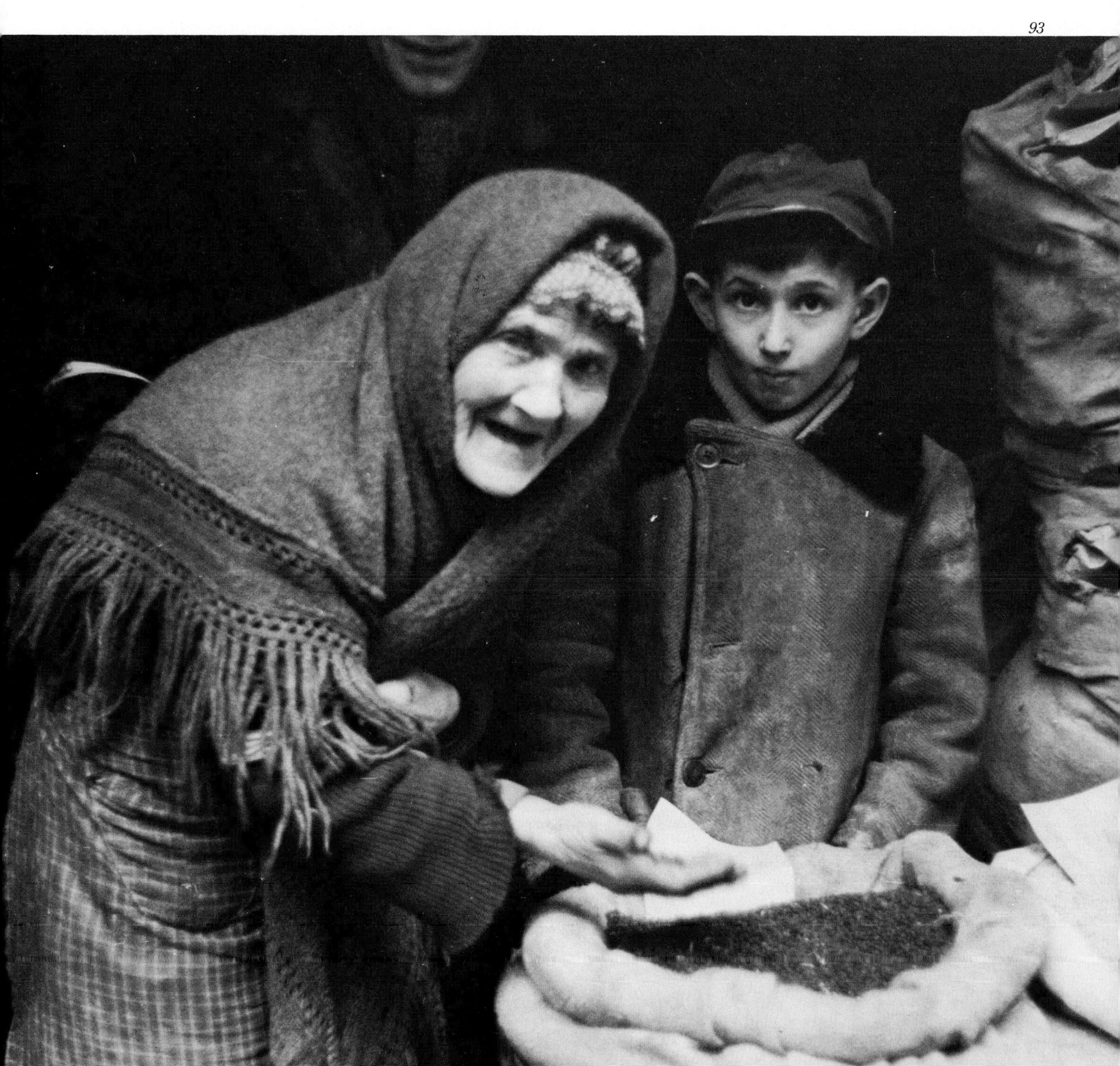

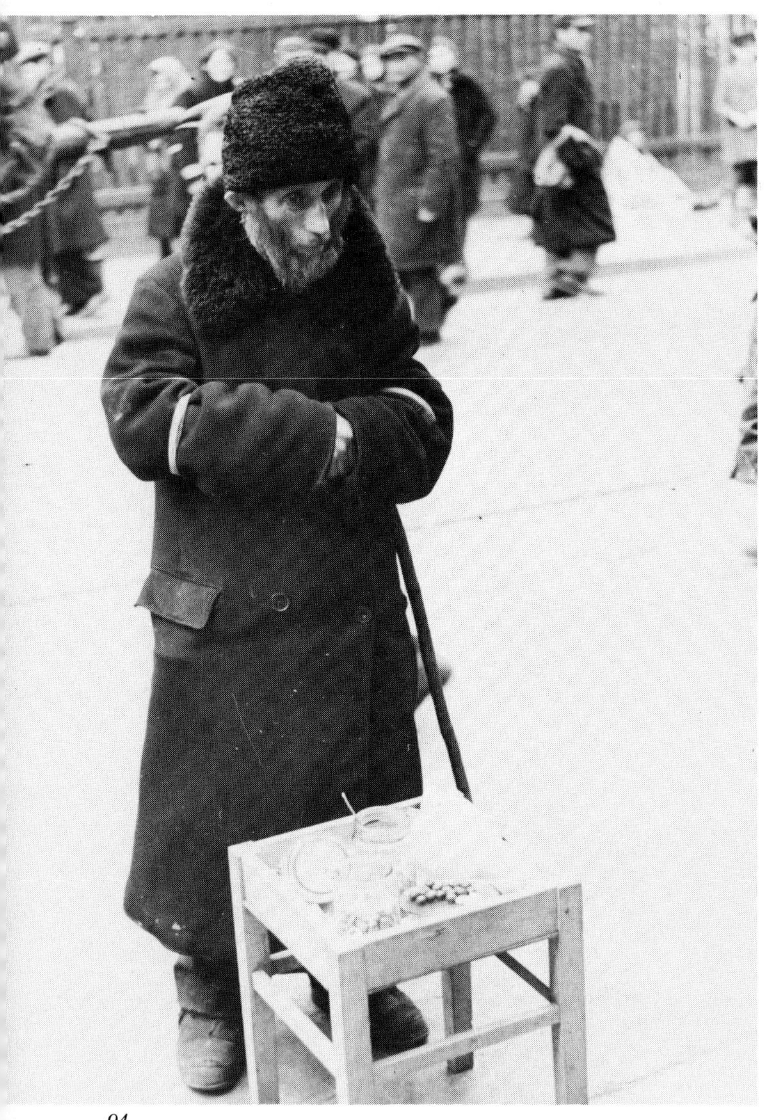

94

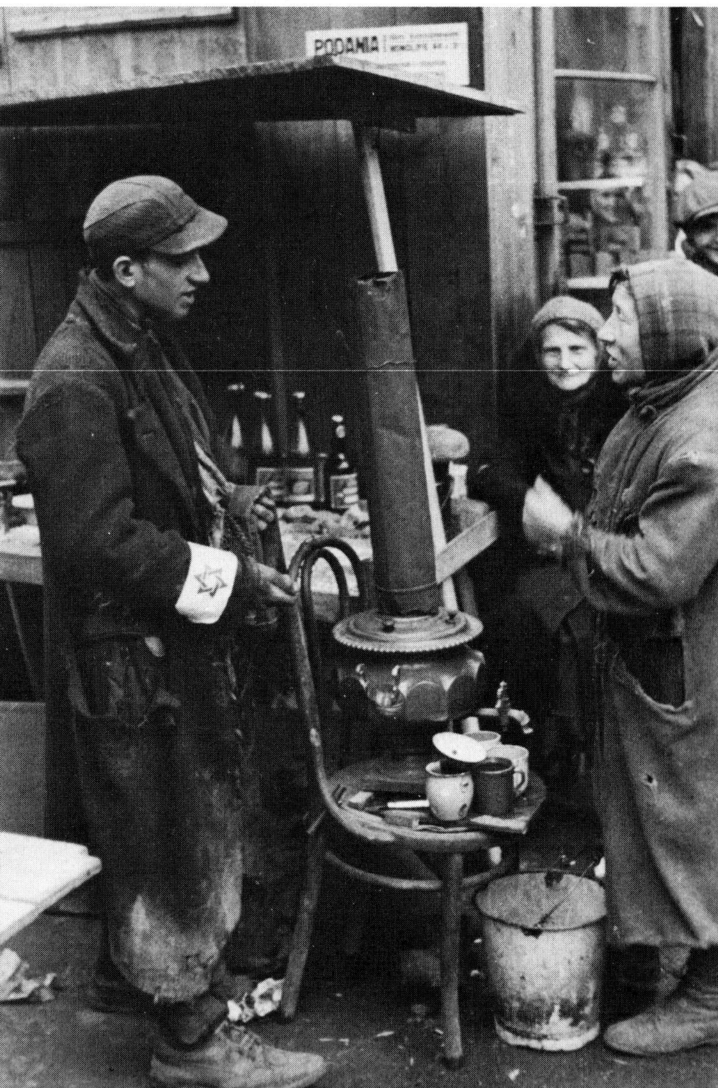

95

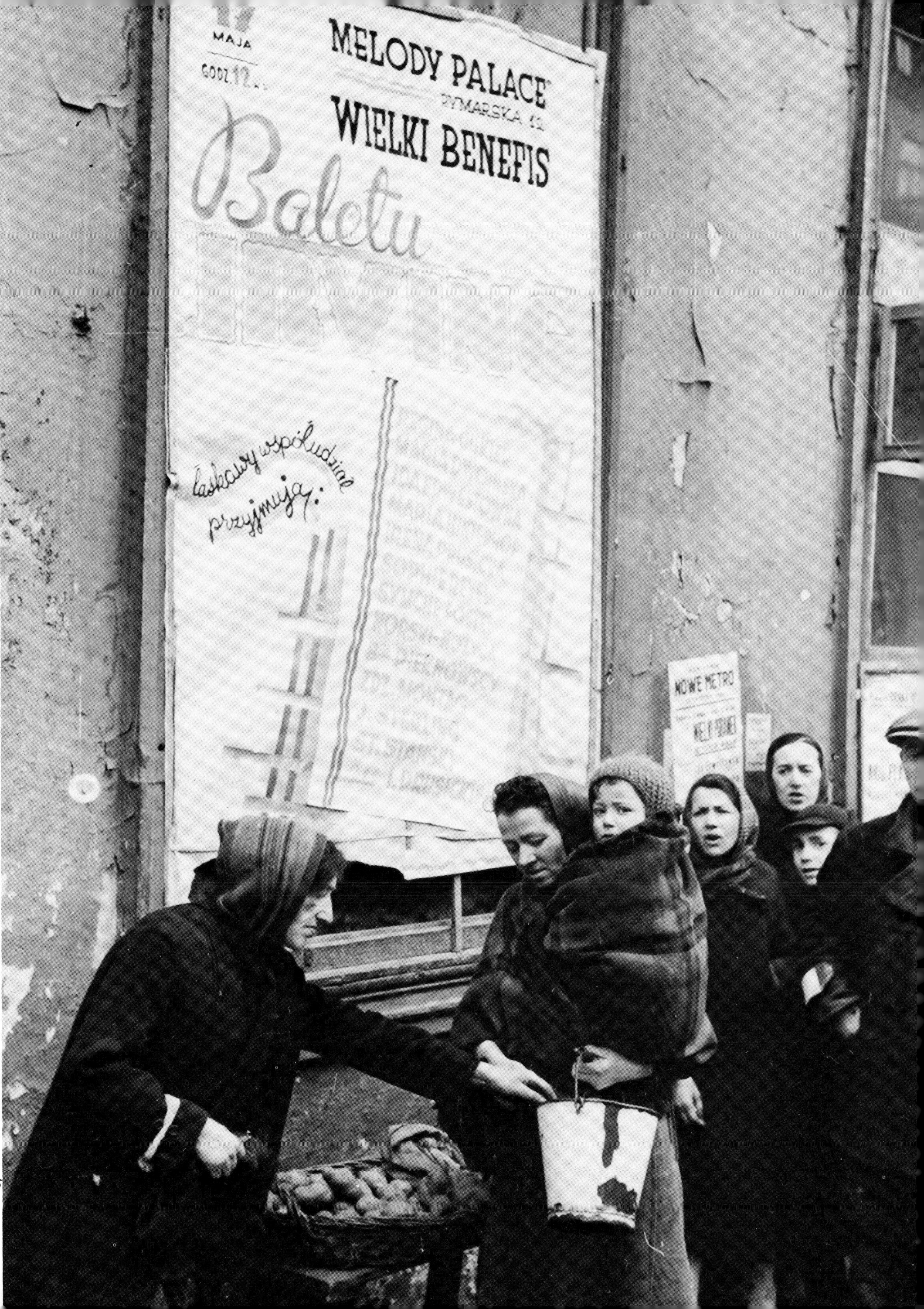

17 MAJA
GODZ. 12...
MELODY PALACE
RYMARSKA 4?
WIELKI BENEFIS
Baletu IRVINGA
łaskawy współudział przyjmują:
REGINA CUKIER
MARIA DWOJSKA
IDA ERWESTÓWNA
MARIA HINTERHOF
IRENA DRUSICKA
SOPHIE REYEL
SYMCHE FOSTEL
NORSKI-NOŻYCA
B-a PIĘKNOWSCY
ZDZ. MONTAG
J. STERLING
ST. SIAŃSKI
I. DRUSICKI
NOWE METRO
WIELKI PROGRAM

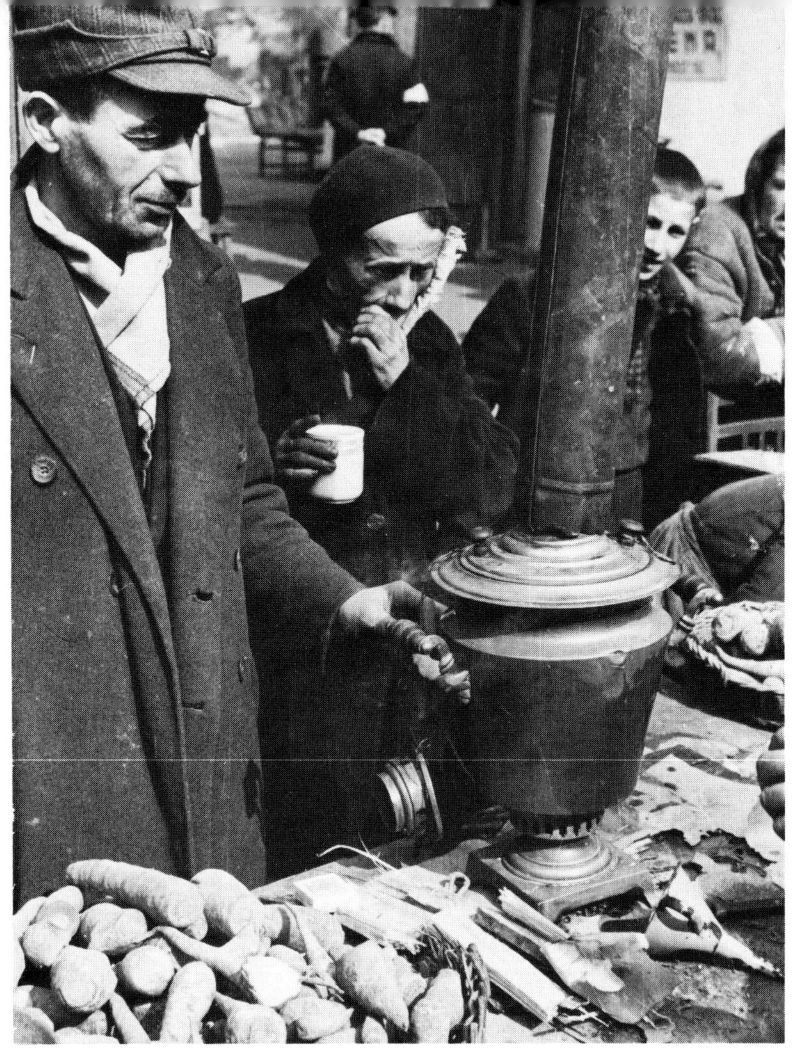

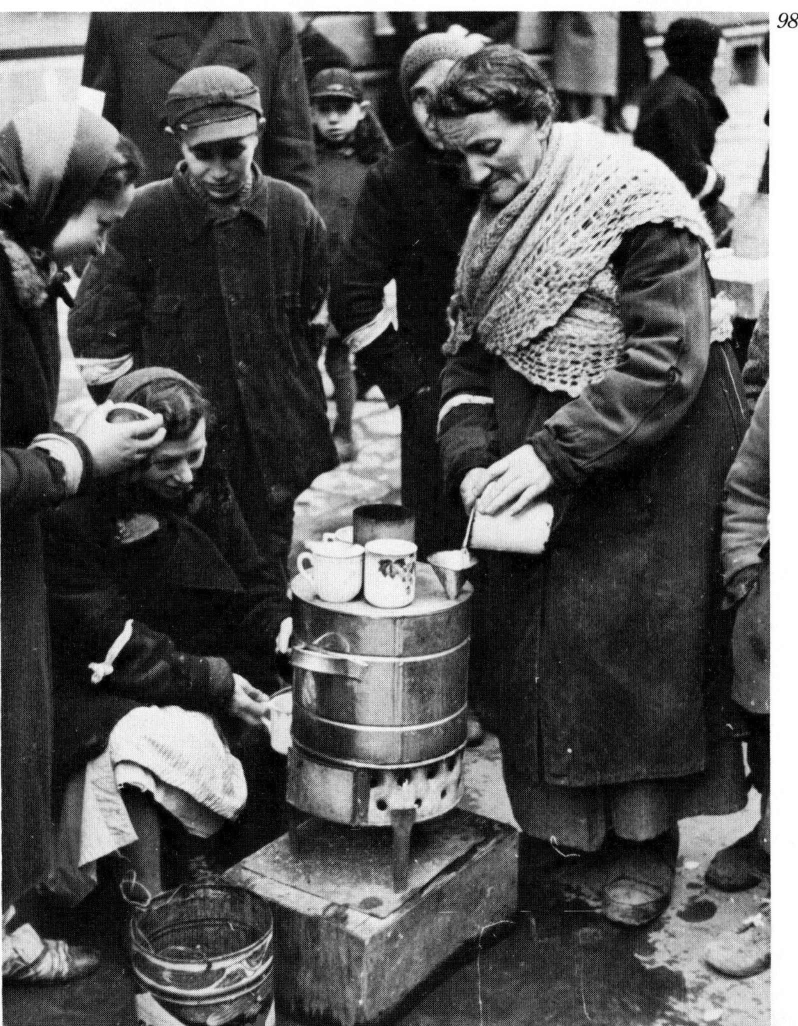

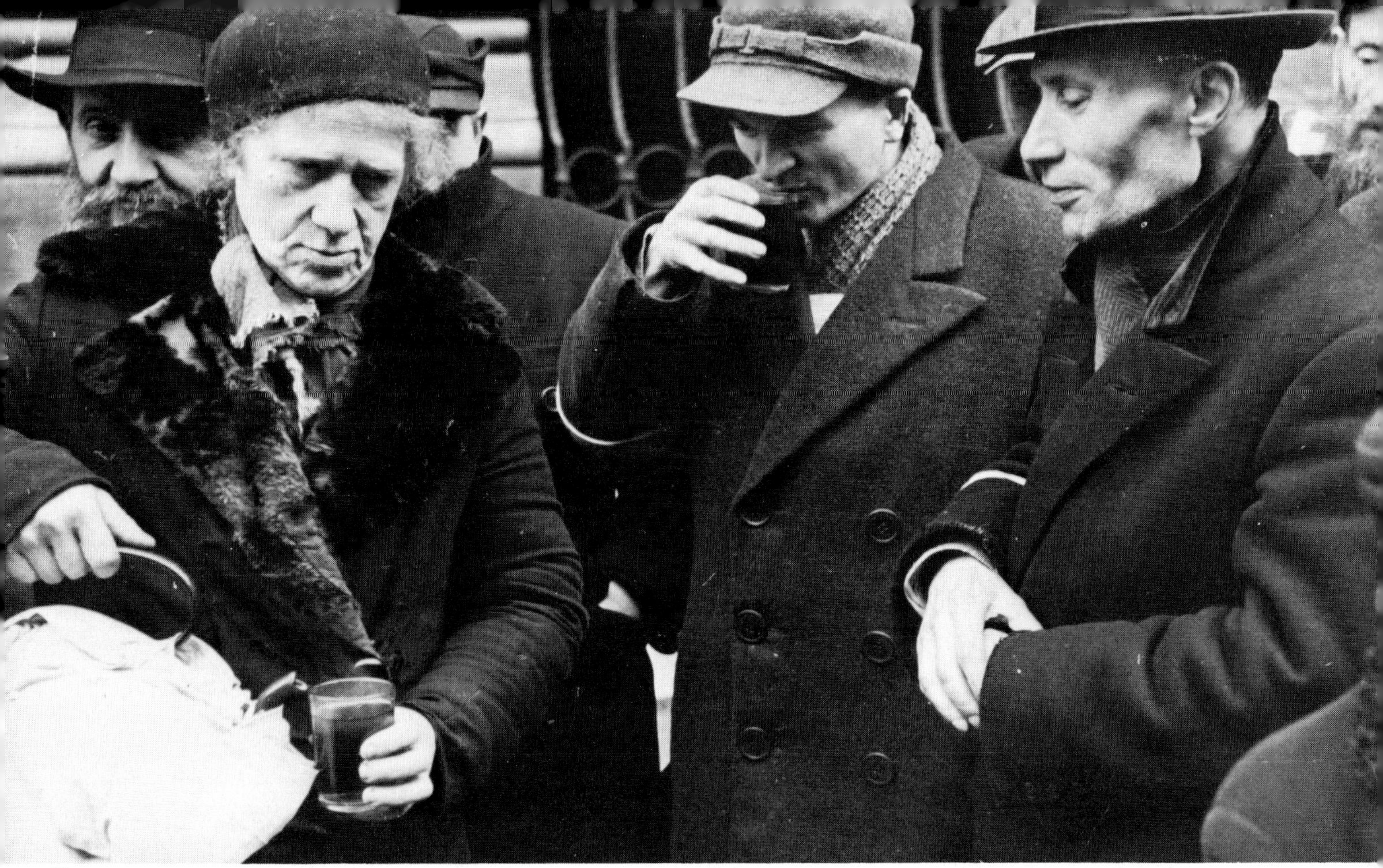

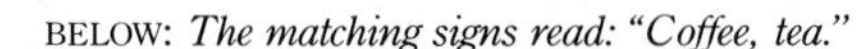

BELOW: *The matching signs read: "Coffee, tea."*

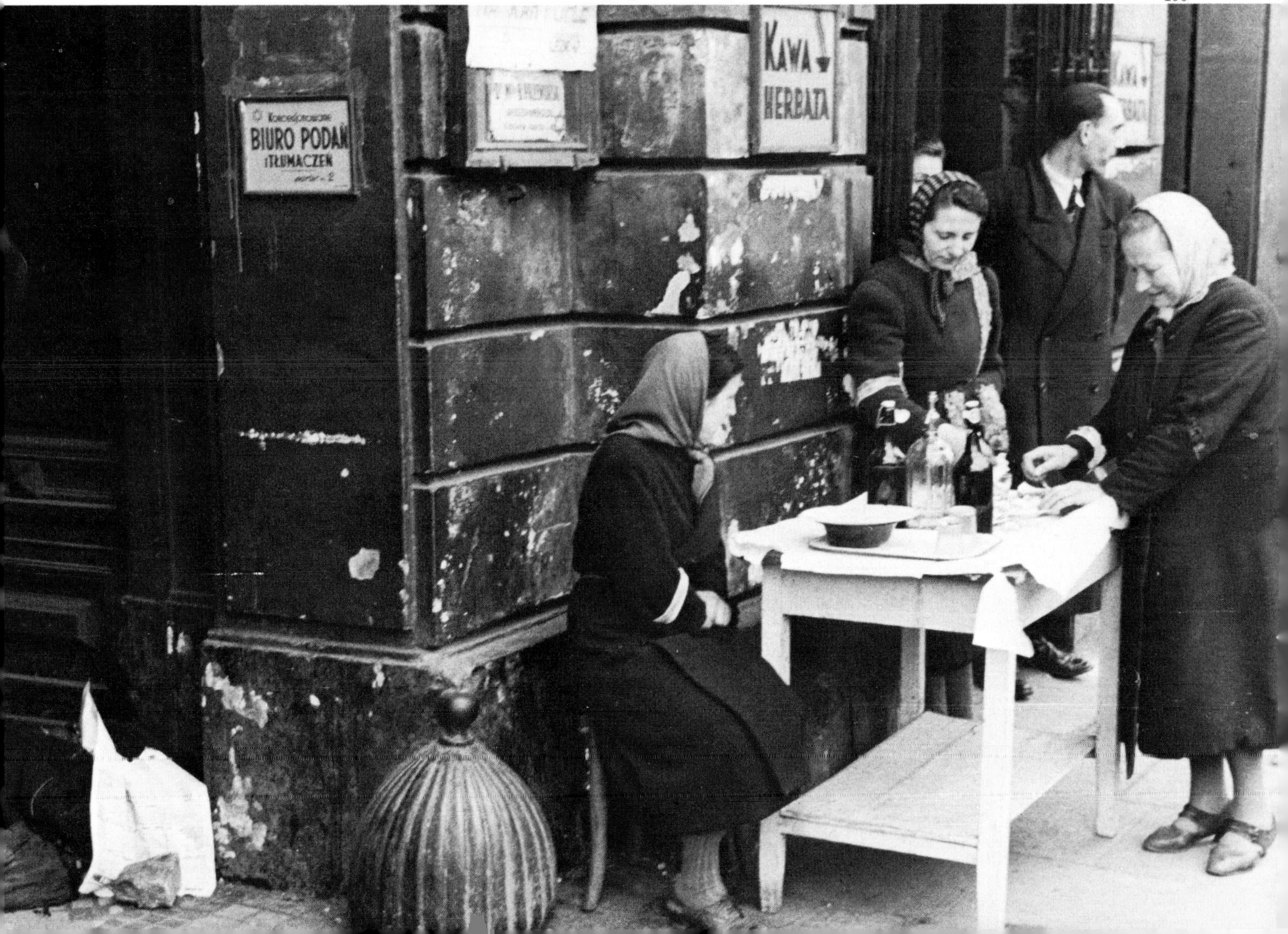

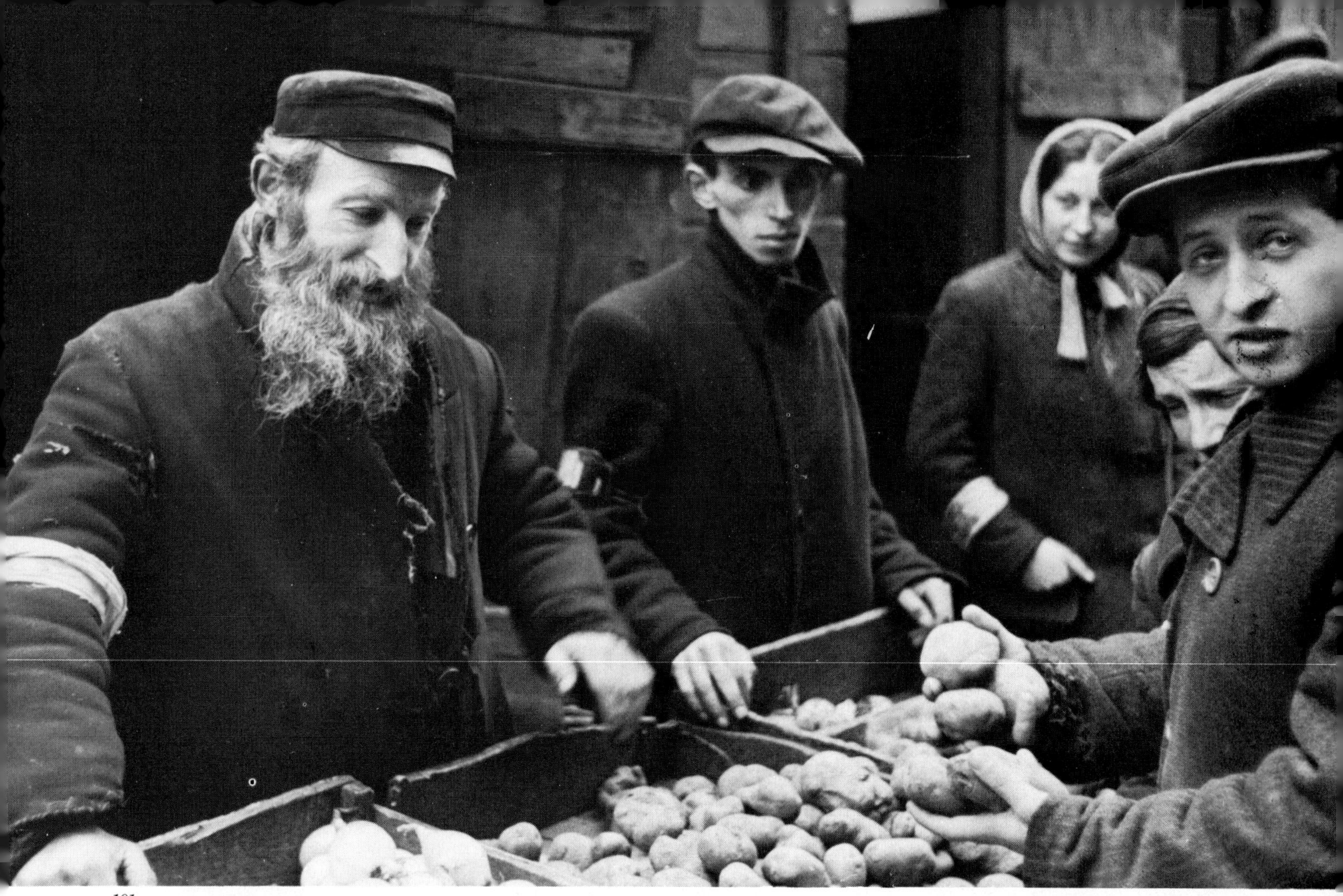

101

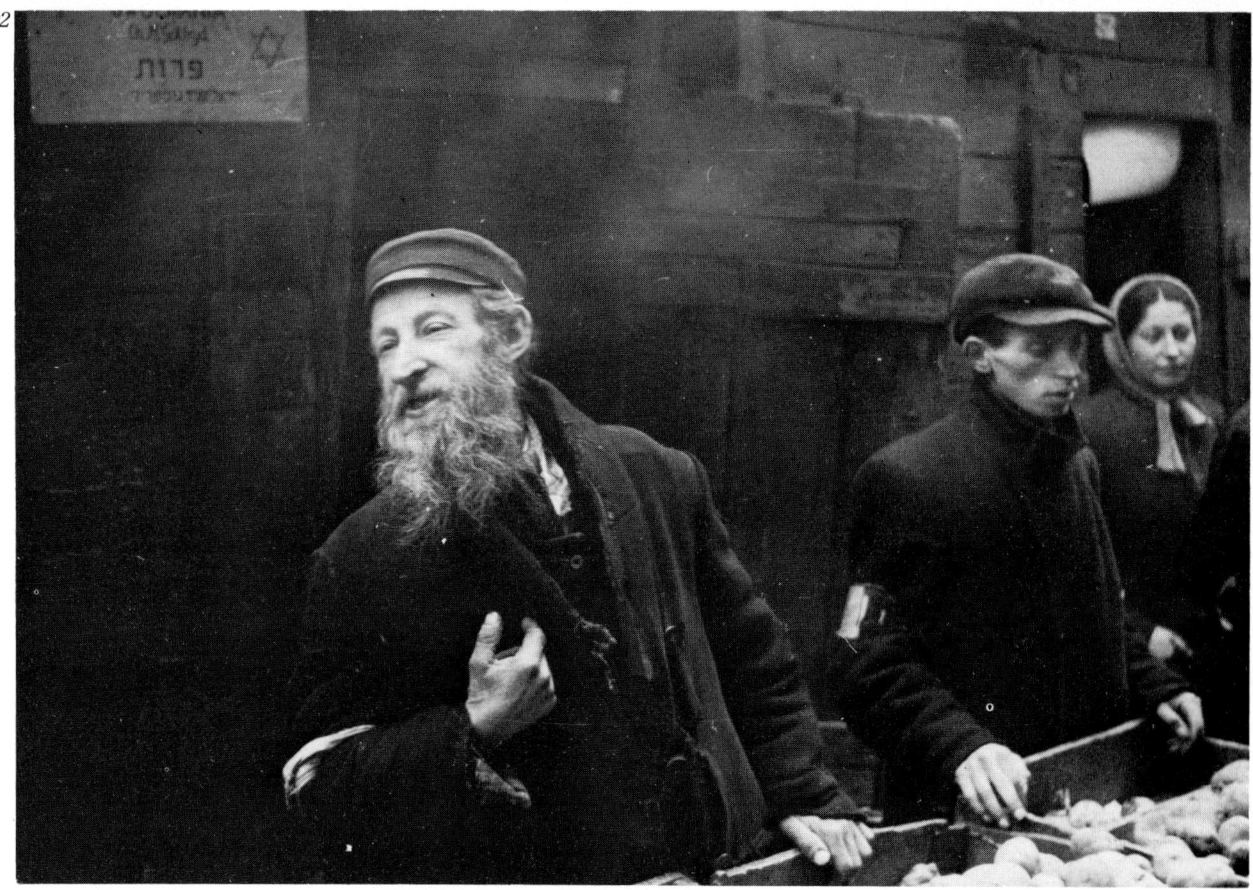

102

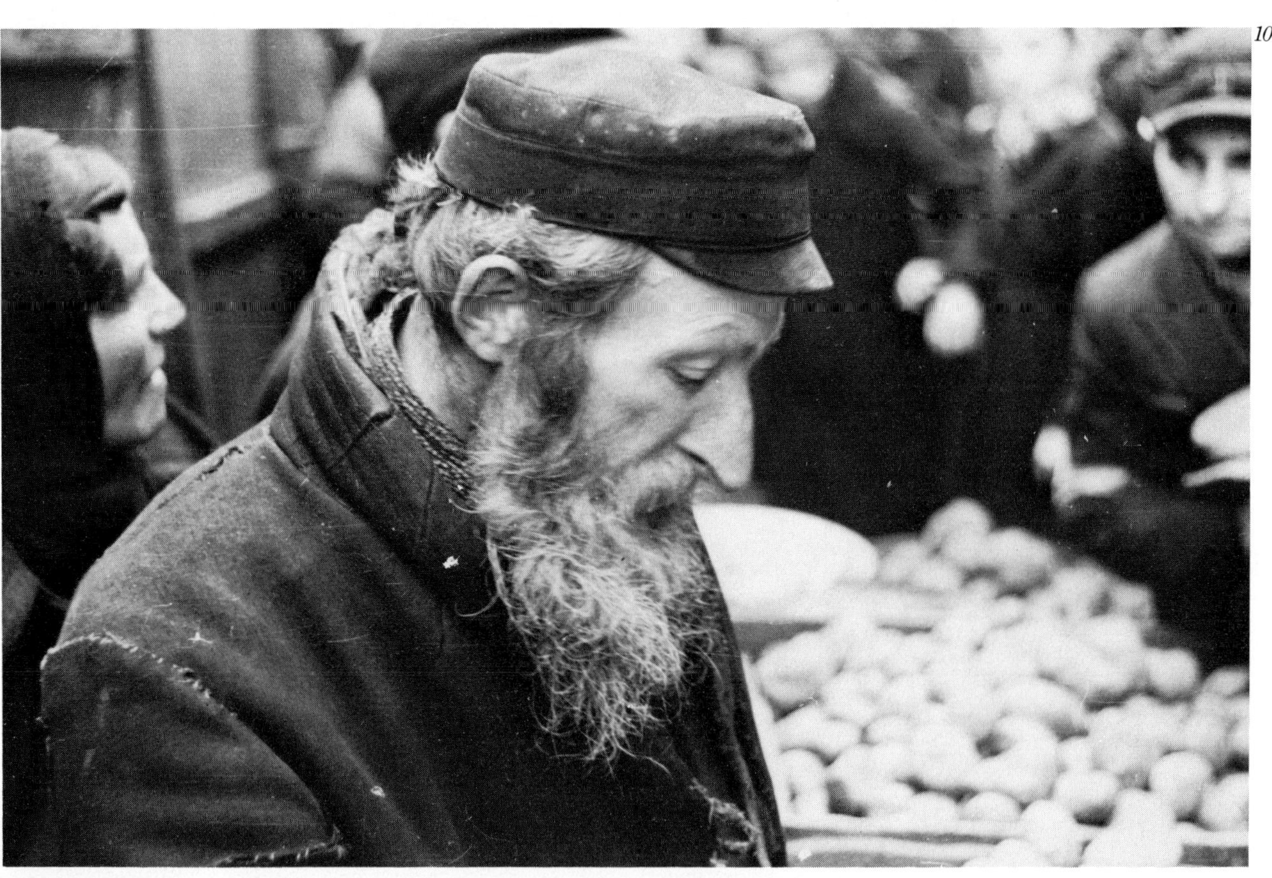

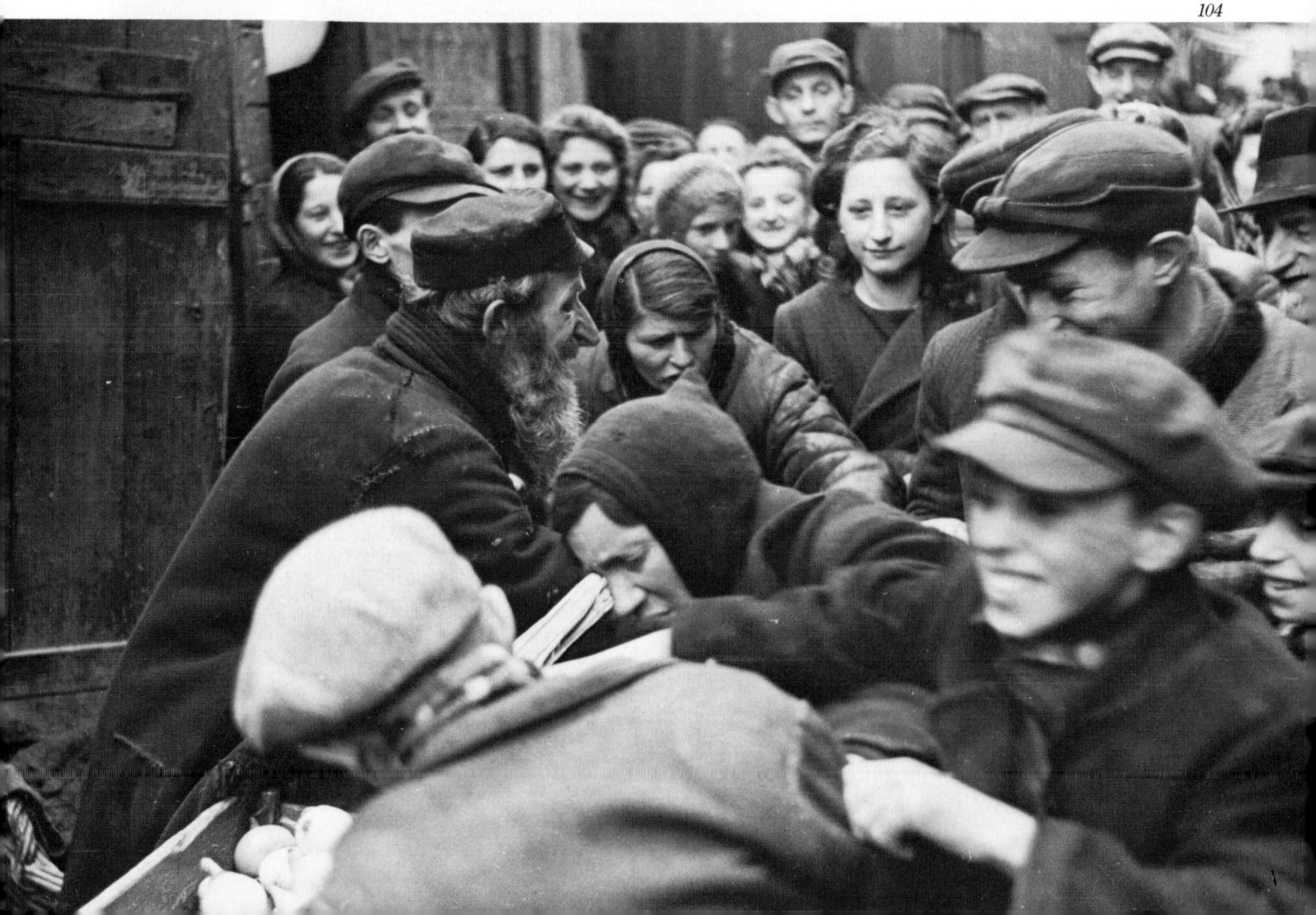

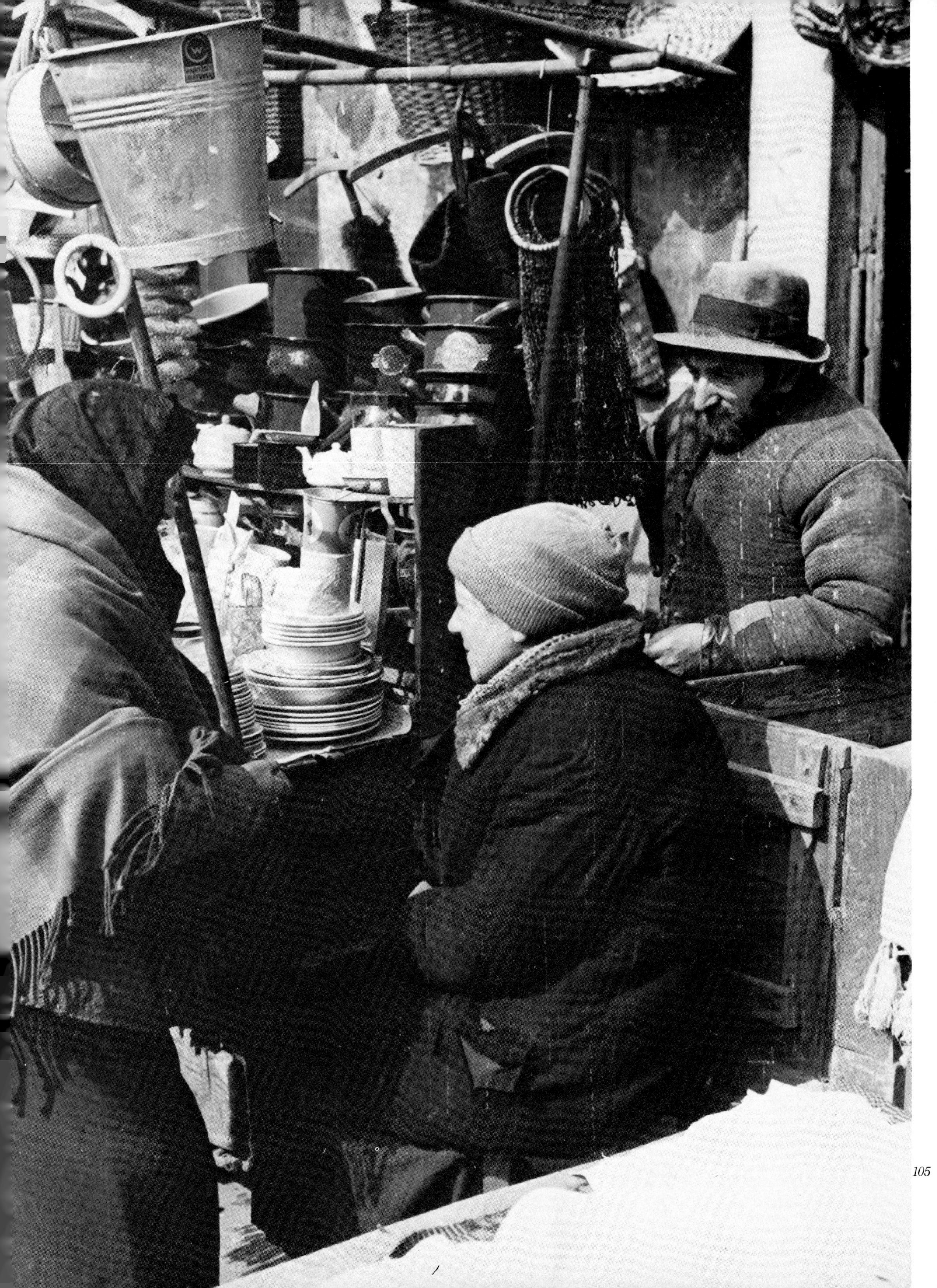

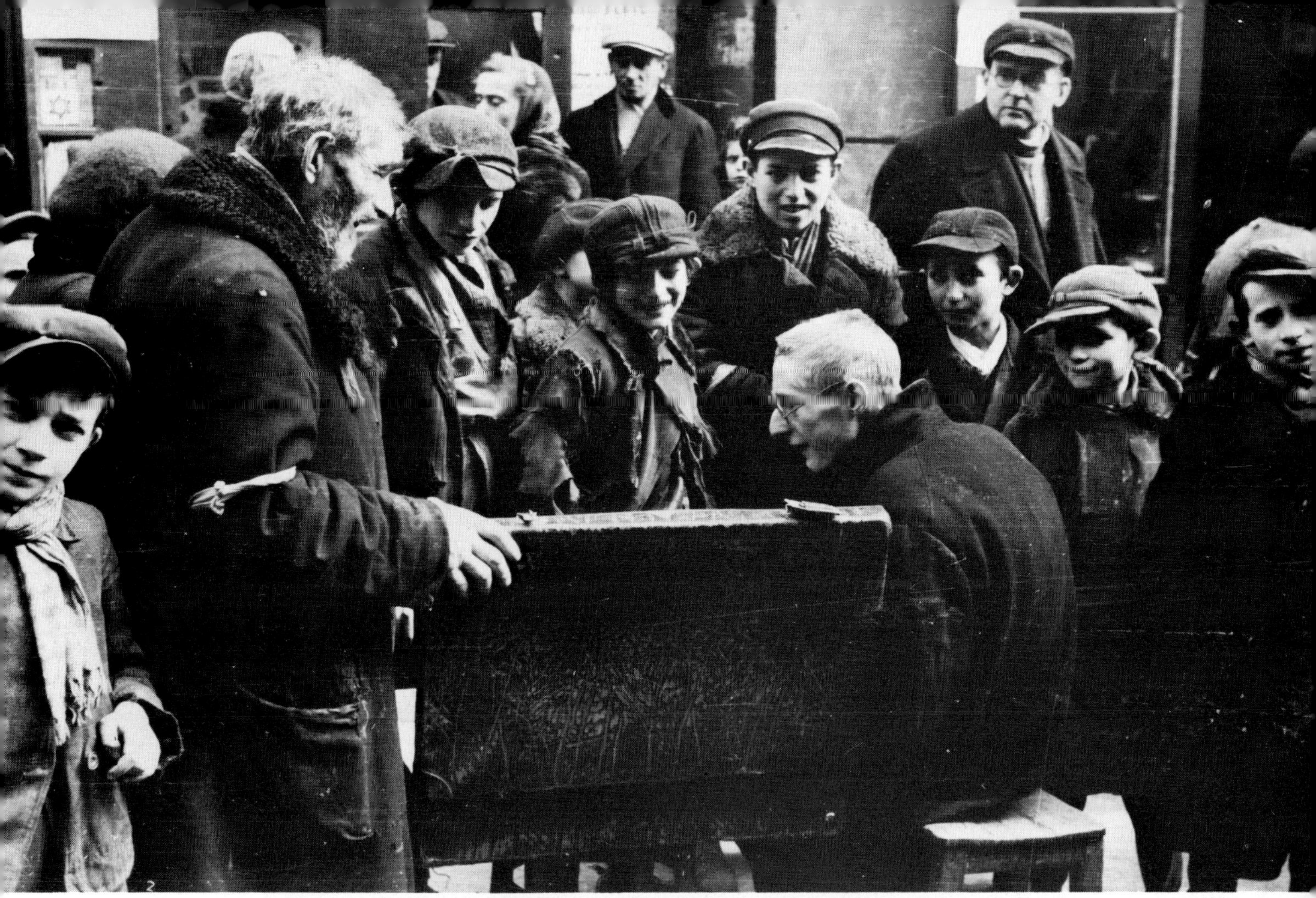

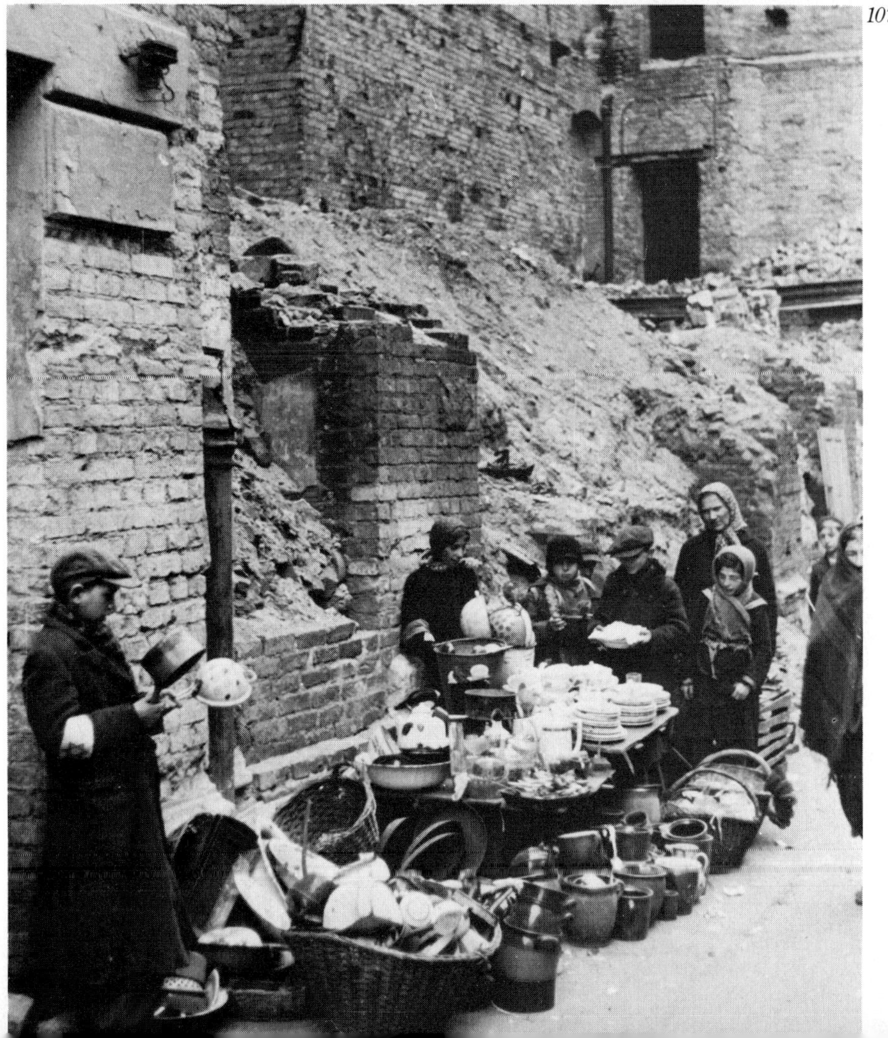

106

107

69

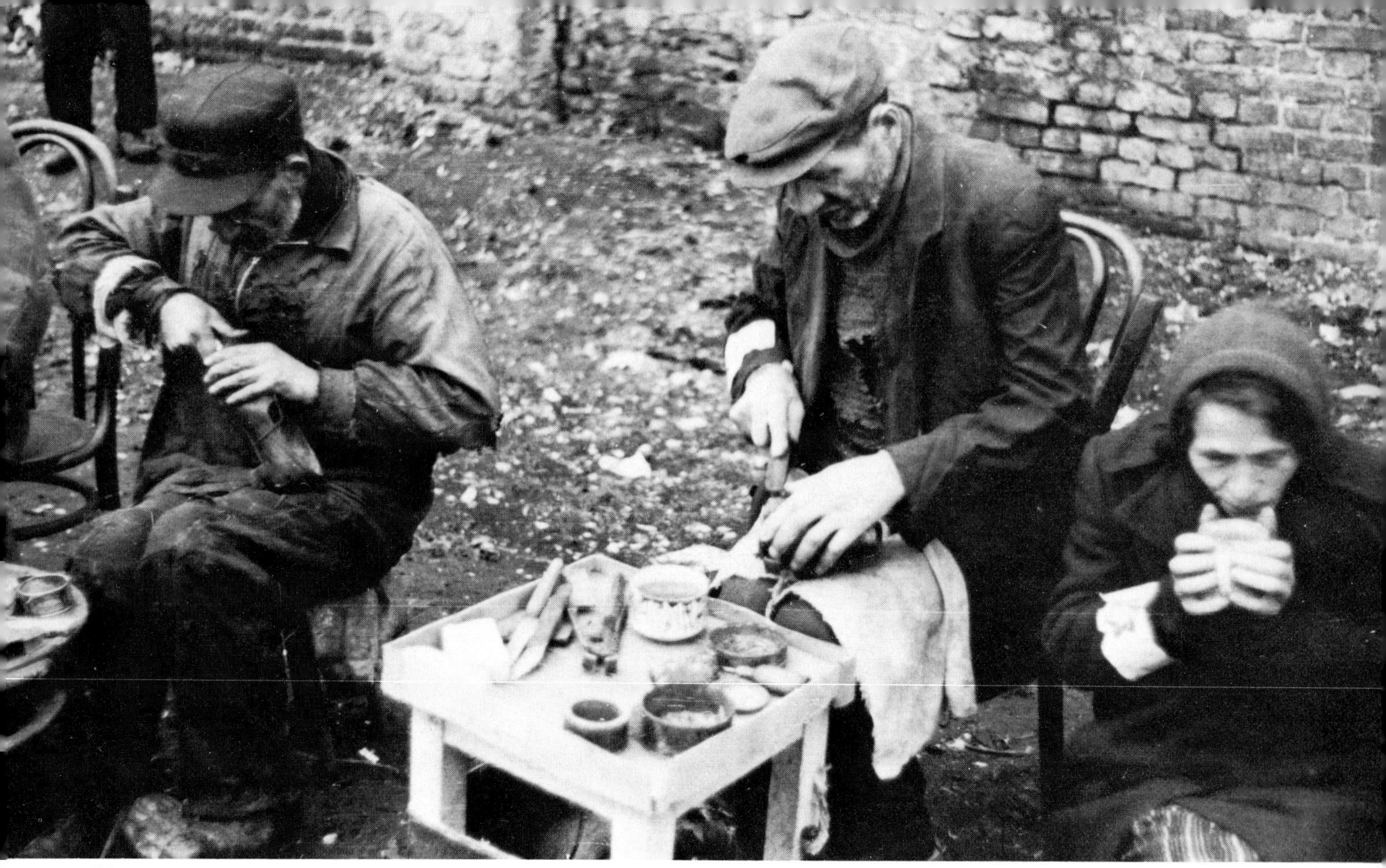

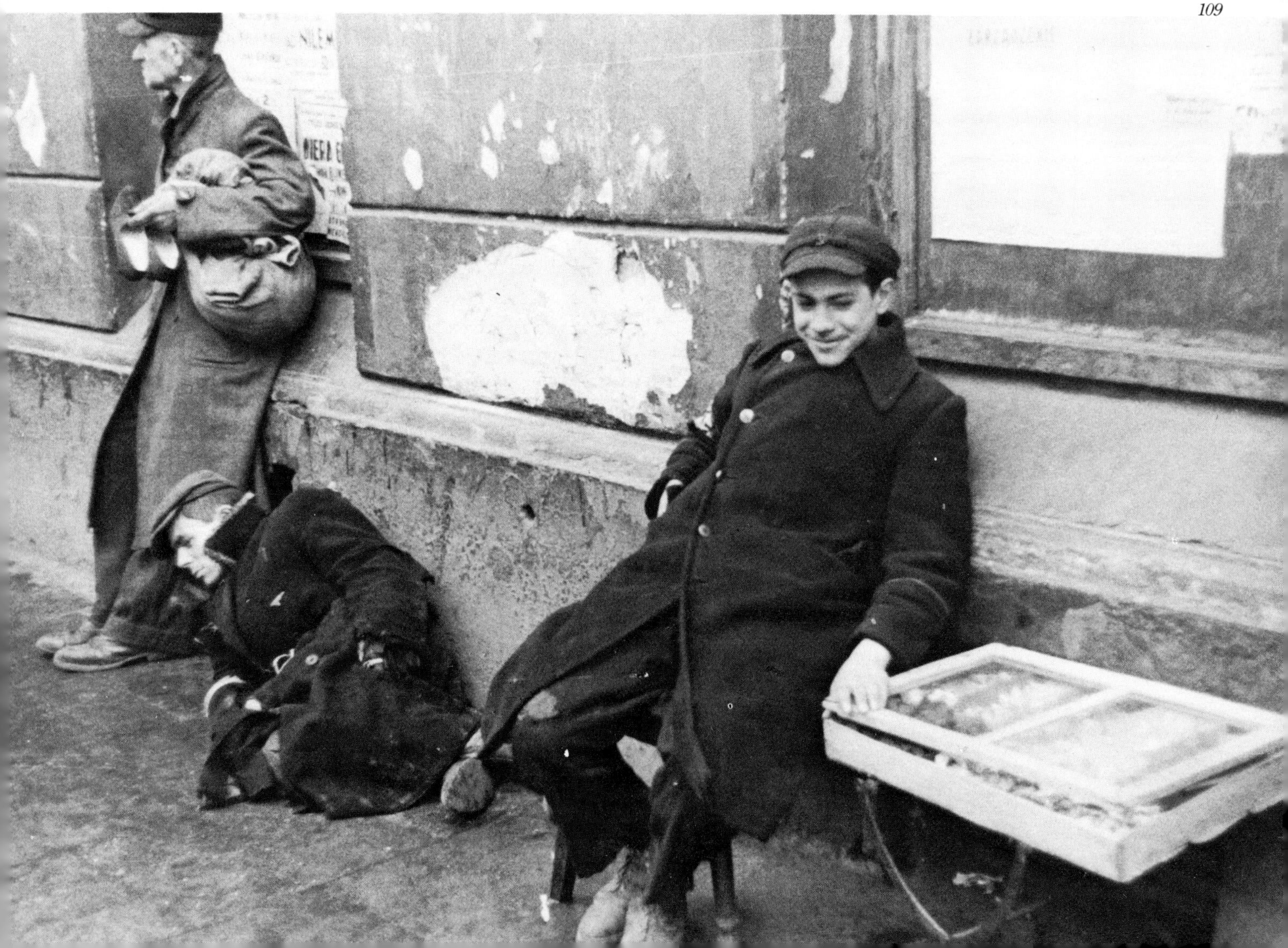

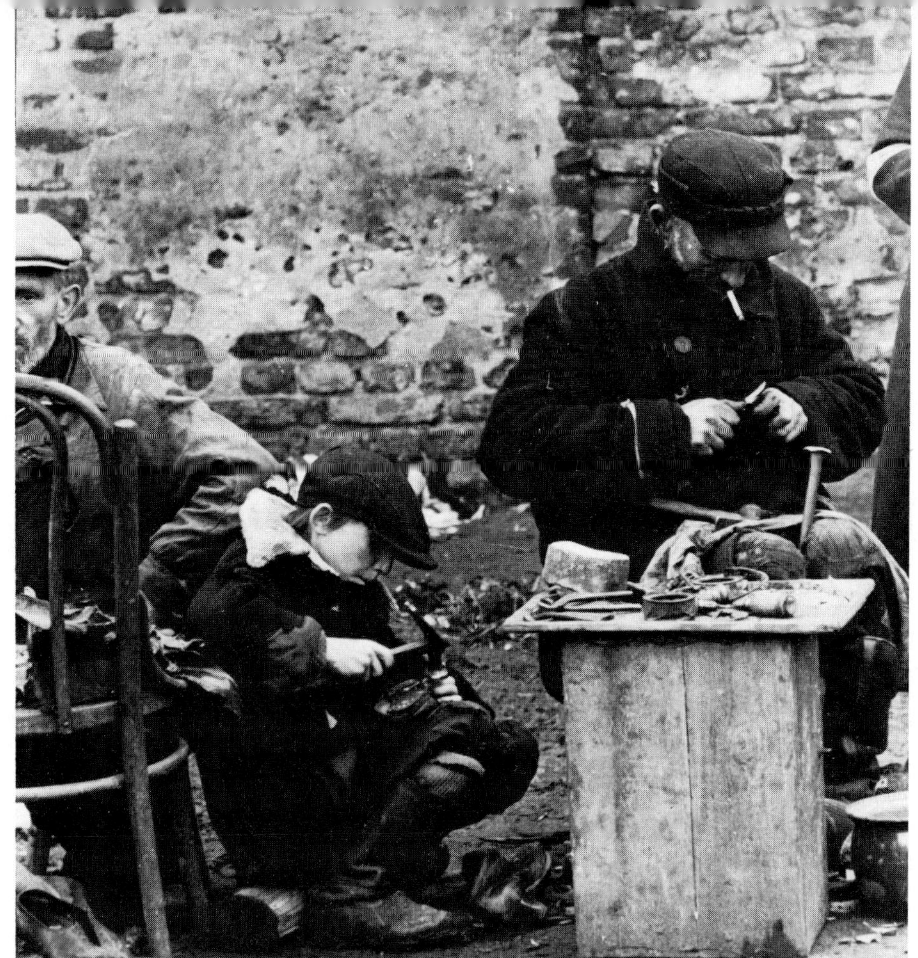

110

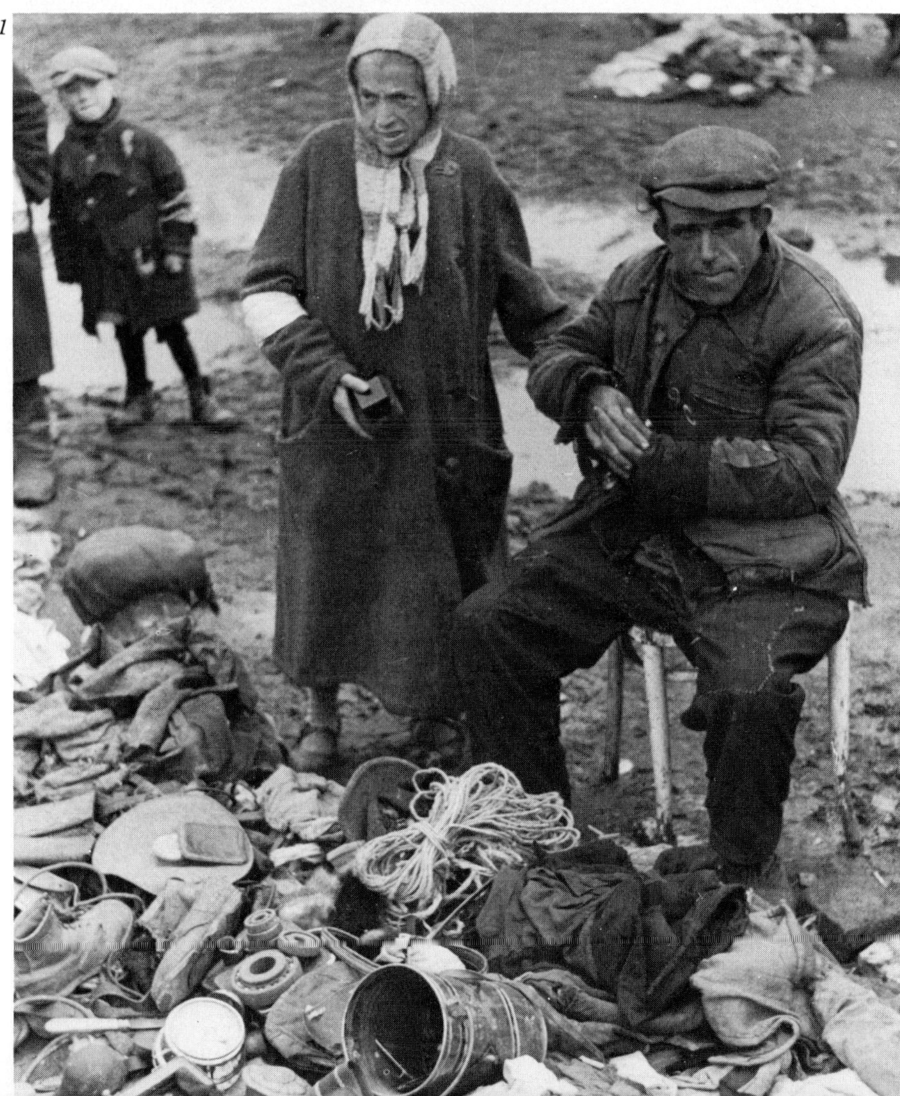

111

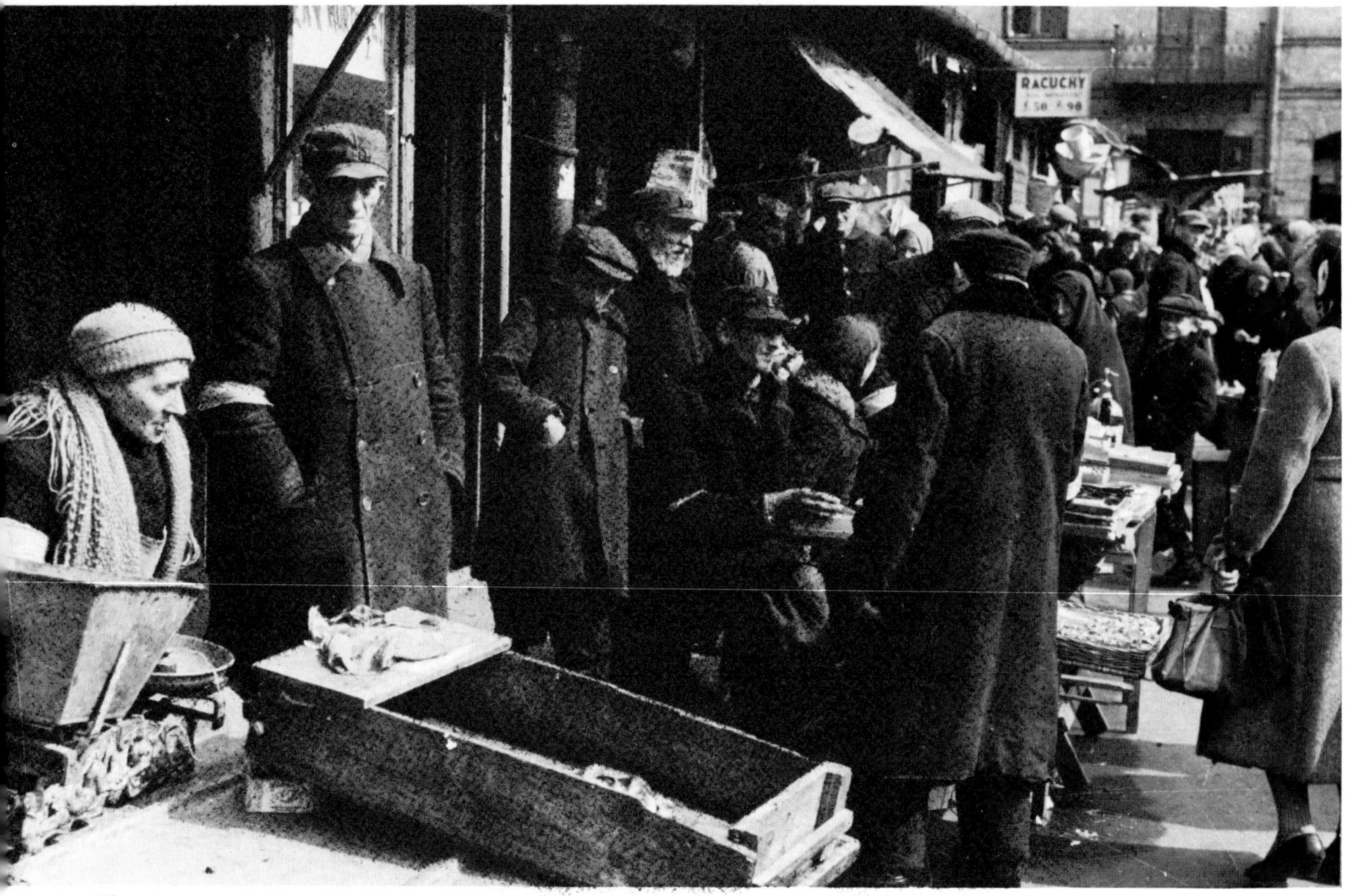

RACUCHY

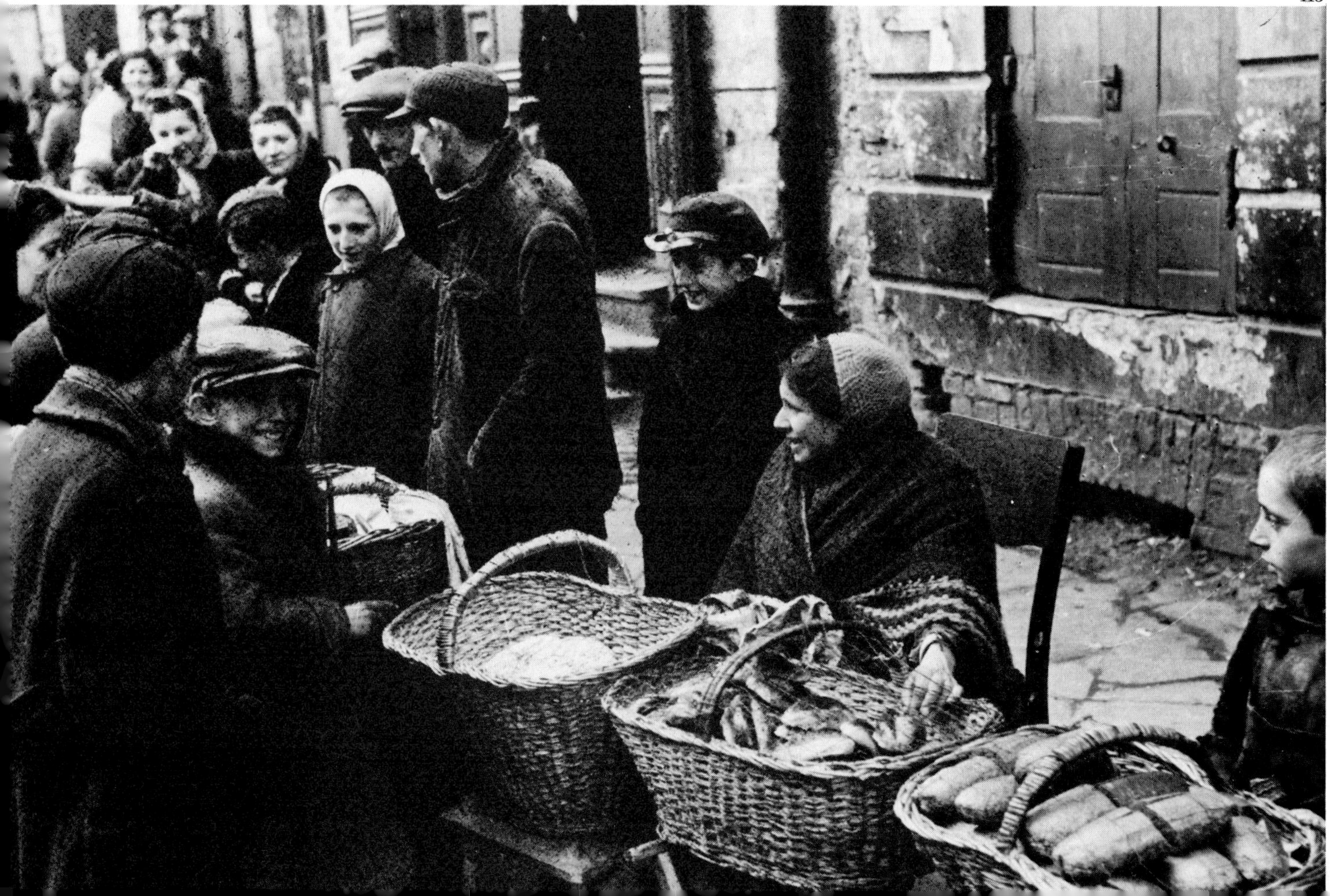

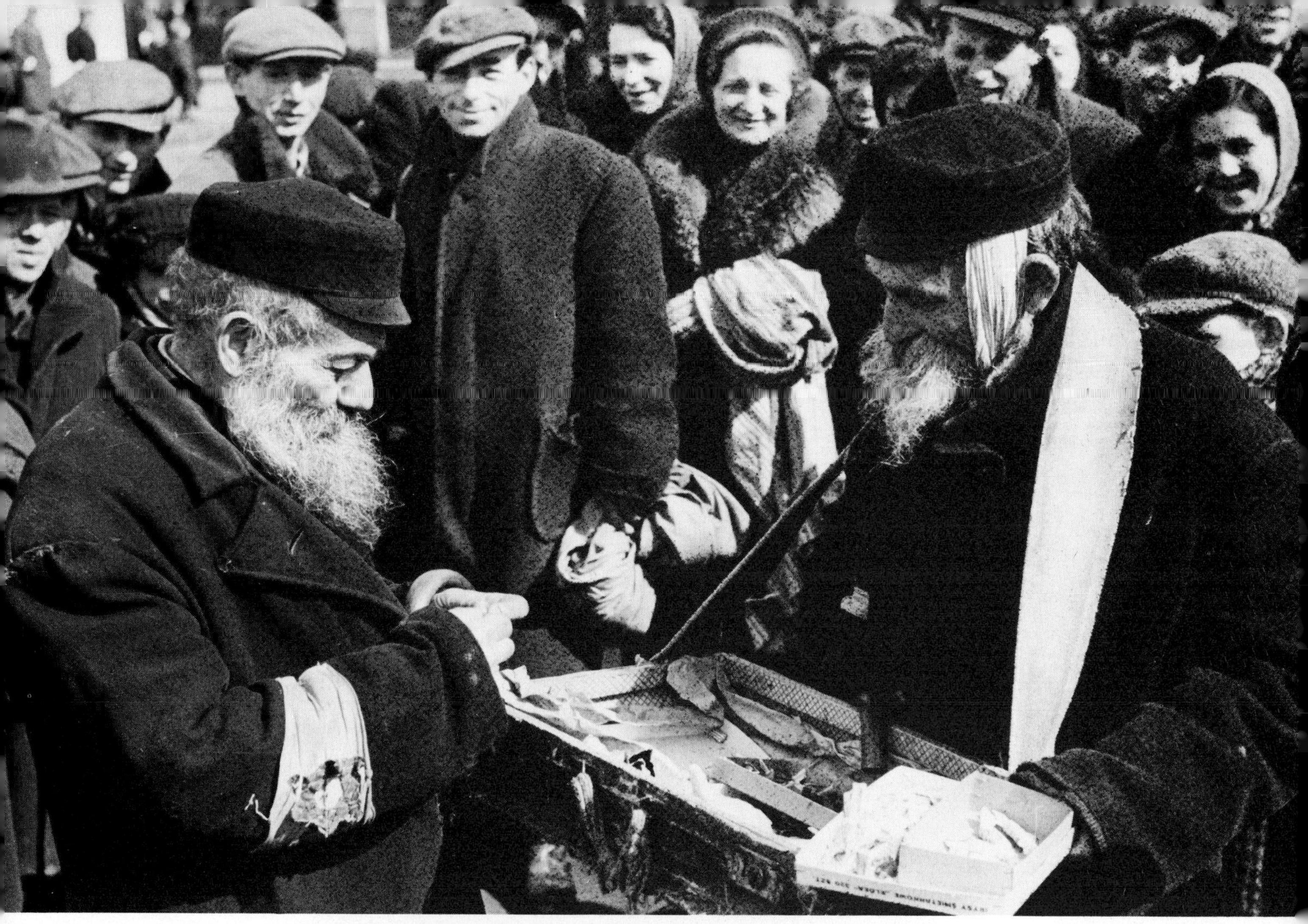

114

115

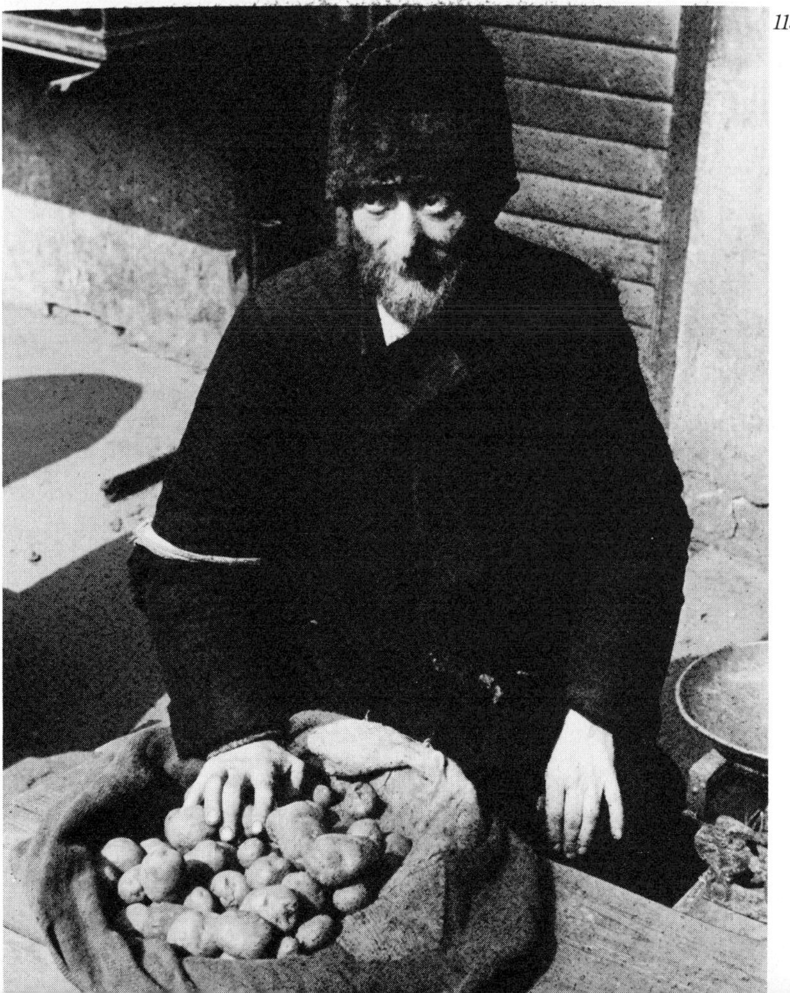

Street Vendors 73

MARKET SCENES AND CHARITY FOOD PROGRAMS
(Nos. 116–130)

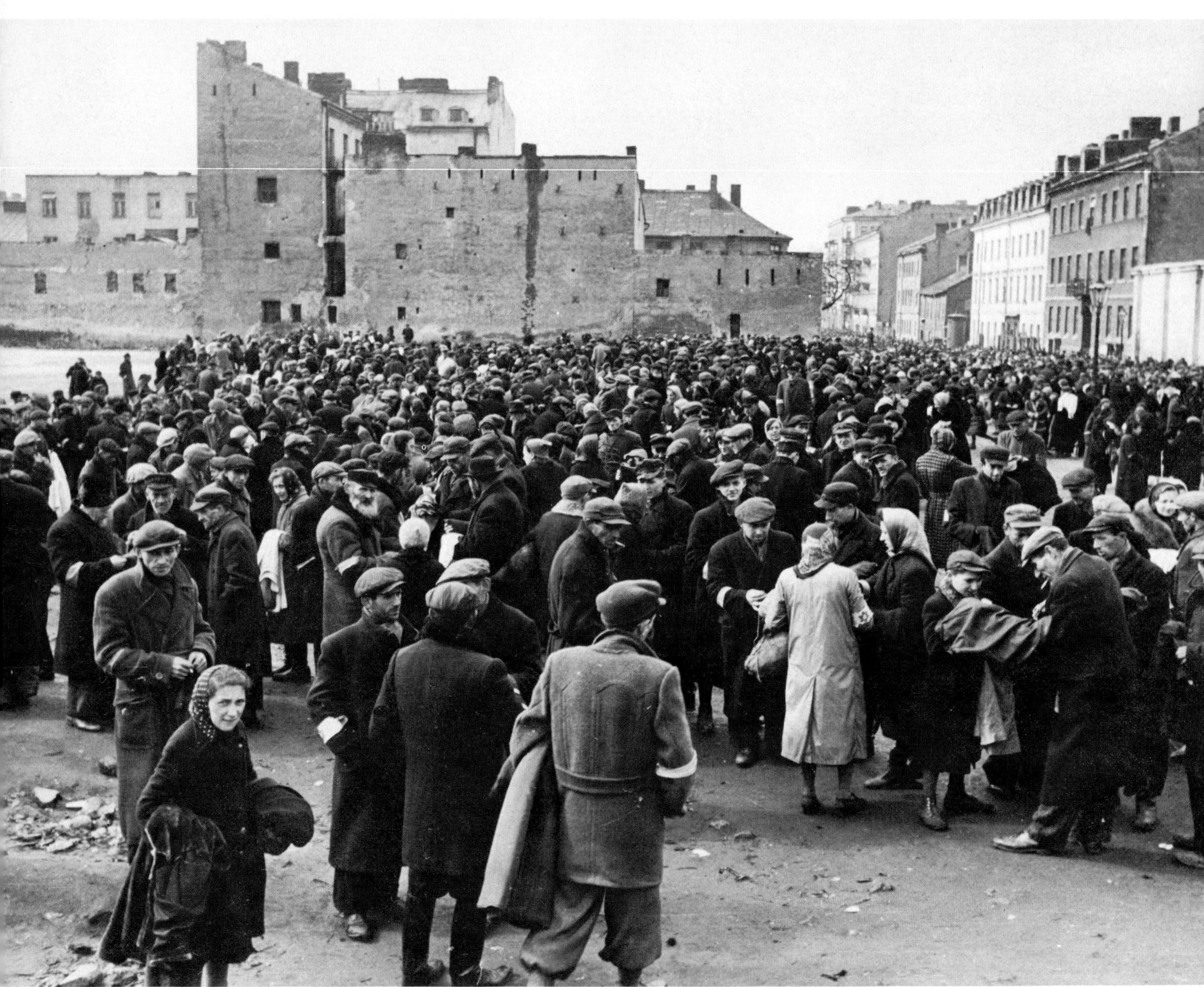

116

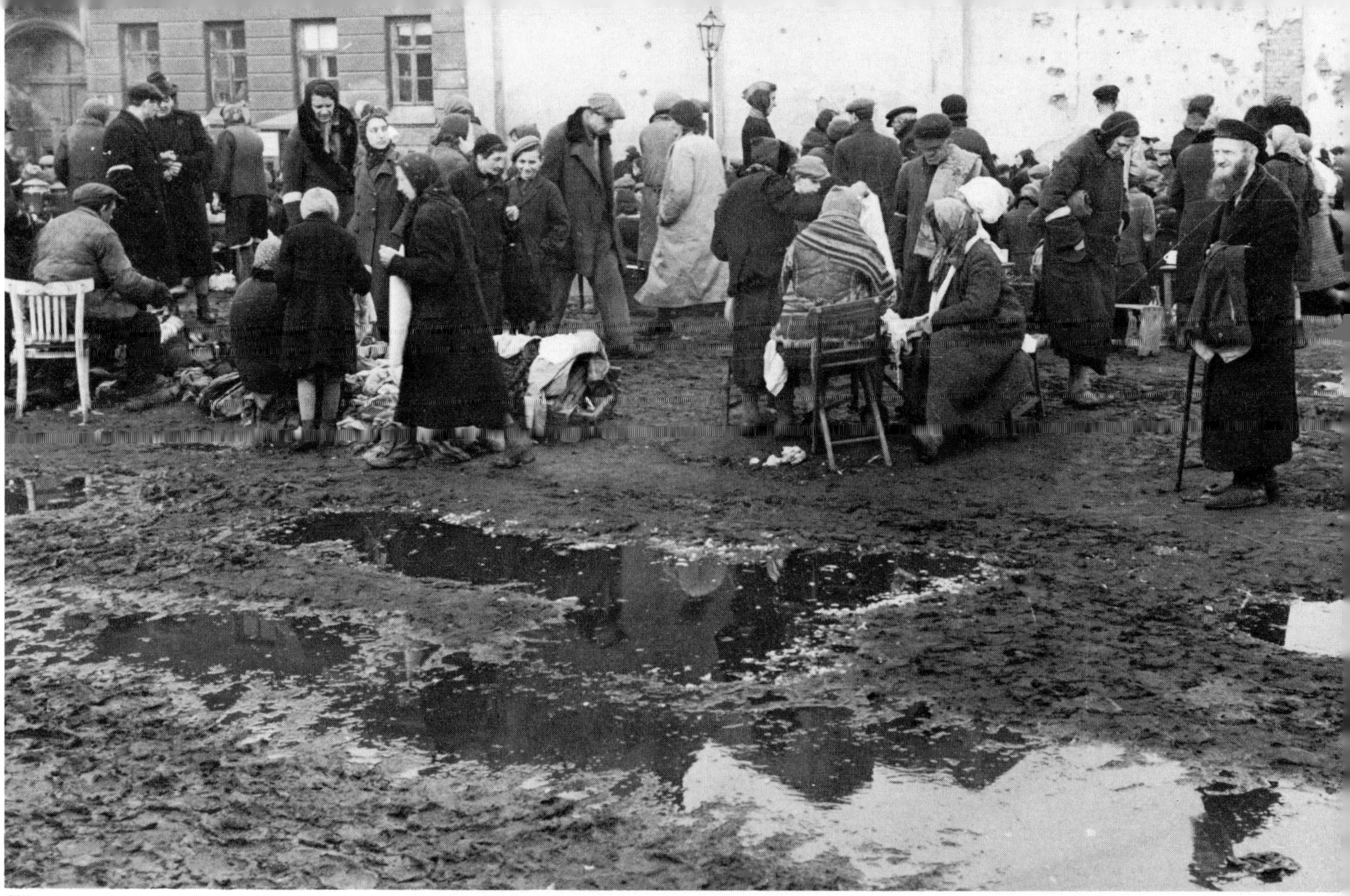

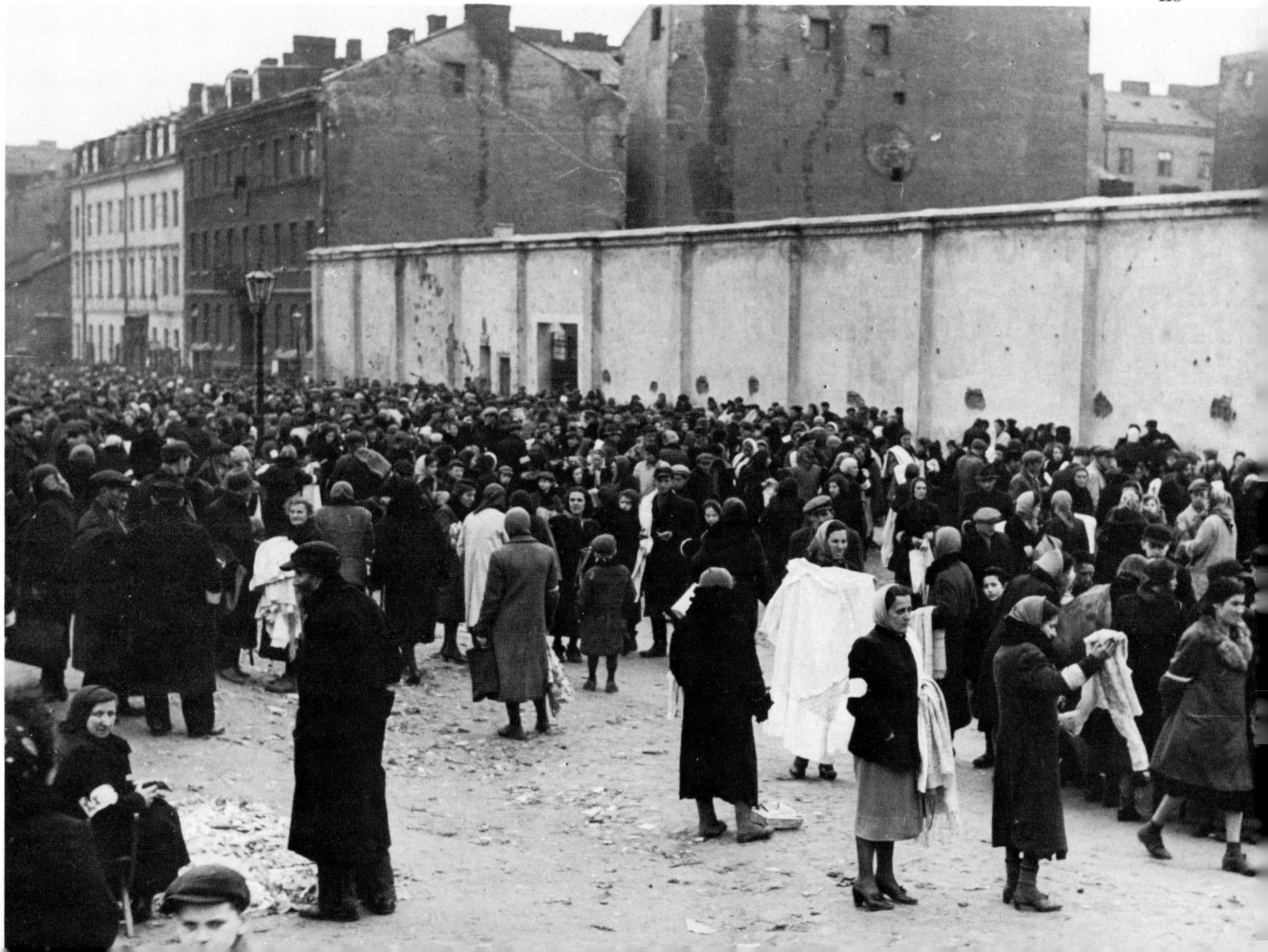

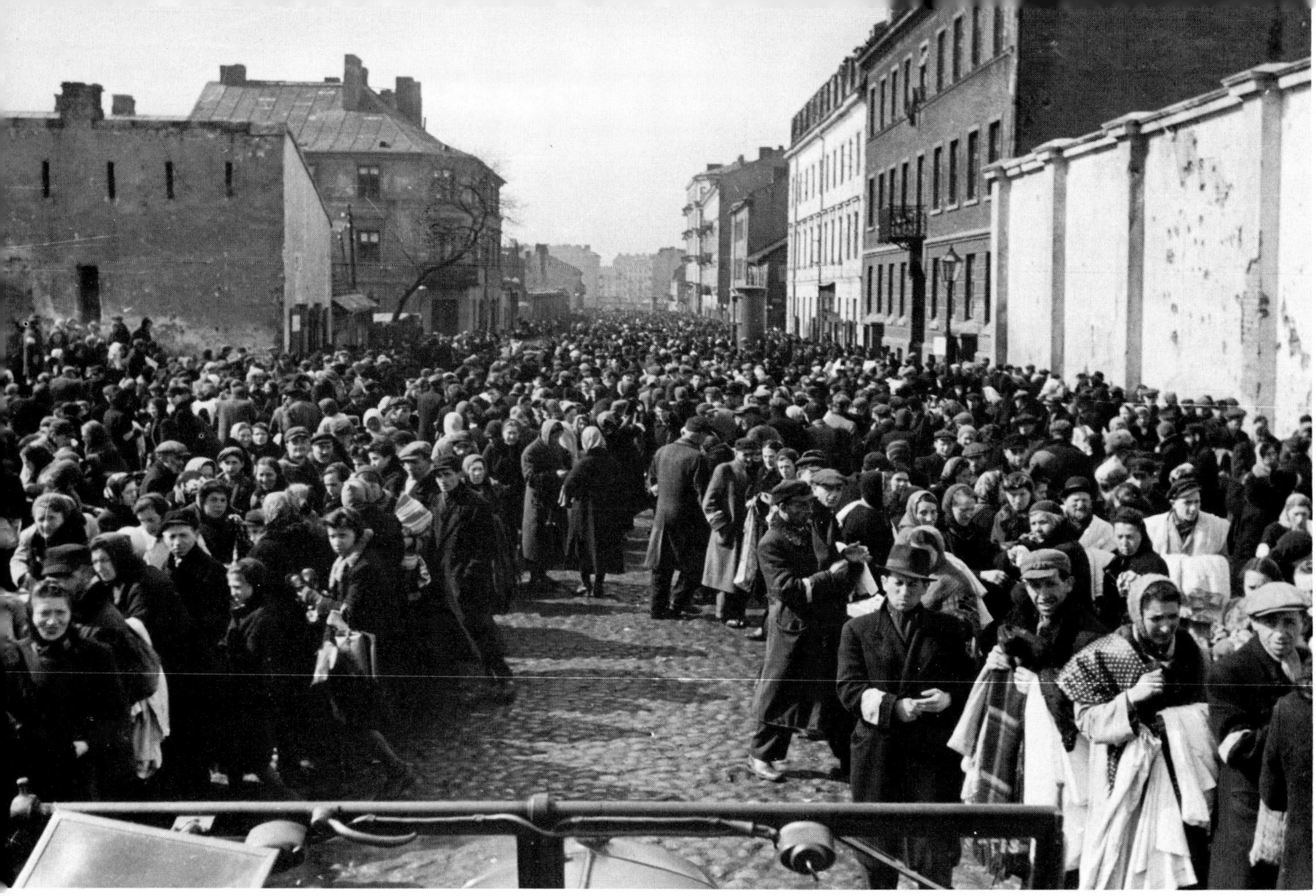

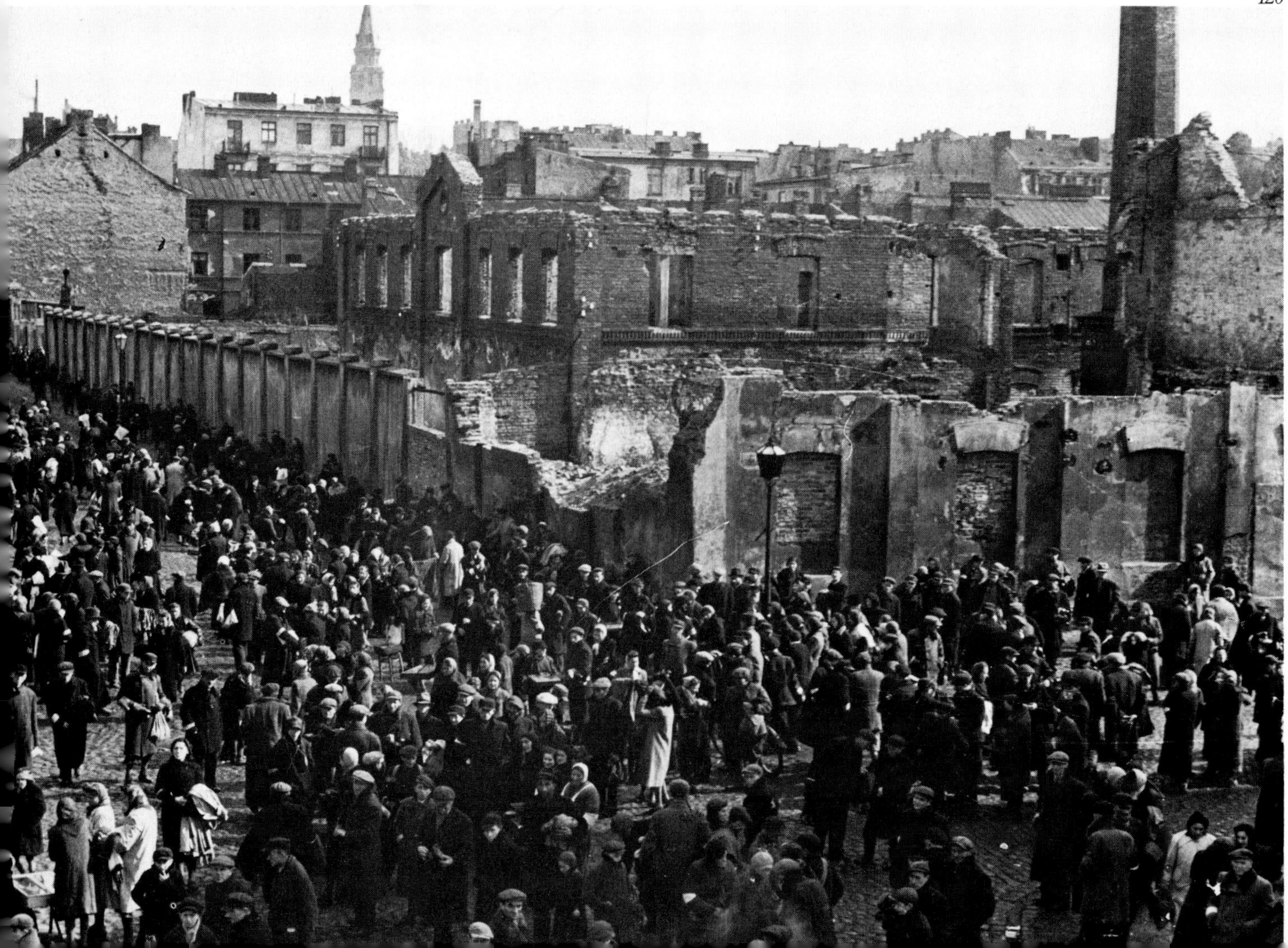

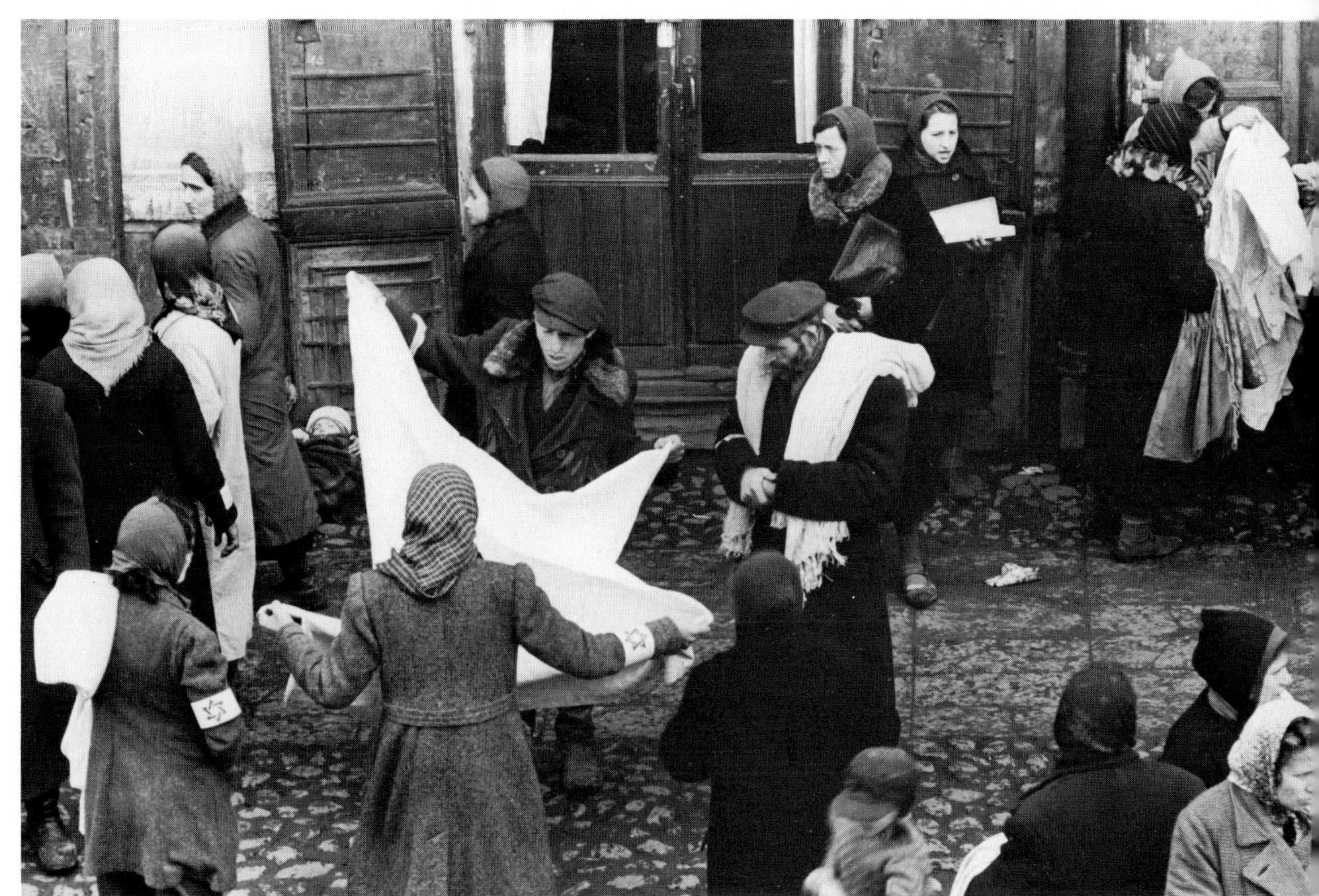

121

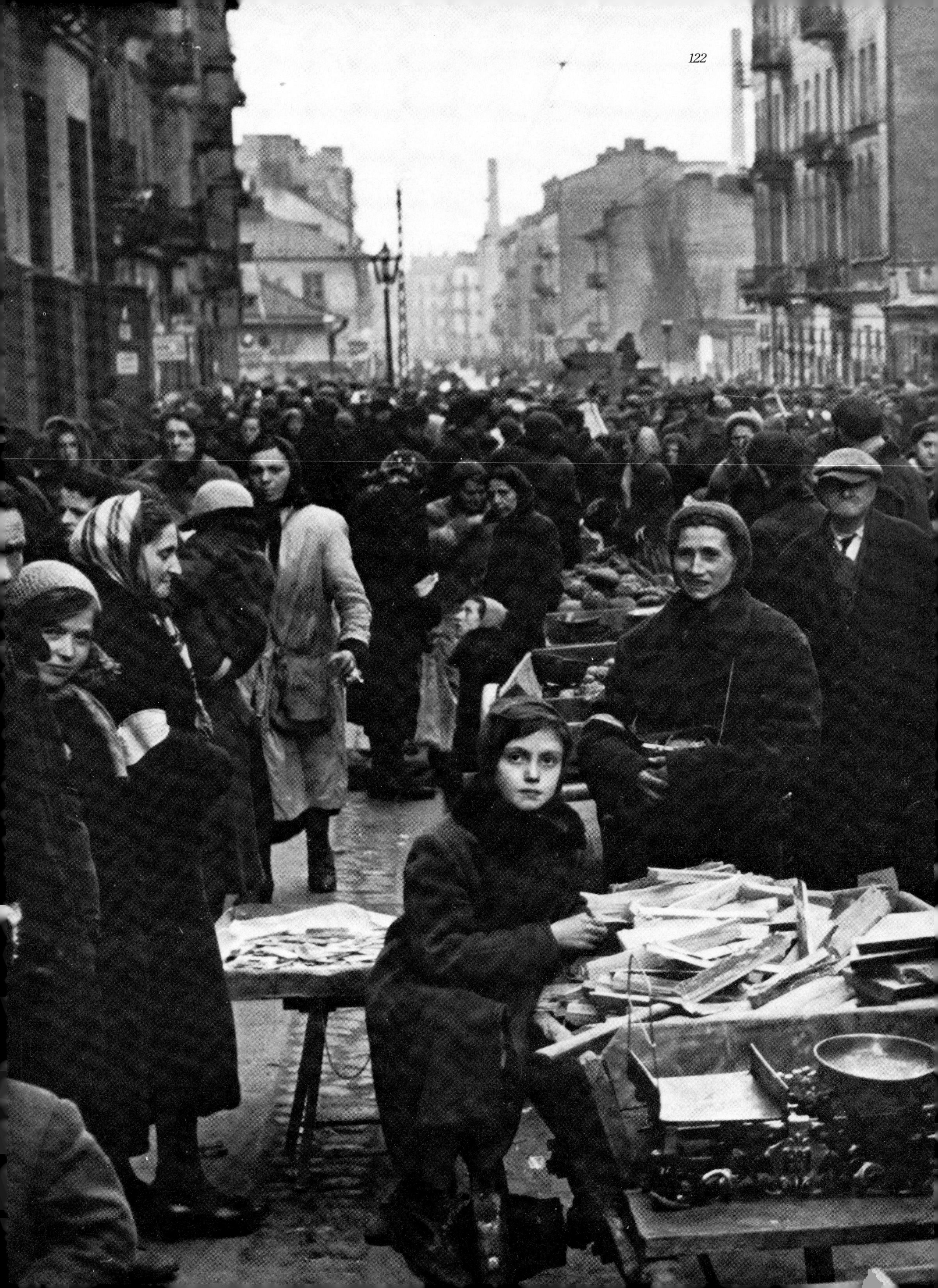

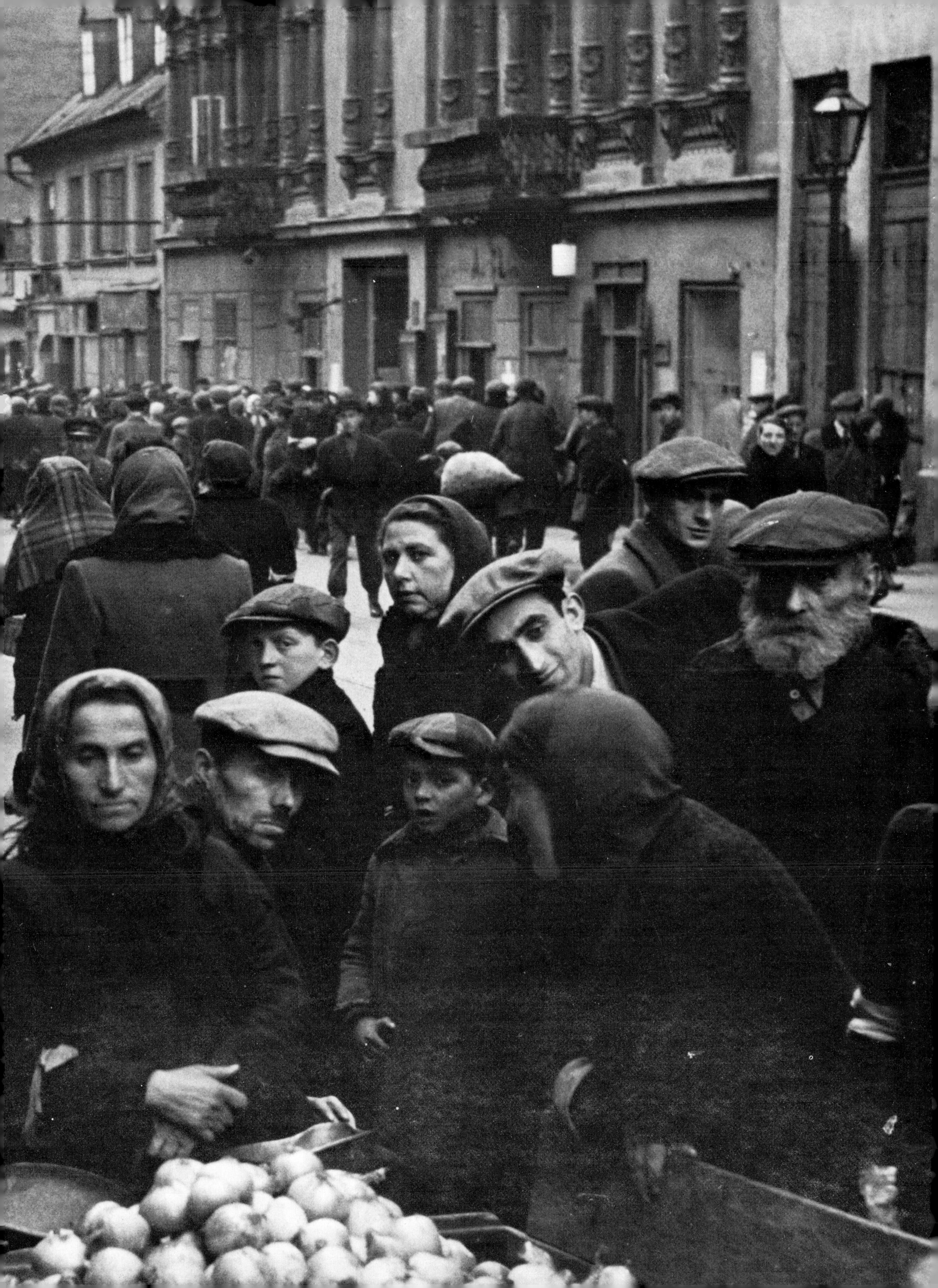

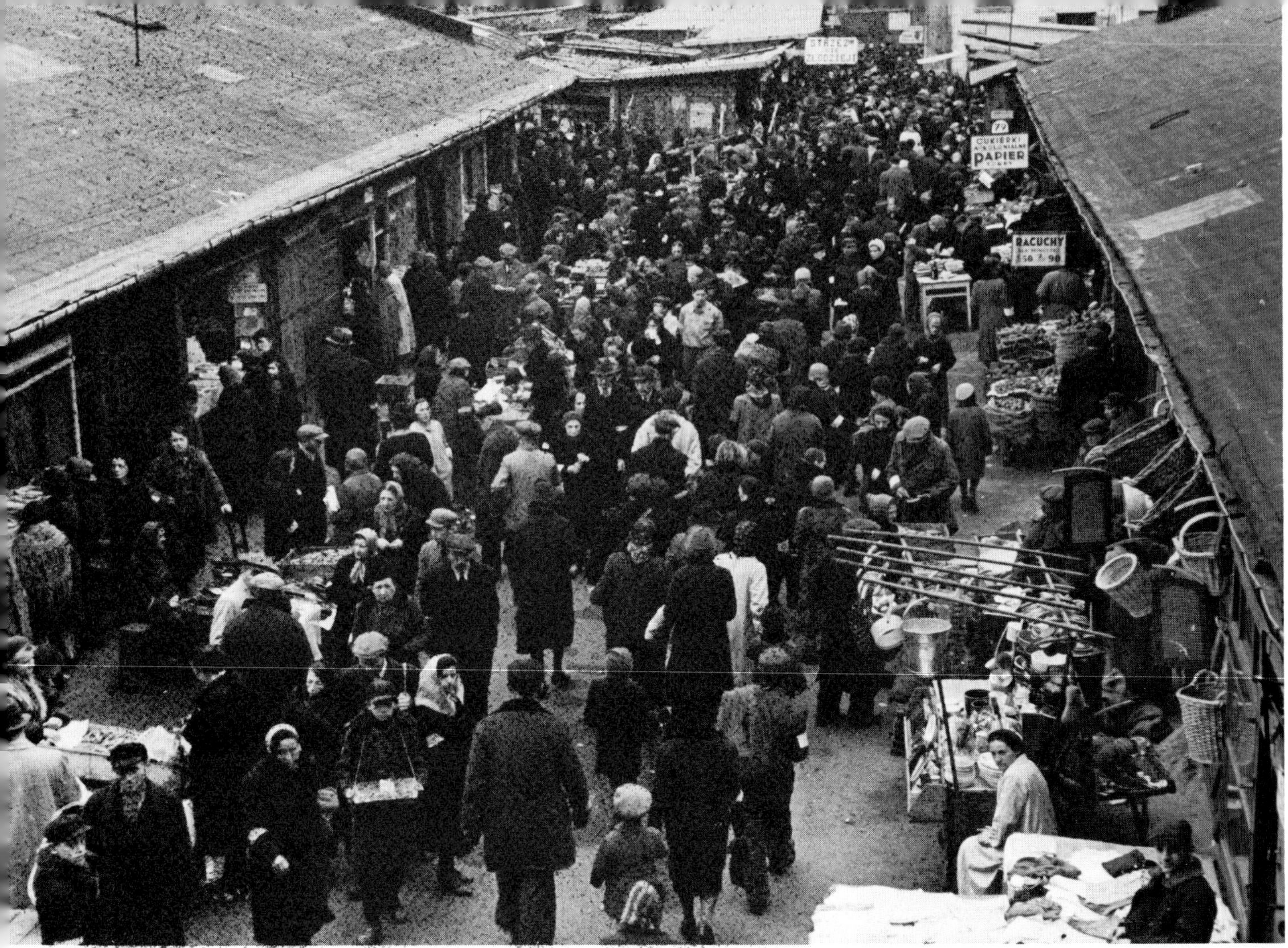

123

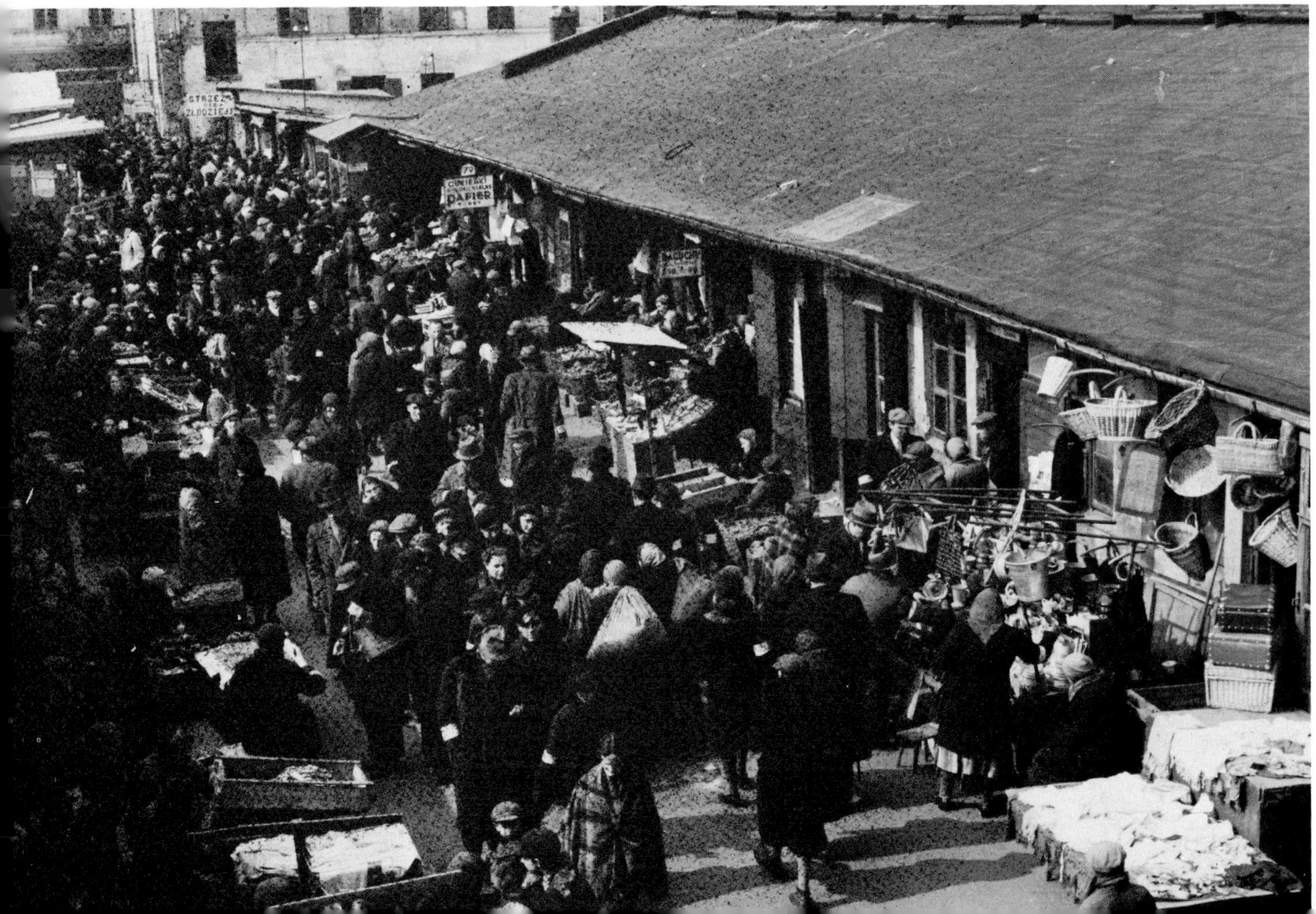

124

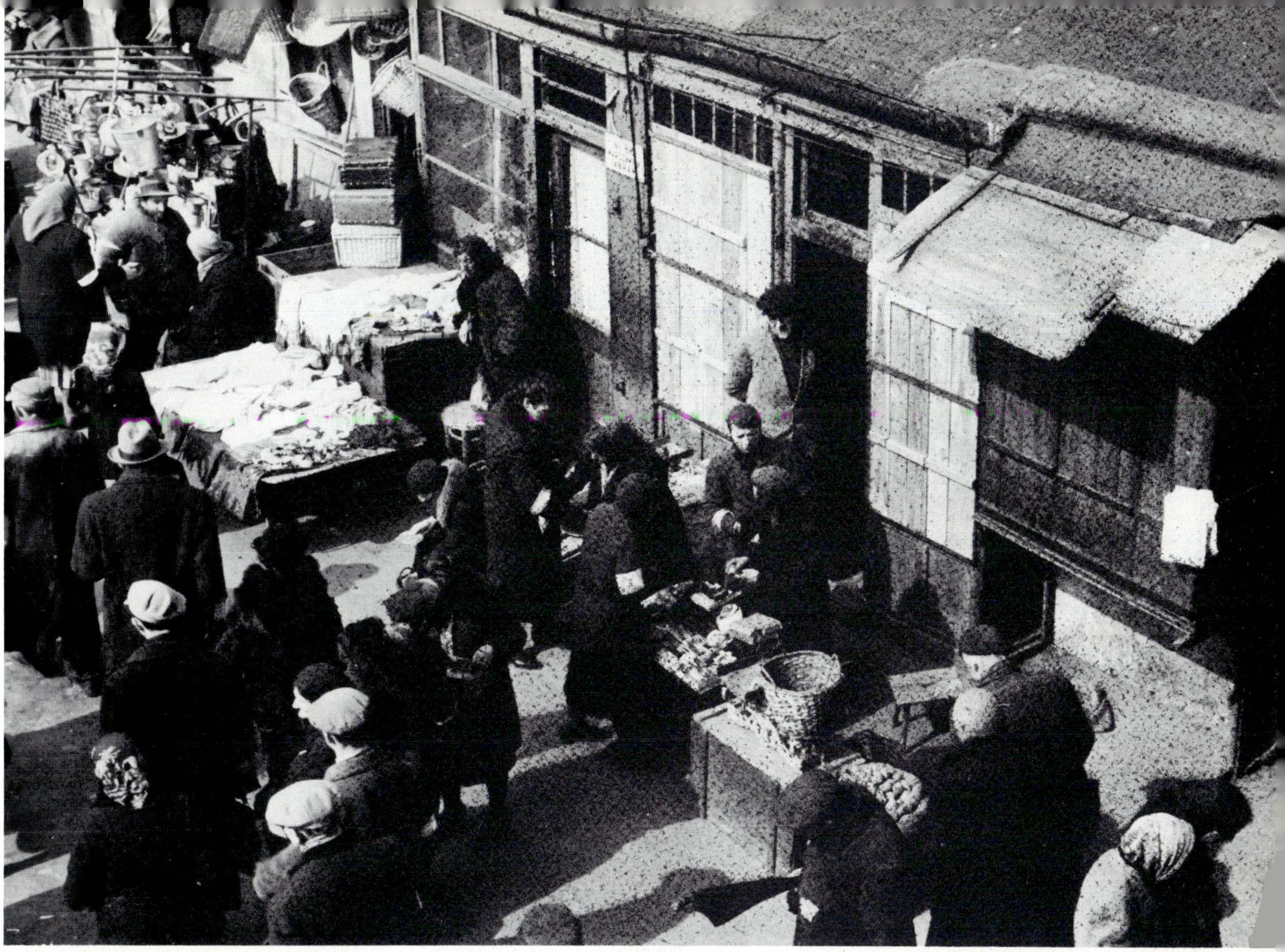

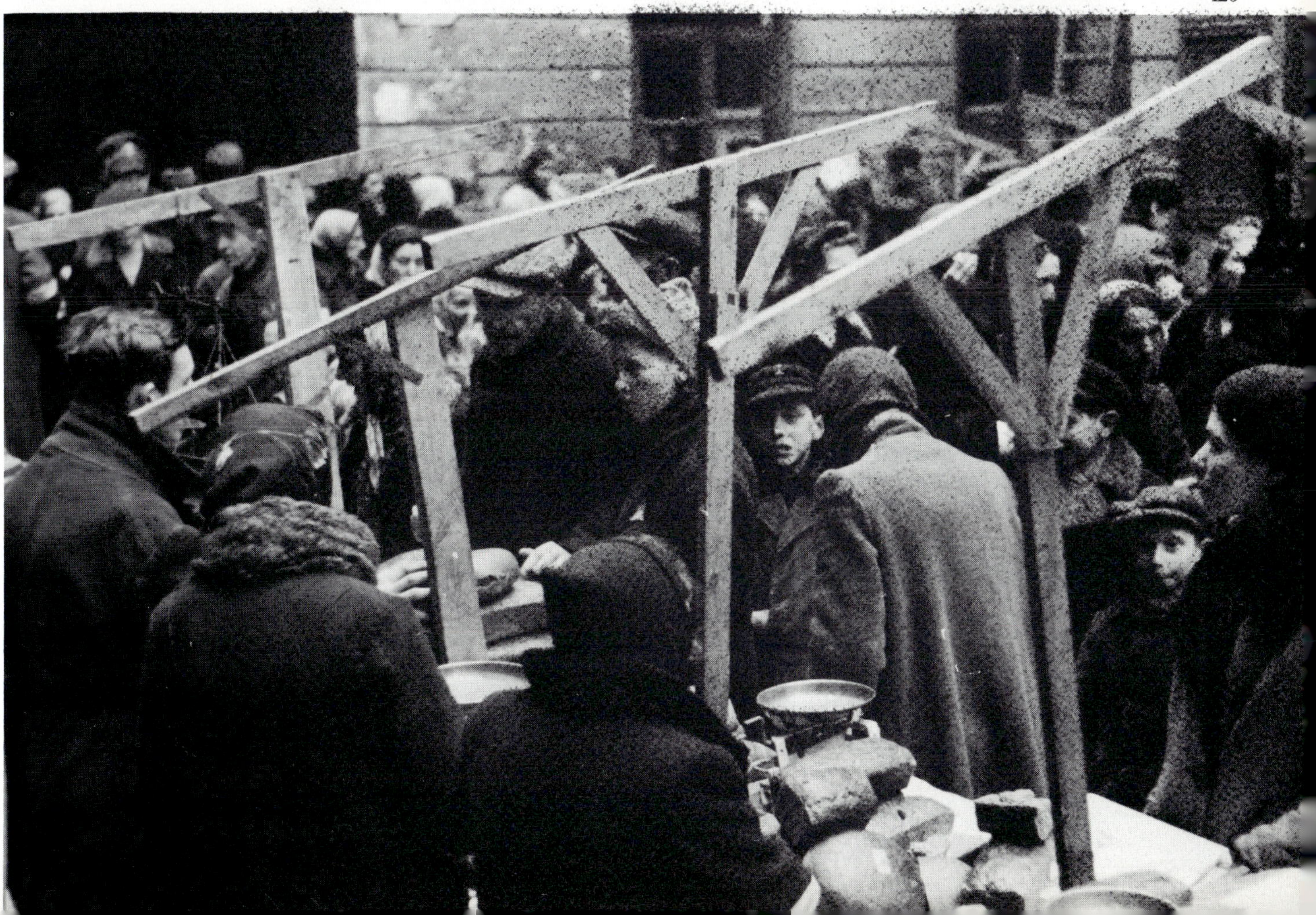

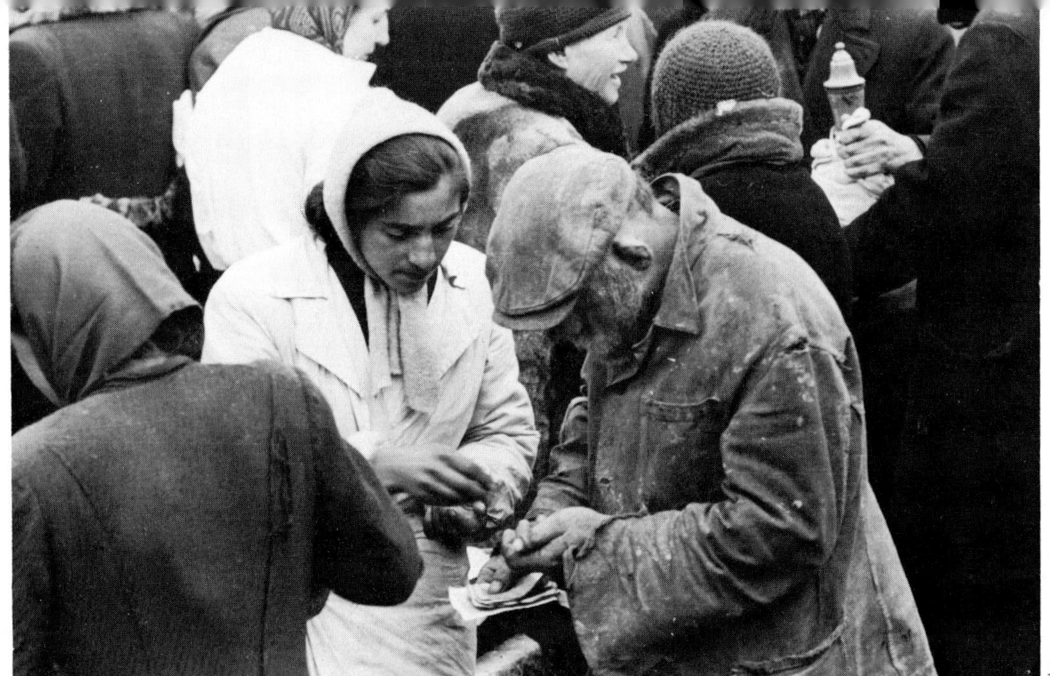

127

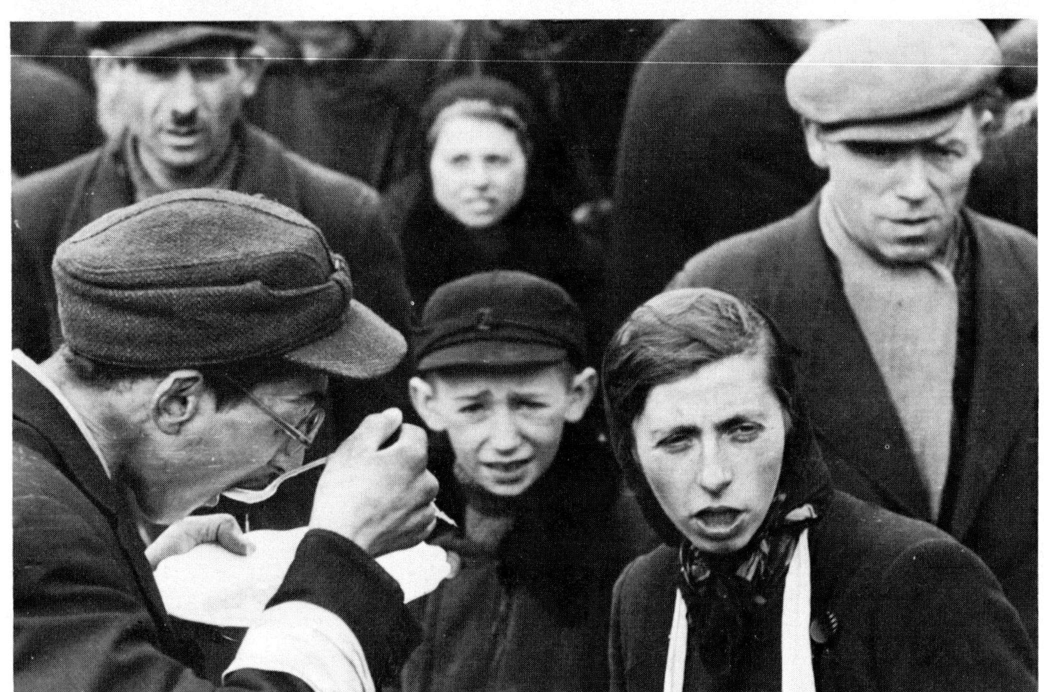

128

129

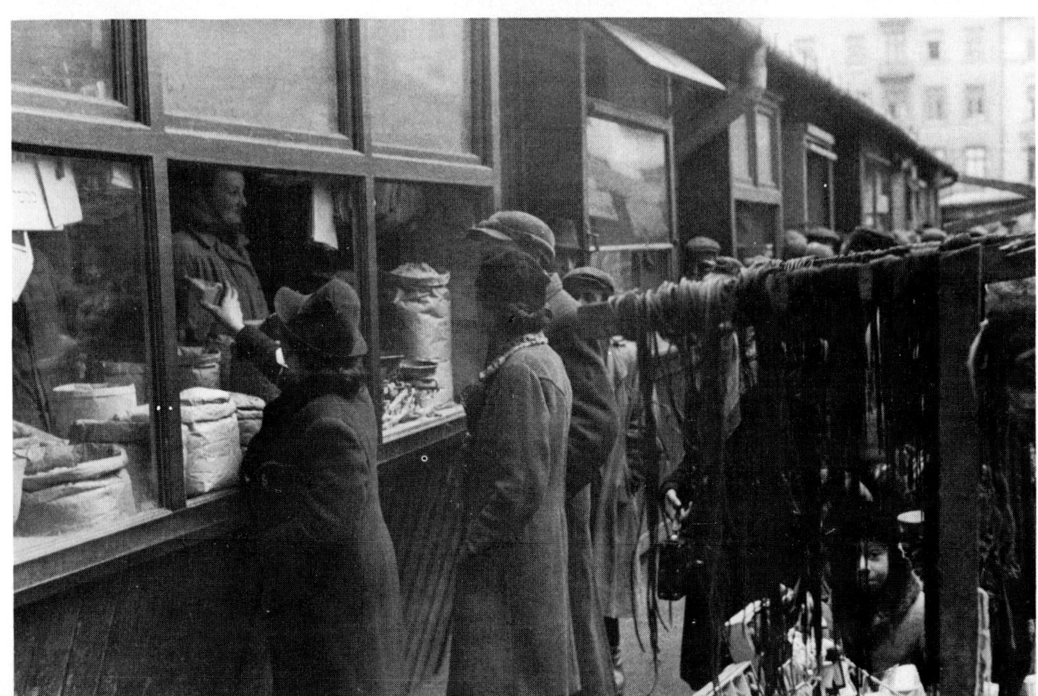

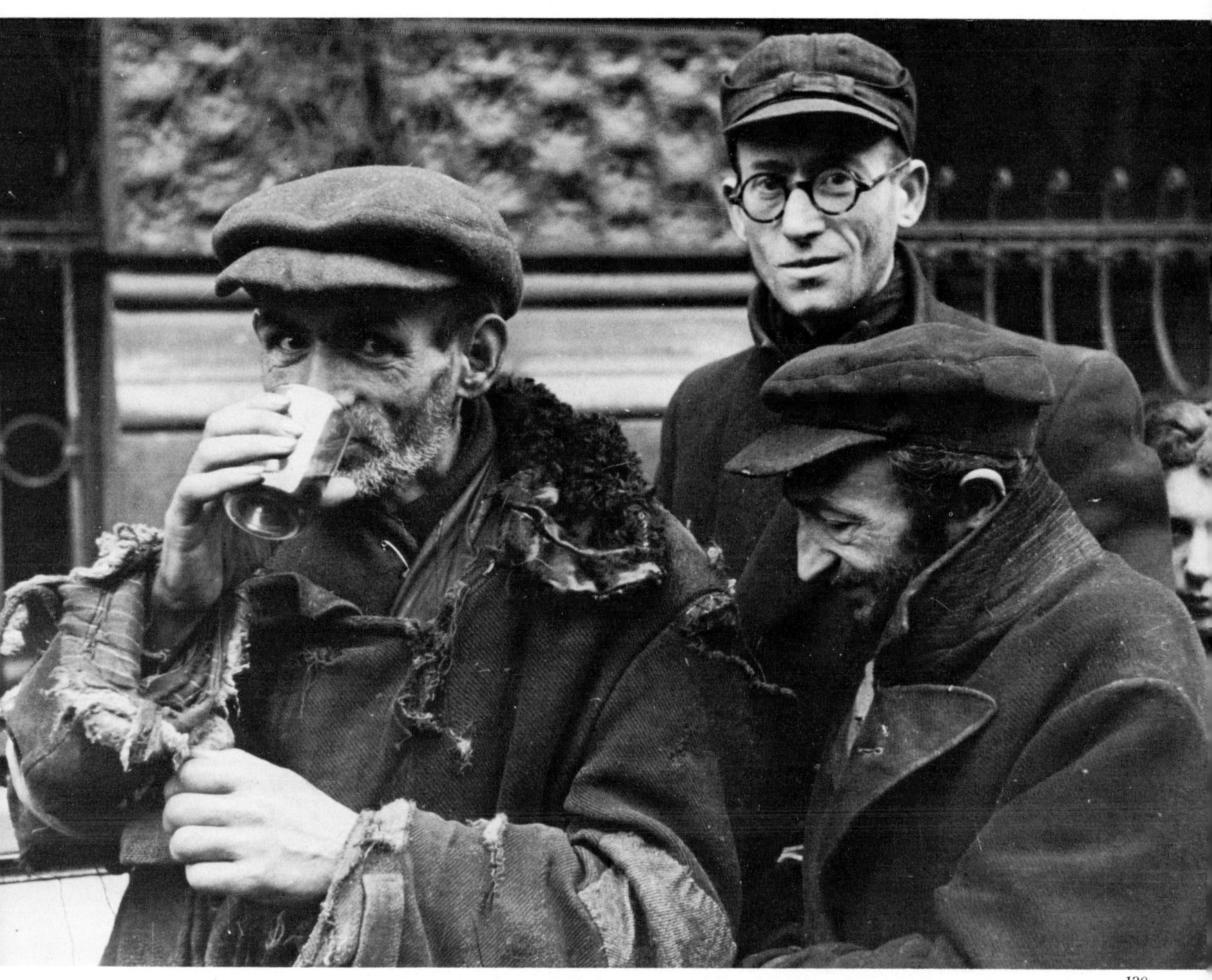

130

BEGGARS
(Nos. 131–139)

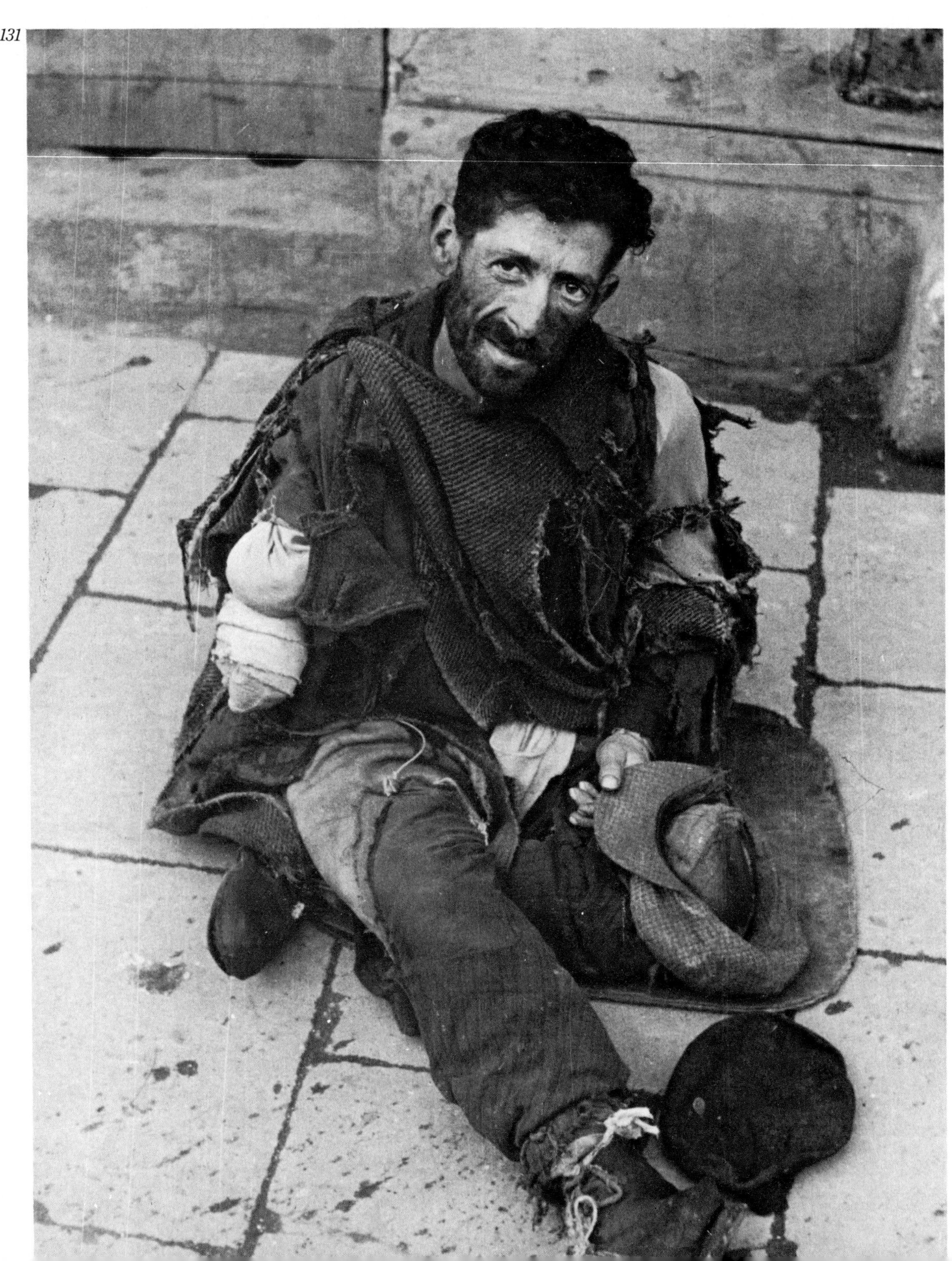

131

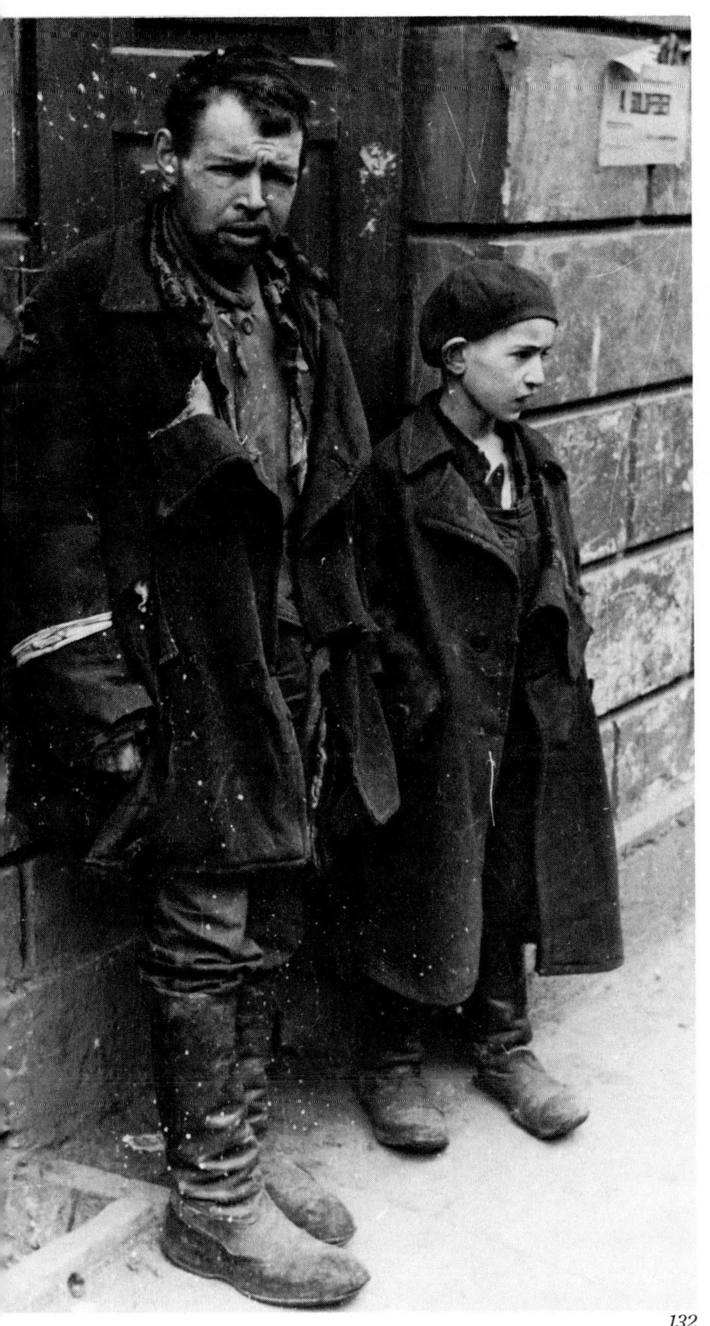

132

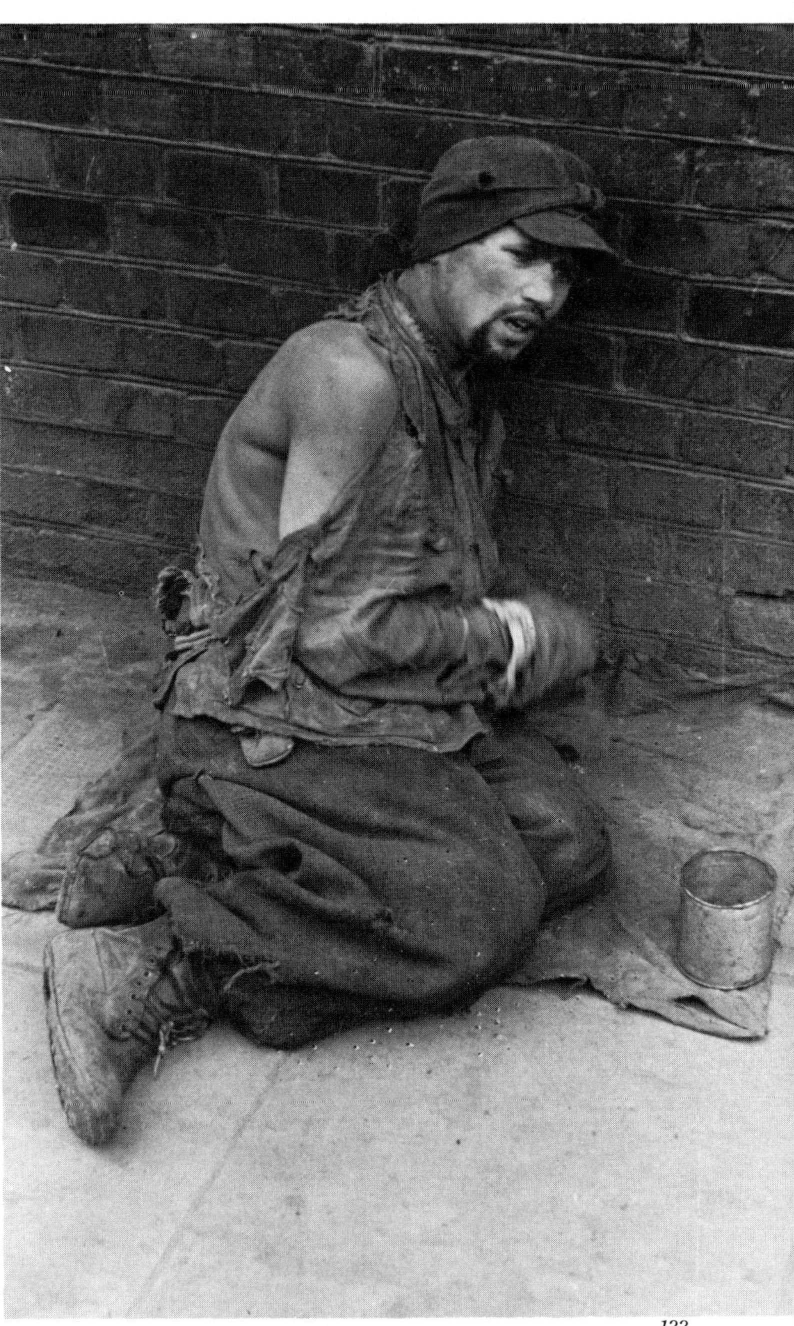

133

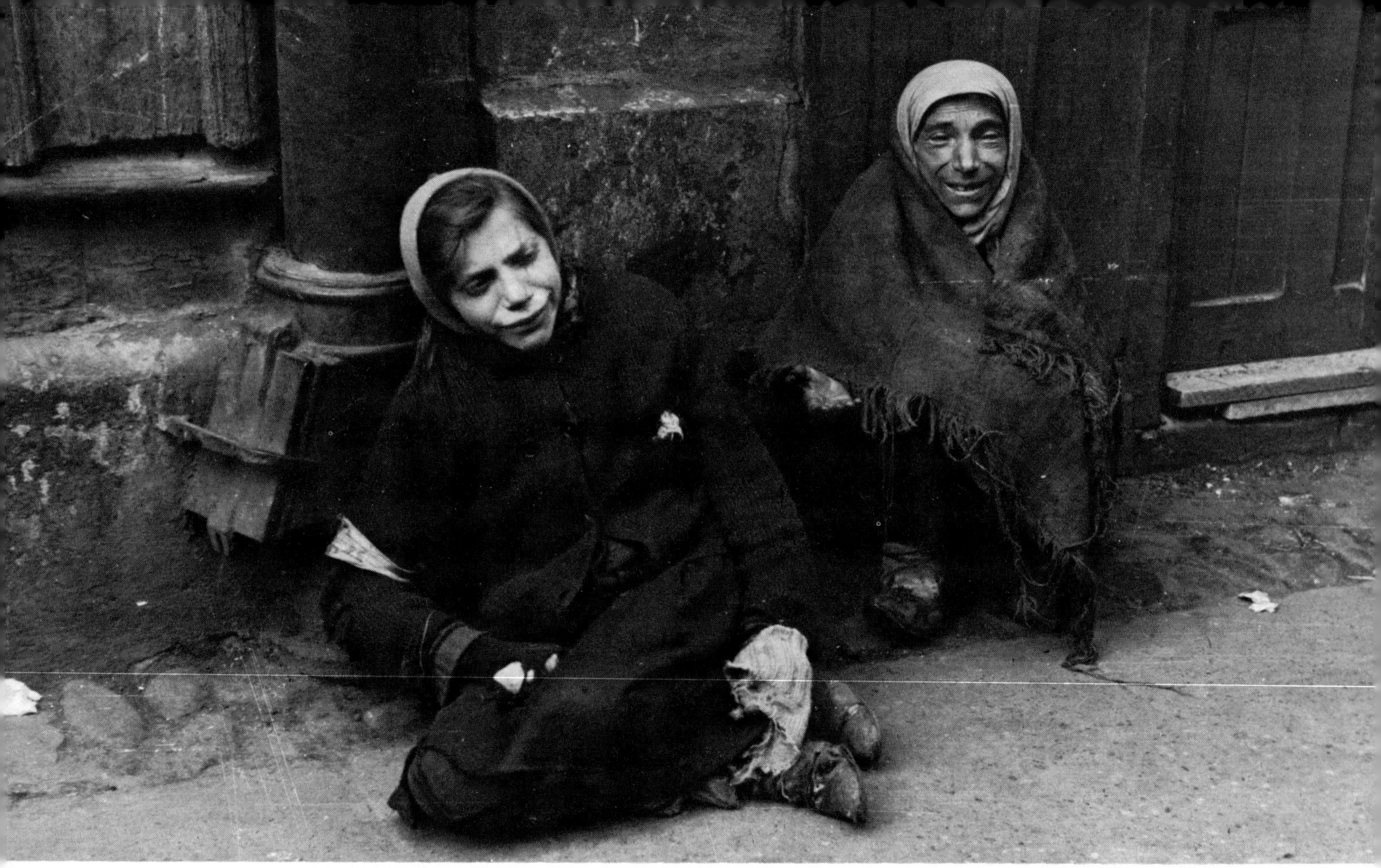

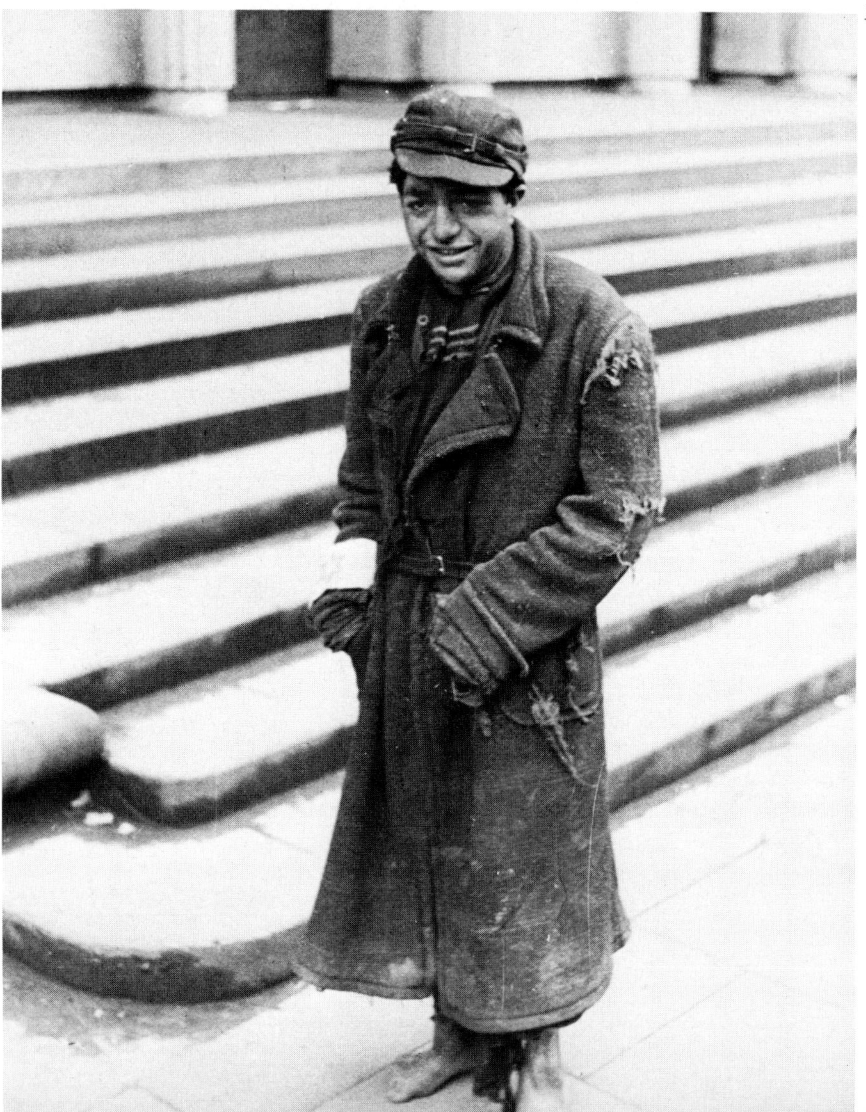

134

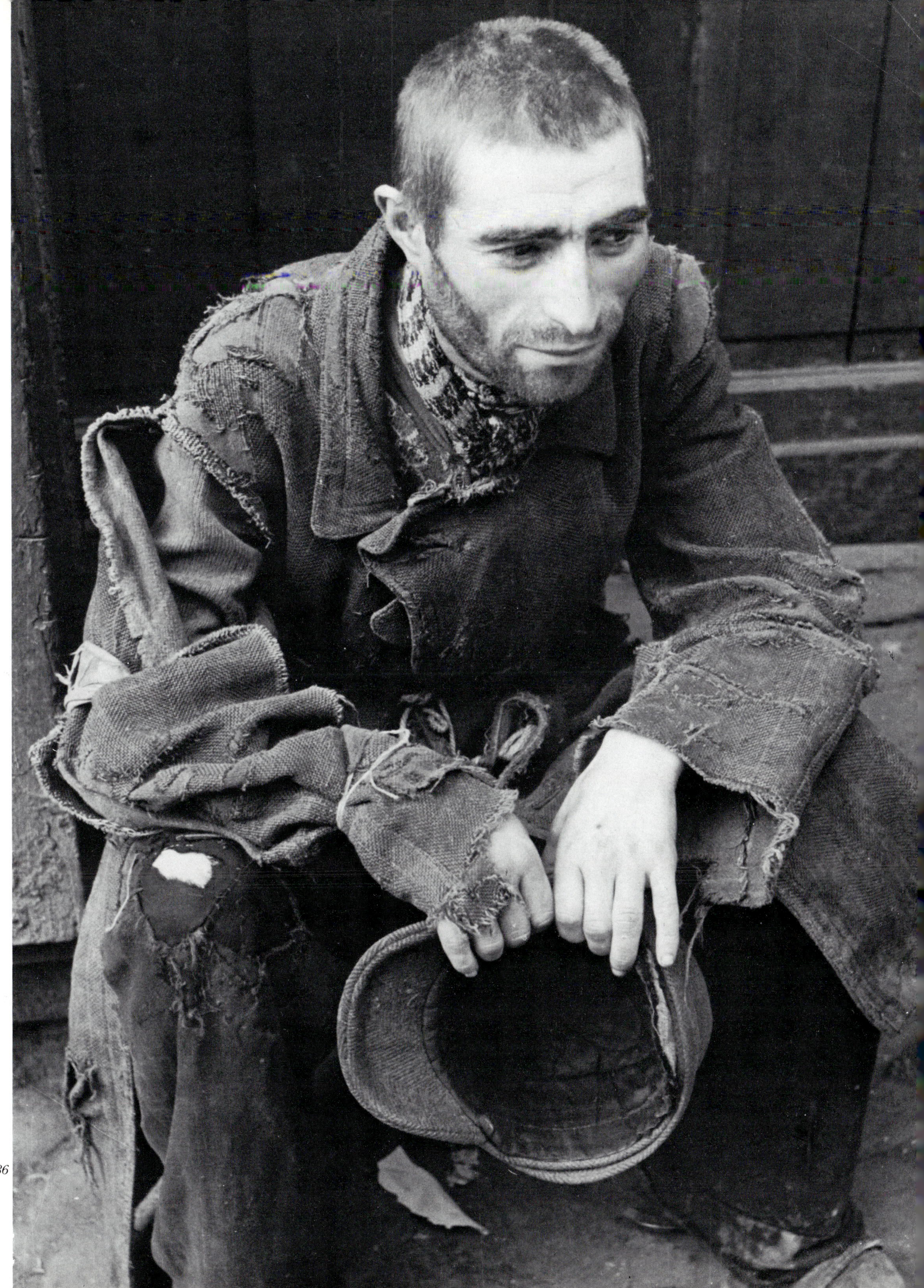

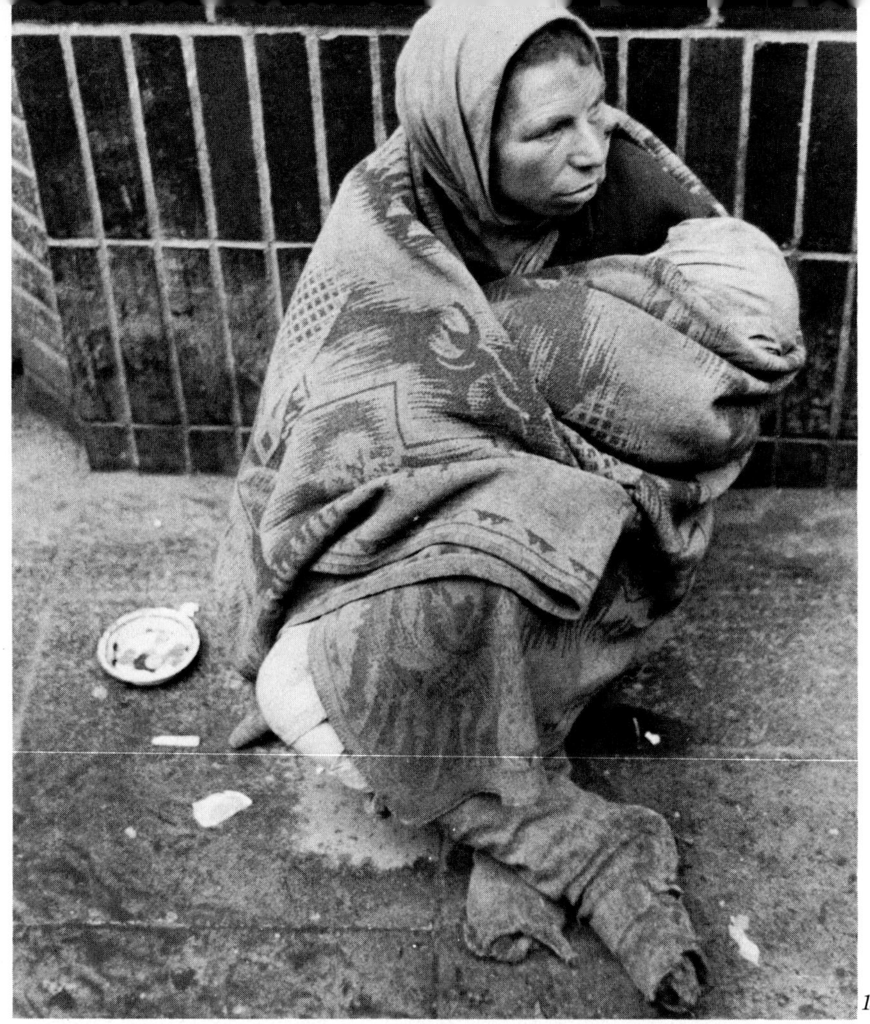

137

138

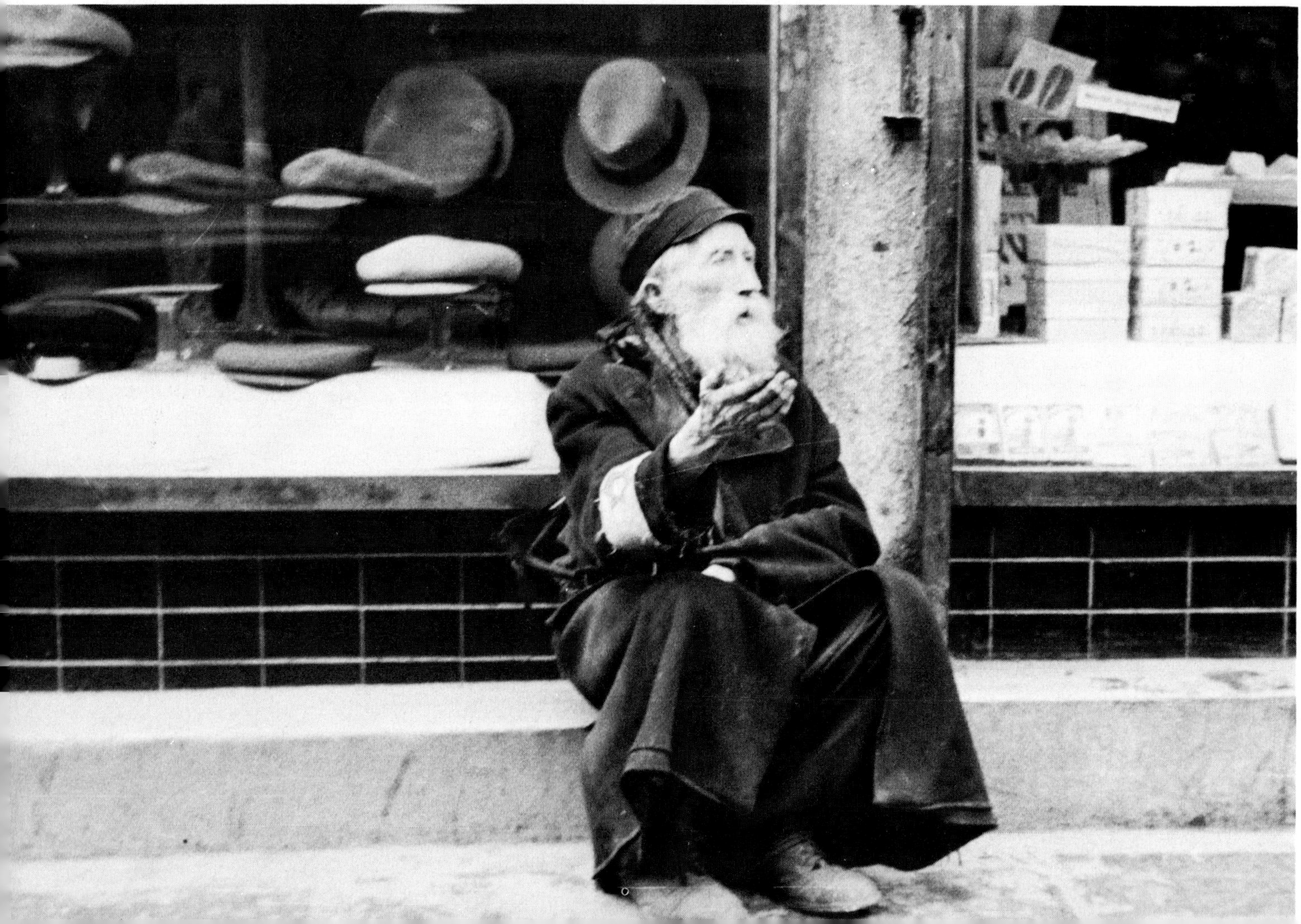

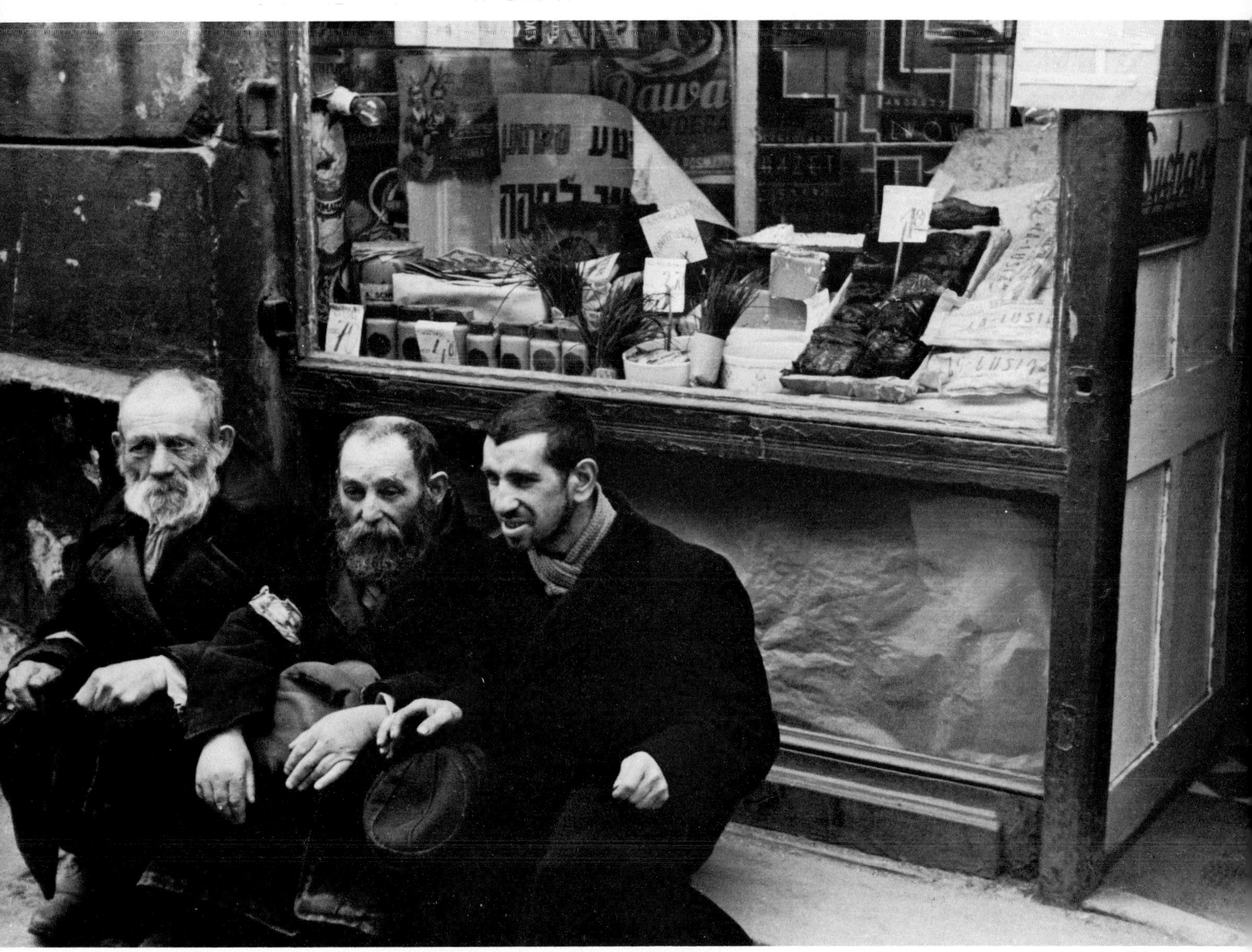

139

CHILDREN
(Nos. 140–151)

140

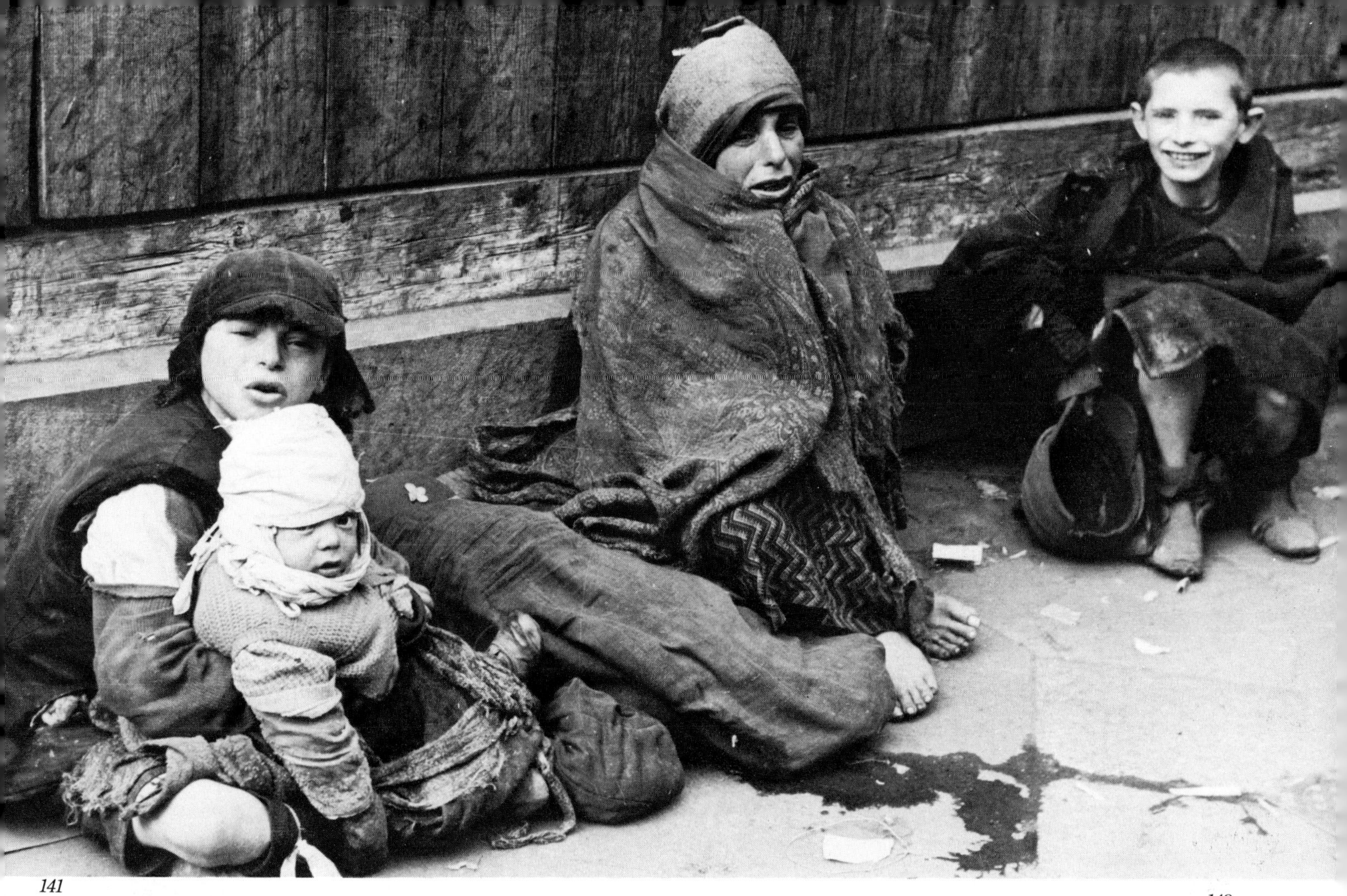

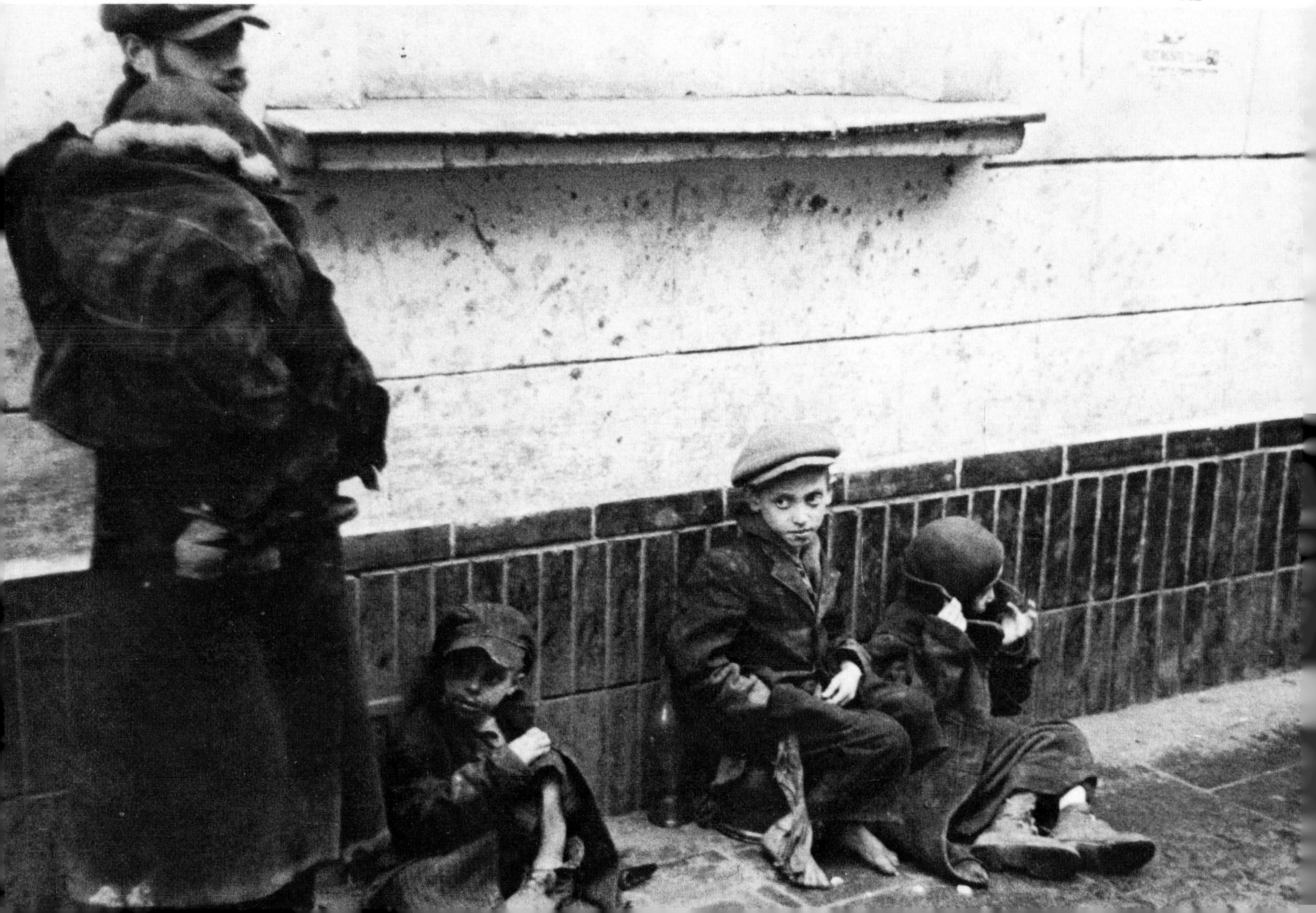

KAPELUSZ
ODSWIEŻEN
DAMSK
PRASOWANIA FASON
PRACOWNIA MIEJ
KAWIARNIA BAR
·PALLADIUM·
na porankach i wieczorem
WŁADYSŁAW
LIN
MAKSA MANDELBAUMA

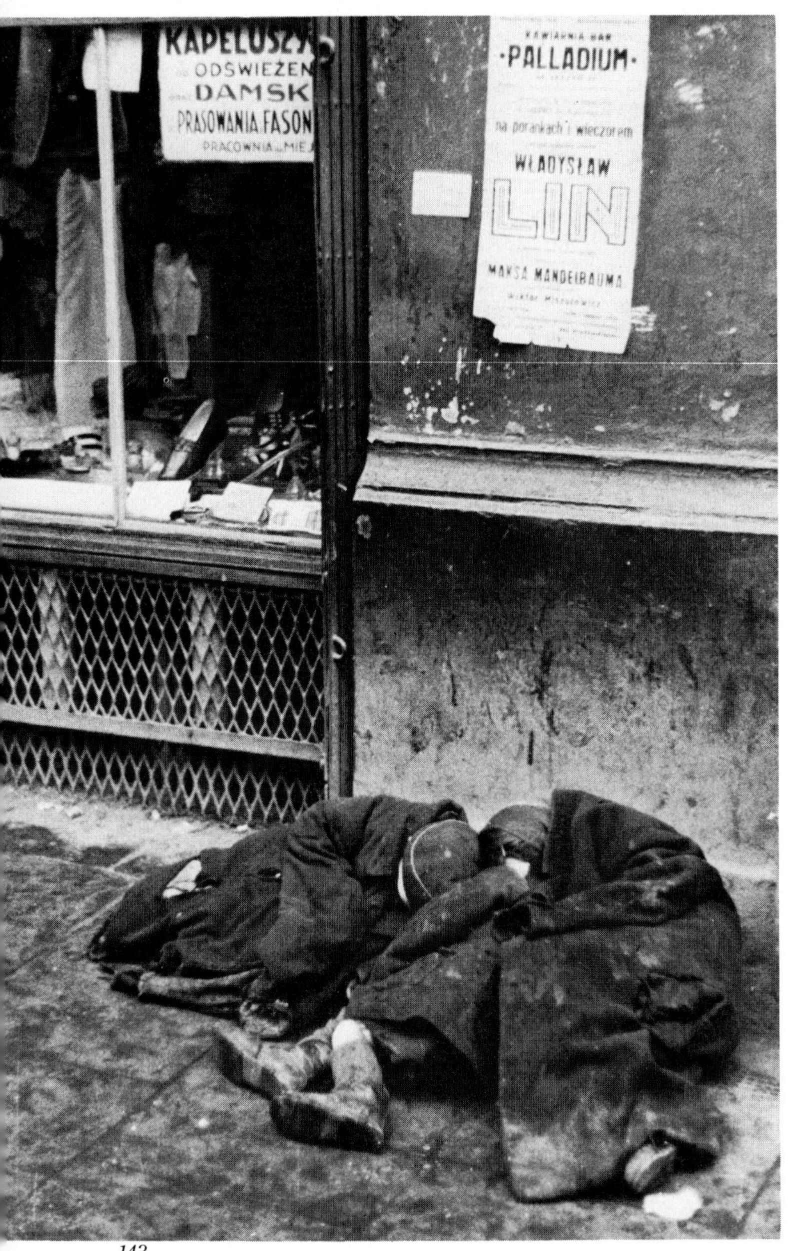

143

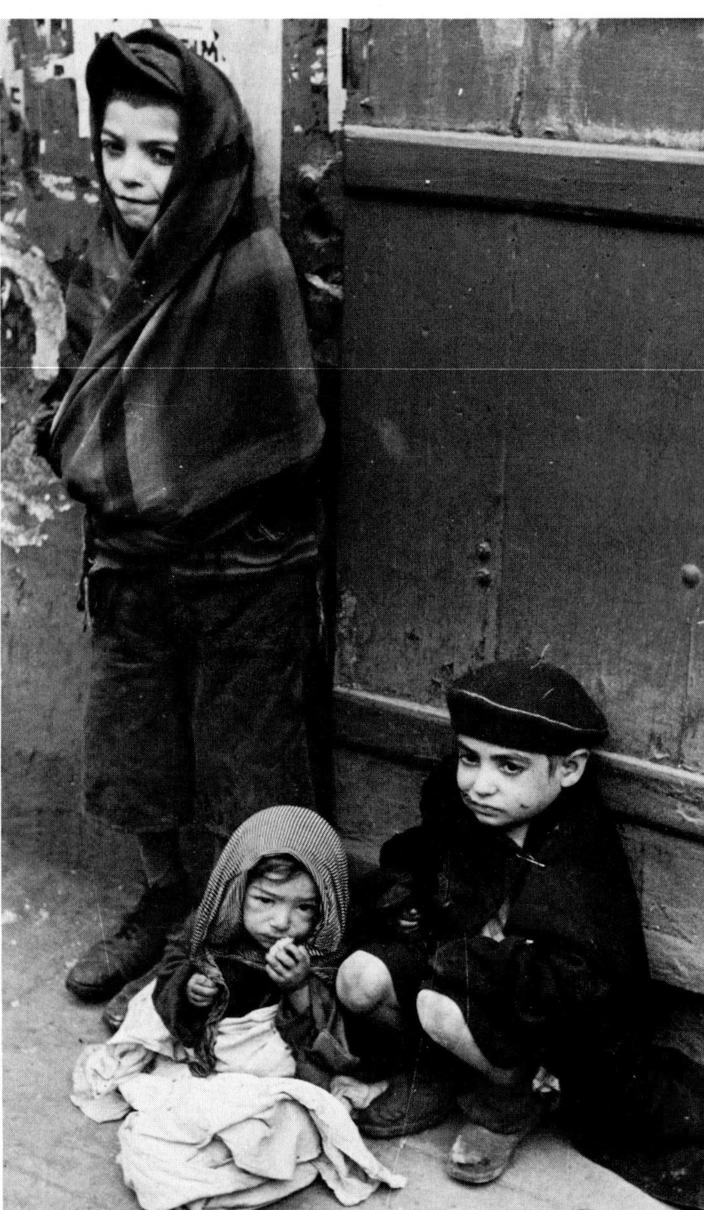

144

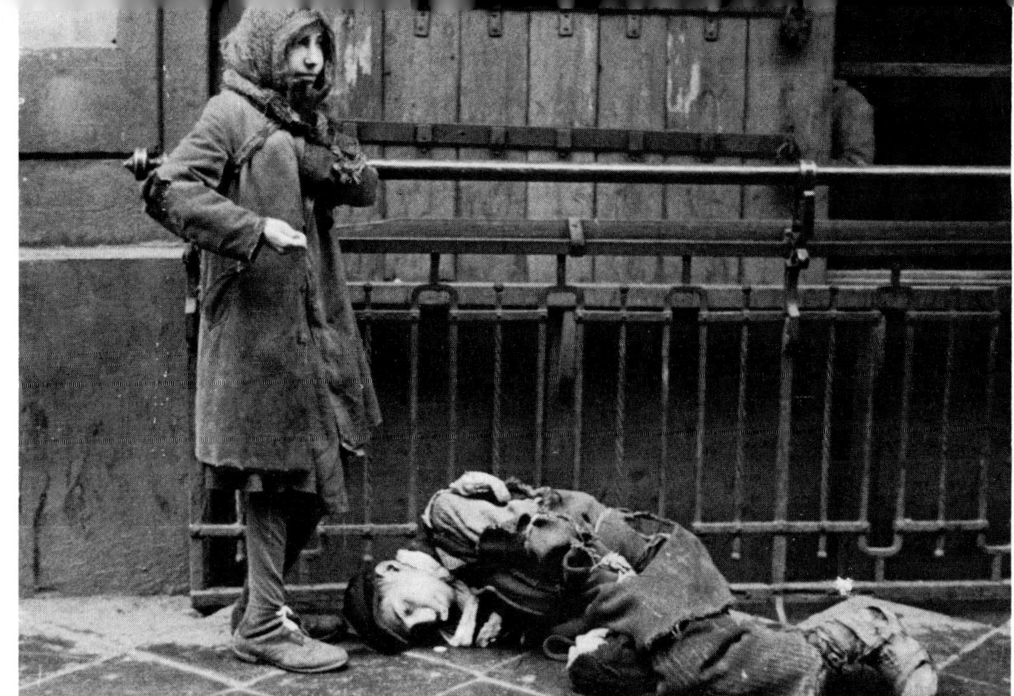

145

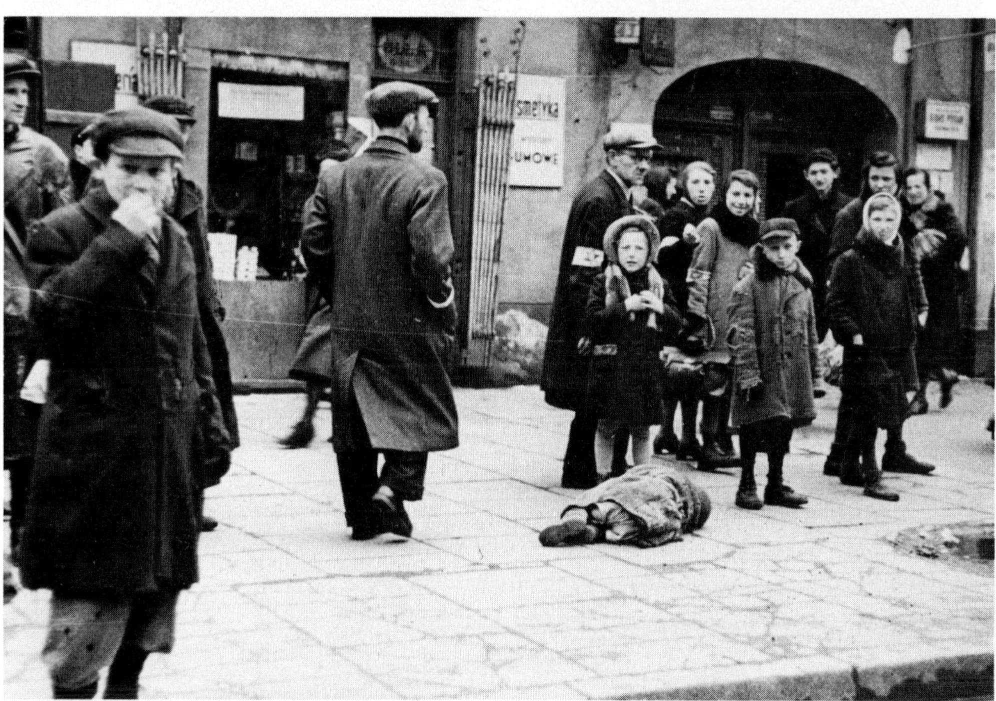

146

147

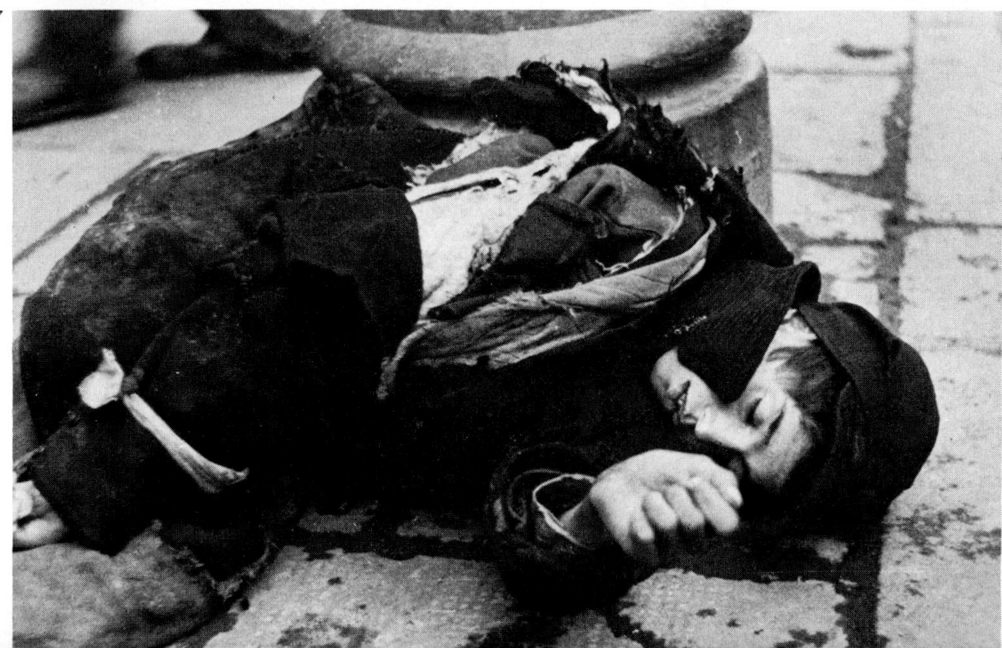

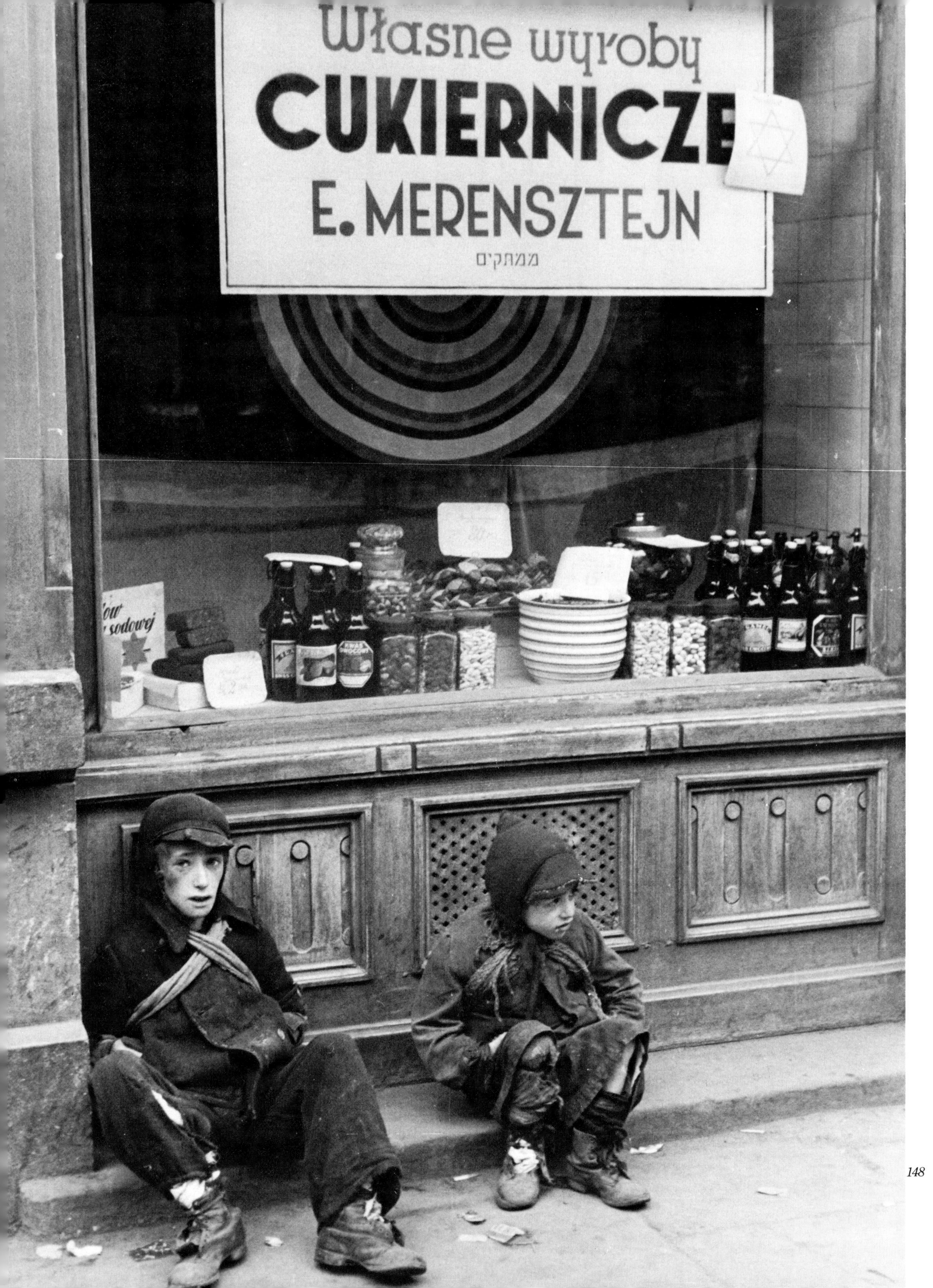

Własne wyroby
CUKIERNICZE
E. MERENSZTEJN
ממתקים

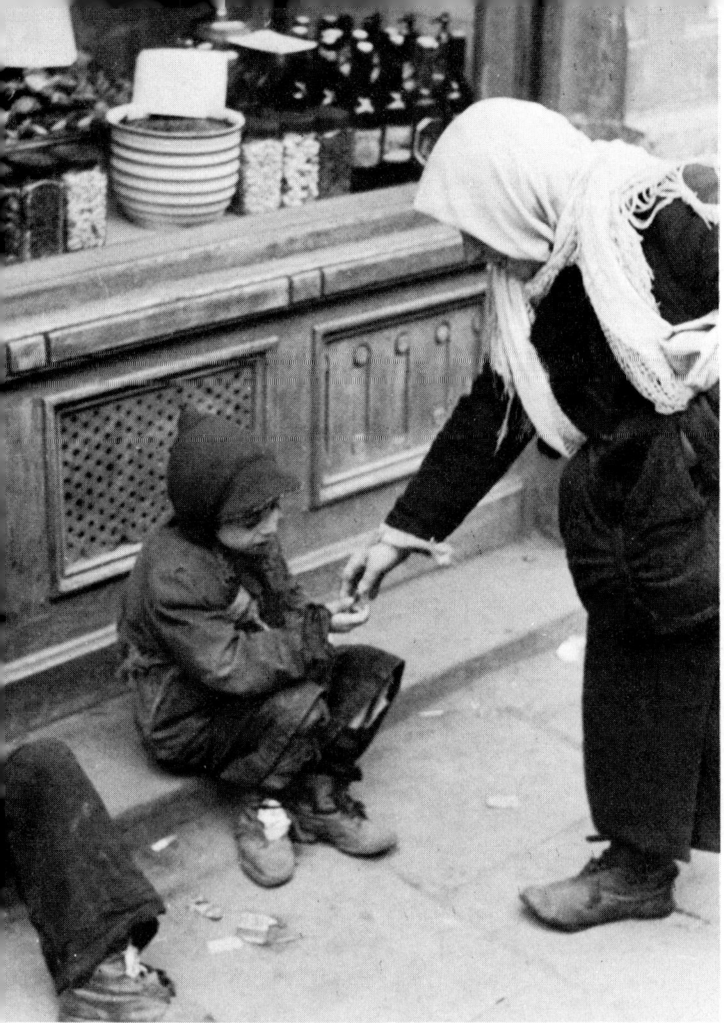

149

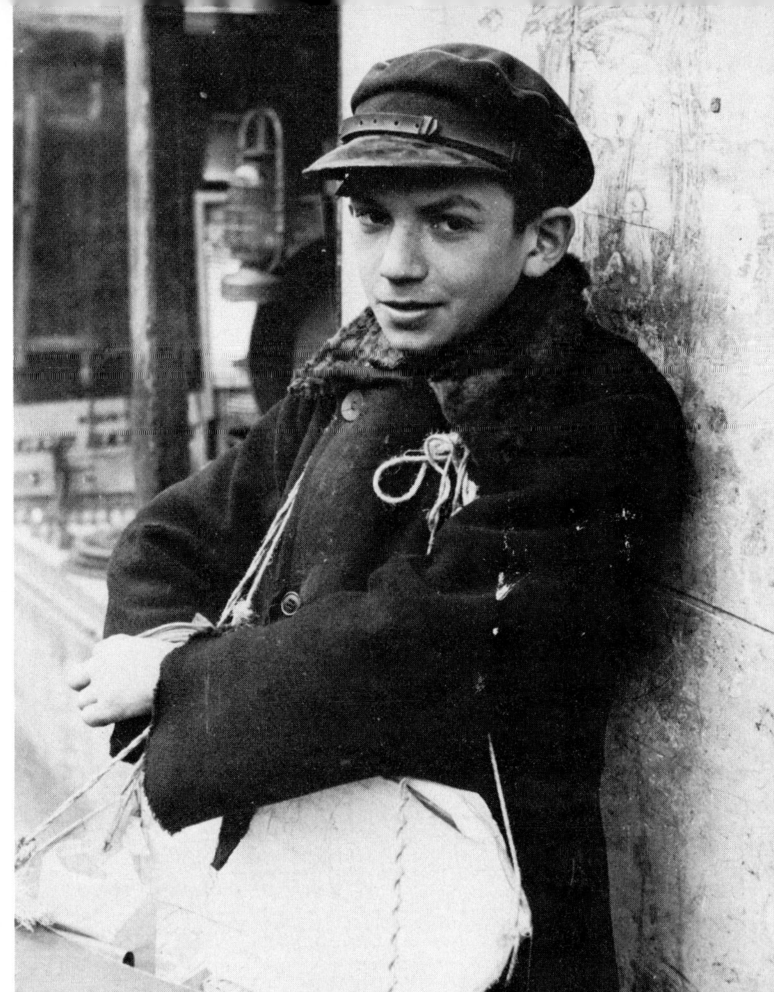

150

151

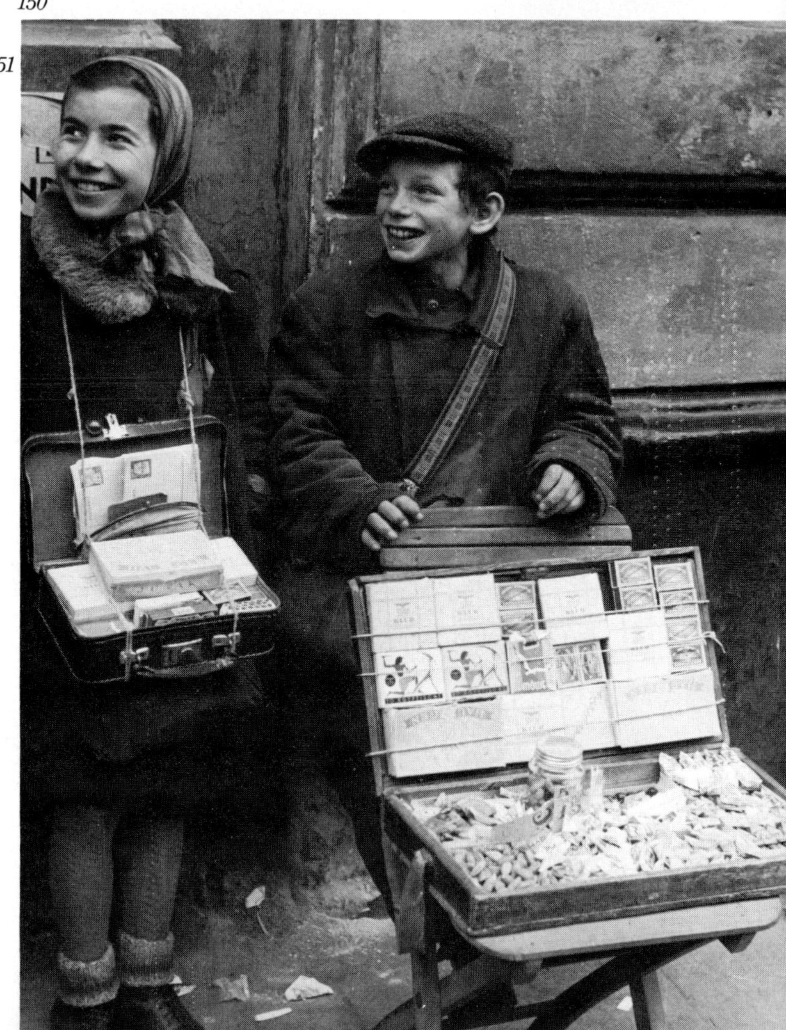

OPPOSITE: *The sign reads: "Homemade confectionery E. Merensztejn."*

PORTRAITS
(Nos. 152–159)

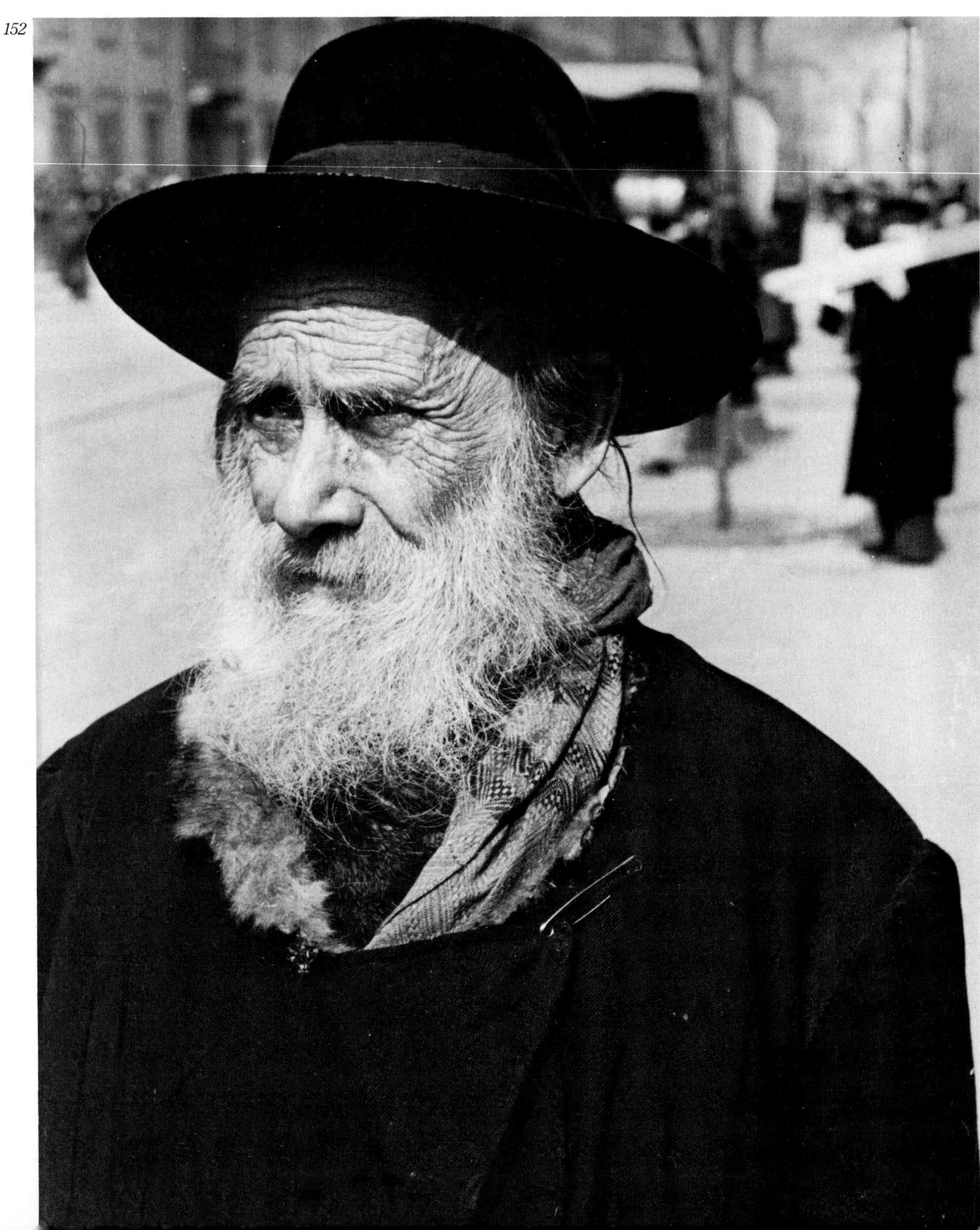

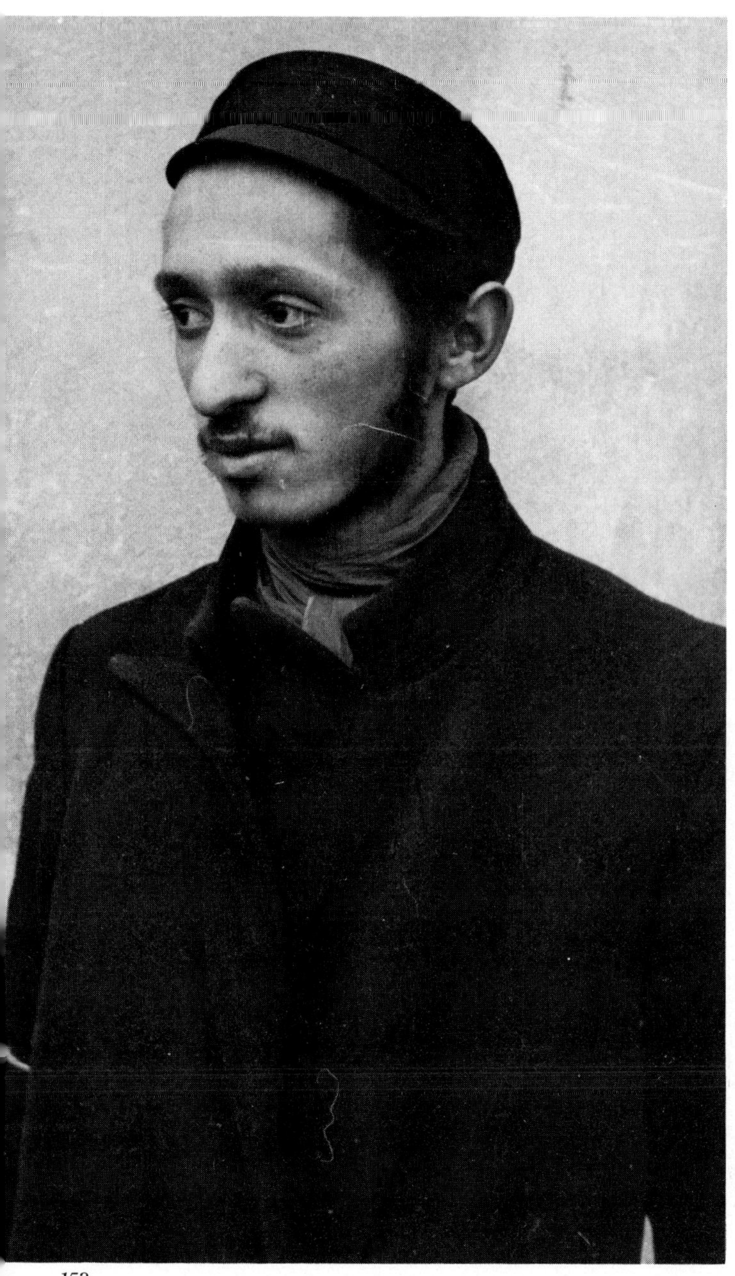

153

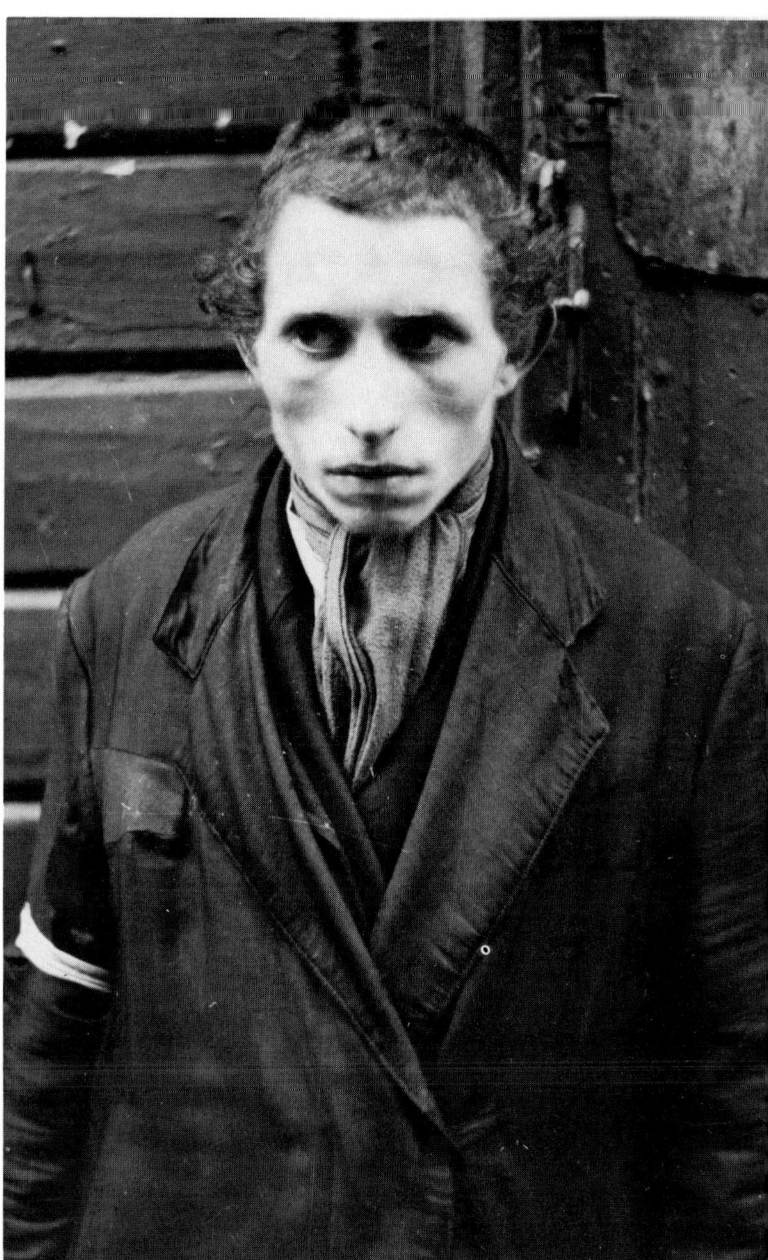

154

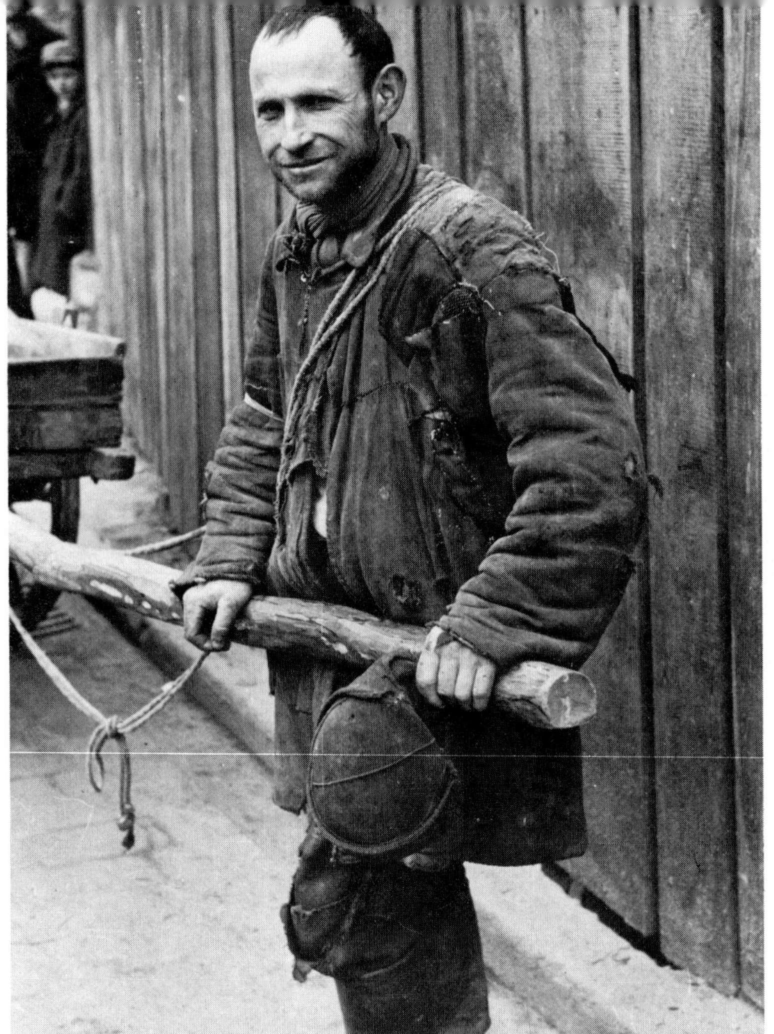

155

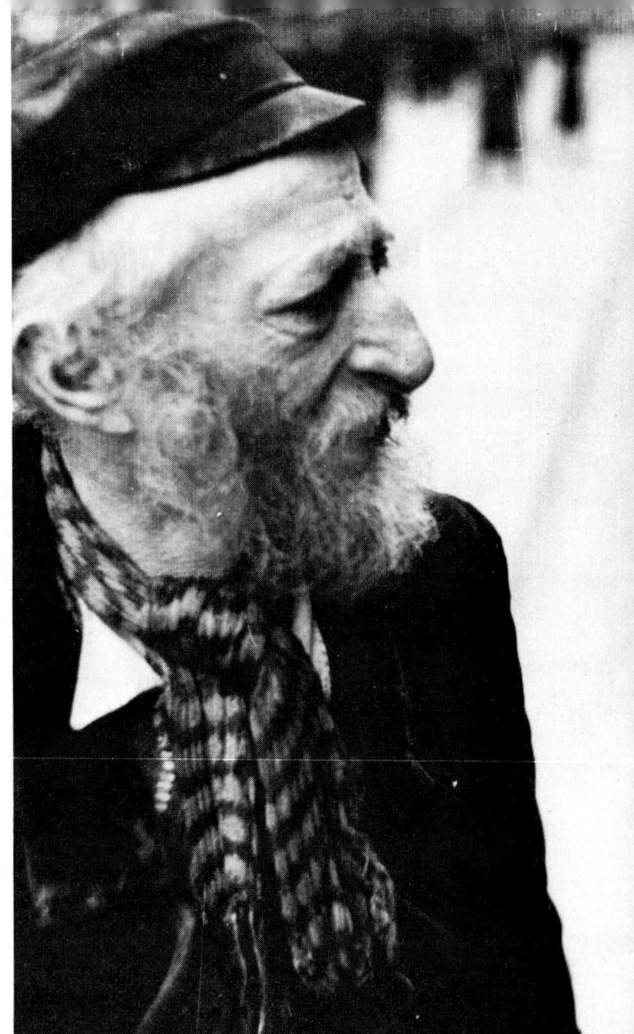

156

157

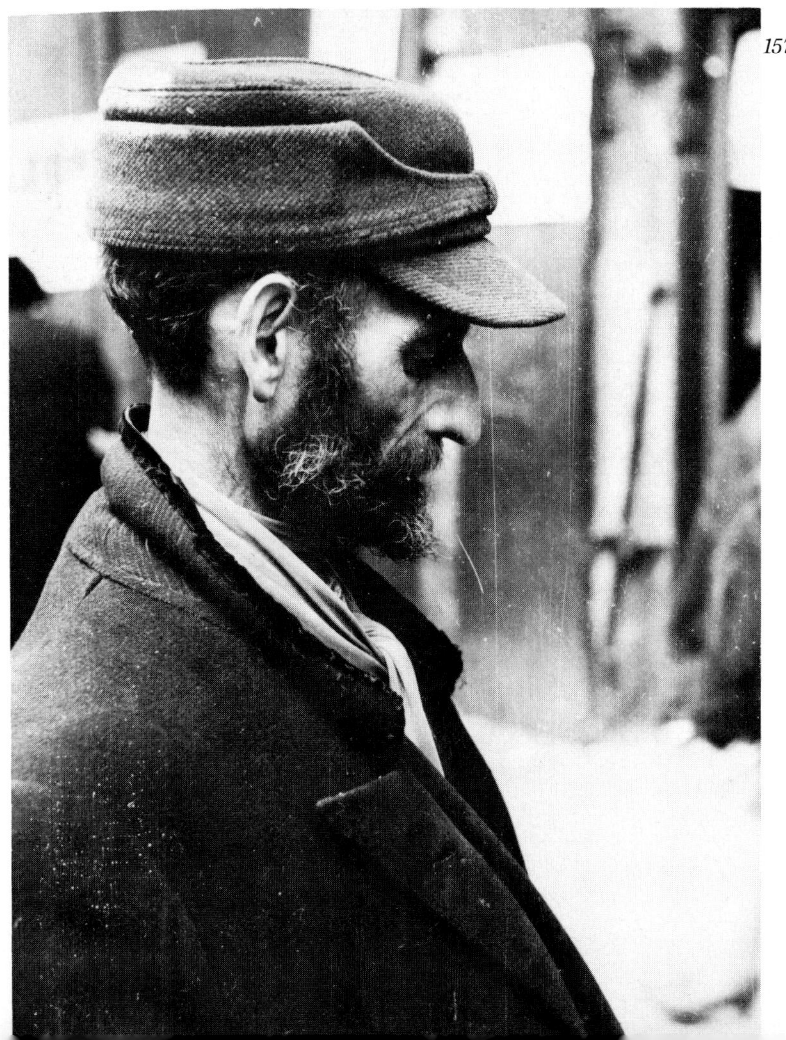

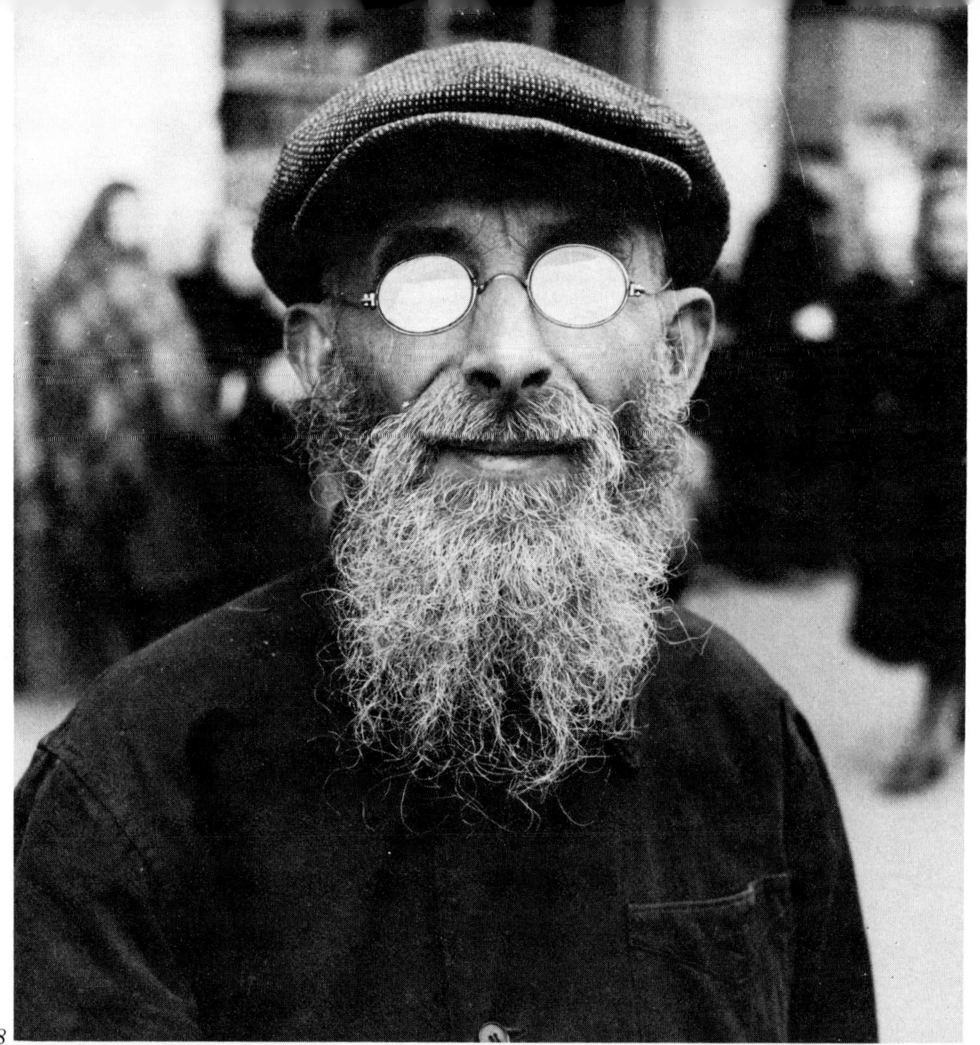

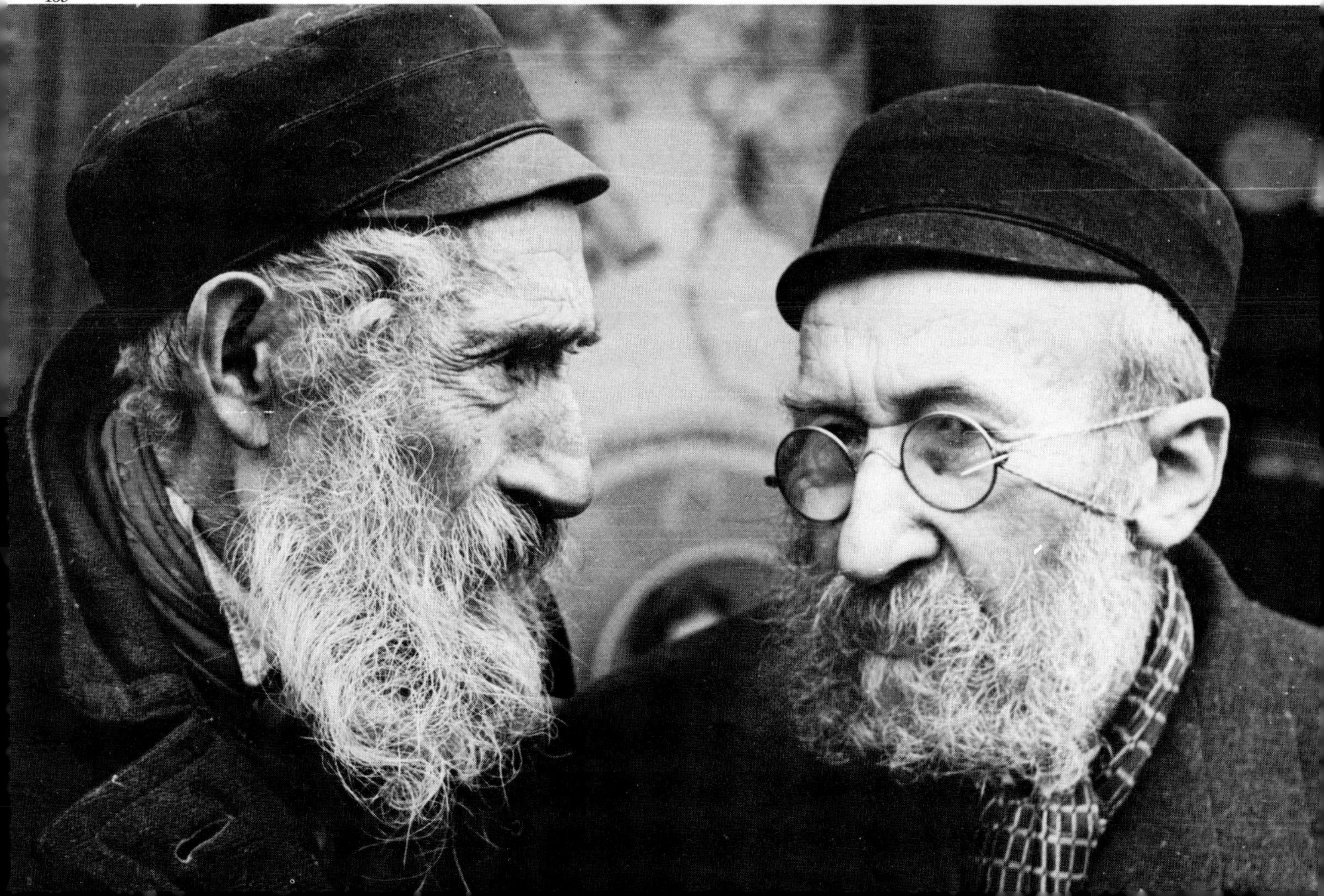

(Nos. 160–170)

The sign reads: "Typhus. Strictly forbidden to enter and leave."

160

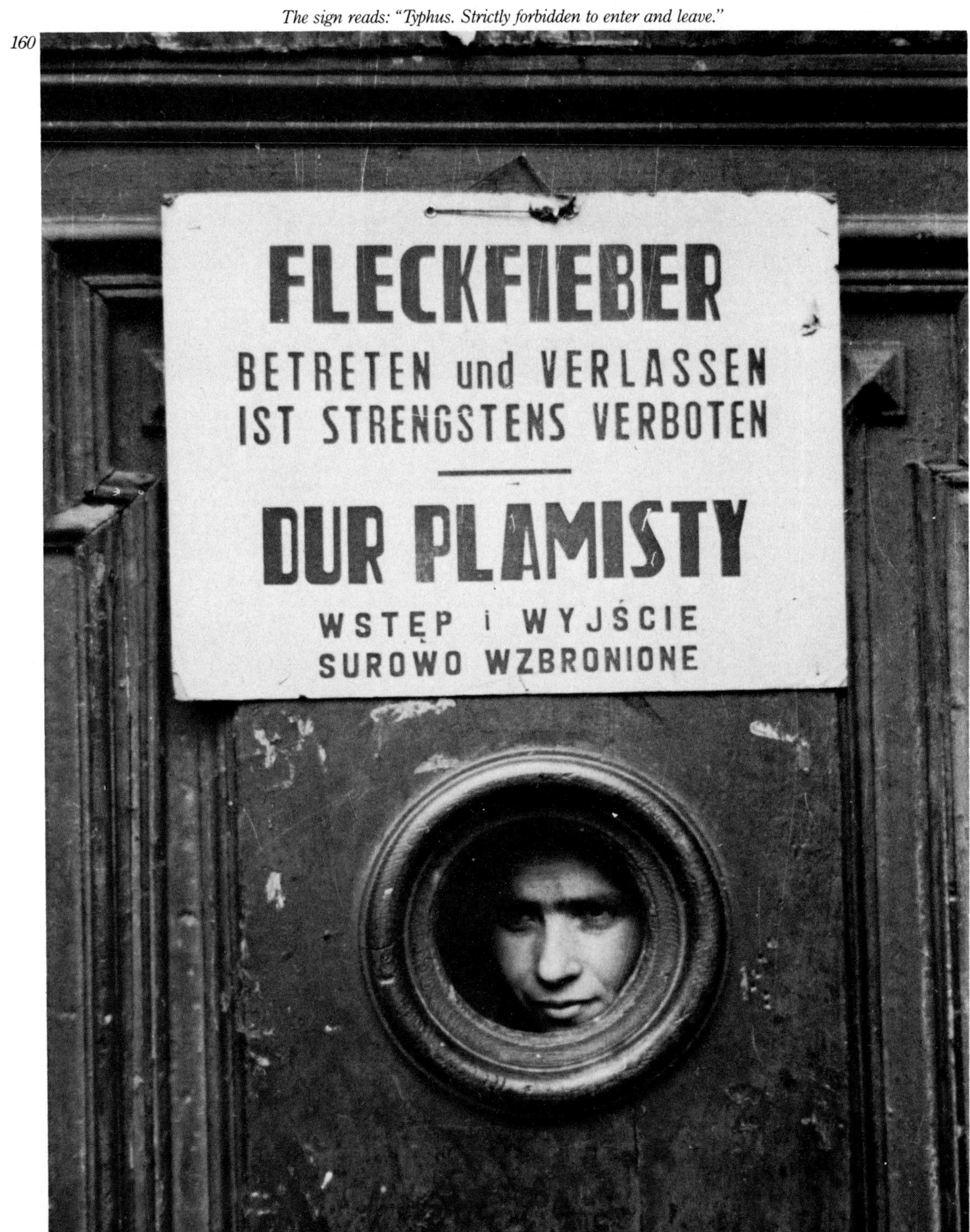

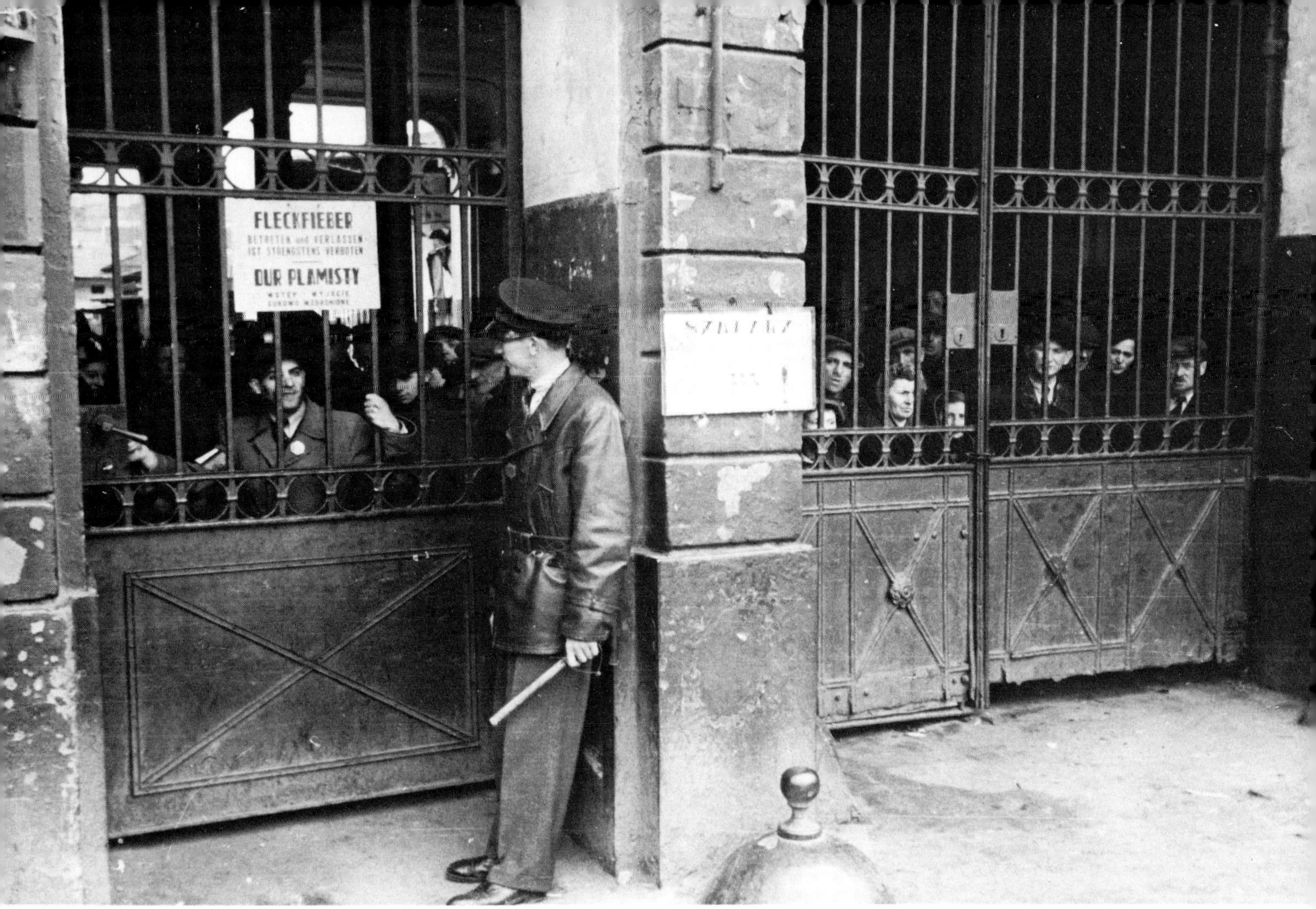

FLECKFIEBER
BETRETEN und VERLASSEN
IST STRENGSTENS VERBOTEN
DUR PLAMISTY
WSTĘP · WYJŚCIE
SUROWO WZBRONIONE
SZMATY

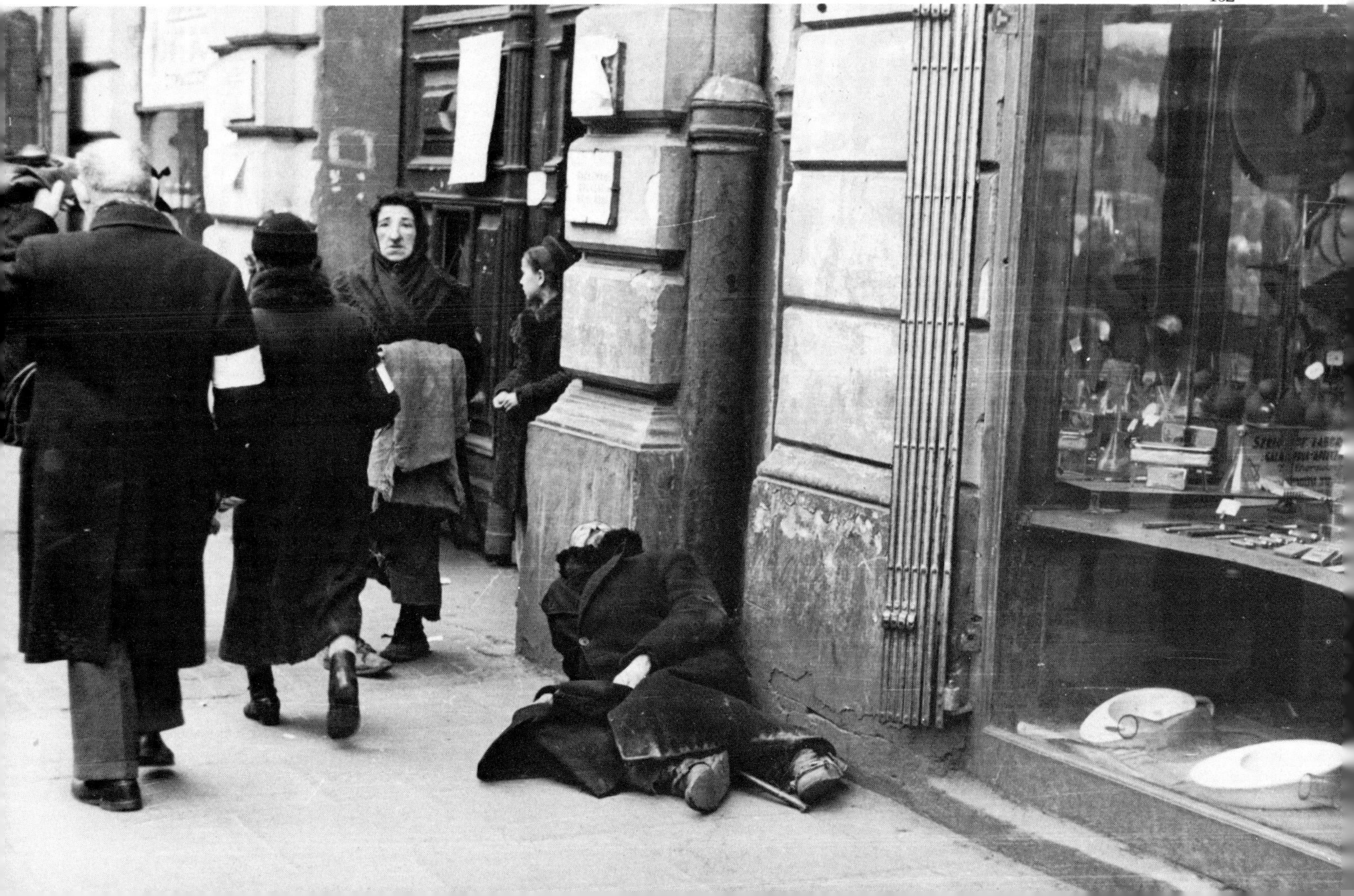

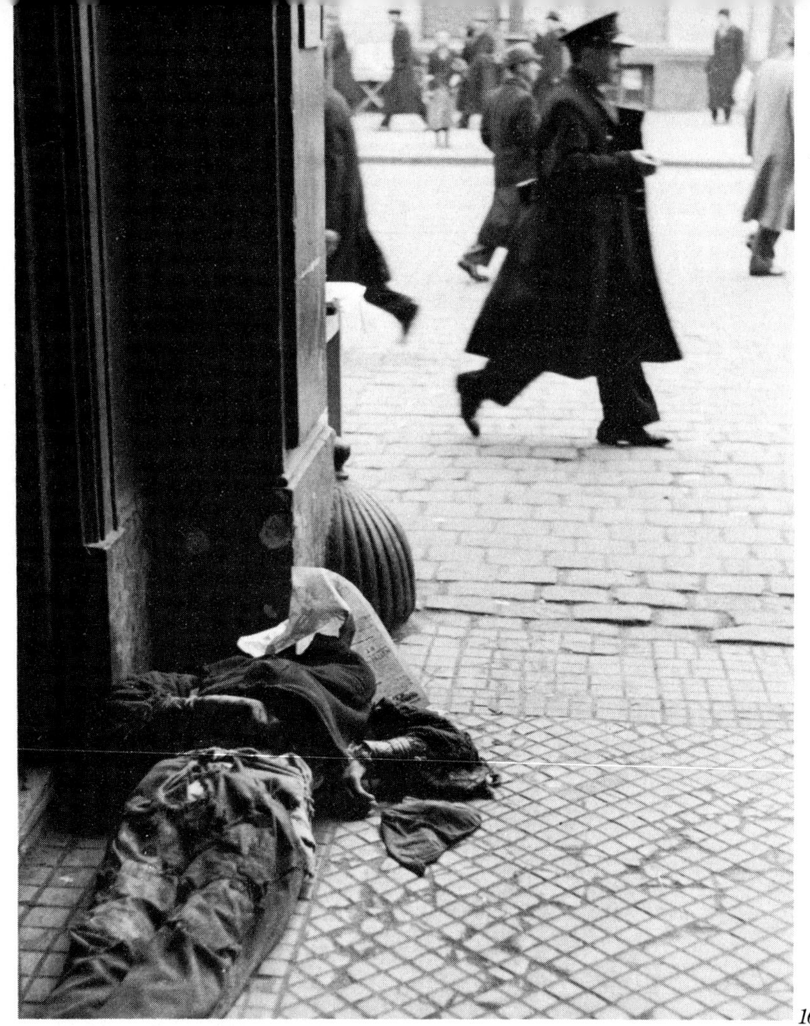

163

164

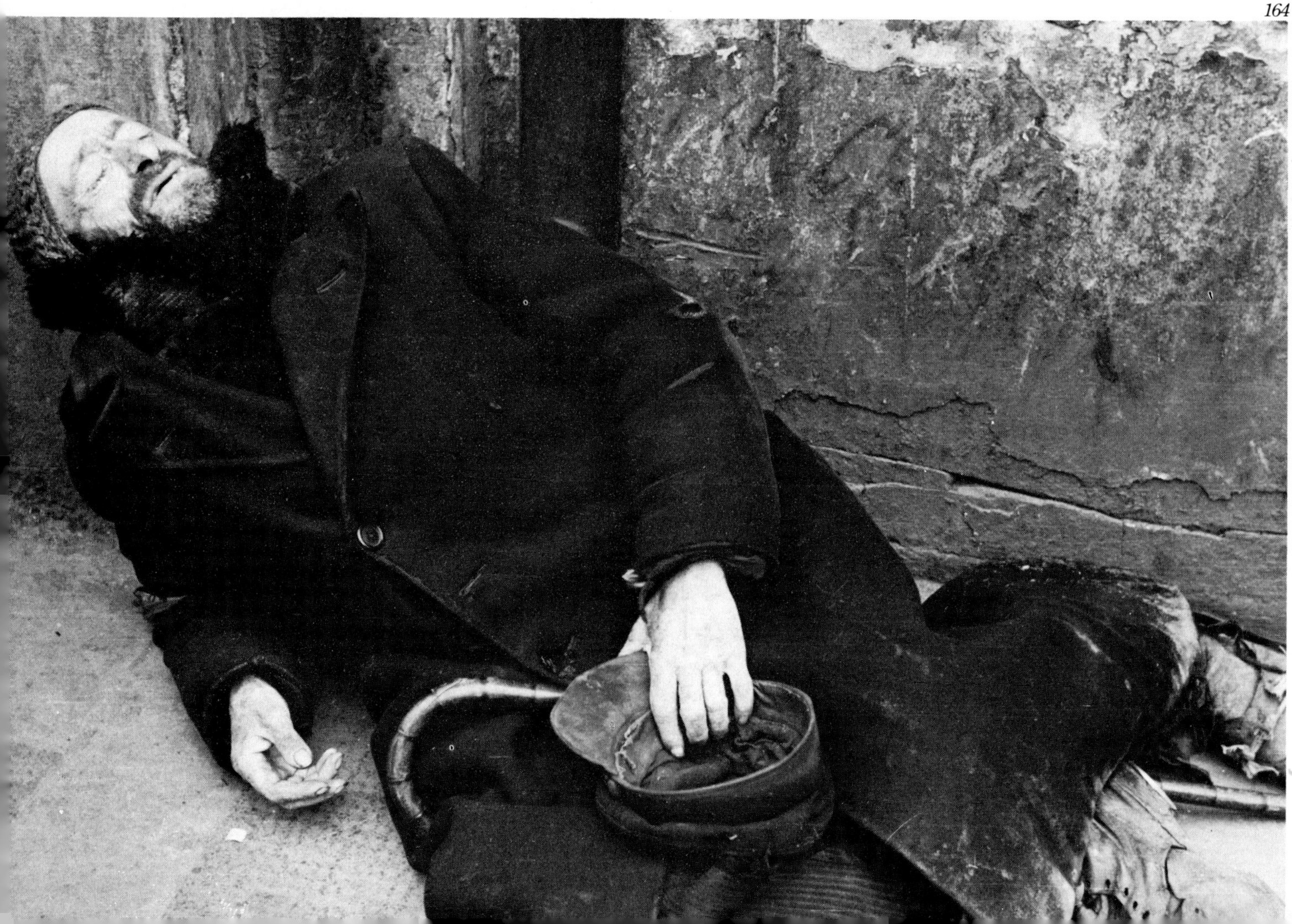

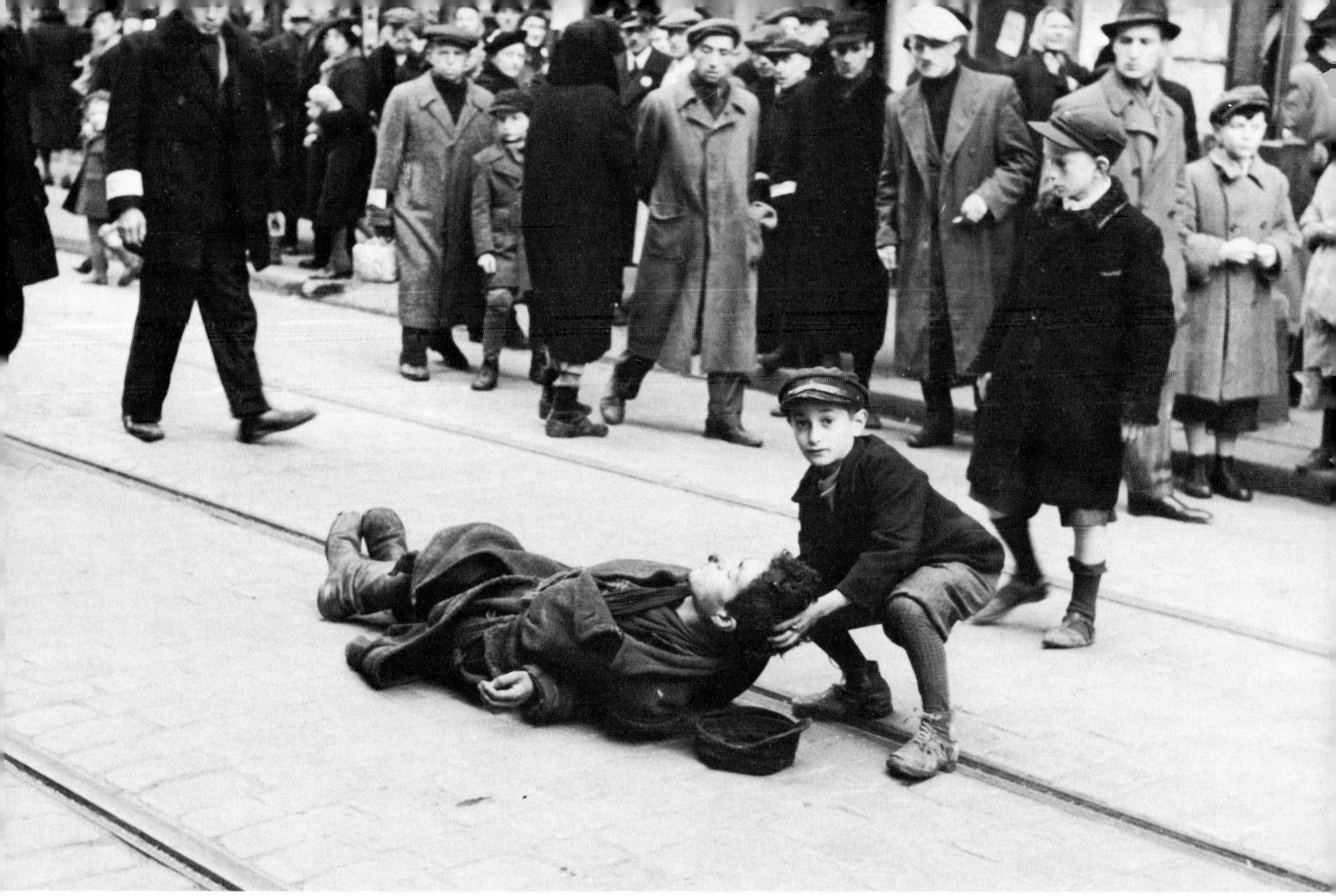

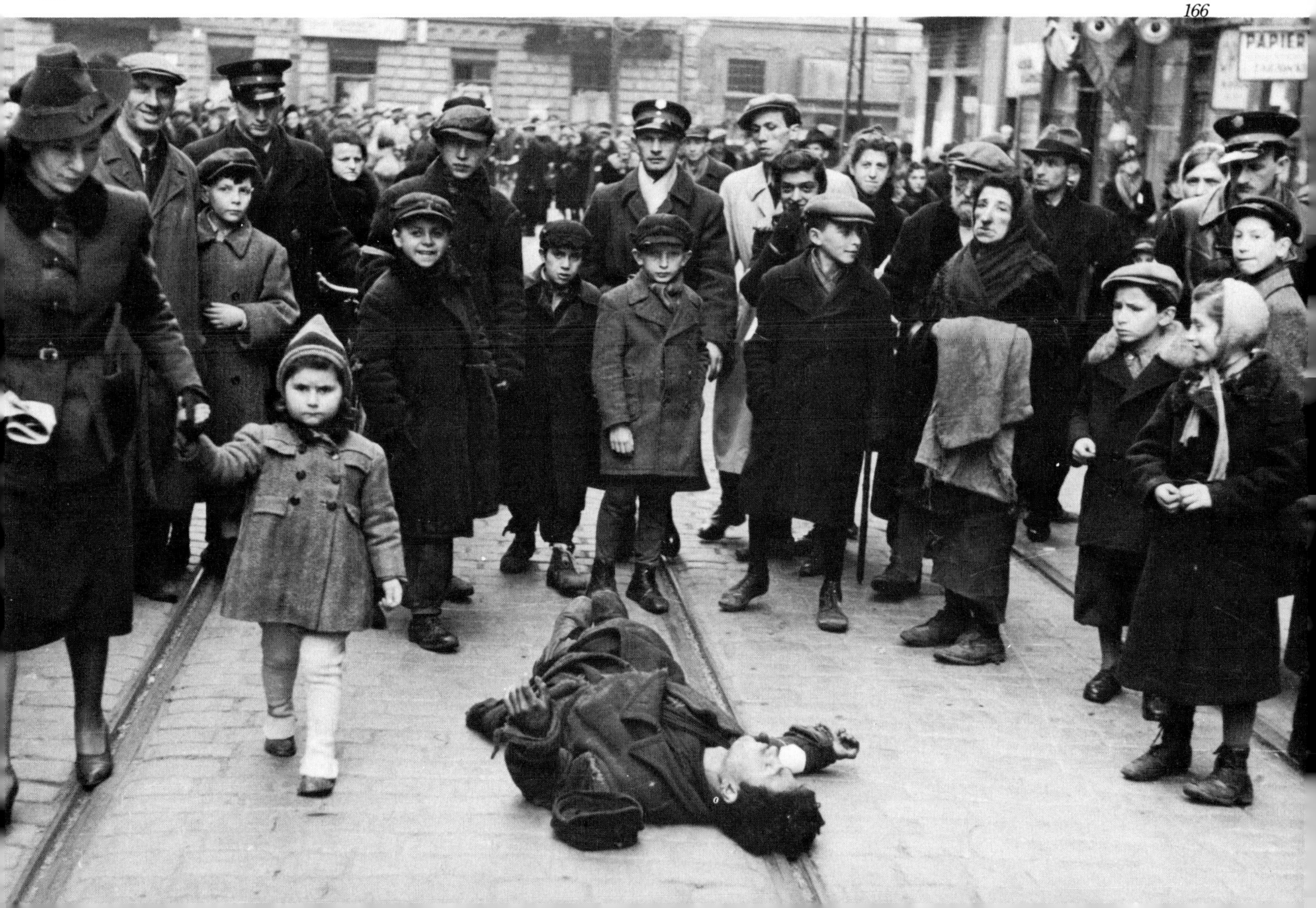

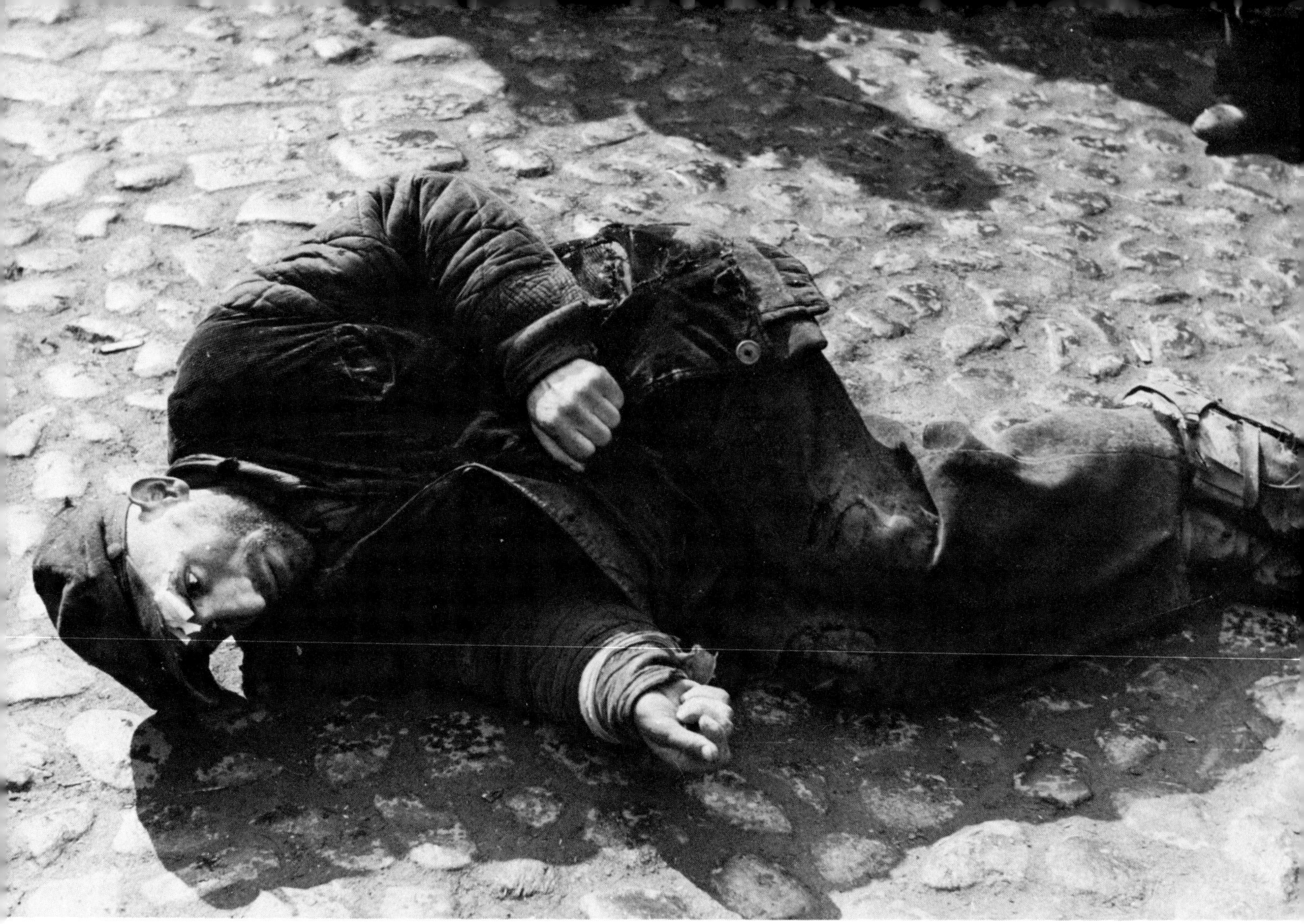

LATARKI BATERIE ŻARÓWKI
DAIMON
tu do nabycia

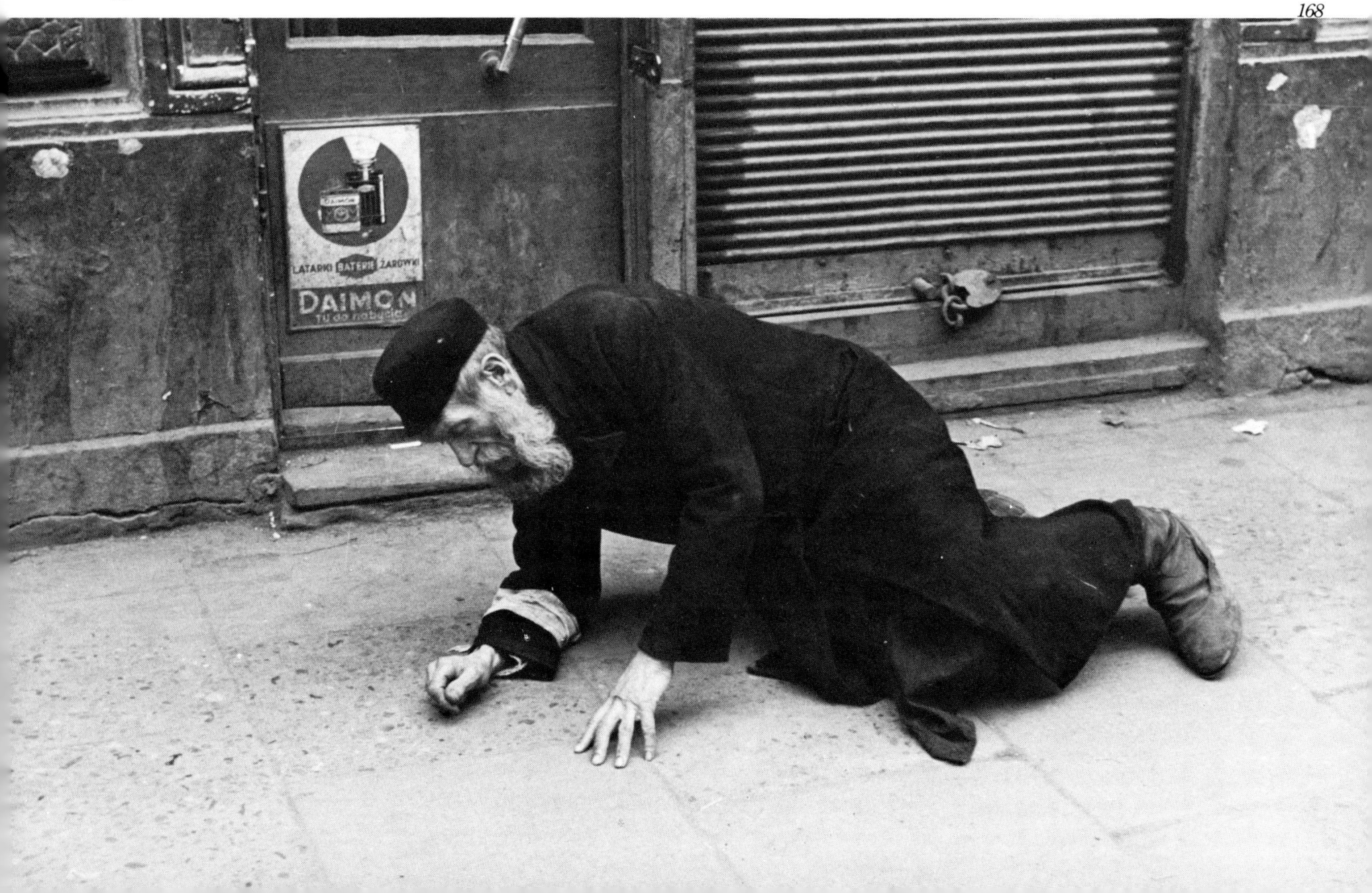

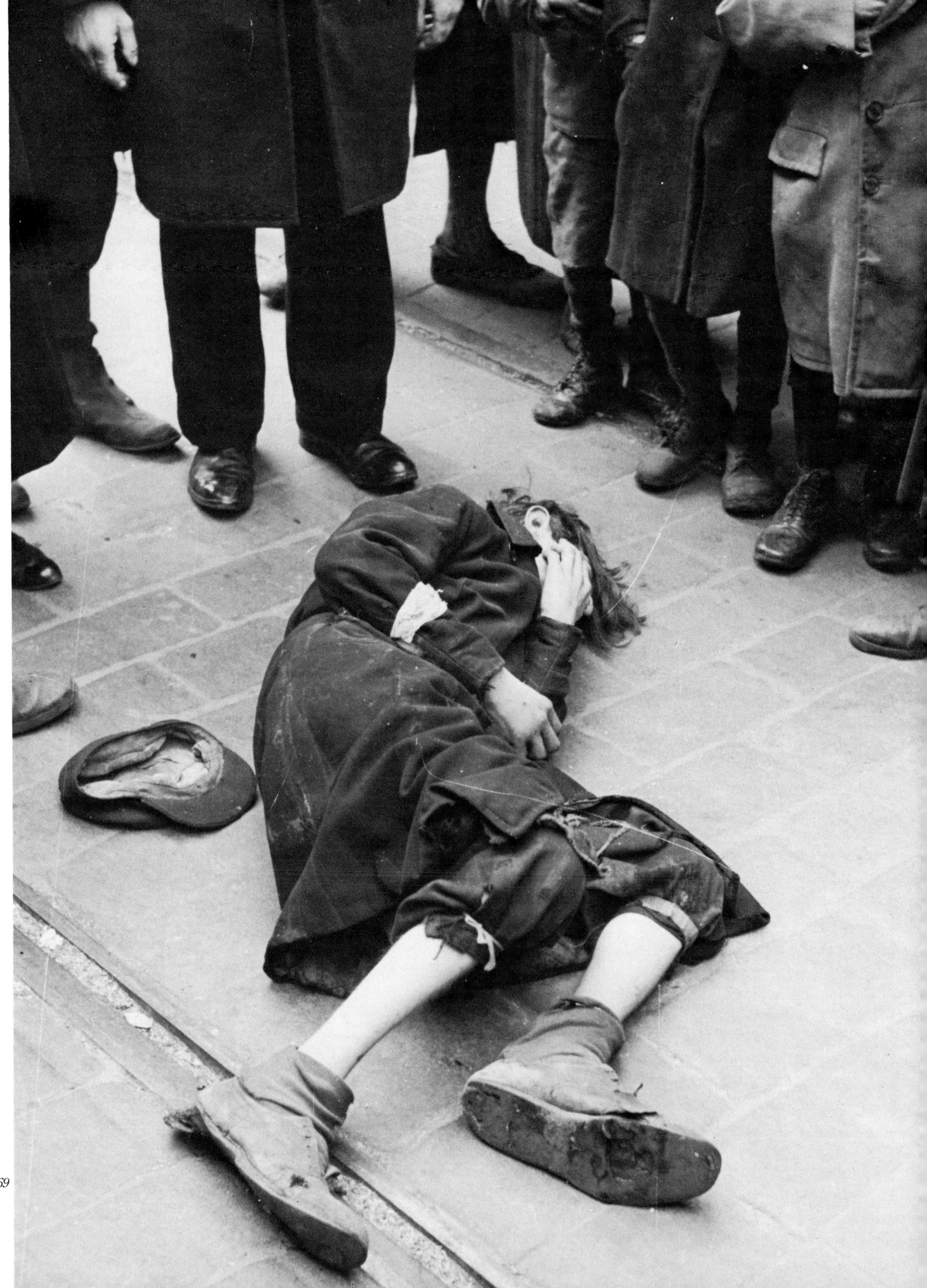

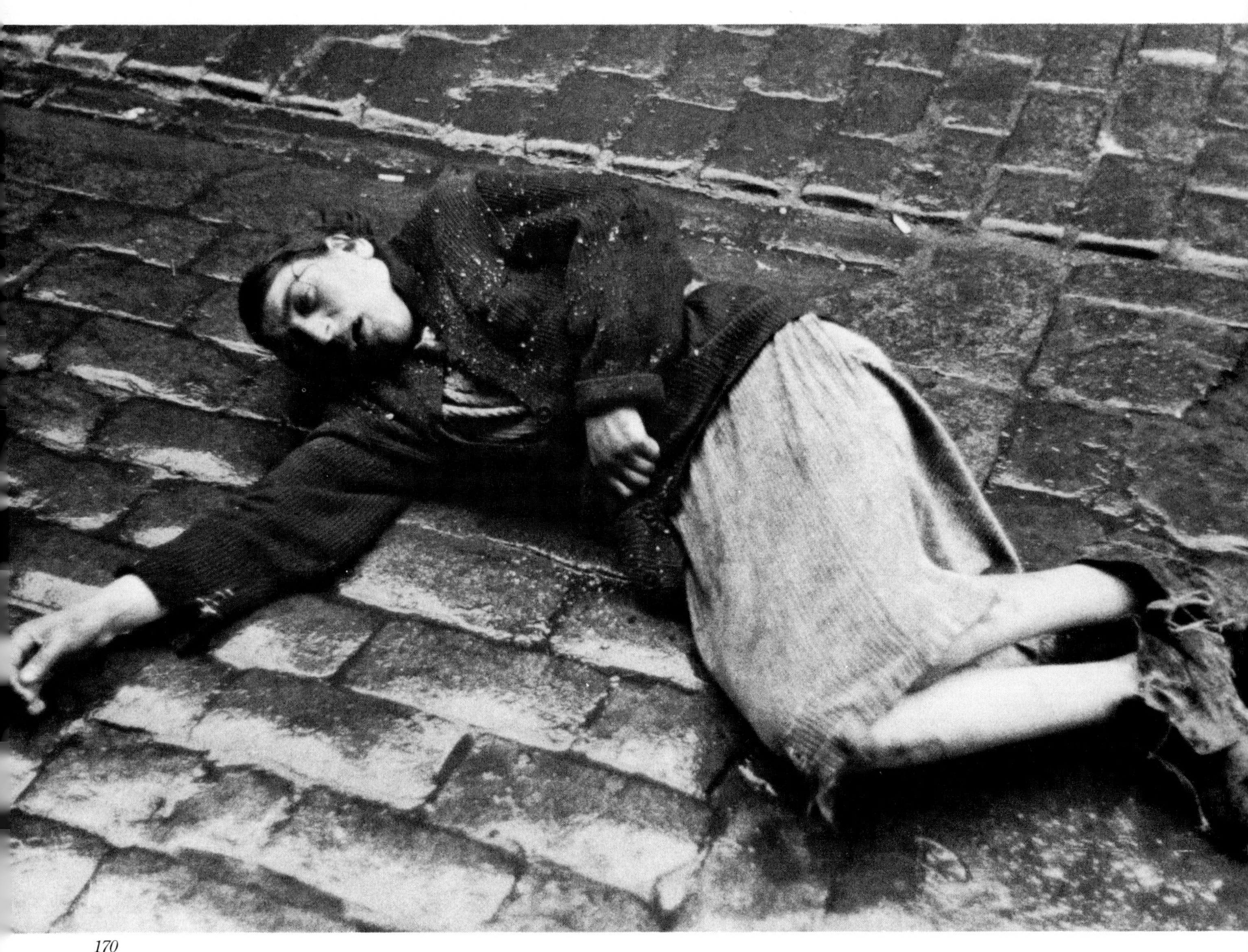

170

BURIALS
(Nos. 171–188)

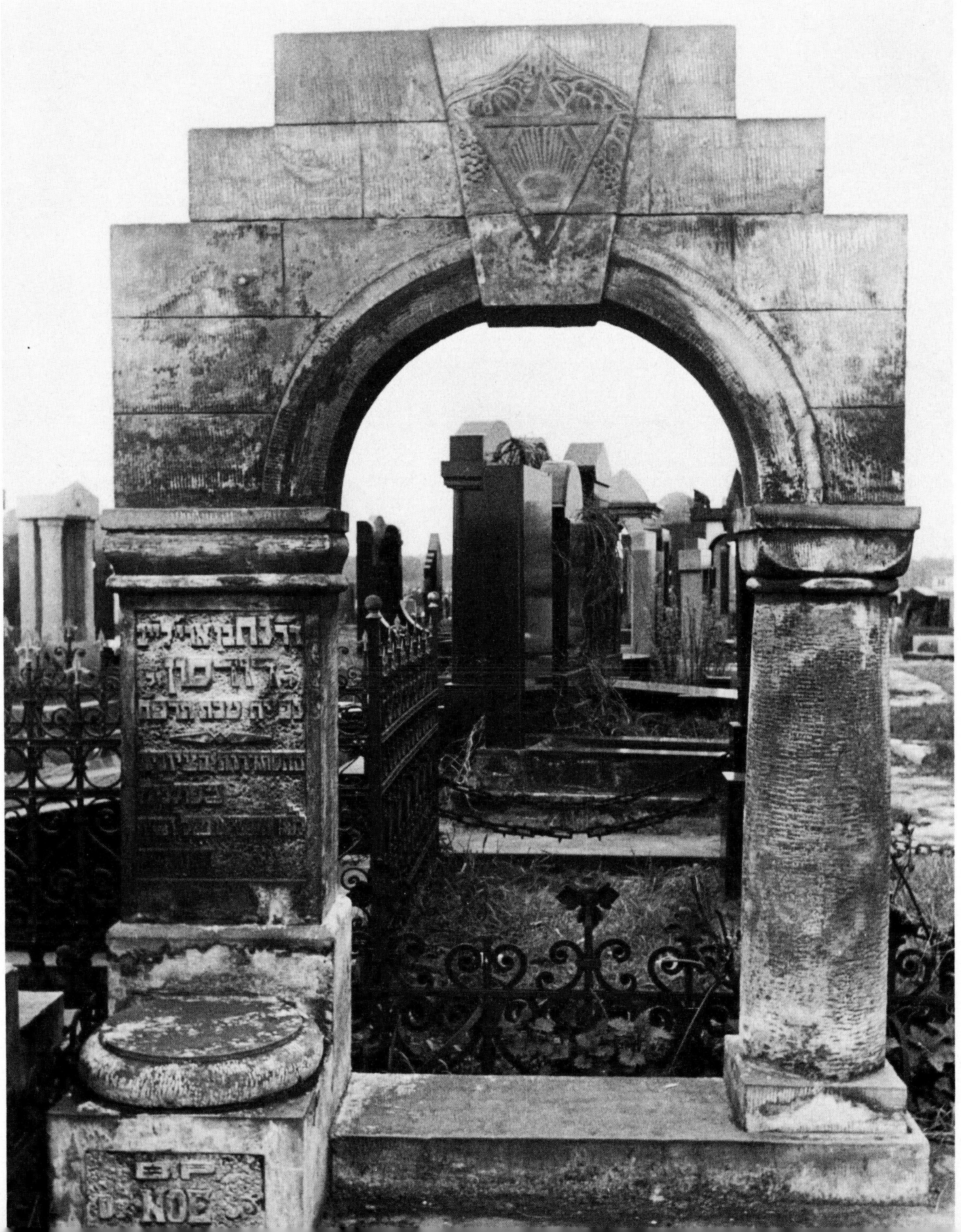

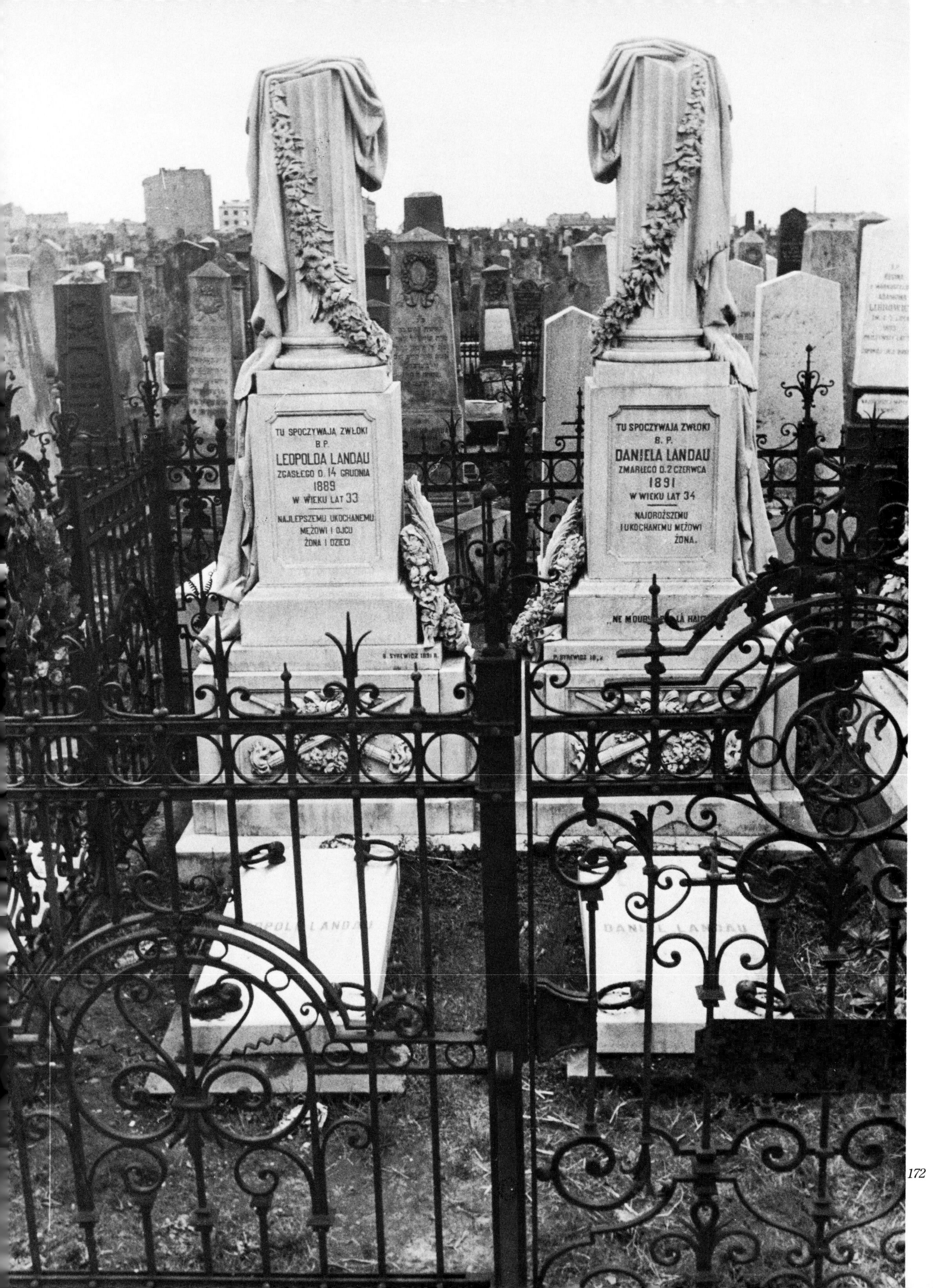

TU SPOCZYWAJĄ ZWŁOKI
B. P.
LEOPOLDA LANDAU
ZGASŁEGO D. 14 GRUDNIA
1889
W WIEKU LAT 33
NAJLEPSZEMU, UKOCHANEMU
MĘŻOWI I OJCU
ŻONA I DZIECI
TU SPOCZYWAJĄ ZWŁOKI
B. P.
DANIELA LANDAU
ZMARŁEGO D. 2 CZERWCA
1891
W WIEKU LAT 34
NAJDROŻSZEMU
I UKOCHANEMU MĘŻOWI
ŻONA.

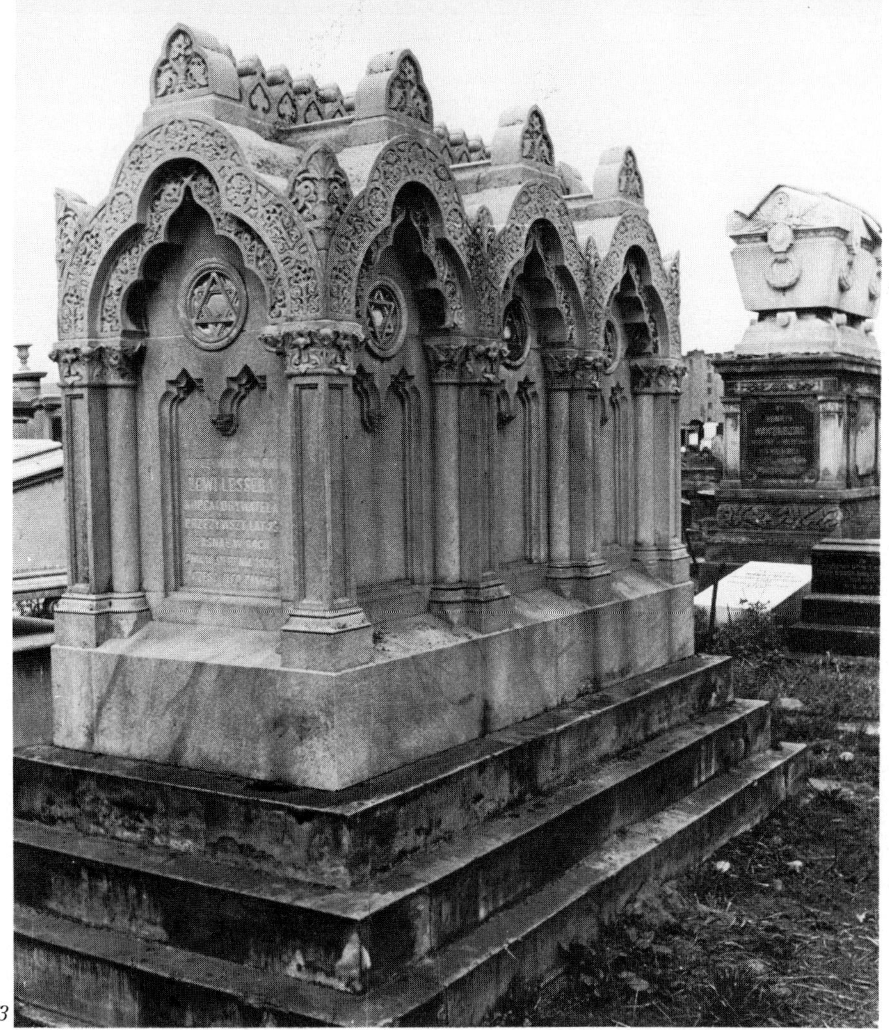

173

174

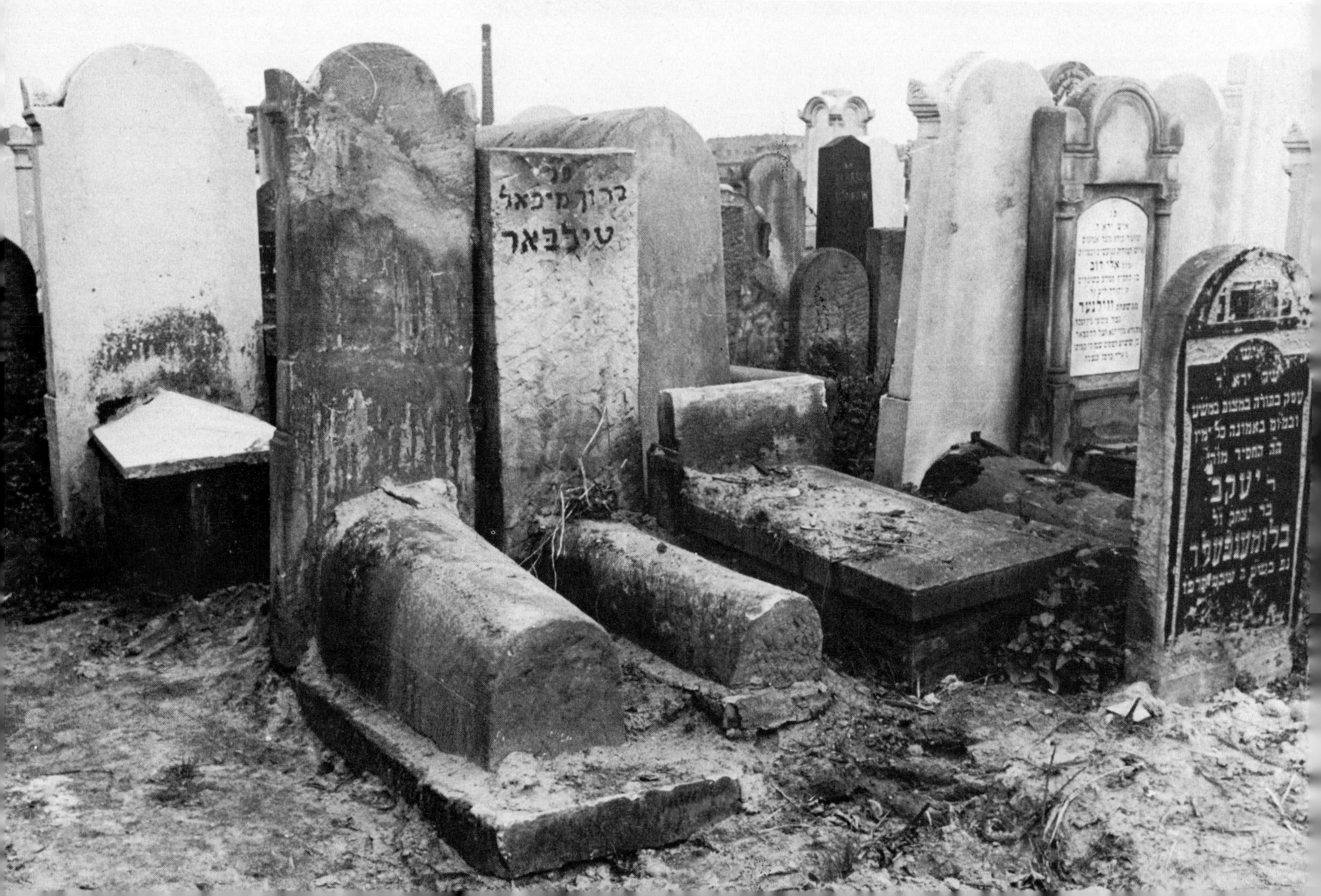

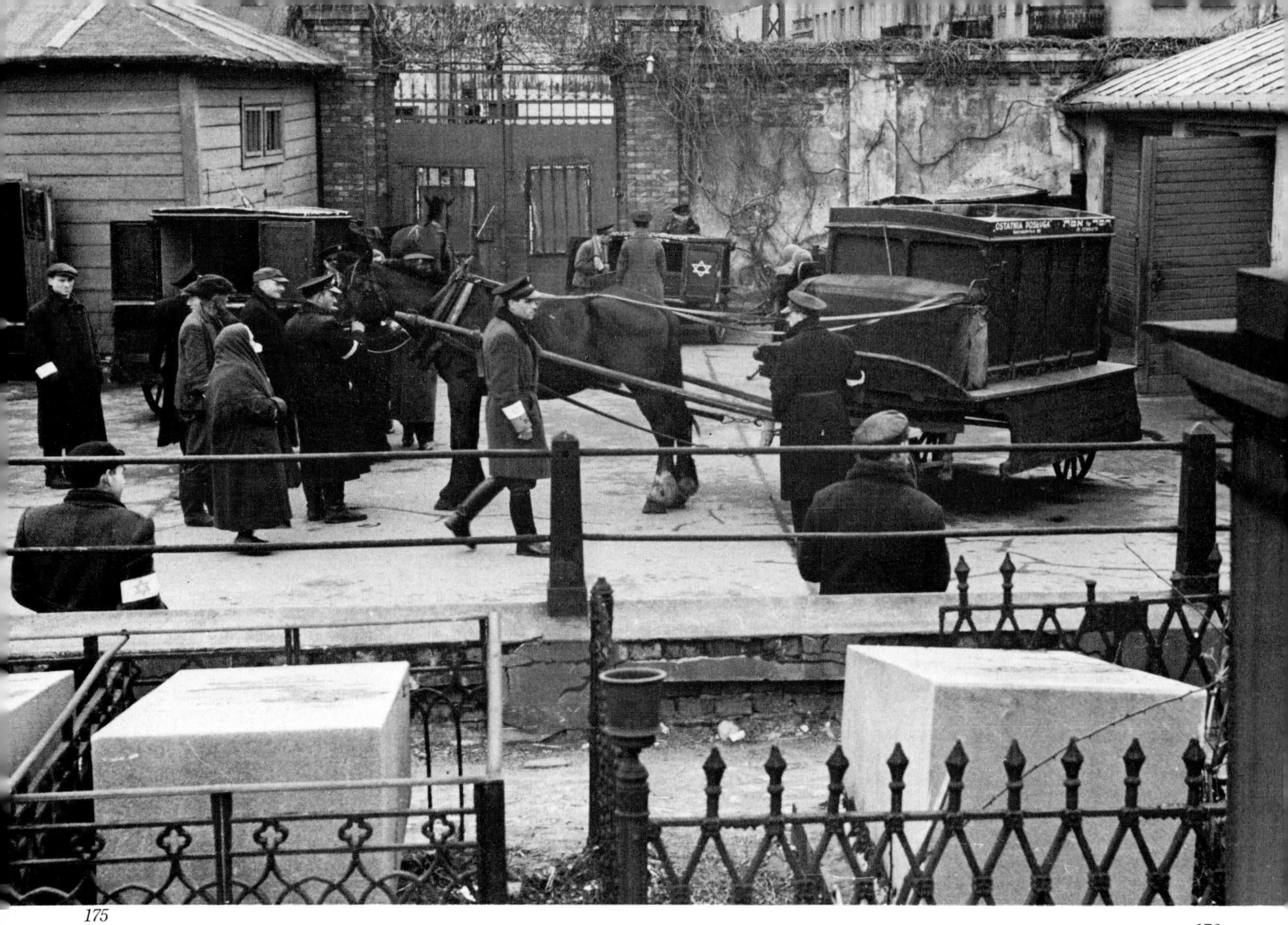

175

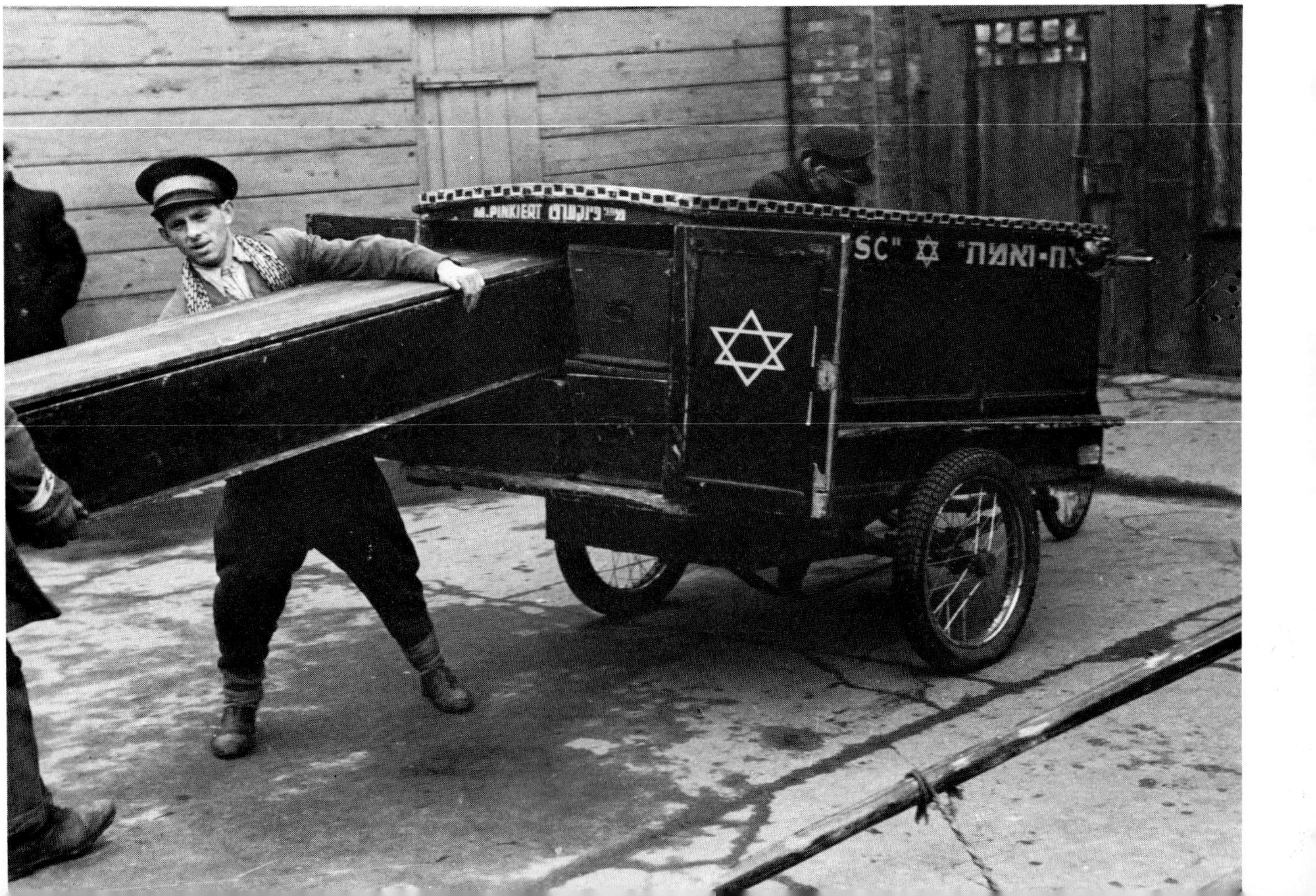

176

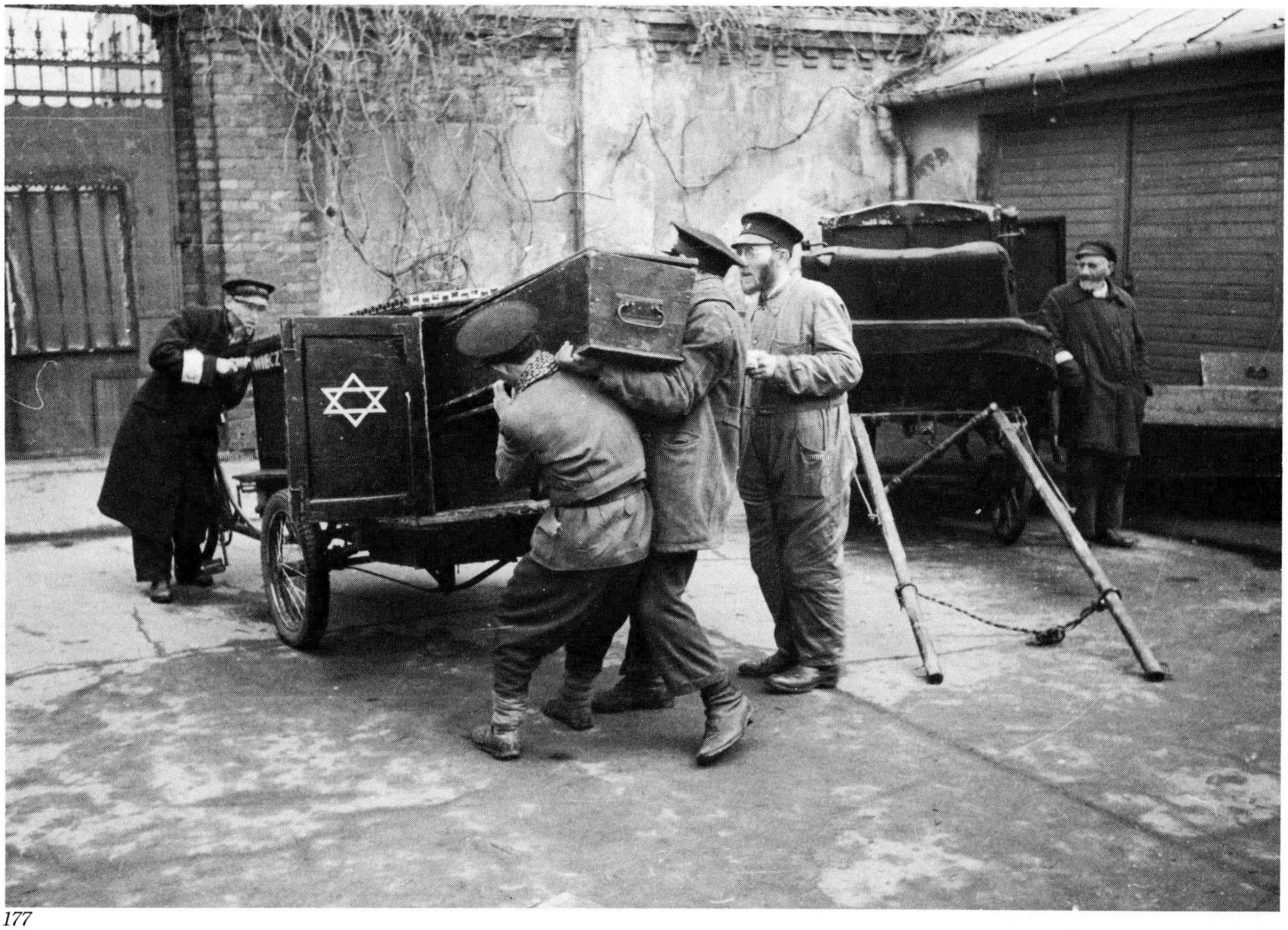

177

178

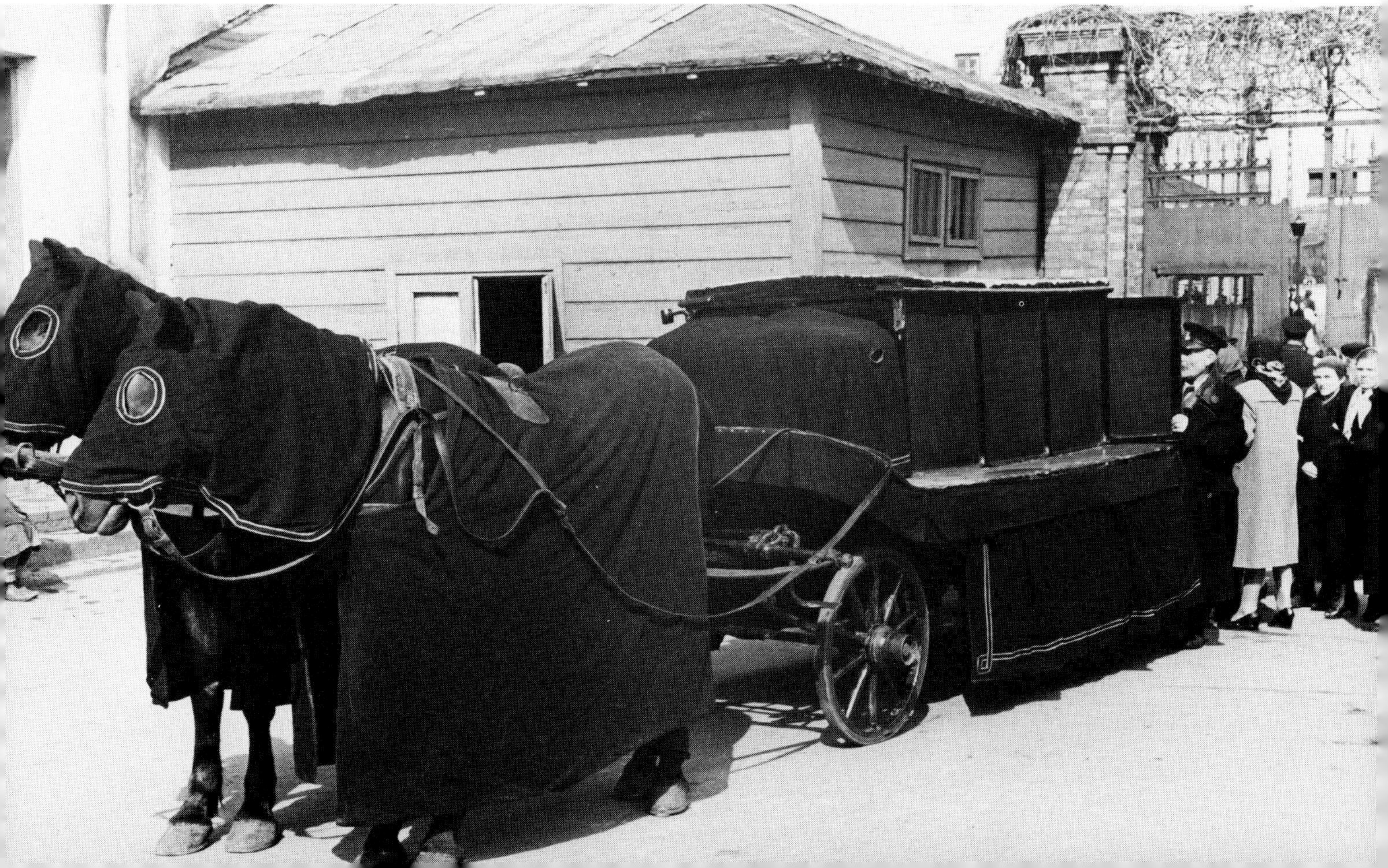

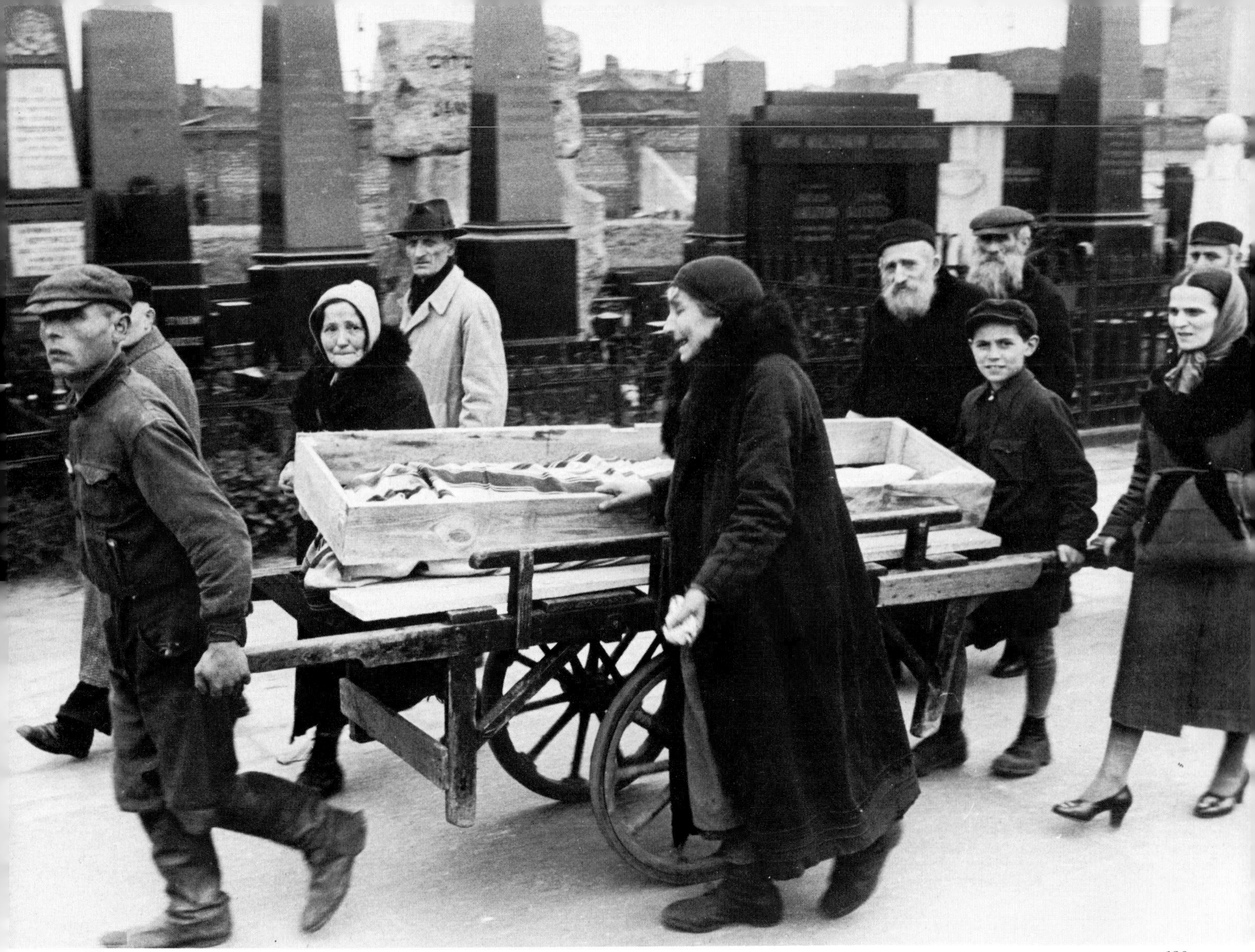

179

180

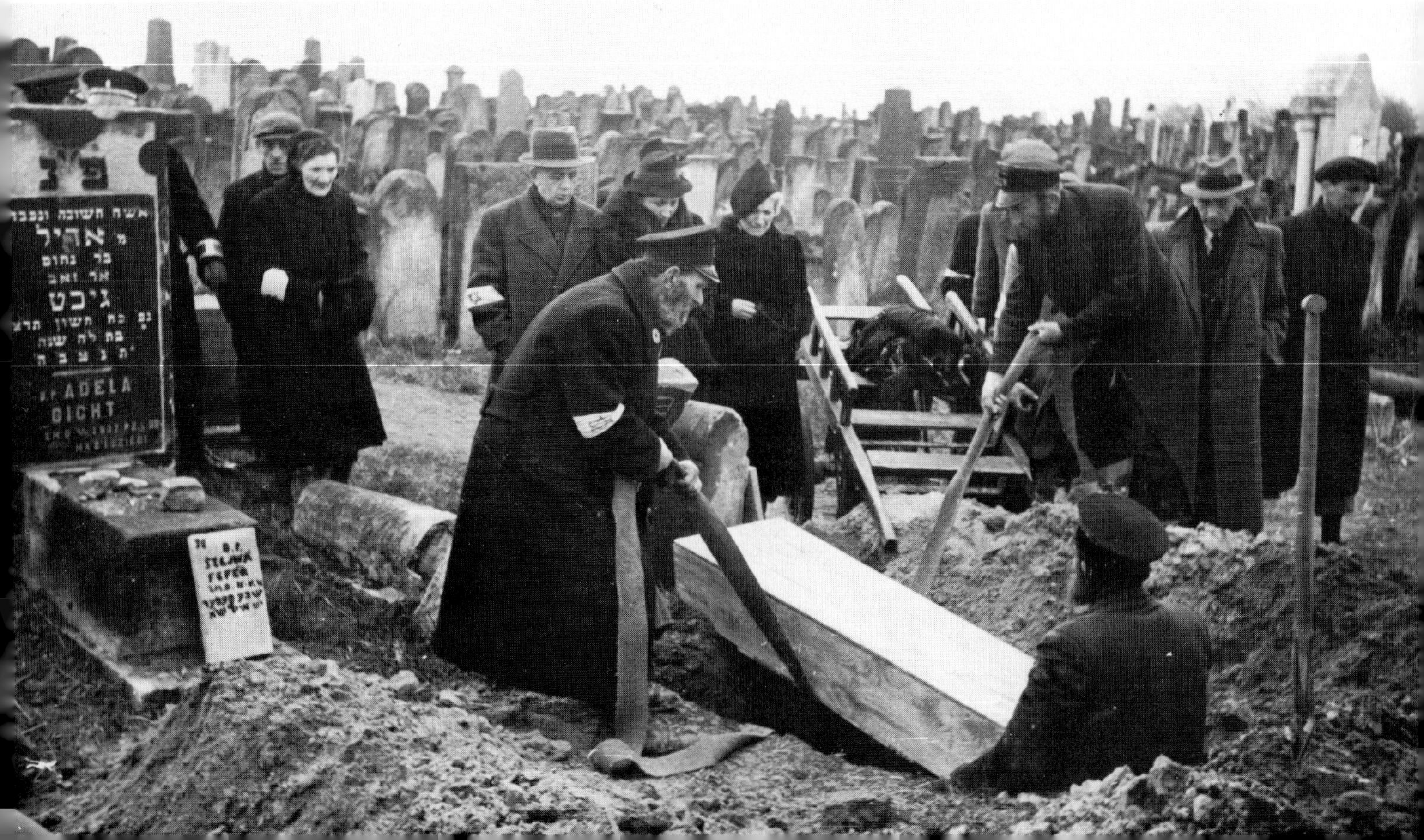

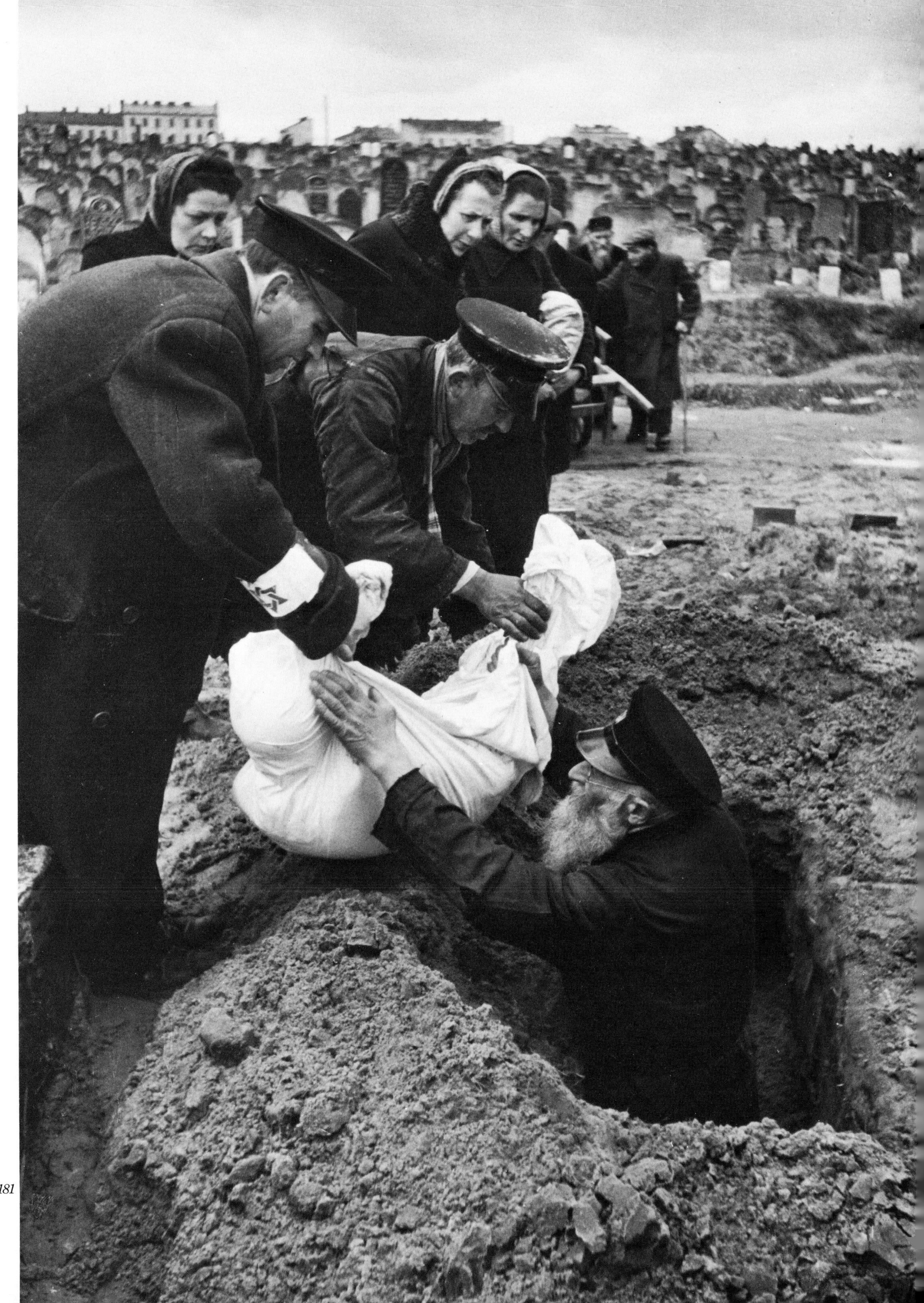

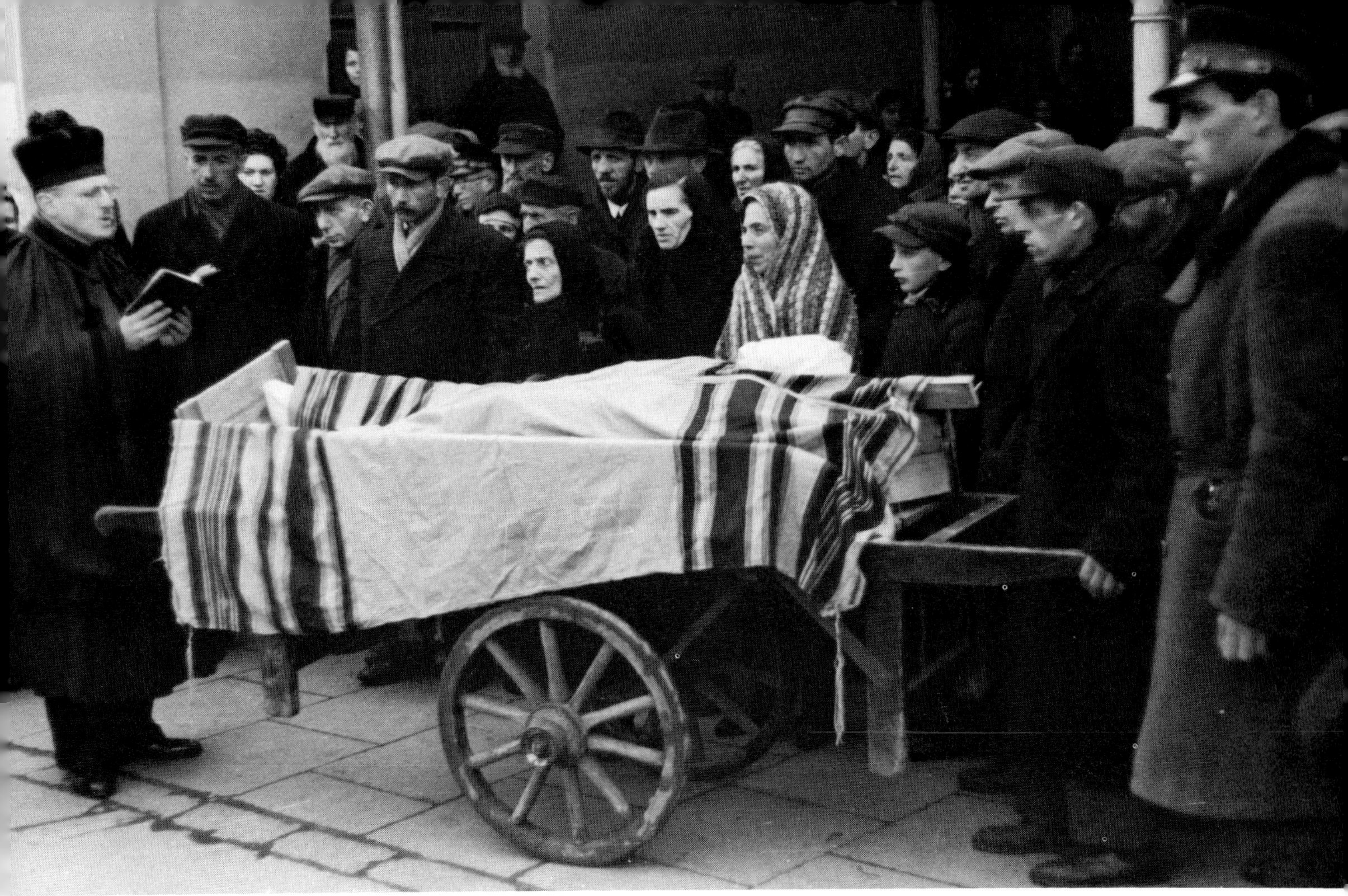

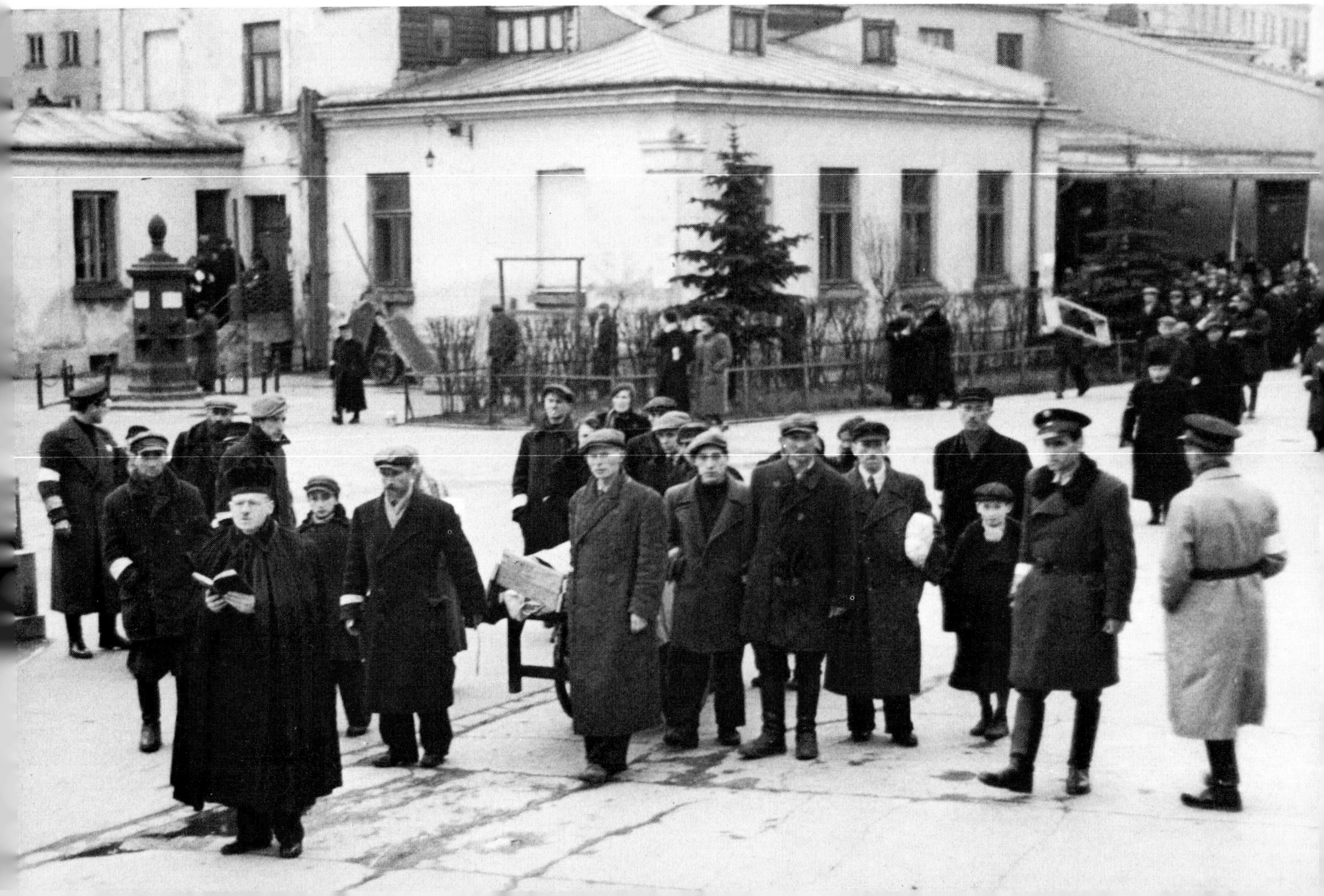

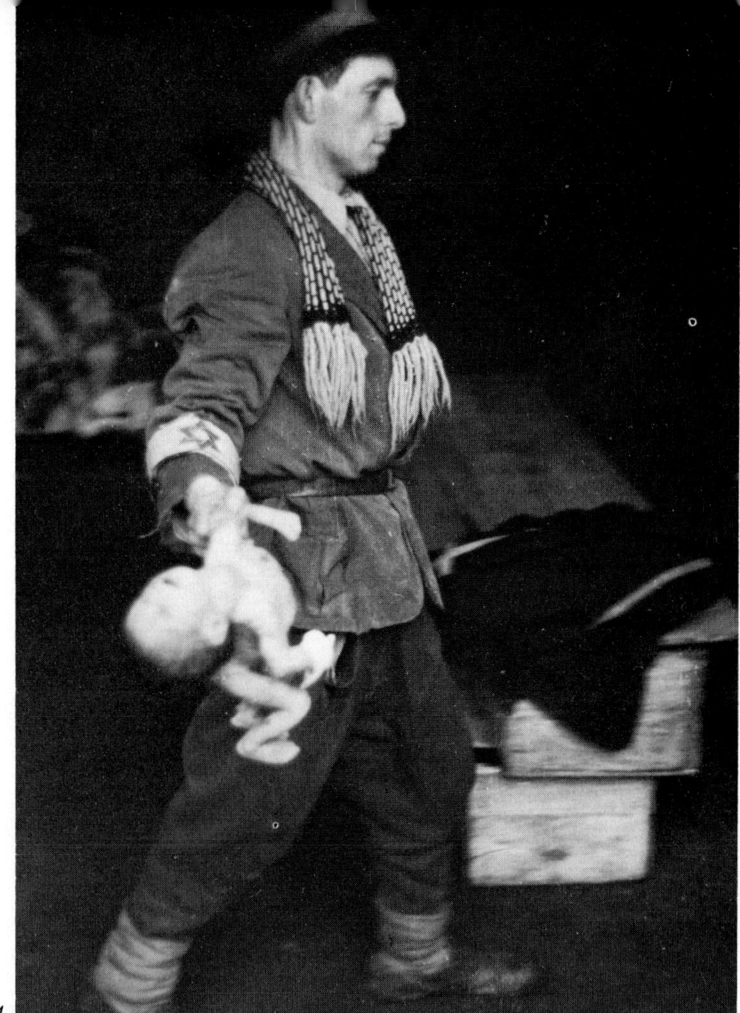

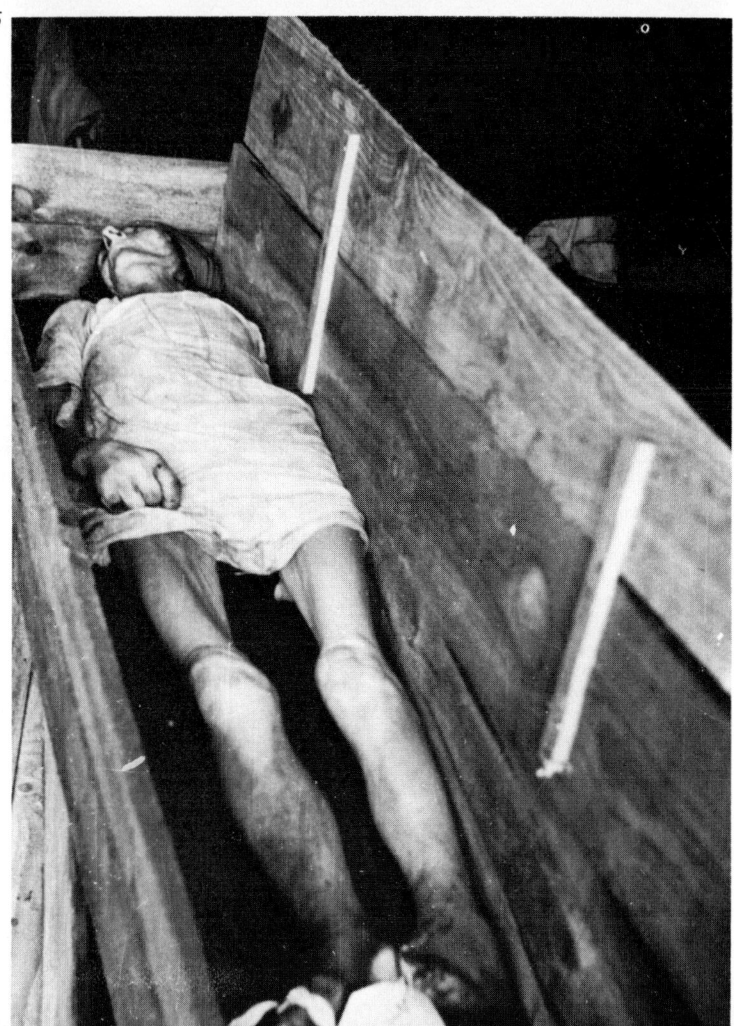

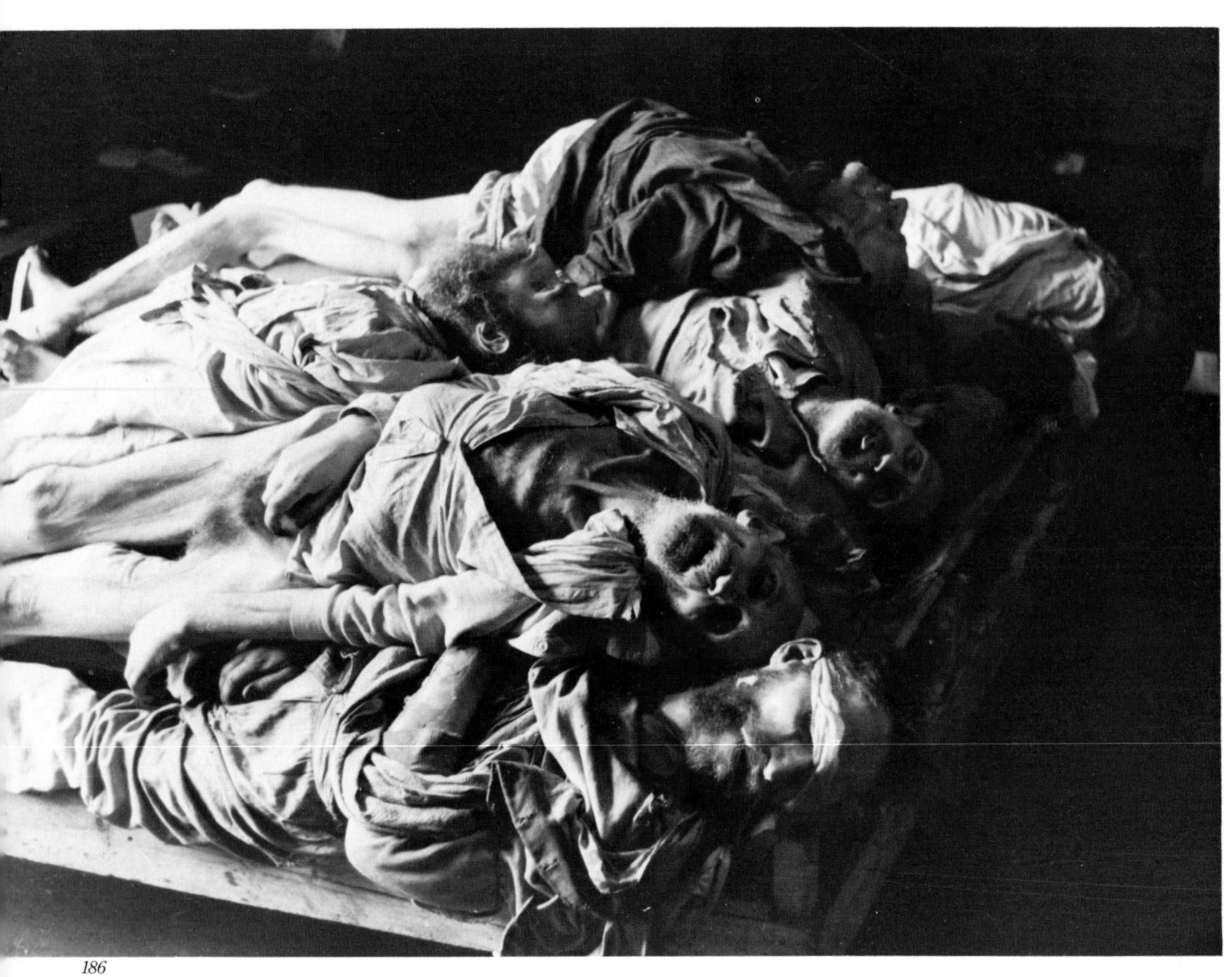

186

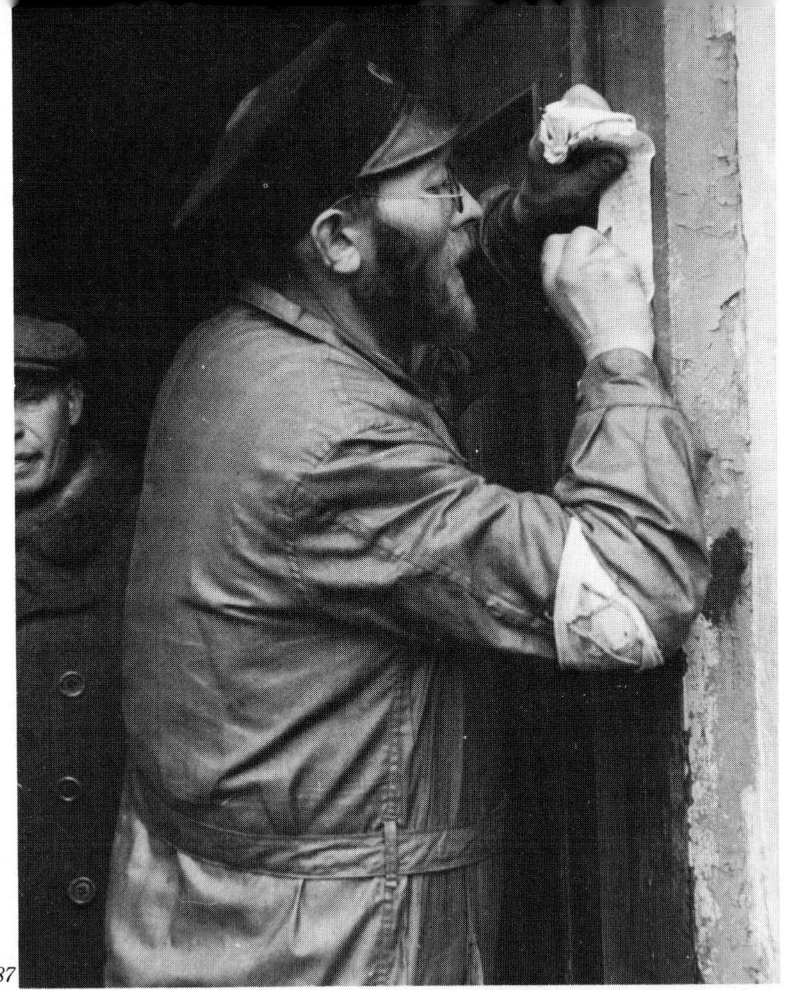

187

188

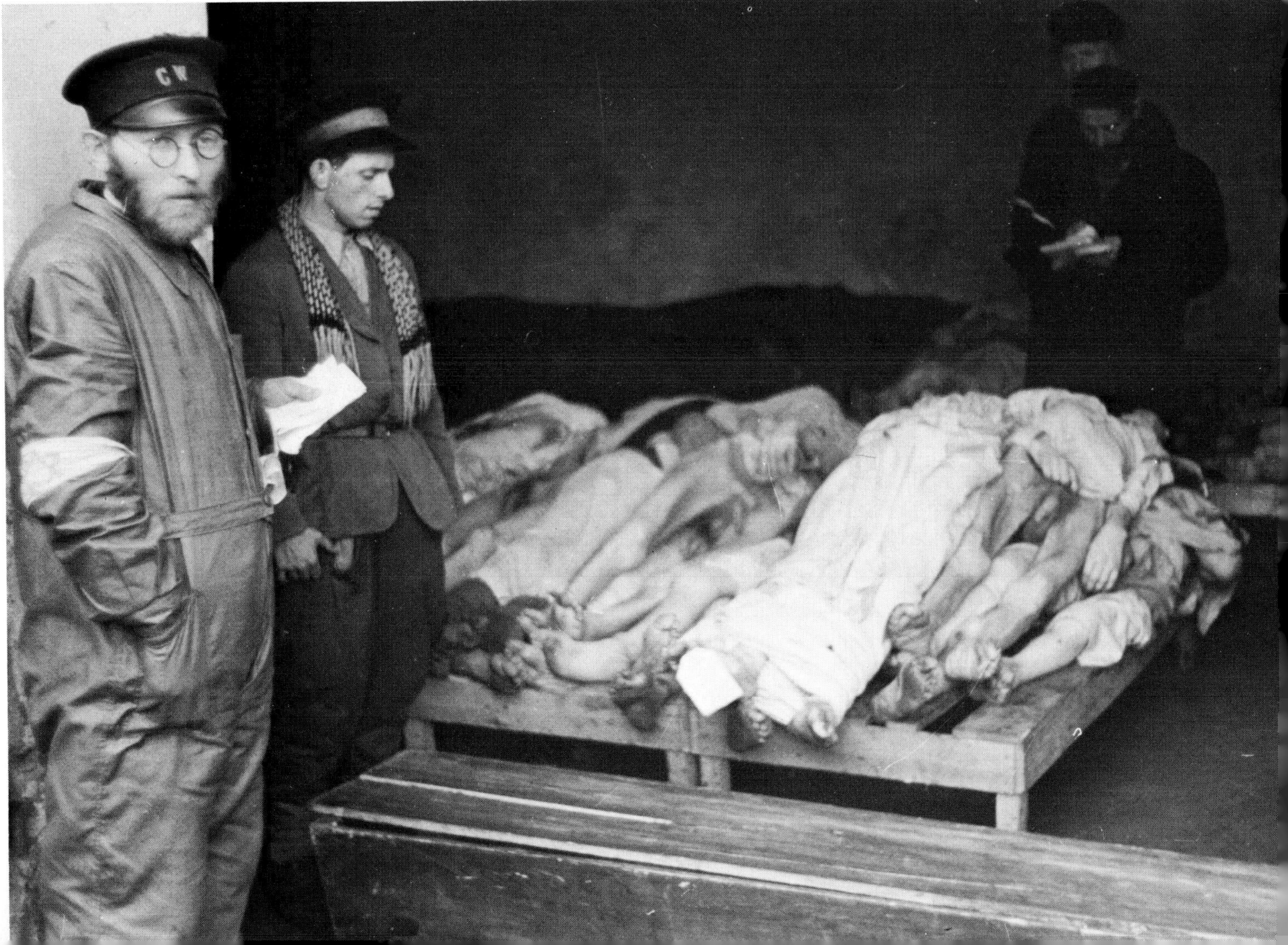

LODZ GHETTO
Entering, Street Scenes, Factory Work
(Nos. 189–206)

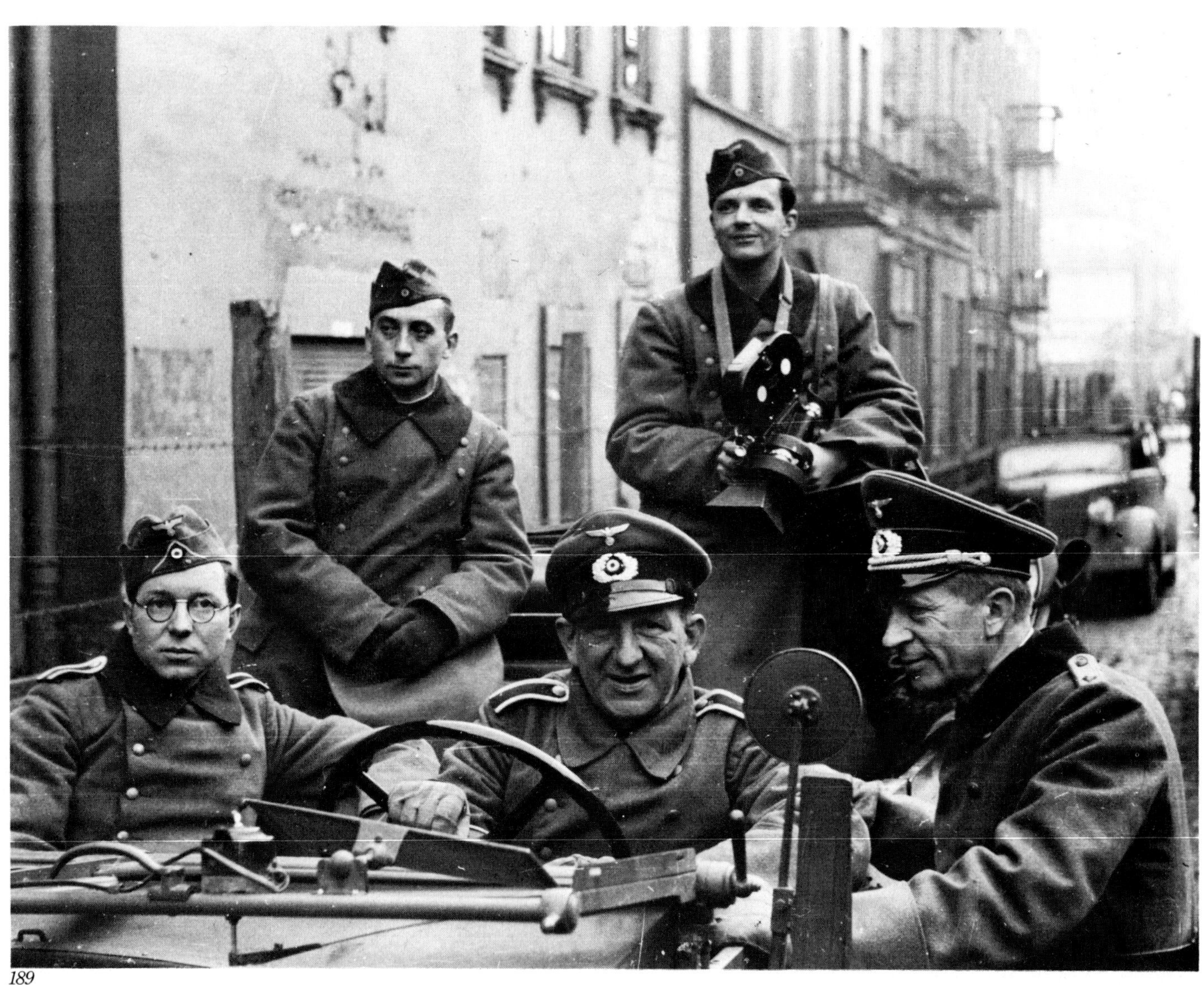

189

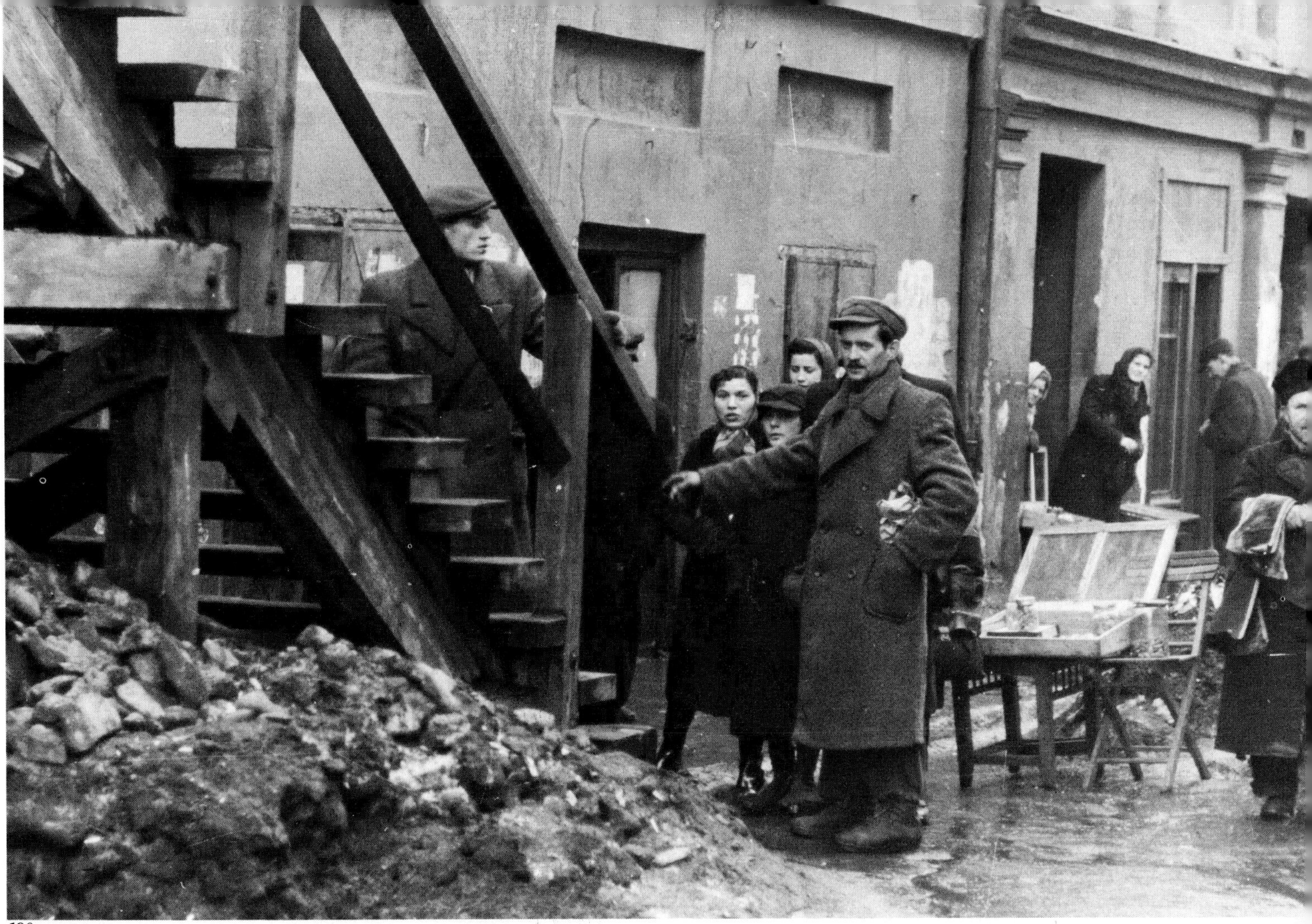

Höhe
5.40 m.
Hochspannung
Vorsicht!
Lebensgefahr

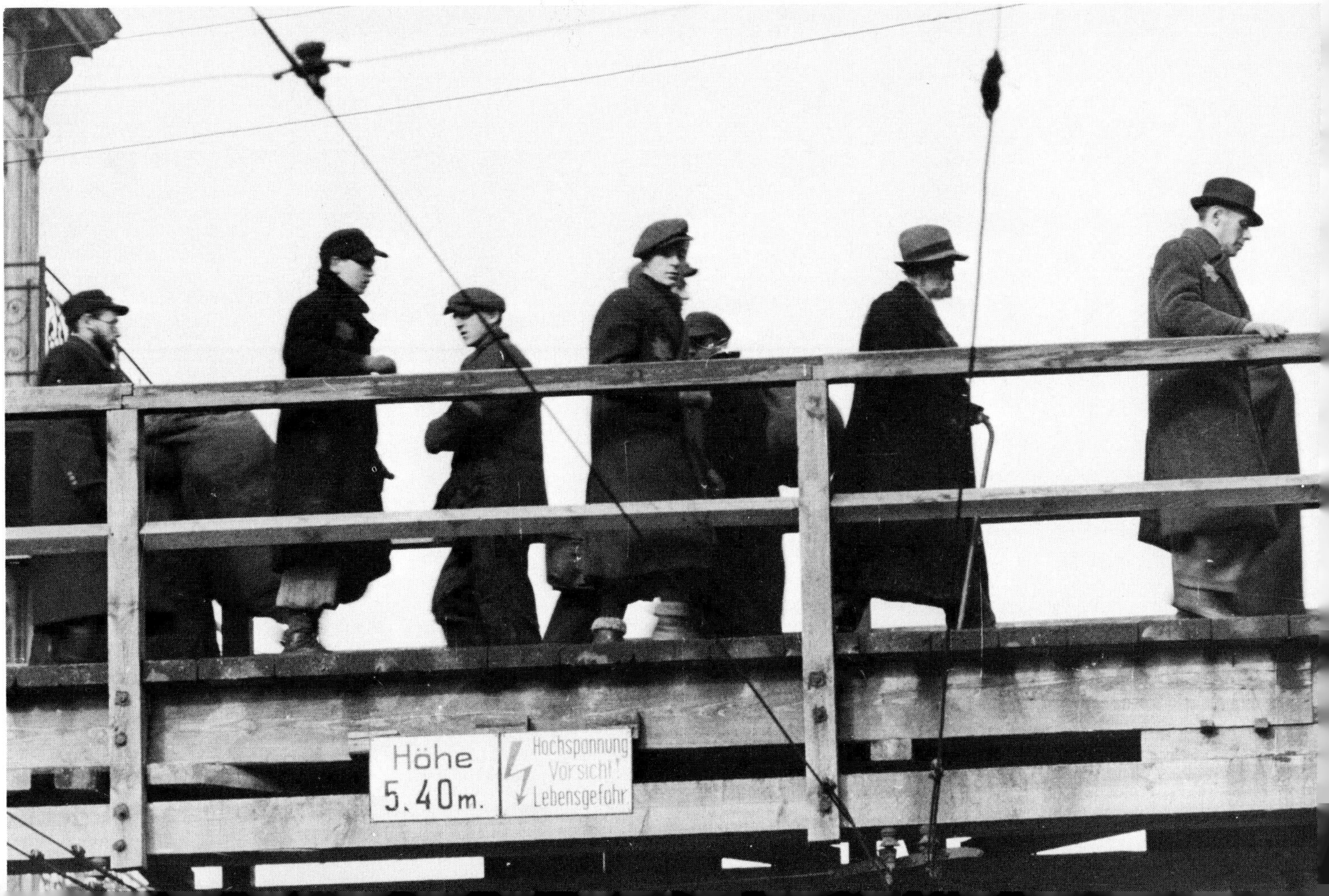

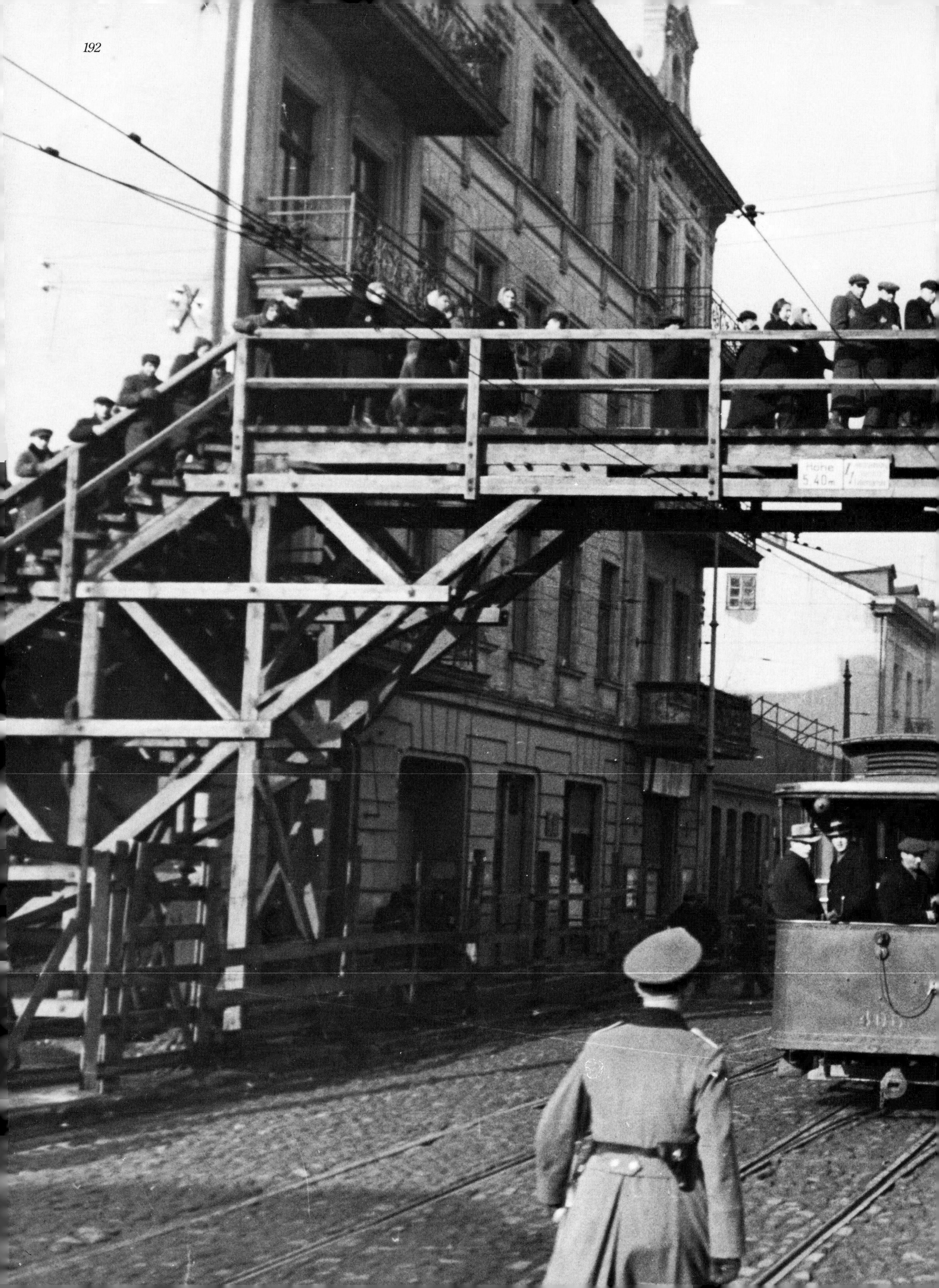

Höhe
5.40 m

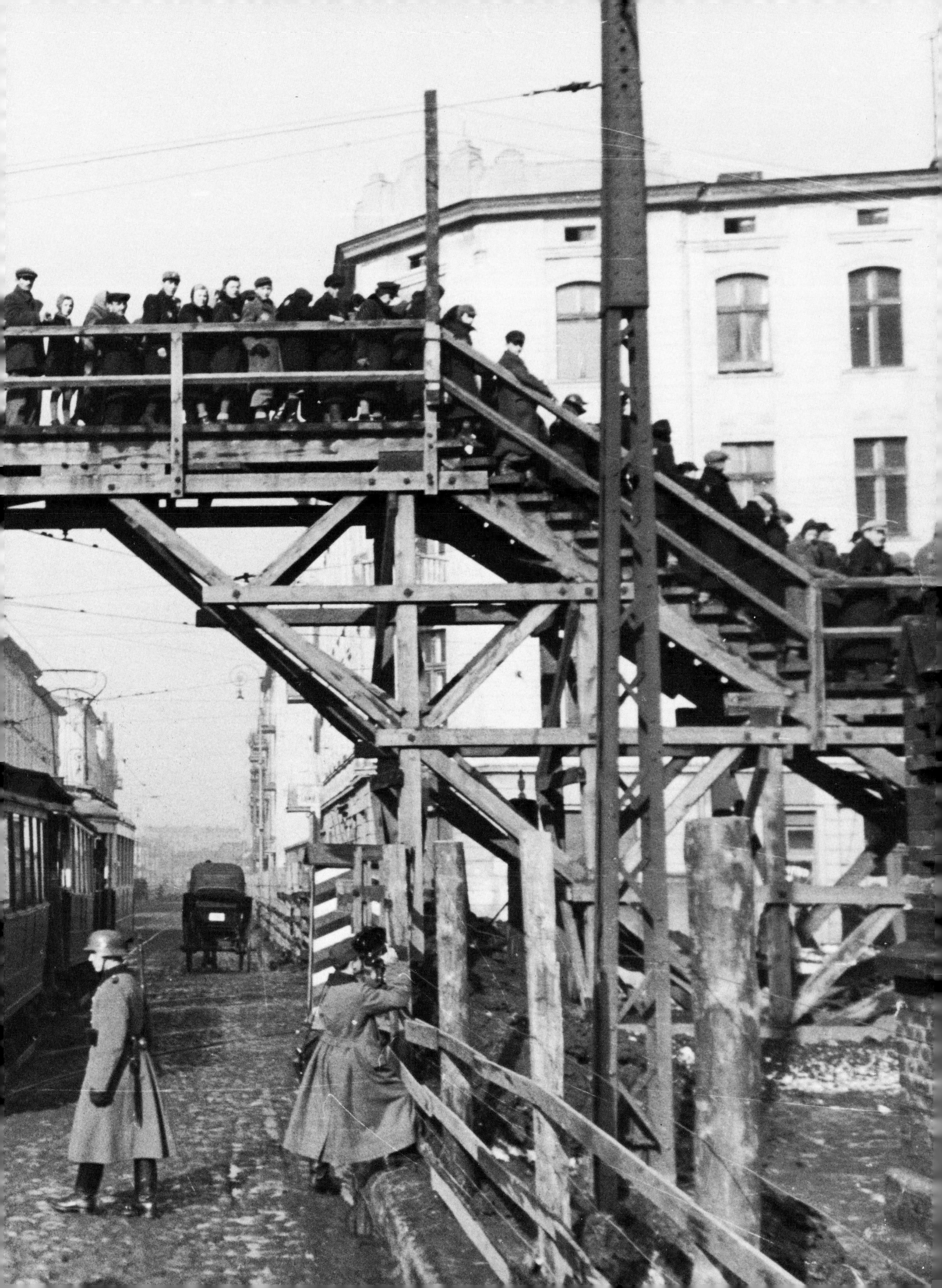

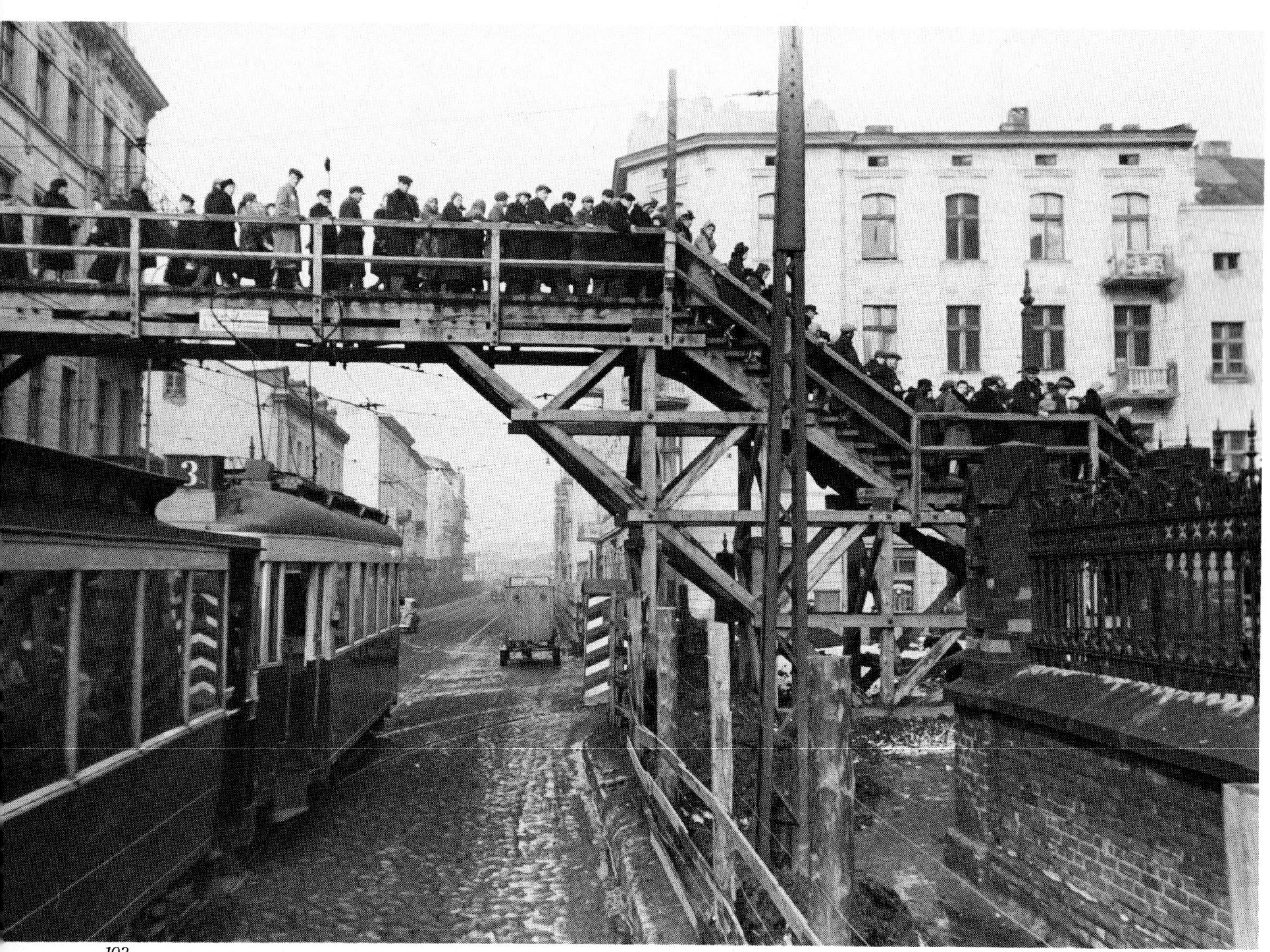

193

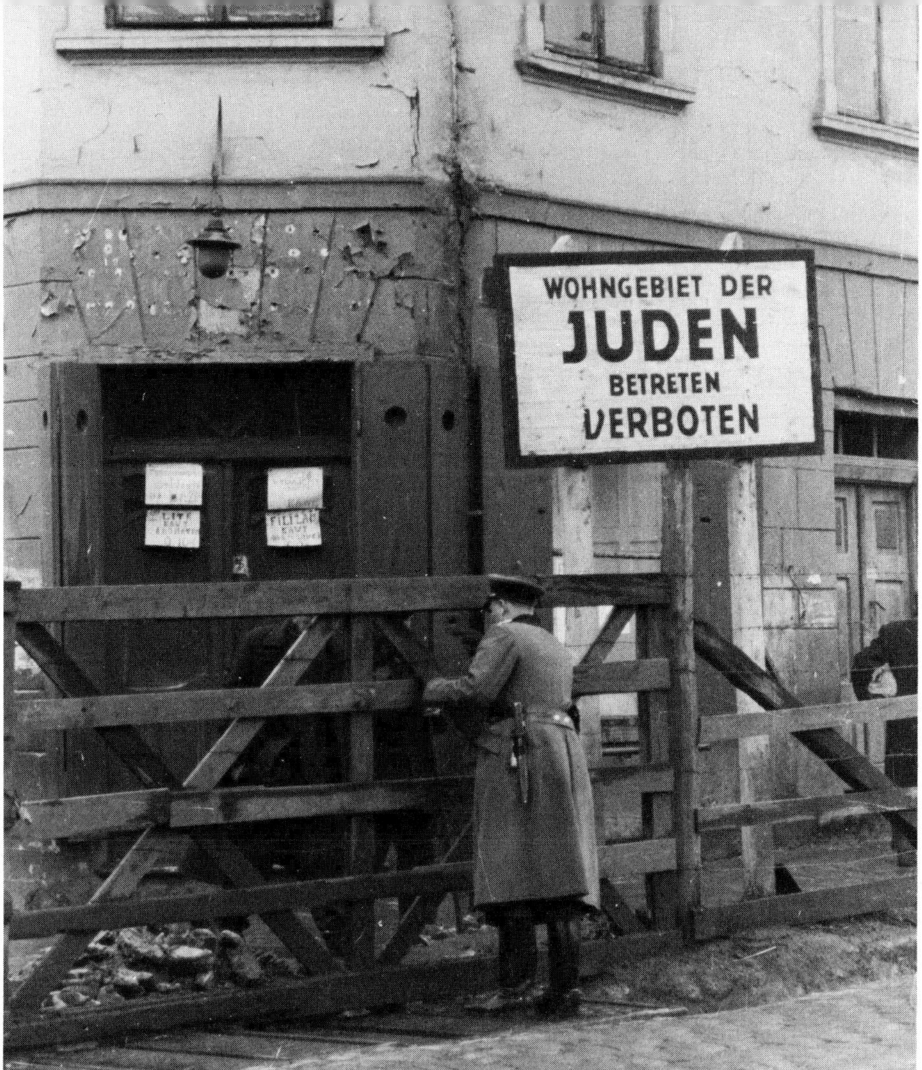

The sign reads: "Residential area of the Jews. No admittance."

194

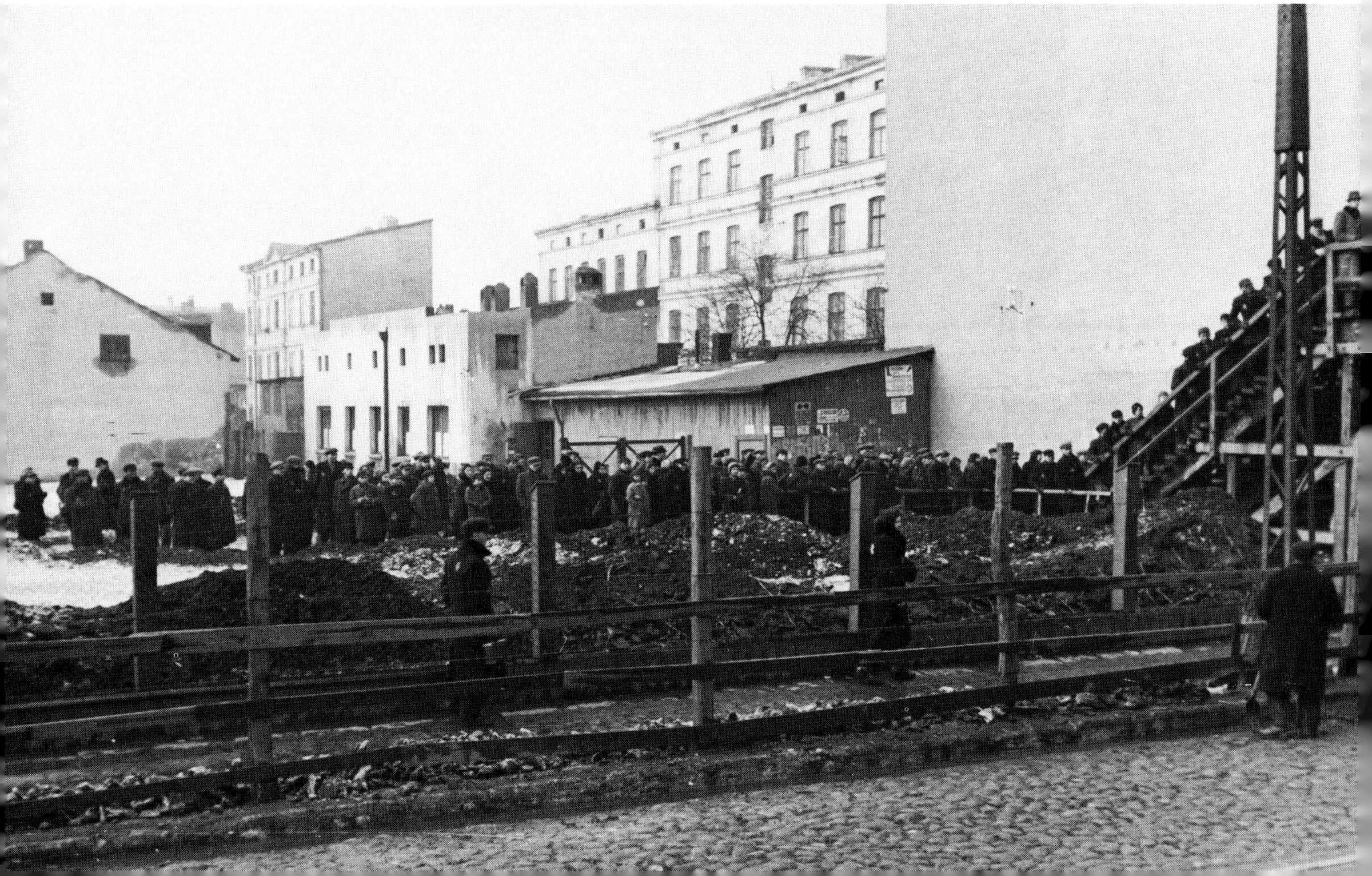

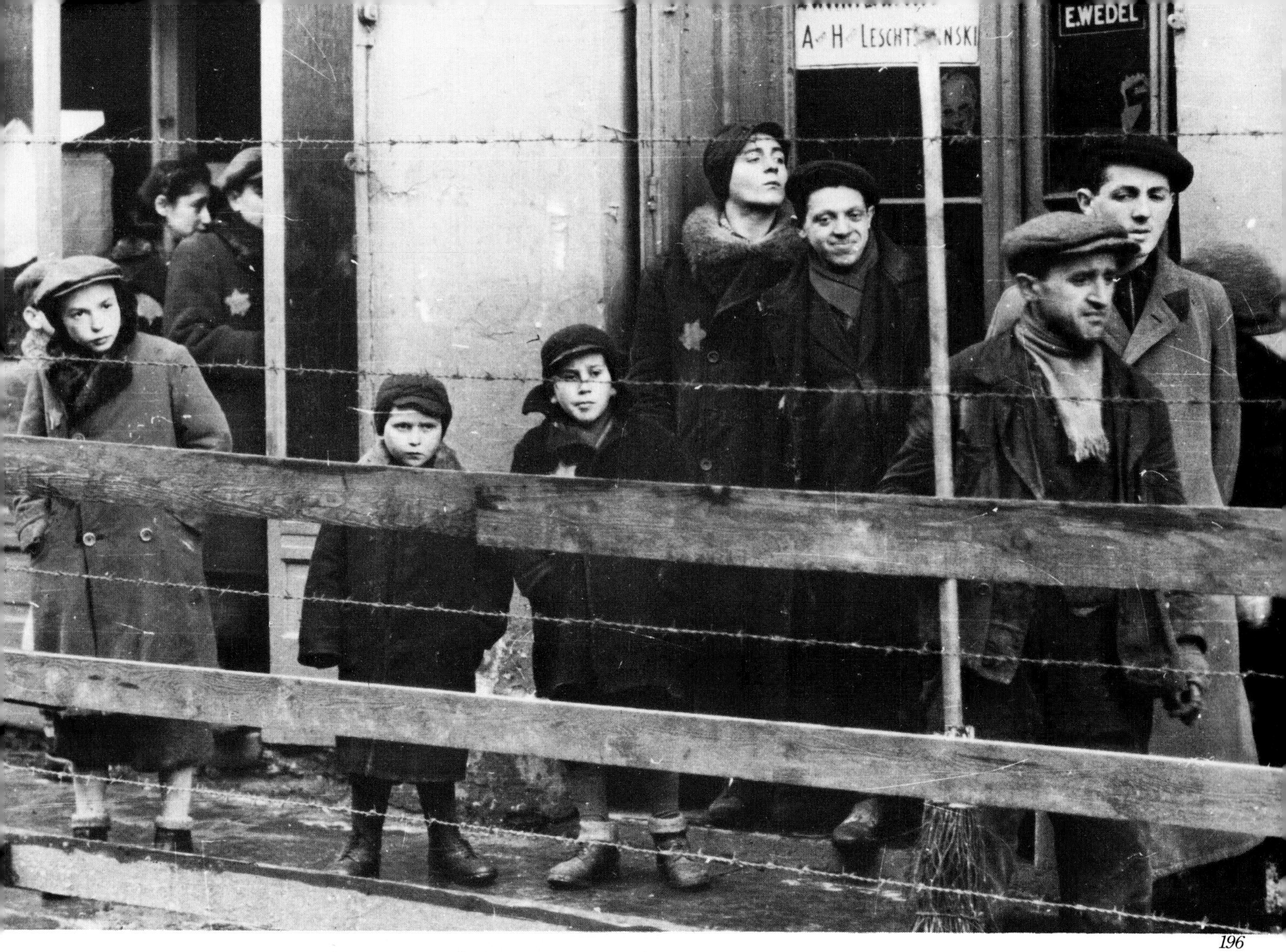

196

197

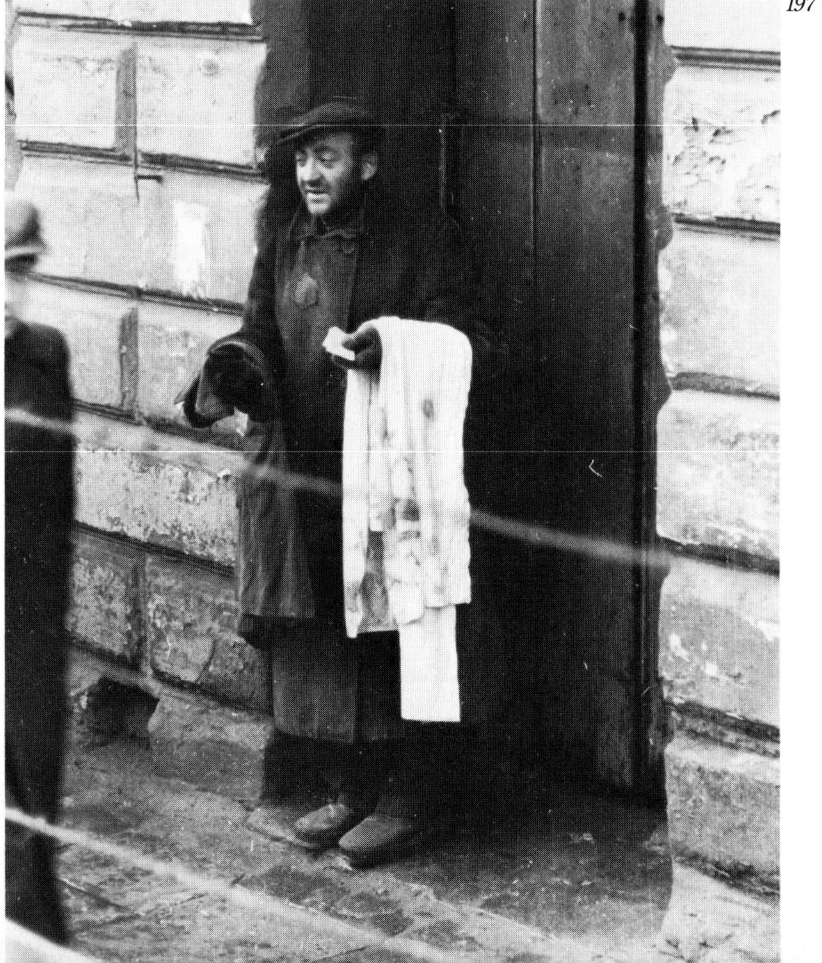

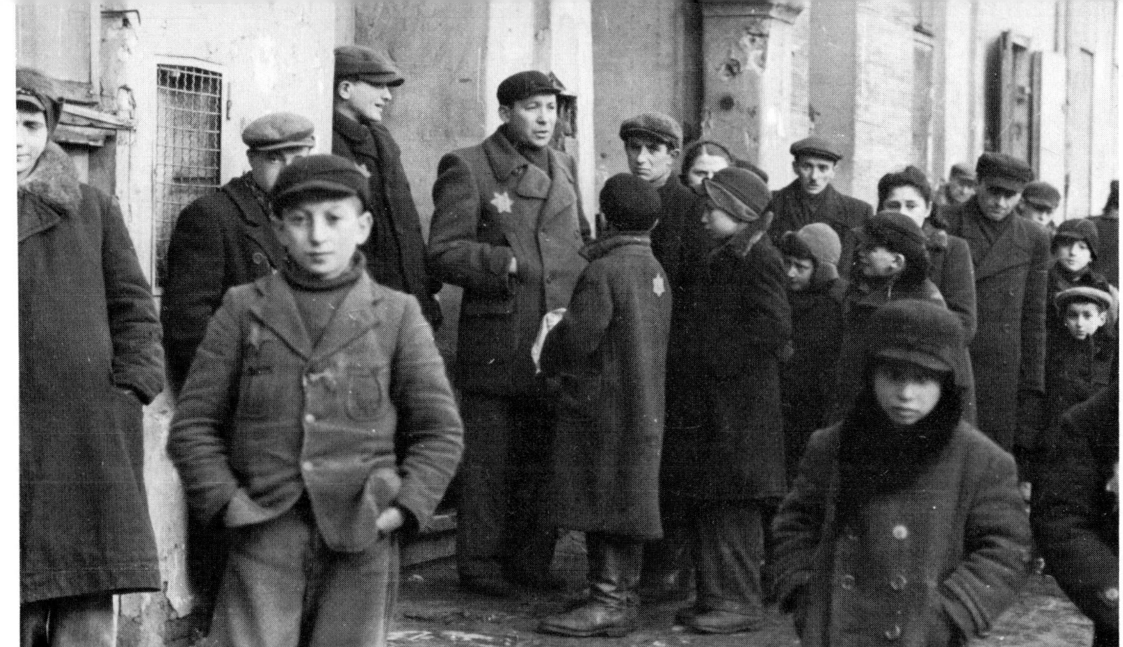

198

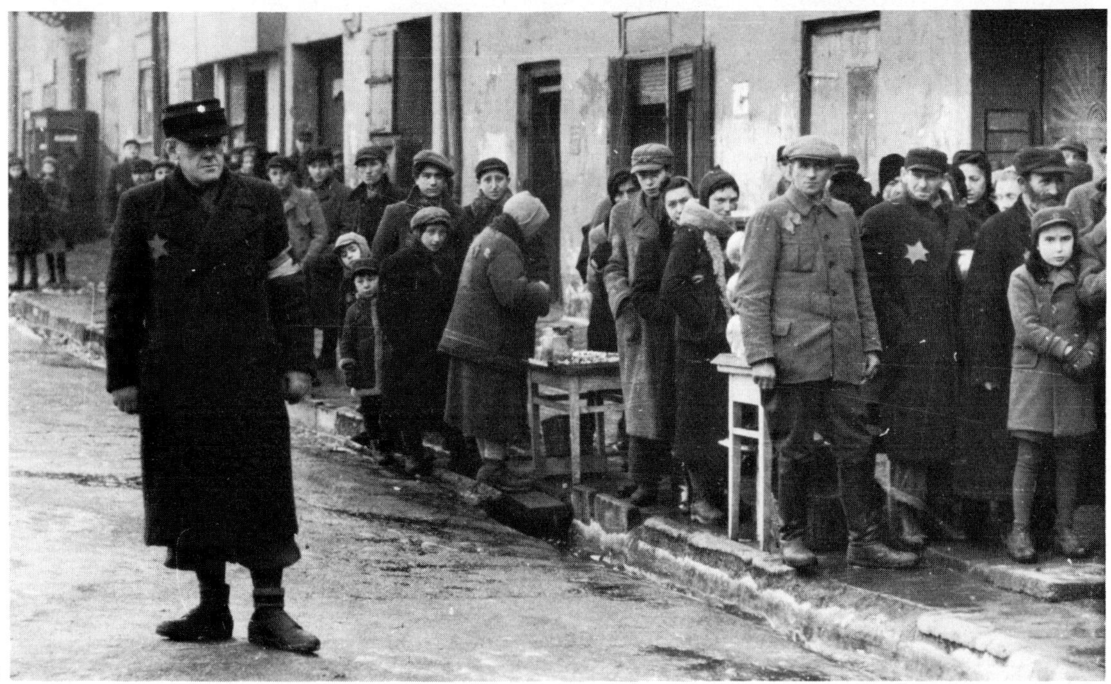

199

200

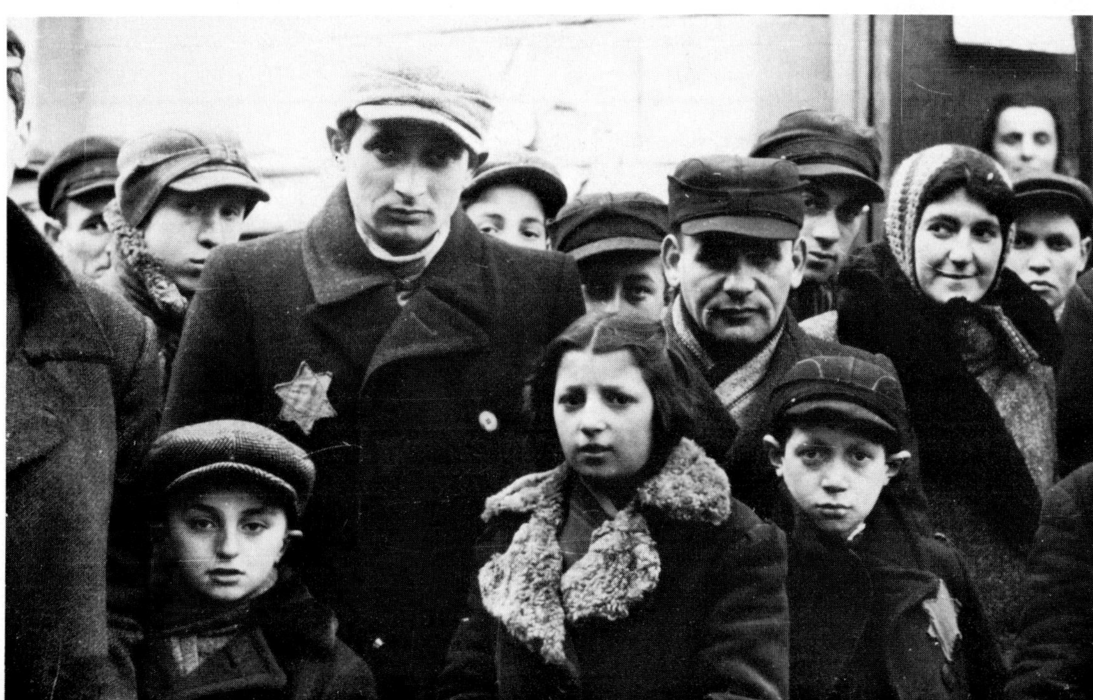

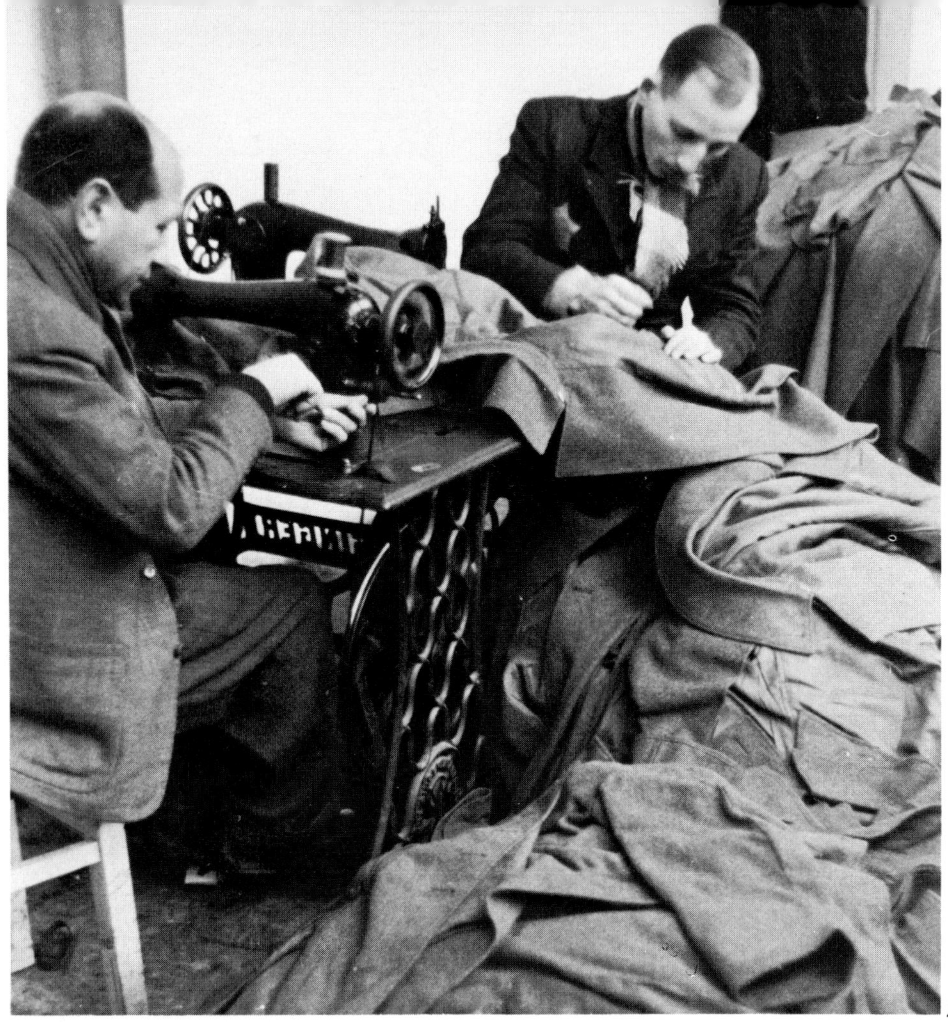

201

202

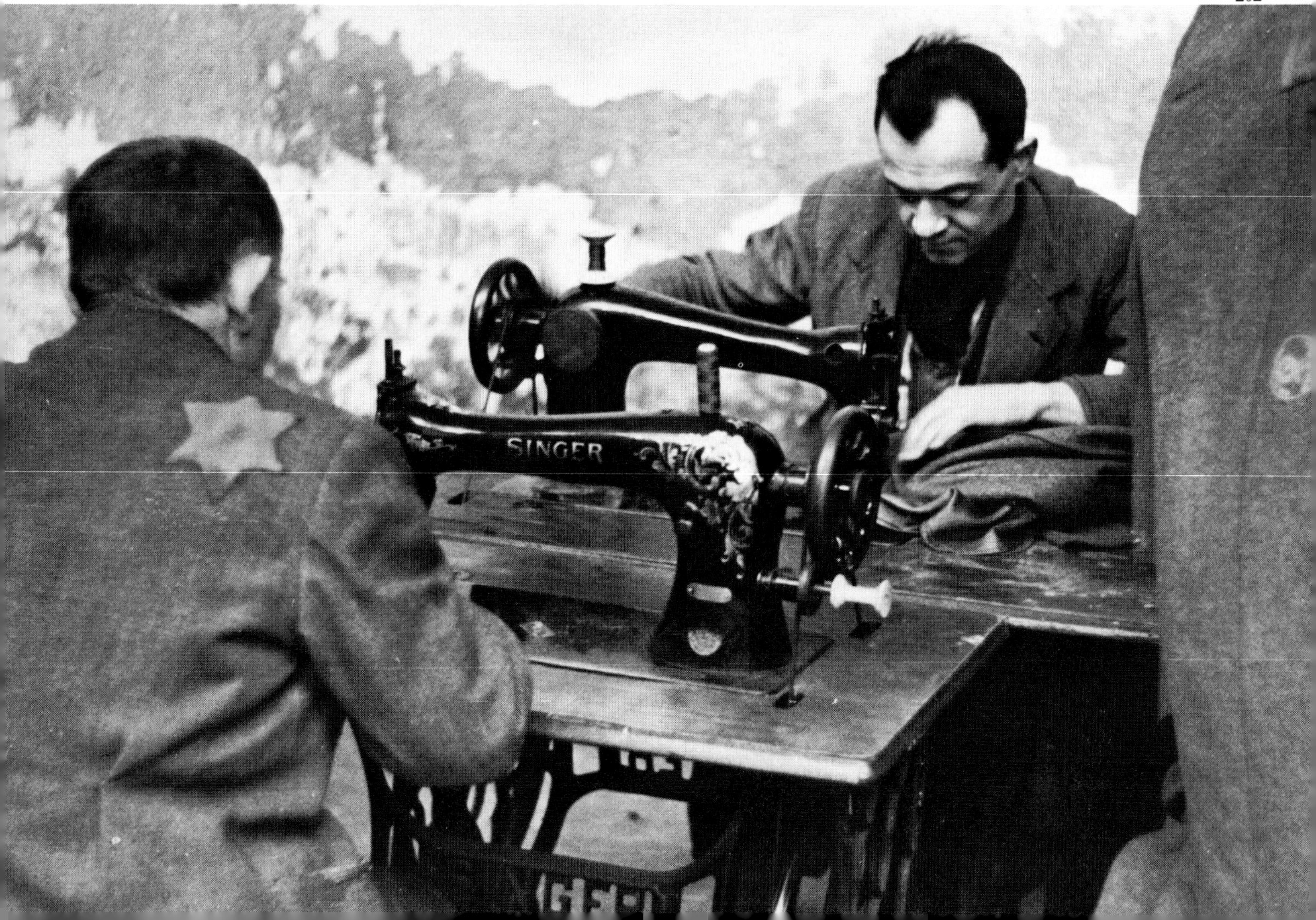

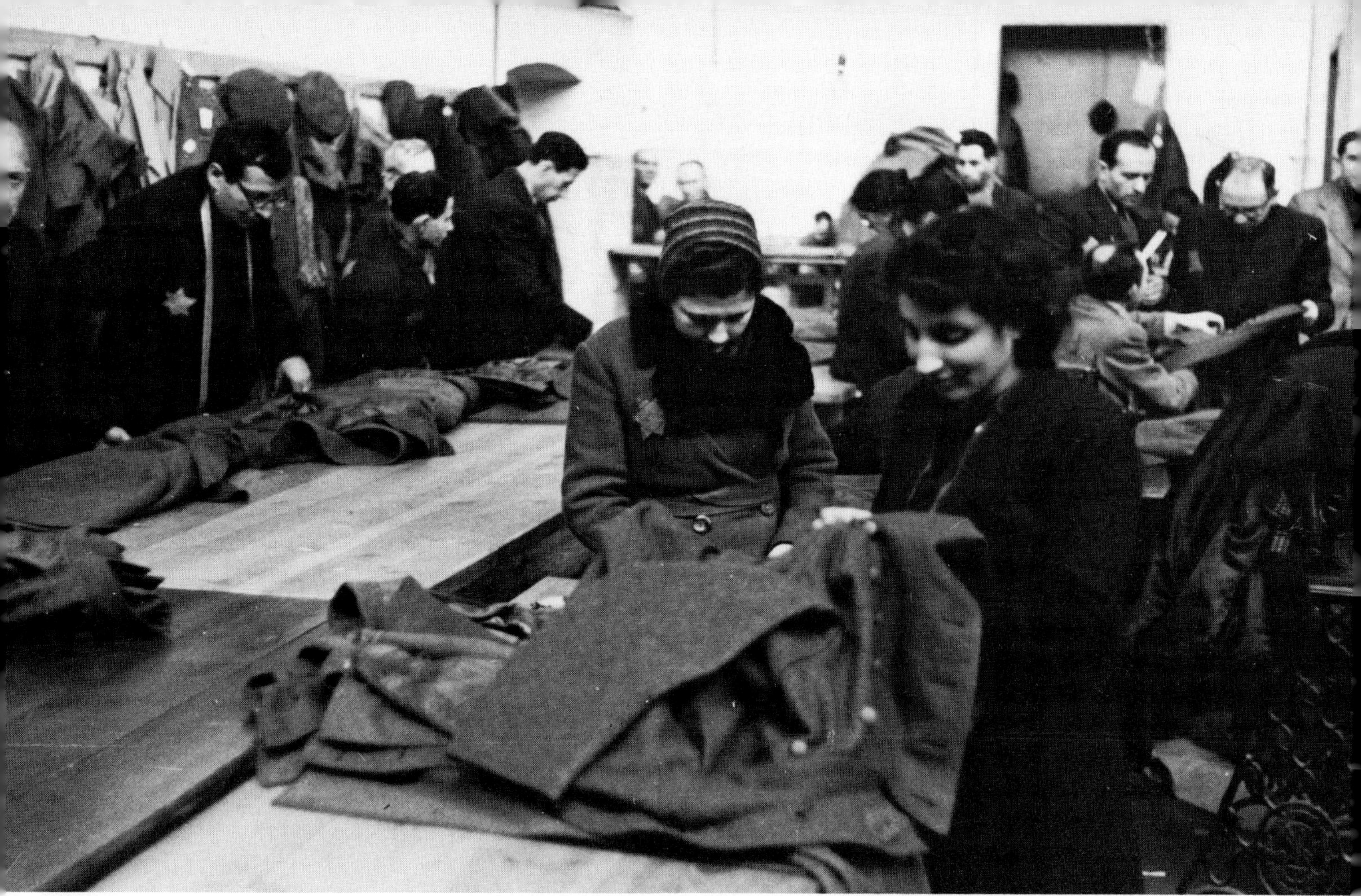

203

204

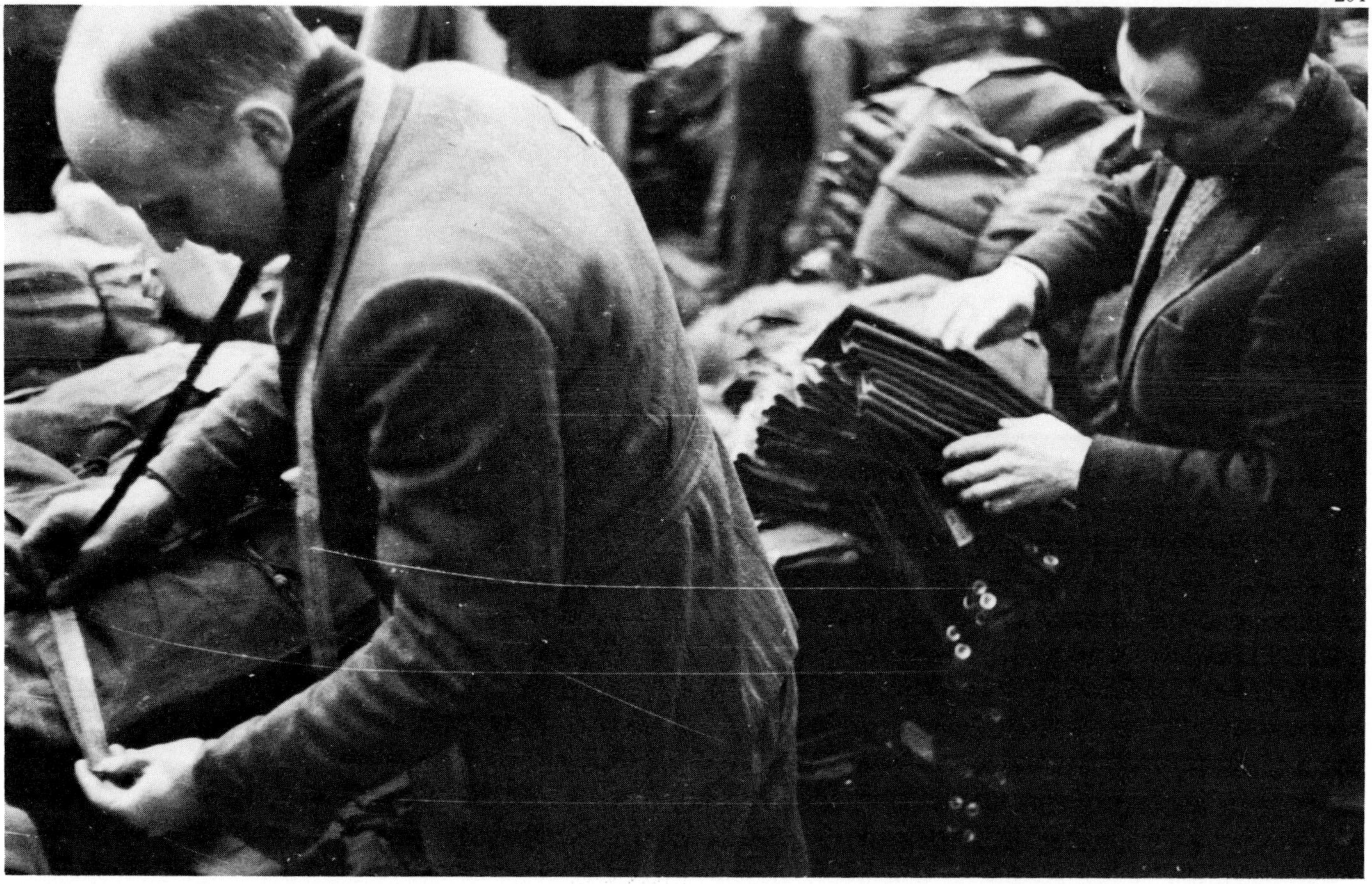

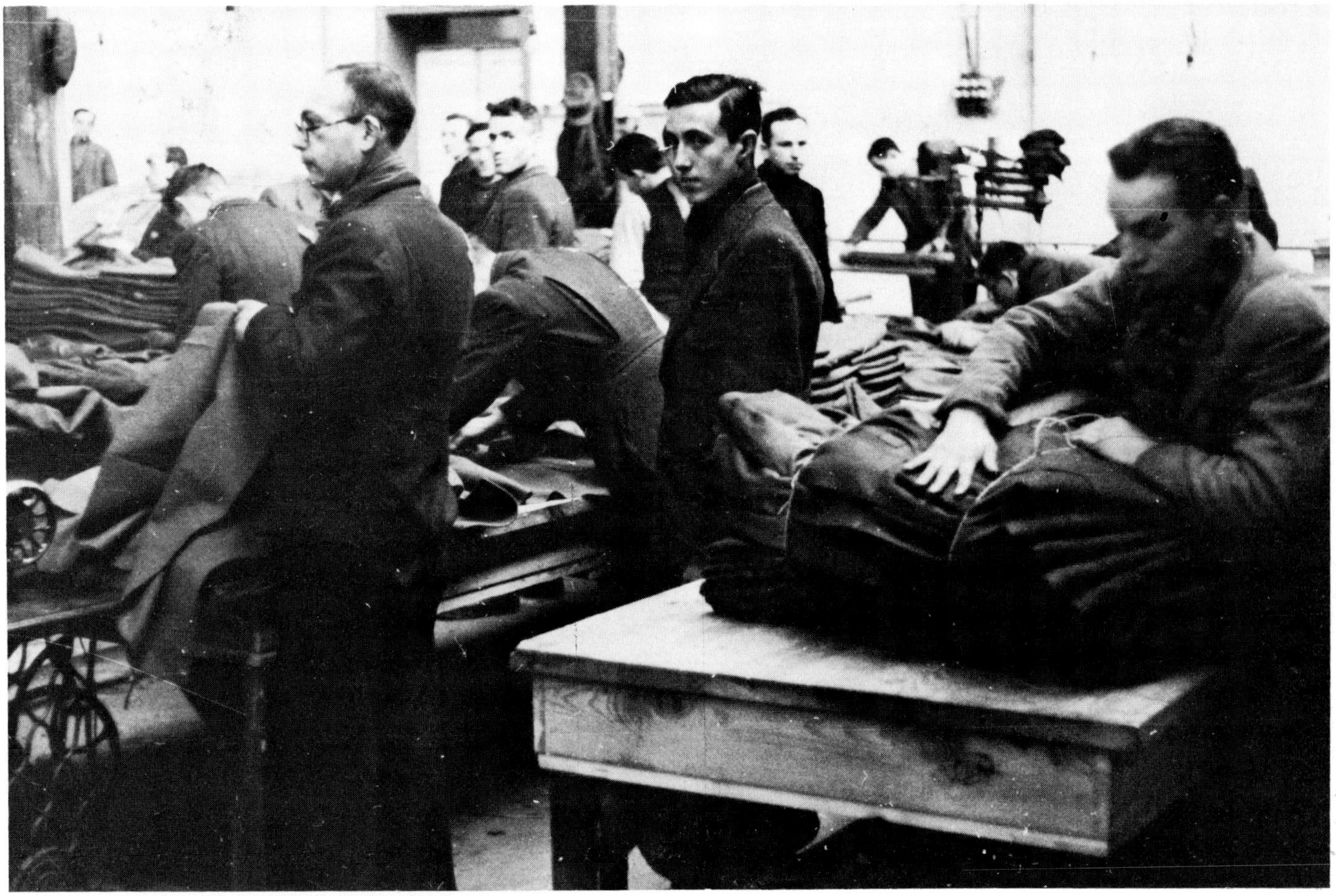

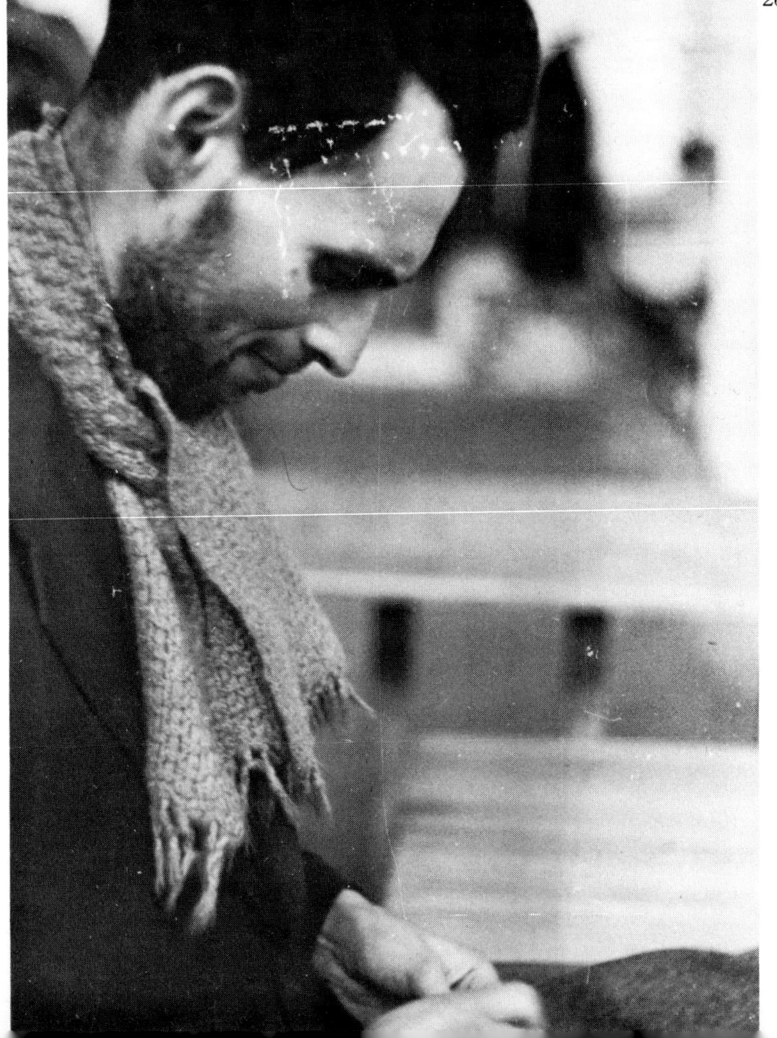

APPENDIX
A Warsaw Ghetto Memoir

The following passages have been selected from Stanisław Rozycki's Warsaw ghetto diary, which seems to have been written in the fall of 1941. Buried in a basement with the rest of Emmanuel Ringelblum's historical archive, it was excavated after the war and is today preserved at the Żydowski Instytut Historyczny, Warsaw. The original is written in Polish. The present translation is based on excerpts published in: *Faschismus—Getto—Massenmord. Dokumentation über Ausrottung und Widerstand der Juden in Polen während des 2. Weltkriegs*, ed. by Żydowski Instytut Historyczny (Warsaw), Frankfurt/M, 1962, pp. 152–156.

I walk further down the street, observing everything and everybody with the eyes of a visitor from foreign lands who enters an exotic, eerie urban landscape. What in the world has happened to me? After all, I know every street, most houses and every other person here, and yet I fail to recognize the people and the streets. I wonder where I am, I cannot find my way home. It is only five minutes from here to my house, but I find myself utterly astray and cannot reach my home. It is these walls, these symbols of shame and humiliation which make my journey so difficult. I am unable to rid myself of the insidious restlessness and anxiety which suddenly take hold of me. I have not been exposed to anything yet; nevertheless, like everybody else, I feel reduced to a hunted animal, pushed deep below the level of human existence.

The crowd is largely composed of shocking caricatures, of ghosts of former people, of wretched rags and miserable ruins of past humanity. The most painful change has affected the faces—faces worn down to the bones by misery, lack of food, vitamins, air and exercise; faces disfigured by overwhelming worries, anxieties, mishaps, sufferings and illnesses. The deeply carved eye sockets, the yellow facial color, the limp, sagging skin, the horrible emaciation and sickliness. And above all this troubled, terrified, restless, yet apathetic and resigned glance reminiscent of a harassed animal. I pass by my dearest friends without recognizing them or reading their past misfortunes. But many of them recognize me; they walk up to me and inquire eagerly how things are "over there," behind the walls; over there where plenty of food, air, exercise and, most of all, freedom is beckoning.

I search for parks, gardens, roses, but such things do not exist here. Even my yearning for modest traces of green is in vain—all this has been eliminated through cunning measures. I move on. I have been here only a few moments, but already something has collapsed within me. It is my faith which fell to pieces here on the threshold of limbo, upon entering these bestially contrived walls.

I look around and find myself immersed in a terrific hum of traffic, a constant rushing, pushing, moaning, crying, bickering. Thousands of people, torrents of pedestrians pour through narrow passages and defiles which formerly were streets. The sidewalks have become insufficient, people are forced onto the traffic lanes, which are already busy. To be sure, German automobiles rarely pass here, but horse carriages, "Jewish" streetcars and the notorious "rickshaws," i.e., tricycles for the transportation of people and goods, are a common sight.

The newcomer is struck by still another gloomy and horrifying phenomenon: almost every house facade is covered with obituary notices. Funerals are in progress everywhere, accompanied by the all-pervasive odor of carbolic acid typical of disinfected buildings. Woefully inadequate ambulances keep rattling through the streets. And everybody's conversation stubbornly returns to that one seductive topic which can so easily be guessed: an epidemic is raging in the city, typhus has gone rampant and literally decimates the emaciated, underfed, hunger-tormented population.

The streets resound with the futile screams of children dying of hunger. They whine, beg, sing, lament and tremble in the cold, without underwear, without clothes, without shoes, covered only by rags and bags which are tied by strings to the meager skeletons. Children swollen from hunger, deformed, semiconscious; children who are perfectly adult, somber and tired of living at age five. They are like hoary old men and know only one thing: "I am freezing, I am hungry," so quickly have they grasped the fundamentals of life. By their terrifying helplessness and innocent suffering these thousands of little beggars represent a powerful indictment of our proud contemporary civilization. Ten percent of the young generation have perished already. Every day and every night hundreds of children literally die on the pavement and there is no prospect of ending this tragedy.

But it is not only the children. Young and old people, men and women, proletariat and bourgeoisie, intellectuals and businessmen are progressively impoverished and degraded. Brutally and recklessly thrown out of their shelters, they are swallowed by the street; they resort to begging for a month, or two or three—but inevitably they approach the end, eventually dying in the streets or in a hospital of hunger, cold, illness and depression. Thus perish those who are not needed any more—former human beings, former citizens, former "useful members of society."

I don't look at these people any more. When moaning and sobbing strike my ear I switch to the other side of the street. When I detect an anonymous bundle huddled on the pavement, wrapped in rags and shaking in the cold, I turn away and refuse to look. I can't do it. It's too much for me. After all, only one hour has passed since my arrival.

The cruel struggle for a slice of bread, for a few square feet of shelter, for the preservation of health, energy and life leaves hardly any strength that could be devoted to spiritual matters, and this is not even taking into account the German restrictions and injunctions. It is forbidden to print, teach, learn anything; it is illegal to form associations and to engage in any kind of cultural exchange. We are cut off from the world of books; we are not allowed to open libraries, schools or scientific institutions. There are no movie theaters, no radio stations, no contacts with the cultural activities in the rest of the world. Nothing reaches us, the creations of the human mind are not permitted to enter our prison. Not only groceries and industrial goods, but cultural products as well have to be smuggled into the ghetto. This is why everything we can obtain and accomplish in this field deserves recognition, regardless of quantity and quality.

How is it possible to discuss cleanliness in view of cleverly devised sanitary conditions which are equivalent to a death sentence and make even the strictest hygiene a futile undertaking? For various reasons, hygiene has sunk to an alarmingly low level. Most strikingly, there is a dreadful

population density which has no parallel in Europe. The deadly overcrowding is particularly noticeable in the streets, where people literally rub against each other, unable to cross from one sidewalk to the other without endless obstruction. Add to this the lack of lighting, gas and heating material. Even the water supply is severely limited; people wash themselves much less frequently and must do without bathrooms and warm water. Bed linen and personal clothes are changed rarely since soap, coal and hot water are difficult to obtain.

To speak of balanced diet would appear as mockery and provocation under the prevailing circumstances. One eats what is available, how much is available and when it is available—these are the only known nutritional principles. All this said the consequences can easily be guessed: typhus, dysentery, tuberculosis, pneumonia, influenza, metabolic disturbances, the usual digestive malfunctions, vitamin deficiencies and all the other diseases caused by lack of food, air, clothing and heating.

The typhus epidemic reduces the population steadily and systematically. There are victims in every family; up to a thousand fatalities are registered per month. In the early morning hours the streets are strewn with the corpses of beggars, children, young men, old men, women—victims of hunger and cold. The hospitals are so horribly overcrowded that two to three patients have to share one bed. Those who cannot get as much as that lie on the floors of rooms and hallways. The scarcity of medication makes it impossible to treat patients effectively, not to mention the lack of adequate food. Only soup and tea are offered.

Anticipated and actual monthly family budgets tend to be separated by great discrepancies as can be gathered from the following example which is by no means fictitious but corresponds all too closely to reality:

Expected income		*Actual income*	
Father's wages	Złoty 235	Father's wages	Zł 235
Son's wages	Zł 120	Son's wages	Zł 120
Welfare	Zł 45	Welfare	——
Side income	Zł 200	Side income	Zł 80
	Total Zł 600		Zł 435

How can the deficit of Zł 165 be made up? By selling family possessions? But let us first discuss the expenditure side.

Expected expenditures		*Actual expenditures*	
Rent	Zł 70	Rent	Zł 70
Bread	Zł 300	Bread	Zł 328
Potatoes	Zł 105	Potatoes	Zł 115
Cooking fat	Zł 54	Cooking fat	Zł 56
Various food rations	Zł 45	Various rations	Zł 80
Various fees	Zł 6	Various fees	Zł 11
Electricity, candles	Zł 20	Electricity, candles	Zł 28
		Heating fuel	Zł 65
		Medication	Zł 45
		Soap	Zł 9
		Various items	Zł 3
	Total Zł 600		Zł 810